ANTI-JUDAISM IN GALATIANS?

ANTI-JUDAISM IN GALATIANS?

*Exegetical Studies on a Polemical Letter
and on Paul's Theology*

Michael Bachmann

Translated by Robert L. Brawley

WILLIAM B. EERDMANS PUBLISHING COMPANY
GRAND RAPIDS, MICHIGAN / CAMBRIDGE, U.K.

Originally published in German under the title *Antijudaismus im Galaterbrief?*
Exegetische Studien zu einem polemischen Schreiben und zur Theologie des Apostels Paulus
© 1999 Universitätsverlag Freiburg Schweiz and Vandenhoeck & Ruprecht

This English-language edition © 2008 Wm. B. Eerdmans Publishing Co.
All rights reserved

Wm. B. Eerdmans Publishing Co.
2140 Oak Industrial Drive N.E., Grand Rapids, Michigan 49505 /
P.O. Box 163, Cambridge CB3 9PU U.K.

Library of Congress Cataloging-in-Publication Data

Bachmann, Michael.
   [Antijudaismus im Galaterbrief? English]
   Anti-Judaism in Galatians?: exegetical studies on a polemical letter and on Paul's theology /
     Michael Bachmann ; translated by Robert L. Brawley.
     p.   cm.
   Includes bibliographical references (p.   ) and indexes.
   ISBN 978-0-8028-6291-4 (pbk. : alk. paper)
   1. Bible. N.T. Galatians — Criticism, interpretation, etc. 2. Paul, the Apostle,
Saint — Relations with Jews. 3. Jewish law. I. Title.

BS2685.52.B3313 2009
227'.406 — dc22

                                        2008036151

www.eerdmans.com

To Ursula

Contents

Preface ix

Preface to the 1999 Edition xi

1. Justification and Works of the Law in Paul
   Orig.: *Theologische Zeitschrift* 49 (1993), 1-33   1

2. 4QMMT and Galatians, מעשי התורה and ΕΡΓΑ ΝΟΜΟΥ
   Orig.: *Zeitschrift für die neutestamentliche Wissenschaft und die Kunde der älteren Kirche* 89 (1998), 91-113   19

3. Jewish Covenantal Nomism and the Pauline Understanding of the Law, the Mosaic Floor of Beth-Alpha and Gal 3:15-29
   Orig.: *Kirche und Israel. Neukirchener Theologische Zeitschrift* 9 (1994), 168-91   32

   Supplement (1999)   58

4. Investigations on the Mediator: Gal 3:20 and the Character of the Mosaic Law
   Cf. *Amt und Gemeinde* (ed. Bischof der Evangelischen Kirche A.B. in Österreich) 48 (1997), 78-85   60

5. The Other Woman: Synchronic and Diachronic Observations on Gal 4:21–5:1
   Cf. *Judaica. Beiträge zum Verstehen des Judentums* 54 (1998), 144-64   85

6. The Church and the Israel of God: On the Meaning and

Ecclesiastical Relevance of the Benediction at the
End of Galatians (1999) 101

Notes 124

Bibliographical Appendix 207

Index of Scripture and Other Literature 210

Index of Authors 228

Preface

This volume marks the English-language publication of a collection of my studies on Galatians which were originally published as volume 40 of the series Novum Testamentum et Orbis Antiquus (NTOA 40) in 1999. This is especially rewarding to me because the issues dealt with in the essays, which relate to the relationship between early Christians and Jews as characterized or at least mentioned by Paul, are still a matter of some controversy. My claim that the Apostle's remarks are not to be taken as an expression of anti-Judaism is, at least in German-speaking countries, not (yet) generally accepted[1] — although there is no lack of concurring opinions.[2] Up to this point, the reception of my studies in the context of English-language exegesis[3] has been somewhat hindered by my German style, which, admittedly, can be demanding for the reader, especially if German is a foreign language. (Perhaps, with my way of expressing myself in my native tongue, I may be able to make claims to achieving a certain precision.) Many of these difficulties should now be remedied by the English translation, which also provides an opportunity to correct several errors and imprecise references in the original edition.

Several persons and institutions have been especially helpful in realizing this translation. Robert L. Brawley and James D. G. Dunn aroused the interest of the W. B. Eerdmans Publishing Co. in the project. The University Press of Freiburg, Switzerland (now Academic Press Fribourg/Paulusverlag) and Vandenhoeck & Ruprecht (Göttingen) agreed to an English-language edition without any hesitation. The major responsibility for this new edition was borne by Robert L. Brawley, who translated the book. A New Testament scholar very familiar with both source and target languages, he not only agreed to this challenging task but accomplished it brilliantly. In Siegen, my similarly well-versed assistant, Johannes Woyke, spent a number of days proofreading the translation, designing illustrations, and formatting the text. My best thanks are due to all of those named above, but especially to these two, Robert and Johannes.

In addition, Nicola Bruch, Stefanie Elshoff, and Isabell Klapheck checked the translation of parts of the German text, and Mareike Dörr prepared the indexes. But, of course, I assume the full responsibility for any errors or inaccuracies.[4] Elisabeth Dörnemann was involved with the paperwork, and Eva Meyer did some of the proofreading. I am especially grateful to all of these friendly and helpful members of my staff and to Thomas La Presti (University of Siegen), who translated both prefaces and the supplement to chapter 3. Additionally, concerning questions regarding English I was able to ask Dr. Stephen Amador (Kirchzarten) on several occasions for his opinion. Last but certainly not least I wish to express my heartfelt gratitude for the seemingly endless number of modifications which my wife Ursula readily and with great patience entered into the computer.

The Wm. B. Eerdmans Publishing company has edited the book very carefully. In this regard A. Myers has to be mentioned, and especially Dr. J. W. Simpson, Jr., who has made numerous suggestions for improvement.

My research work has, of course, developed further since 1999, especially in reference to Paul and to Galatians. To a great extent, this work has exhibited a certain continuity with the articles translated here. In particular, the justification for and the limitations of the New Perspective on Paul are issues that have captivated my interest.[5] I sincerely hope that this translation might help to promote work on these areas of exegesis and contribute to a fuller understanding of early Christian utterances related to Judaism.

MICHAEL BACHMANN
St. Märgen
November 23, 2008

Preface to the 1999 Edition

The six studies compiled in this volume deal with topics which interested me as early as the time of my work on a postdoctoral thesis *(Habilitationsschrift)*, which was then published in 1992 (WUNT 59). But at that time I did not have the opportunity to pursue these matters in much detail. My attention was focused on the structure of Gal 2:15-21 and on the function of this passage in the context of the entire letter to the churches of Galatia. Ensuing debates on these matters, the mostly positive reviews of my book, and insights gained from other authors (especially Jan Lambrecht and Andreas Wechsler)[1] have at least given me the impression that my "labors were not in vain." Meticulous scrutiny of Paul's arguments in the Letter to the Galatians, a document certainly not free of polemics, had prompted me at various points to question a view which maintains that here Paul is sharply criticizing "justification by good works *(Werkgerechtigkeit)*," above all Jewish convictions concerning "justification by good works." That view did not seem convincing to me for several reasons, among them the fact that the Apostle was addressing Galatian *Christians,* (primarily) Gentile Christians, and was attempting to influence their behavior. Issues such as these, which were for the most part treated marginally in my postdoctoral thesis, have become the major focus of the studies collected here.

The keyword "anti-Judaism," not a particularly clear concept itself, may in the meantime even provoke dismissive reactions, if used in the context of debates on New Testament issues. Yet, in light of our present historical situation and of current exegetical debates, this term would seem to be anything but obsolete with reference to Paul and to Galatians. A few quotations might demonstrate this. On the basis of extensive knowledge and insight, H. Schreckenberg (*Umfeld*, 89)[2] comments: "Jews have seen and still see in the letter to the churches in Galatia a major source of animosity toward Jews within the theological and political spheres during the Christian era." That there is still reason to hold this view is evident from R. Ruether's opinion (based not least on sections of Galatians): "Without a doubt, Paul's position is that of anti-Judaism" (*Nächstenliebe*, 101 [cf. p. 104]). Even according to the more recent formulations of W. Kraus (*Volk Gottes*, 254), for "unbelieving Israel" rejection is "objectively performed" at least in Galatians and specifically there by "excluding [this people] from the inheritance and identifying the Sinai covenant with slavery." In our present historical situation and in such a constellation of the history of research, it is no slight matter to determine whether or not Galatians is to be understood in terms of anti-Judaism: Should we, indeed, discern Pauline anti-Judaism here and thus, in light of an appropriate critique *(Sachkritik)*, emancipate ourselves from this standpoint (cf. Ruether, *Nächstenliebe*, 112, 210-12; cf. ibid., p. 246, where P. von der Osten-Sacken finds "the quintessence of Ruether's study . . . in the necessity of theological abandonment of possession [*Besitzverzicht*]")? Or should the position expressed in Galatians be characterized as "a polemical overstatement" that is "not to be understood as the last word on the matter" (Kraus, *Volk Gottes*, 355), is it, to a certain extent, "revised" in Romans (ibid., 359), and can it be corrected from there?

Working on the studies compiled here has brought me to the hardly conventional conviction that not Galatians itself, but, instead, only its reception (history of interpretation) exhibits evidence of anti-Judaism. Admittedly, the letter's polemics did encourage such a reception. In addition, already soon afterward the language — with reference to ἔργα νόμου:[3] technical terminology — and Paul's Jewish-shaped hermeneutics of Scripture were no longer sufficiently understood, and, increasingly, problems of later times, especially those of the 16th century, were read into Galatians. In this sense, then, these articles — which consciously refer to aspects related to the history of reception — deal not only with numerous, often controversial, issues involved in the exegesis of Paul's letters, but also touch earlier and current relationships between Jews and Christians, as well as philological and ecumenical debates on the so-called doctrine of justification.

Chapters 1, 2, and 3 are reprinted here as in their first publication[4] but with a new, uniform layout — to which end the marginal notes of the original version of chapter 3 have now been excluded. The manuscripts were

Preface to the 1999 Edition

checked for typographical and other errors; in particular, figure 4 in chapter 3, an illustration of the mosaic floor in the Beth-Alpha synagogue, has now been realigned (in accordance with the article: correctly) so that Abraham is, so to speak, upside down. Those additions to notes 138, 147, 151, 158, and 160 in chapter 1 which originally appeared as a supplement (*TZ* 49 [1993], 331) have now been integrated into the notes themselves (and adapted with reference to bibliographical data), whereas now a Supplement has been added to chapter 3.

The remaining three studies have not been published before in this form. Nevertheless, only the concluding essay is an original publication in the strict sense. Shorter versions of chapters 4 and 5 have appeared earlier. The main distinction in the version of chapter 5 published here is the more comprehensive series of notes added.

Many people contributed to the realization of this collection of studies, which was not originally planned as a unit and therefore exhibits some overlap, e.g., between chapters 1 and 2 and between 3 and 4. I have included only those essays on Paul which are focused on the topic expressed in the main title.[5] Gerd Theißen suggested the place of publication, and Max Küchler not only concurred but also made some of the relevant literature available to me. The publishing houses Friedrich Reinhardt (Basel), de Gruyter (Berlin), and Neukirchener Verlag (Neukirchen-Vluyn) readily agreed to reprinting chapters 1, 2, and 3. The difficult job of transforming handwriting into typescript was originally carried out by Monika Glockner in Freiburg/Breisgau and later by Ruth Schumacher, Rosemarie Reimann, and Elisabeth Dörnemann in Siegen. Under the direction and support of an experienced computer duo consisting of my wife Ursula and above all our son Philipp, Matthias Schüring assumed responsibility for the uniform layout and the design of the illustrations. Karl Friedrich Ulrichs, who had now become a member of my staff, once again took over the difficult tasks of proofreading and compiling the indexes. Katrin Irle and Christian Eberhard also helped in the search to eradicate typographical errors. Kerstin Rhode and Michael Büchner took care of the pages with illustrations. I wish to express my sincere thanks to all these people.

MICHAEL BACHMANN
St. Märgen/Siegen
May 28, 1999

1. Justification and Works of the Law in Paul

In memoriam Karl Heinrich Rengstorf

(10/1/1903–3/24/1992)

1

Rather presumptuous and somewhat tedious — this is how the chosen theme might appear. Is it not too much of a good thing, and would it not be unproductive for a brief lecture to take on the doctrine of justification, which for almost 2000 years was and still is heatedly discussed in church and theology and which played a considerable role in the schism of the church in the 16th century — a division that until today has not been overcome?[1] To look at the doctrine of justification in its entirety would indeed be presumptuous and tedious. Therefore the first restriction is: the lecture will be about the Pauline sphere. However, this qualification helps only a little, because our exegesis of Paul is inconceivable apart from the history of the church that lies behind us, and concerning this history the Reformation is especially committed to the interpretation of Paul. According to Luther's own famous testimony in 1545,[2] it was indeed the exposition of the term *iustitia dei* from Rom 1:17 that led to his turnaround: this phrase was not to be understood, as he had learned, *"de iustitia (ut vocant) formali seu activa"*; rather, what was at stake was passive justification, *"qua nos Deus misericors iustificat per fidem," "qua nos iustificemur."* To employ conventional contemporary terminology:[3] "Righteousness of God" is not to be

---

The material in this chapter was first presented as a public lecture given in Basel June 3, 1991, on the occasion of the author's qualifying as a university lecturer. It appears here in a slightly revised and enlarged form with notes.

conceived of as a *genitivus subiectivus*, that is, as God's own justice, but rather as a *genitivus obiectivus*, more precisely as a *genitivus auctoris*. It has to do with the righteousness that counts before God,[4] for which human beings are indebted to God. In view of this history it is no wonder that Protestant and incidentally also Catholic exegesis of Paul especially over the past decades has been intensely focused on this genitive construction, δικαιοσύνη θεοῦ in Greek, though admittedly without reaching a consensus — and this shows finally that our first attempt to set some limits helps only partially. For instance, E. Käsemann's proposal that alongside the character of God's righteousness as a gift, its character as God's power should be taken into consideration. That is, in contrast to Luther, we should consider different nuances of the subjective genitive (and indeed going beyond Rom 3:5, 25-26), an idea that many have adopted, although others have vehemently rejected it.[5] As gratifying as it is to see that, as Käsemann's judgment and as more recent Catholic contributions to the discussion also show, 16th-century positions are not simply extended into the contemporary exegetical discussion, and rather work on the Pauline texts themselves can lead to theses that do not stem from the confessional tradition of the exegete,[6] even so it is equally regrettable that our first attempt to set limits — to stick with Paul — is not yet really sufficient.

So let us try for a second limitation! This further qualification is intimated in the title by the conjunction "and," which here does not mean an expansion but expresses rather something like the intersection between the doctrine of justification and works of the law — and this precisely in Paul. Justification ought not to be of interest primarily or exclusively under the aspect of the genitive construction "God's righteousness," but rather of another genitive construction: "works of the law," ἔργα νόμου.[7] That *this* will lead to further or innovative statements is now certainly all the more probable for the following reasons: In the first place this expression "works of the law" occurs only in very few passages. In Paul, if one sticks with that noun that governs a case *and* the other noun governed by a case, it is a matter of only six verses (Gal 2:16 [3 times]; 3:2, 5, 10; Rom 3:20, 28; cf. further 9:32 variant reading). Beyond these passages the expression or a Hebrew equivalent is completely absent in biblical literature. At the most only a few more verses in Romans could be added in which, instead of "apart from works of the law" (Rom 3:28) or "by/from works of the law" (Rom 3:20; Gal 2:16; 3:2, 5, 10), Paul more briefly writes "apart from works" (Rom 4:6) or "by/from works" (Rom 4:2; 9:12, 32; 11:6).[8] He evidently does this not least because he is referring to events that predate the Mosaic law.⁹ To speak of "works *of the law*" at that time would be rather anachronistic.¹⁰ With such a manageable number of references one should indeed be able to find out something! This should be true all the more because, in the second place, this field oddly enough has not yet been grazed or disfigured by bunkers dug in exegetical battles to the point of being unrecognizable.¹¹ Although the kind of genitive remains a bit in the dark,¹² interpreters are rather in agreement on the meaning of the expression;¹³ to give some actual instances: "fulfillments of commands" (P. Billerbeck), "duty *(Dienst)* of the law" (E. Lohmeyer), "Torah observance in a completely comprehensive sense" (O. Hofius).¹⁴

2

Thus, it should be possible to orient oneself in this field. Moreover, it is advisable because, for one thing, with the expression "works of the law" we also have been loaded with a heavy burden in the history of the church; for another,¹⁵ because this phrase itself is not particularly controversial; indeed, rather, the question is how "the key statement of the Pauline doctrine of justification" (to use E. Lohmeyer's formulation)¹⁶ is to be understood, namely the statement in Rom 3:28 or the formulation that Paul chooses in Rom 3:20 and Gal 2:16 in connection with Ps 143(142):2, according to which "no human being is (to be) justified by works of the law." If now both that burden and these differences of opinion are looked at briefly, this would make one attentive not only to problems which ought to be considered but simultaneously aware of a problematic intercourse with the expression "works of the law."

Let us begin again with Luther and thus with the burden in church history! For the Reformer this key statement was of significance similar to that of Rom 1:17. This can be seen, for example, in that Luther "produced different series of theses on Rom 3:28,"¹⁷ and further, for instance, in the famous *Sendbrief vom Dolmetschen* of the year 1530.¹⁸ There the translation of 3:28 is defended, more precisely the addition of the word "alone" over against the Latin (or Greek) text: "We hold that a person is justified apart from works of the law, by faith alone."¹⁹ Of only little interest for us is the reason for this free procedure. A well-known passage²⁰ deals with the fact that one has to recognize the particularity of the German language and to try to correspond to it: One has to "look at the mouth [of the people], how they speak, and translate accordingly."²¹

More important for our context is the following argument,²² and indeed first because Luther here expressly states that in Rom 3:28 Paul deals with "the primary item of Christian teaching, namely, that we are justified by faith in Christ without any works of the law."²³ Furthermore and above all, since in these remarks something of the — so to express it — *Sitz im Leben* becomes clear that the "main doctrine" has for Luther. If I might formulate it again in a questionable way, it is determined by *anti-Catholic* sentiments.²⁴ Luther actually says that the doctrine is "especially [necessary] for this time, since they [i.e., the people] have been accustomed for so long to works and they must be pulled away from this with force."²⁵ That it has to do, among other things, with anti-Catholicism is confirmed when one adds further passages in which the Reformer is concerned with Pauline works of the law. This is what is said in the *Themata de Votis* of 1521²⁶ in theses 29-31:²⁷

xxix *Votum religionum aut quodcunque omnino quaedam lex est conscientiam natura captivans.*
xxx   *Et vita religiosa aut devotaria non nisi opera legis natura sunt.*
xxxi *Quaecunque ergo de lege et operibus Paulus sentit, de votis et religiosis sentienda sunt.*

29 The monks' vow or whatever else besides is altogether some kind of law and by nature takes the conscience captive.
30 And the life of a monk is by nature nothing other than works of the law.
31 Consequently whatever Paul thinks about the law and works, this must also be the thinking about vows and monks.

Especially this Luther thinks — according to theses 13 and 14:²⁸

xiii   *Opus bonum fit aliquando opinione iustitiae et salutis querendae per ipsum.*
xiiii *Haec opinio universa impietas, infidelitas et idolatria est.*

13 In the particular case [or: at times] the "good work" is done with the intention thereby to obtain justification and salvation.
14 This intention is sheer godlessness, sheer unbelief, and sheer worship of idols.

A slight anti-Judaism can also be combined with this anti-Catholicism, to the degree that the Reformer sees a correspondence[29] between his situation and that of the early Christians. In his Commentary on Galatians of 1519,[30] in which Luther in the exposition of 2:16 turns especially against the contemporary doctrine that *"remissio peccatorum"* supposedly happens *"per satisfactiunculas, per contritiones coactas"* ("by little works of satisfaction and coerced remorse"),[31] the interpreter had earlier named the Pharisees from New Testament times as an example of behavior that to be sure finds recognition in this manner of life,[32] but nevertheless is to be evaluated differently, as *"iusticia servilis, mercennaria, ficta, speciosa, externa, temporalis, mundana, humana"* ("a servile, day laborer's, counterfeit, whitewashed, external, temporary, worldly, human righteousness").[33] That one cannot easily avoid this anti-Catholicism and the certain kind of anti-Judaism related to it can be demonstrated by a witness who is quite free from suspicion, Hans Asmussen, who in 1937 wrote in Theologische Existenz heute on the theme "Sola fide — das ist lutherisch!"[34] and therein sought to define "works righteousness" as "*the* quintessential danger of the spiritual life," a danger that in those years, as he thought, manifested itself not least of all in the politically propagated behavior "according to the race *(artgemäss).*"[35] In order to derive this he formulated the following: "The fact that the Reformation cannot be imagined without the discovery that works righteousness is just as much the danger of the Roman Church as it was for Pharisaism can no longer be overlooked."[36] Of course one should ask, and we have to ask ourselves, if the Reformation, the Lutheran Reformation, was the first to employ the Pauline formulation of works of the law against what Asmussen could also call "workery *(Werkerei),*"[37] or if Paul himself already does that. Before we — not the least on account of this question — turn to modern exegesis of Paul, in the meantime it should be noticed that the reproach of religious groups for workery showed up in Protestantism not only against outsiders but also within: The larger intra-Lutheran debates which preceded the Formula of Concord — that is, the dispute about Antinomianism and the Majorist and Synergistic controversies — after all have to do to a great extent in one way or another with the question of "works" in Christian life.[38] And concerning the Swiss Protestantism of that time, to mention only this example, Melanchthon (1529) in Marburg accused Zwingli and his supporters of works righteousness because, as he said, they "speak . . . and write improperly about how the human being is reckoned before God *('für got recht* geschetzt werde'), and they do not press the doctrine of faith sufficiently, but speak rather as if works, which follow faith, were the same righteousness."[39] That the reproach of workery thus comes in in a wide variety of places might take a bit of the edge off the problem at hand with anti-Catholicism and anti-Judaism; at the same time, however, it draws attention to at least one problematic side — not only, but also — with Luther's position and argumentation: as too easily escapes notice, he deals with the expression "works of the law" very generously.[40] Not only that, for example, as we saw the fulfillment of monk's vows was subsumed under this expression, although these vows had quite little to do with the Torah; also, to cite only a few examples from the *Sendbrief vom Dolmetschen*,[41] works of the law are equated with "our works," with "external works,"[42] with "good" and "bad works."[43] Of course in Rom 3:28 there is nothing of the sort, and just as little in Gal 2:16, concerning which Luther said in 1519[44] in commenting: "*Opera legis . . . sunt bona in specie, mala in corde*" ("*The works of the law . . . are good in appearances, but evil in the heart*").[45] Such generous philology, especially equating "works" or "works of the law" with "good works," is, of course, not to be blamed on Luther alone, even less so when in view of the ecclesiastical tradition and his anti-Catholic orientation the issue of good works had to suggest itself.[46] Moreover, we will immediately run across such generosity in association with Paul's way of expressing himself[47] as, after this glance at the burden in church history associated with the expression "works of the law," we now turn briefly to the present differences of opinion with respect to why, according to Paul, works of the law do not justify.

In loose dependence on a listing that the Belgian New Testament scholar J. Lambrecht presented some years ago,[48] I would like to name three positions:

(1) Above all, R. Bultmann with his view of things stands very close to Luther:[49] "no human being can obtain his 'righteousness' by works of the law — namely . . . because he cannot present them."[50] And: "The human being is . . . therefore not to be 'justified' by works of the law, because he should not think that he is able to obtain his salvation from his own power."[51] Also according to the famous exegete from Marburg, human action at best produces seeming good works. Even worse: according to him, one should understand Paul such that "human effort to win salvation by fulfilling the law only brings one into sin; indeed, it itself already is the sin,"[52] insofar as at the same time "the law . . . is grasped by human beings

as a means of their self-glorification."⁵³ "One gets," to characterize and to caricature this position a bit with the words of another exegete, "the impression that zeal for the law is more damaging than transgression" of the regulations of Torah.⁵⁴ So, according to Bultmann, there is always something fishy in the doing of good, the fish of self-justification. Against this the two other positions take their turn:

(2) U. Wilckens represents a view that should be especially valid for Rom 3:28: "it is in no way the case, that he [i.e., Paul] criticizes as such the effort of human beings to prove to be righteous before God by fulfilling the law[so Wilckens], let alone, then, that he disputes the righteousness of one who really is righteous on the basis of works. Rather, Paul judges all human beings actually as sinners, because all have sinned."⁵⁵

(3) E. P. Sanders likewise turns against Bultmann. This can be seen in two distinctive and imaginatively formulated central statements of his influential book *Paul and Palestinian Judaism*, namely, that the Apostle simply "holds Judaism to be false . . . in that it is not Christianity,"⁵⁶ and that Paul does not think from plight to solution but "from solution to plight."⁵⁷ With direct reference to Bultmann is the formulation: "What is wrong with following the law," with the works of the law, "is not the effort itself, but the fact that the observer of the law is not seeking the righteousness which is given by God through the coming of Christ."⁵⁸

When we survey these recent positions on the reason for not being justified by works of the law, two further items are added to the problem of whether Paul with this terminology may have expressed himself in a slightly anti-Jewish way (and whether he lends encouragement to anti-Catholicism and perhaps also to an anti-Reformed bias). First, the question of how the Apostle would respond to the "main doctrine" of the Lutheran Reformation, to the *articulus stantis et cadentis ecclesiae*,⁵⁹ which after the intense oscillations that have been presented seems itself to be oscillating. Unfortunately the representatives of the considerably divergent positions who have been named are also exclusively Protestants! Does Paul's way of expressing himself here possibly permit a clarification or indeed a decision? Meanwhile on *one* point all the opinions that have been presented fortunately or at least interestingly agree, namely, that at issue with the works of the law is in some way or other the notion of acting according to regulations of the law, the Torah, or at least of attempting to act in such a way. In spite of this consensus, which has already been pointed out with the mention of P. Billerbeck's widely accepted suggested translation, i.e., "fulfillments of commands,"⁶⁰ a further, a final problem arises: is this translation reasonably correct, or does it miss the meaning of the expression "works of the law"?

That there is a problem here has already been touched on with the reference to Luther's problematic equating of "works of the law" with "our," "external," "good," and "bad works."⁶¹ Similarly loose, similarly problematic, however, is, e.g., Wilckens's procedure, when he says in connection with the formulation already cited: "Within the scope of the law even a single sin is capable of making a human being a sinner; and therefore it stands that a sinner cannot liberate himself by any *good work* from the sin he has done. . . . It is the *sinful work* which has the effect of disaster on the fate of the sinner."⁶² "Works of the law" correspond here to good *and* bad works, to acting according to the law *and* to transgressing the law. What authorizes this peculiar equation? Indeed in the passage that is thematic for Wilckens, Rom 3:28, Paul says nothing about "works of lawlessness," but rather only something about "works of the law." A basis for the identification is hinted at in Bultmann's dictum, which is no less peculiar, even if it is carefully formulated, "that he [i.e., Paul] does not shrink from speaking about judgment according to works in what is at least an apparent contradiction to his doctrine of justification by faith alone."⁶³ Here — as similarly in Sanders⁶⁴ — the expressions "*according to/on the basis of* works" and "*by/from* works of the law" relating to judgment on the one hand and justification on the other are implicitly set in relationship with each other, as if the prepositions "according to" (κατά) and "by/from" (ἐκ) were identical and as if the genitive (τοῦ) νόμου could be ignored beyond all question.⁶⁵ If one were allowed to proceed in this way, then one would naturally also have to have no scruples to bring into play with respect to the expression "works of the law," also "good" or "bad," indeed also "my" and "your" works, because what is at stake with "judgment according to works," both for Paul and his milieu, is the clarification of how the action of a concrete human being is eventually to be evaluated. But is this equation of "*by/from* works," and "*according to/on the basis of* works of the law," likewise on the level of action, really correct? Should we not take into consideration that Paul does not intend to contradict himself when he speaks of justification "apart from works of the law" and of judgment "according to works," and that he chooses consciously distinct ways of expressing himself? We will now track this down and along with that take a stand on the problem just named,⁶⁶ namely whether works of the law — in accordance with the *opinio communis* — can be placed directly on the level of action.

3

My thesis, which I will have to establish exegetically, can be formulated here: with the expression "works of the law" Paul does not mean something that lies at the level marked out by action according to the regulations of the law, especially not the fulfillments of (a) command(s); rather, with the syntagm "works of the law" Paul means the regulations of the law themselves. One could also say that he means the *mṣwt*, the *hlkwt* that are to be observed.[67]

In the argument in favor of this assertion I would like to proceed in such a way that a first and longer stage takes the New Testament into view and within the New Testament then focuses more and more on Paul. After this, the horizon will be widened and comparative material outside the New Testament will be of interest.

The argument for this view! The thesis in question might seem to some to be abstruse, and probably it has never been seriously[68] or consistently advocated[69] because linguistic history points in another direction or at least appears to; for Greek ἔργον is, to say it with the article on ἔργον in Kittel's *Theologisches Wörterbuch zum Neuen Testament,* "from the same Indo-Germanic stem and has the same meaning as the German 'Werk'"[70] — and as the English "work." Therefore, when one says "Werke des Gesetzes" or "works of the law," one is supposed to know straightaway what ἔργα νόμου means. Since by "Werk" — or correspondingly by "work" — one thinks without question of effective action,[71] so naturally the conclusion suggests itself that the expression "works of the law" is equivalent to "actions according to the law (or according to its individual regulations)." This conclusion is, however, too simple. For instance, a glance at the account of the letter to the church in Thyatira (or to its angel) in Rev 2:18-29 will show this. Close to the beginning, in 2:19, ἔργα, "works," are mentioned in such a way that the level of action is unquestionably emphasized: "I know your works and your love and your faith and your service and your patient endurance, and the last to be more than the first."[72] When the text then turns to what is said negatively about Jezebel and those who are said to have been beguiled by her, this statement appears (2:23): "I will give to each of you as your works deserve,"[73] then it is clear that with this judgment terminology, here related to Jesus, ἔργα is again thought of as part of the sphere of behavior, indeed even denoting good *and* bad behavior.[74] But the use of the word is completely different afterward in 2:26, where it appears not with a second person pronoun but with a first person pronoun, which designates Jesus: "And to the one who conquers and keeps *my works* unto the end I will give power over the nations." Obviously this cannot mean Jesus' *action(s)* but only keeping his *commandments*,[75] especially since 3:8 (cf. 3:10) or 12:17 and 14:12 respectively speak similarly of keeping Jesus' words or God's commands (ἐντολαί).[76] Thus the first conclusion: "Work," ἔργον, can have to do not only with the level of effective activity or doing — as for the most part[77] — but can also designate the norm that should be obeyed, the command.[78] The second conclusion: The genitive accompanying "work" can be not only — as it is often[79] — a *genitivus subiectivus* marking the subject of the action, but also a kind of genitive that characterizes in some way the quality of the work, that is, of the command. As a confirmation it should be taken into account that at least the Johannine writings[80] offer parallels; so John 6:28, 29, possibly also John 4:34 and 9:4 (cf. 5:36; 17:4).[81][82] Briefly put: in view of such passages — contrary to the impression of the diachronic argument which concerns the linguistic history — the thesis is indeed possible, and the genitive νόμου in the phrase ἔργα νόμου could thus clarify the commands in regard to their quality as, e.g., τὰ ἔργα τοῦ θεοῦ — in John 6:28 — does by means of the attribute that brings the commands into association with God.[83]

A glance at the Epistle of James is also instructive, so far as it[84] is in development and in — supposedly indirect[85] — dispute with what Paul said about ἔργα νόμου and πίστις Χριστοῦ.[86] The passage that is decisive for this dispute — Jas 2:14-26, which ends with the emphatic statement: "faith without works is dead" — remarkably does not contain the genitive νόμου,[87] and likewise does not contain the other genitive, Χριστοῦ. At the least that is a clear clue that James is at cross-purposes likely not with his addressees but possibly with Paul, for whom in the contexts where the expression "works of the law" occurs the issue is quite patently the groundshaking Christ event and therefore precisely the πίστις Χριστοῦ (see only Rom 3:22, 24; Gal 2:16-17, 20-21; 3:1, 13-14).[88] This terminological digression from Paul has an equivalent in that in spite of the use of the apparently Pauline prepositional terminology "by/from works" (Jas 2:18, 21, 22, 24, 25) and "without works" (2:18, 26),[89] the author of James — Luther, consequently, was not the first — has no scruples in adding a personal pronoun, namely μοῦ.[90] Jas 2:18 says (cf. 2:22; 3:13): "I will show you the faith by my works."

Just this, however, as E. Lohmeyer emphasized in an important essay on the term "works of the law" that first appeared in 1929,[91] is never the case in Paul's writings: "in no passage did Paul connect the expression 'works of the law' with the genitive of a person"; "it is also absent where the terminology is abbreviated to the simple word 'work.'"[92] Rather, the Apostle makes a, so to say, clinically clean cut between on the one hand the complete and the abbreviated expression[93] and on the other hand the other formulations that use the term "work." Only in the second type does Paul use pronouns in the genitive,[94] and that, by the way, he does in an entire range of passages (Rom 2:6; 1 Cor 3:14, 15; 9:1; 2 Cor 11:15; Gal 6:4; 1 Thess 1:3;[95] 5:13; cf. 2 Tim 1:9;[96] 4:14, further Tit 3:5,[97] 14[98]). Corresponding to this Paul never — and certainly not in Rom 9:11-12 — designates "works of the law" (or the abbreviated expression "works") directly as good or bad, although beyond these texts he speaks now and then about "good work"[99] (Rom 2:7; 13:3; 2 Cor 9:8; Phil 1:6; cf. Col 1:10; 2 Thess 2:17; 1 Tim 5:10; 2 Tim 2:21; 3:17; Tit 1:16; 3:1).[100] If one realizes this clean division between two terminological domains and thereby disengages oneself from the almost unavoidable compulsion to mix them as in the Epistle of James[101] — and then later, e.g., Luther, Bultmann, Wilckens, and Sanders — then an independent view of Paul's use of the expression "works of the law" becomes possible. Not only has this compulsion now been broken but also the spell exerted by etymology. The Pauline letters themselves then supply considerable evidence for the equation of "works of the law" and "regulations of the law." I will emphasize four points:

(i) If, as has just been presented, there is never any talk here of "my works of the law," or — for example — "yours," and never any talk of "good" or "bad works of the law," then this is sufficient evidence that ἔργα νόμου has nothing immediate to do with individual achievements that are to be judged.[102] Rather it appears as if the issue must be about something independent from me or you and from concrete action. Or the other way around: if it is about regulations of the Torah, about the Torah that God gave, about "God's law" (Rom 7:22, 25; 8:7), then to speak of my or your works of the law and likewise reference to bad works of the law is obviously inadmissible (cf. Rom 7:7), and the analogous reference to good works of the law (cf. Rom 7:12, 14, 16[103]) can in nearly all cases be dispensed with.

(ii) It has already often been noted in the literature that "works of the law" and "law" in Paul can stand parallel to each other.[104] Incidentally this applies to the contexts of all six verses in which Paul presents the syntagm.[105] This correspondence is especially clear in Rom 3:28 and 3:21, where it says "without works of the law" and "without law." The simplest explanation for this parallel[106] is of course that the works of the law are nothing other than the regulations of the law.[107] For then something almost like an equation is under consideration here with "law" and "regulations of the law," an equation that describes the demands of the law.[108]

(iii) Besides the six verses with the plural "works of the law," Paul uses the singular once, in Rom 2:15:[109] "the work of the law."[110] Of course because, according to this passage, the work of the law is — in dependence perhaps on Jer 31:33[111] — inscribed in the hearts of the Gentiles, it cannot mean here action according to the law — an action that naturally takes place primarily in relation to the external world.[112] According to the context of the passage, with the singular the Apostle somehow means the entire demand of the Torah or of something equivalent to the Jewish law.[113] Moreover, at the same time the context also indicates that according to Paul the entire demand is broken down into individual demands and that he nonetheless has certain difficulties in designating these individual regulations. In the previous verse he helps himself with the expression τὰ τοῦ νόμου, leaving out the substantive that governs the formulation. One can hardly understand it any differently from E. Käsemann, who in translating inserts the word "demands."[114] Thus the demands of the law are equivalent to the work of the law, and this of course fits quite well our thesis that the works of the law are to be understood precisely as the demands, the individual regulations of the Torah. It is not at all easy to say why the Apostle expresses himself in this elliptic way in Rom 2:14. At any rate it is clear: He uses νόμος consistently in the singular[115] and mostly with a view to the Mosaic law as a unity,[116] and thus he continues, "the LXX's practice of translating the plural *torot* almost exclusively with singular νόμος."[117] This already reduces Paul's linguistic possibilities to speak of the regulations of the Torah in the plural. Inasmuch as in Romans 7 he uses the term ἐντολή, "command," without exception in the singular and in v. 12 parallel with νόμος, and, moreover, inasmuch as in 1 Cor 7:19 he even sets the ἐντολαὶ θεοῦ over against the requirement for circumcision, for him this word does not come into consideration for the individual regulations of the Torah. Apparently for a similar reason the plural τὰ δικαιώματα τοῦ νόμου in

Rom 2:26 (cf. 8:4, also 1:32) drops out: Paul here treats the fulfillment of these δικαιώματα on the part of "the uncircumcision" (ἡ ἀκροβυστία). Finally, then, only our expression ἔργα νόμου remains. According to the use in Galatians and Romans this expression has to do with the Torah and especially includes the requirement for circumcision,[118] and for that very reason it may have been avoided in Rom 2:14-15, because these verses also consider the question of the fulfillment of the law on the part of those who are uncircumcised. However, according to the indications of just this context the syntagm can mean, as we have seen, the requirements, the regulations of the law. And the formulation τὰ δικαιώματα τοῦ νόμου in Rom 2:26, to which τὸ δικαίωμα τοῦ θεοῦ in 1:32 (cf. 8:4: τὸ δικαίωμα τοῦ νόμου) corresponds to a certain extent, gives a helpful parallel to our genitive construction. One does not have to "establish a *genitivus nomisticus*," as Lohmeyer facetiously introduced into the discussion,[119] nor is it advisable to follow the suggestion of the North American New Testament scholar L. Gaston that a *genitivus subiectivus* is under consideration, similar to the expression "works of the flesh" in Gal 5:19, so that the law — just as the flesh — would be a power that has a negative effect.[120] The genitive τοῦ νόμου indicates rather what constitutes the quality of the ἔργα, and what constitutes it is the domain to which they belong: the domain of the νόμος. Therefore, a quite normal genitive construction is under consideration.[121]

(iv) The six verses[122] with the expression "works of the law" must of course provide the decisive test. And they are, in my opinion, actually to be interpreted without exception in a less problematic way with the new understanding of the syntagm than before. This can for instance be settled, as has already been made thematic under point (ii), in that the parallel formulations of νόμος and ἔργα νόμου with this assumption can be well understood in every context. What otherwise can be asserted[123] in a supporting way should be addressed for reasons of time in only two points.

First: One *crux interpretum* that has occupied interpreters for centuries fades with this new interpretation. This concerns Gal 3:10 — and in a similar way Rom 3:20.[124] Luther for instance, who for his part already in his first lecture on the letter refers to Jerome's difficulties with the passage,[125] and says with respect to the verse (Gal 3:10) in the large commentary on Galatians (1535) that the "two sentences" united in it "clearly contradict each other."[126] And in the small commentary (1519) it says:[127] "Now look at the strange conclusion that the Apostle draws here! He quotes from Deut 27:26 that those who do not do what is written in the book of the law are cursed. From this negation he gets an affirmative sentence, namely this: Those who do the works of the law [*qui operantur opera legis*] are cursed. Does he not then affirm just that which Moses denies?" Whereas Luther refers to the words of the Roman governor Festus from Acts 26:24, that Paul has gone mad from his great learning,[128] C. D. Stanley, who recently devoted an essay to the problem, speaks of something like a facetious riddle: "the Pauline text does present something of a conundrum."[129] Now, as it seems to me, this riddle can be resolved,[130] though quite differently from how Stanley would prefer.[131] The problem arises only if one comprehends the first half of the verse in the sense of the characterization of those persons whose working corresponds to the Torah, *qui operantur opera legis*, to express it once more in Luther's words. If, however, works of the law are a matter not at all of action according to the Torah but rather of the regulations of the law themselves, it comes off without any tension because then this part of the verse still has nothing at all to do with the fulfillment of the law but rather simply with something like the orientation toward individual commands and prohibitions of the Torah, an orientation that may not be crowned with success. And the point is just that this orientation is entirely *not* crowned in that way, and this point and that the conflict with individual regulations of the Torah leads to the curse are then underlined by the citation from Deuteronomy and substantiated in the following verses.[132] Therefore, on the basis of sinning, everyone who is of the works of the law, who is orientated toward the regulations of the Torah, is under the curse.[133] Thereby a long-established *crux interpretum* is settled!

Moreover and *second*, a glance at Gal 3:2, 5 indicates more clearly what kind of alternative Paul had in view with the rather stereotyped opposition of "by/from works (of the law)" (Rom 3:20; Gal 2:16aα, bγ, c [cf. Rom 4:2; 9:12, 32; 11:6, further Rom 4:13, 14, 16; 10:5; Gal 2:19aα, 21bα; 3:18a, 21cβ; 5:4aβ])[134] and "through (or by/from) faith in (Jesus) Christ (or Christ Jesus)" (Rom 3:22, 26; Gal 2:16aβ, bβ [cf. Rom 9:32; Gal 2:16bα, 17a, further Rom 3:28; 4:3, 5, 13, 16; 9:30; 10:6; Gal 3:8, 9, 11, 12, 14]).[135] What is in mind is not really the somewhat distorted opposition — distorted in view of biblical and Pauline ethics (cf. only Ps 25:4-17; Phil 2:13) — between human and divine action, between the horizontal and vertical, if one does not relate ἔργα νόμου to doing but to the regulations of Torah. Rather what is in mind is the issue that two conceivable sources of salvation, of the Spirit, of God's dealing with human beings are compared. The alternative runs: "from regulations of the law (. . .) or from the preaching of faith." This is a clear alternative, insofar as it refers twice to an *extra nos* from which the individual can understand himself or herself and from which the individual can shape his or her life.¹³⁶ And it is also clear that for the Apostle only the second possibility comes into consideration.

Alongside these four points, which plead in favor of our thesis about the Pauline use of the expression "works of the law," diachrony should also come into play a little, though not without accentuation. The question needs to be raised whether labeling the typical etymological argument as specious¹³⁷ leaves behind a gap in the history of comparative linguistics. If one therefore searches for a Hebrew equivalent to the expression "works of the law," which Paul uses in such a strikingly invariable and apparently technical way, one runs into — it is already mentioned in "Billerbeck" — *m'śy twrh*.¹³⁸ Of course for this combination neither Billerbeck nor Lohmeyer could provide even one reference from antiquity.¹³⁹ When they claim instead the expression *opera praeceptorum*, "works of the commandments," in 2 *Bar.* 57:2 as a close equivalent to the syntagm "works of the law,"¹⁴⁰ then this passage is not completely uninteresting for us; for "works" and "law" are set in parallel here as in Paul,¹⁴¹ and, moreover, doing is distinguished from the "works," as already Lohmeyer saw.¹⁴² By way of confirmation it can be added that (particularly) the Septuagint employs ἔργον in the sense of command or prescription in quite a number of passages.¹⁴³ This fact ought to cause less astonishment since ἔργον in the domain of secular Greek can mean not only effective action¹⁴⁴ but also a task to be mastered.¹⁴⁵ But ἔργα νόμου is not found in the Greek Old Testament. The situation has, however, changed decisively for the better with the discoveries at Qumran, more precisely with the successive publication of the more or less well preserved documents. To be sure, the "parallel," already published for more than 30 years¹⁴⁶ and until recently the only one noted (and clearly designated) in secondary literature,¹⁴⁷ that appears in a "Florilegium" found in the fourth cave has been under considerable doubt for a good 20 years; because 4QFlor 1:7 possibly reads not *m'śy twrh*, works of the law, but rather, with daleth, *m'śy twdh*, works of the thank offering.¹⁴⁸ Meanwhile, however, fortunately, at least in a kind of pirated edition,¹⁴⁹ a document from the same cave that is interesting in many respects has become known, a letter that perhaps even originates from the Teacher of Righteousness himself.¹⁵⁰ And this letter to a nonparticipant in the Teacher's group, dealing with more than 20 halakhic questions, especially concerning "calendar, purity and temple cult, laws of marriage,"¹⁵¹ offers now in its epilogue the only certain parallel to the Pauline expression "works of the law." If it says regarding what precedes *mqṣt m'śy htwrh*[152] (C29 [cf. B1-2 and C32]), there can hardly be any doubt that this is about prescriptions, regulations of the law, not about doing according to the regulations. So then the (proper) editors of the text translate the expression, which they incidentally choose as the designation of the document (4QMMT), "some of the precepts of the Torah."[153] Evidently Paul joins in just such a use of language! And this should be all the less open to doubt because, first, the noun *m'śh* — already in Exod 18:20, where it stands in parallel with *ḥqym* (statutes) and *twrt* (instructions[154]) — means what is to be done[155] and because rabbinic interpretation refers to just this passage and points here to "the line of the law,"[156] to judging "according to the letter of the law."[157] Second, Paul and this Qumran letter also stand quite strikingly close to each other even beyond the sheer expression "works of the law." This terminology is closely associated not only in Romans and Galatians (Rom 4:3; Gal 3:6) with the question, inspired by the text about Abraham in Gen 15:6 (cf. 1 Macc 2:52, further Ps 106:31), of what is reckoned as righteousness; also the epilogue of the letter from Qumran (C33; cf. C29) provides precisely this association![158] Moreover, by means of similar modes of speech both Paul and the "Teacher of Righteousness" say that works of the law, prescriptions of the Torah, need to be taken into careful consideration with regard to what is to be done; for whereas in the older halakhic document the verb *'śh* surfaces in connection with these "works," prescriptions[159] (C33; cf. C24, also B2), the verb that the Apostle uses in Rom 4:4-5 (cf. 2:10; 13:10; Gal 6:10, further 1 Cor 16:10, also 1 Cor 9:13) is ἐργάζεσθαι.[160] In brief, in view of these points of contact one cannot speak, or can no longer speak, about a gap in the history of comparative linguistics.

4

As a result our thesis recommends itself on the basis of both diachronic and synchronic aspects. This also means, in a paradoxical way so to speak, that just that conviction must be abandoned which connects the three answers presented above to the question of why, according to Paul, works of the law do not justify — the conviction that works of the law have to do in Paul directly with the level of doing. That is just not the way it is! Thus whereas what has been the consensus until now must be abandoned, the dissent outlined above may possibly be overcome. Certainly it appears overhasty to condemn wholesale the positions of Bultmann, Wilckens, and Sanders, or indeed Luther's interpretation. Without doubt, however, these views appear in a different light with this new understanding of the expression "works of the law." Concerning Bultmann, it is unquestionably correct that Paul has something against self-glorification of human beings, but not because "fulfilling the law . . . is the sin," but rather because those who take glory in themselves (according to Romans 2–3) transgress the law publicly or in secret[161] and so according to Gal 3:10 become victims of the curse.[162] Wilckens has seen this quite correctly, but Paul does not arrive at the thought that "all human beings actually" are "sinners" on the basis of a statistical survey; rather, as for example the opposition "from works of the law (. . .) or from the preaching of faith" in Gal 3:2, 5 makes clear,[163] he does so on the basis of the Christ event, which according to the Apostle cannot have been causeless (see Gal 2:21b).[164] Sanders grasps this quite well, in exactly the same way that he perceives the sociological dimension of the ἔργα,[165] but the dreadful state, the dreadful state of sin, which Paul actually derives from the Christ event, is for the Apostle just as real as the death of Jesus itself, in which precisely the overcoming of sin(s) was at stake (see only Rom 3:23-26; Gal 1:4; 2:20[-21]; 3:14).[166]

Of course this sinning should not now be confused with the works of the law — neither in the sense of successful doing nor in the sense of action that misses its target. Rather, the works of the law have to do directly with the νόμος, which according to Rom 7:12 is holy, and in this respect they have to do with none other than God. Where Paul speaks of ἔργα νόμου, he will not encourage in any way a discrediting of action according to the works of the law, whether it is the good action of the Catholic, the Jew, the Reformed, or even the Lutheran. For according to Rom 2:13, "it is not the hearers of the law who are righteous in God's sight, but the doers." We have to give serious consideration to this in view of the burden of our theological and ecclesiastical history and in view of what corresponded to and corresponds to it in the history of our social life, or more accurately, in the history of our often pathological social life. This is demanded not only by the event of the Holocaust and by the era of ecumenism; this is demanded, it seems, also by Paul. Of course this will not go beyond — as in exegetical work — knowing in part (cf. 1 Cor 13:9), completely in accordance with that which Paul and, following him, Luther all the more never tire of emphasizing over against all triumphalism. To cite the Apostle one last time — more precisely Rom 3:20:[167] "no flesh is (to be) justified before him [i.e., God] by/from the regulations of the law, for through the law comes the knowledge of sin."[168]

2. 4QMMT and Galatians, מעשי התורה and ΕΡΓΑ ΝΟΜΟΥ

1

In his essay on 4QMMT and Galatians,[1] J. D. G. Dunn listed in a commendable way important parallels between the two documents,[2] and from these similarities he derived some conclusions concerning the situation (in Antioch and) in Galatia.[3] One can highlight further similarities, even though they are not quite as spectacular as the correspondence between מעשי התורה (C27; cf. B2) and ἔργα νόμου (Gal 2:16 [3 times]; 3:2, 5, 10). Thus, for example, terminological contacts in the way of speaking about "seed," that is, descent, stand out (B81 [cf. B75] and Gal 3:16, 19, 29), and further the metaphor of keeping to the path (see C12 [cf. C25] and Gal 2:14 [cf., e.g., Gal 2:18; 3:19]).[4] Substantially the almost eschatological tones — involving the theme of Israel[5] — are particularly evident (see esp. C16, 21, 30-32; Gal 1:4; 4:4; 5:5; 6:15-16). And in no case should one overlook that the document 4QMMT, originally described by its editors E. Qimron and J. Strugnell as a letter of polemical style,[6] stands strikingly close in its literary character especially to the Pauline letters and among them precisely to the one sent to "the churches of Galatia" (Gal 1:2).[7]

This assessment is ultimately not dependent on whether the introduction to the text, which does not appear in any of the manuscripts of this document, contained the prescript of a letter.[8] What is decisive, rather, is that the two sections that follow the calendrical information (A), the first of which is defined by halakhic material (B) and the second of which bears a stronger parenetic character (C), are reminiscent of Paul's letters in two ways, in the sequence of what is thematic and what is of rather personal nature,⁹ and, above all, in the constellation of three groups that are found in these two sections:¹⁰ In the "Qumran document" a group designated by "we" (B1; C7 and *passim*) turns in a quite friendly tone to a group designated by "you" plural (B68; C8 and *passim*) or to a specific "you" singular (C26, 28 and *passim*) representing a larger circle (see C27; cf. C31-32); whereas it is without doubt intended to convince the one who is addressed by "you" singular and his circle concerning the mentioned halakhot (see esp. C30), a group designated by "they" emerges in the phraseology without any friendliness, which judges these points differently (B6, 10 and *passim*).¹¹ There is probably a reference to these people in the by now well-known formulation, which represents the earliest instance of פרש in the sense of delimiting a religious community, a sect, here the "we" group: "we have separated ourselves from the multitude of the people [and from all their impurity] and from being involved with these matters and from participating with [them] in these things" (C7-8).¹²

This constellation of three groups obviously parallels the Pauline literature, especially clearly Galatians.¹³ For Paul claims to write that letter in the name of the "brothers" who are with him (Gal 1:2), and he frequently makes use of the first person plural, leaving the impression of a "we" group;¹⁴ the polemic over against a "they" group is clear as well,¹⁵ whereas the addressees — no differently from the cowriters (or co-senders) — are designated as "brothers" as well as "you" (plural),¹⁶ and the Apostle endeavors to prevent them from following the line of the "they" group and from allowing themselves to be circumcised.¹⁷

How close the two constellations of three groups are to each other can be particularly observed in the conclusions of the two documents. In Gal 6:14-16 Paul connects the recommended obedience to his (christological) maxim with a hopeful view of the "Israel of God," and in 4QMMT C28-32 the desired recognition and realization of the presented halakhot is correspondingly combined with the well-being of Israel.¹⁸

In view of the far-reaching correspondences in both content and structure between 4QMMT and the Pauline Epistles, especially Galatians, the thought suggests itself that the "vocabulary and manner of theologizing,"¹⁹ as represented by the "Qumran Document," could not only be claimed for "opponents" of the Apostle (having an effect in Antioch and becoming effective in Galatia),²⁰ but also quite reasonably for his own argumentation — although it is obviously not aiming for demarcation and particularism (see only Gal 1:16; 2:7-9; 3:8, 20, 26-29). Inasmuch, however, as 4QMMT also intends to win the "you" (singular) and the circle associated with him for a particular (halakhic) understanding and action,[21] the mentioned contacts are of high interest first of all for the epistolographic assessment (of the Pauline Epistles and above all) of Galatians. It can now hardly be regarded primarily against the background of the *genus iudiciale* of ancient rhetoric and of the minutely few examples of "apologetic letters,"[22] but rather should be classified much more as a polemical document just like 4QMMT — or even as a polemical halakhic letter. For the intended effect this means that the polemic especially aims at modifying the addressees' attitude and behavior (not at a defense of the Apostle against attacks).[23]

Since Paul, as has been mentioned, speaks against attempts to accept circumcision and opposes particularist tendencies, the conviction he seeks to mediate is, concerning its substance, rather directly opposed to the persuasive intent of 4QMMT. One could get the impression that in the triangle of "we," "you" (singular and plural), and "they" that characterizes the "Qumran text," Paul belongs to the "they" group and from there engages in polemics against the "we" group in order to convince the circle of addressees as well. This is of course an anachronism, because the composition of 4QMMT lies about 200 years before that of Galatians,[24] and *in the triangle of Galatians* the individual positions are occupied by members of the Christian communities:[25]

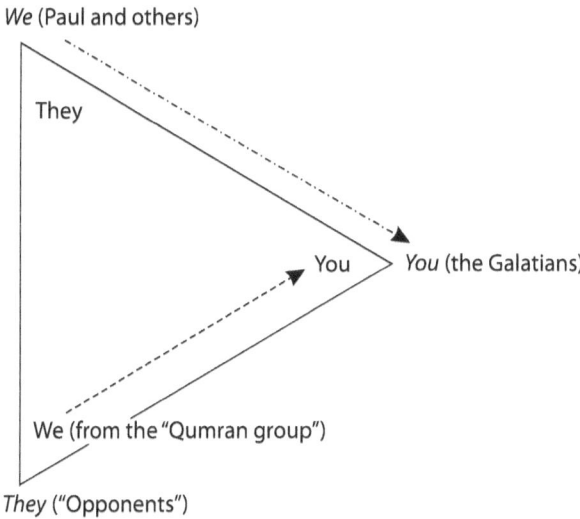

However, this working model helps us to draw attention more sharply to the fact that in Galatians Paul advocates an inclusive idea of salvation and in Gal 3:1–4:7 no fewer than three times brings "the inclusion of the Gentiles" before the readers' eyes.[26] He evidently does this because he considers the attitude of *his* "*they*" group, which at least propagates circumcision — something halakhic — as if it means the exclusion of those who do not agree with this norm of behavior (see 4:17: ἐκκλεῖσαι ὑμᾶς θέλουσιν).[27] In relation to Peter and capable of referring to everyone belonging to this "*they*" group, 2:12 describes the other side of the process of exclusion: ἀφώριζεν ἑαυτόν — and this is indeed a remarkable parallel to the action of the "we" group in 4QMMT, as it is described in C7-8.[28] The Apostle opposes the coercion that derives from such exclusivity as well as the zeal that is connected with it (see 4:17-18), particularly in 4:8–5:1.[29]

Moreover, the working model is not *completely* anachronistic: Paul characterizes himself in 1:13-14 as one who at one time did not shrink back from harsh proceedings as an extreme ζηλωτής . . . τῶν πατρικῶν μου παραδόσεων,[30] and he writes this before the Qumran settlement is destroyed by the Romans and while 4QMMT is still in effect there. To be sure, Paul evidently does not adopt his stance[31] directed against exclusivism grounded in halakhah because he, on the basis of his religious upbringing, would be accustomed to thinking as a lenient Pharisee, differently from the "Qumran people" standing behind that letter. Such a view is well nigh excluded by the term Φαρισαῖος in Phil 3:4-6 (which comes to mind because of its close connection to Gal 1:13-14) — where the concept must be used differently, namely, precisely with the meaning of 4QMMT C7-8![32] Rather what is decisive for the Apostle is his experience of a call (Gal 1:15-16), which turned him around from a persecutor who advocated exclusivity to a proclaimer of faith (see esp. Gal 1:23), and thus it is the Christ event which for Paul means inclusiveness. According to Gal 2:15-17(-21) justification for other Jewish Christians is also tied to Christ alone, not to ἔργα νόμου, and according to 3:1ff. this holds also for the (Galatian) Gentile Christians.[33] Therefore Paul attempts precisely not to persuade the "Qumran people" to give up their exclusivity but rather to convince the Galatian community that a tendency for Christians toward exclusivity grounded in halakha could come about only at the price of breaking with the Christ event and hence ought not to come about (see esp. 5:2-12; 6:11-16[34]).

The points of contact between 4QMMT and Galatians provide, as we have seen, benefits for resolving important epistolary and historical prob-

4QMMT and Galatians, מעשׂי התורה *and* ΕΡΓΑ ΝΟΜΟΥ

lems which are presented by this Pauline letter (and the analogies vice versa contribute to the understanding [of the genre] of the "Qumran document"). Only if the parallels can be traced back to Paul himself and not simply to his "opponents," is it moreover explainable why the contacts with 4QMMT are not confined to the letter to the Galatian communities. They are also relevant for Romans, which, for example, contains the motifs of "seed" (4:13, 16, 18 and *passim*) and "Israel" (9:6; 11:26 and *passim*) as well. What is more, Romans offers with 4:5-9 in the context of the theme of justification, that is, with the reference to the forgiveness that is asserted for David, an additional remarkable parallel to this "Qumran document" (see C23-32, esp. C25-26, 31).[35] As is well known, this Pauline letter does not lack the expression ἔργα νόμου (Rom 3:20, 28; cf. 9:32 variant reading); indeed an enormous effect has spread out from Rom 3:28, and particularly Luther's rendering "on des gesetzes werck, allein durch den glauben" ("without works of the law, by faith alone"), inserting the little word "alone," accented the relationship between πίστις and ἔργα νόμου as even more charged with tension.[36] If this expression, which has been so important in the history of the West and which remarkably has never been attested in Greek literature before or beside Paul so far, now for the first time finds a close parallel with מעשׂי התורה in 4QMMT C27,[37] this is of course of the highest interest.

2

A considerable opportunity for understanding is wasted, however, if the two expressions מעשׂי התורה and ἔργα νόμου — out of a legitimate interest of accenting their proximity — are translated by "works (or deeds) of the law," thus minimizing the relevance of evidence that demonstrates other connotations. That is what eventually happened with Dunn in the essay mentioned above (i.e., at the beginning of section 1), when he, with regard to the expression מעשׂי התורה, highlights: "The closeness of the parallel with Paul's phrase, ἔργα νόμου, has unfortunately been obscured by the translations so far adopted — 'the precepts of the Torah' . . . , 'observances of the Law.'"[38] As will now be worked out just in a few points, the rendering "works of the law,"[39] which is favored instead and for which it is put forward that "'deed' or 'act' is the most natural meaning for מעשׂה,"[40] is difficult to maintain if the "Qumran document" is taken into account

(2.1). Further for Paul one should not translate ἔργα νόμου with "works of the law," but with "regulations of the law" or with "halakhot," as will be summed up afterward (2.2) in connection with former remarks on the matter.[41]

2.1

As indicated previously, the expression in 4QMMT C27 so far lacks a genuine parallel in ancient Hebrew literature. In particular, such a parallel cannot be claimed to exist in 4Q174 3:7 (formerly called 4QFlor 1:7), where, if one were to follow Dunn, "works of the law" is documented an additional time;[42] that the reading there is not מעשי תורה but מעשי תודה should by now be regarded as sufficiently certain.[43] One can of course compare parallels that are not as close, for instance מעשי הצדקה (1QH 9:26 [formerly 1:26]; 12:31 [formerly 4:31]) and מעשי בתורה (1QS 5:21; 6:18; cf. 5:23 [מעשיו], 24 [מעשיהם]).[44] But the distinctions are considerable indeed since, in 9:26, not Torah but righteousness in the construct state is connected with "works" and, in 5:21, etc., the construct state does not appear at all and מעשים is used without exception with a suffix,[45] connecting the "works" with a person (or persons).

One is therefore — and on methodological grounds — directed primarily to the literary context of the expression מקצת מעשי התורה, which has, as it were, given the document 4QMMT its name.[46] There can accordingly be no doubt — merely on account of מקצת and the distribution of evidence — that the expression finds a particularly close parallel in the formulation מקצת דברינו, which is used two times.[47] First, with this formulation in B1 "a series of halakhic rulings, chiefly relating to the temple, priesthood, sacrifices and purity" is introduced,[48] and then in C30 what was said before is mentioned so once again, that is, described in summary fashion.[49] The fact then that one must take this formulation as a reference to halakhic regulations[50] and that it stands in the background of the expression that is to be interpreted is not denied by Dunn, who in view of his plea for "works" must then employ a peculiar doubling of terms such as "rulings/practices."[51] If regulations are meant, by means of which the writer and those about him contrast themselves with the "they" group, as we have seen,[52] it is only natural to speak of "some of *our* 'sayings.'"[53] Indeed, this does not actualize the *fulfillment* — in principle difficult to guarentee⁵⁴ — of these regulations designated by "our words" for those in the circle about the author, but rather the specific *judgment* of halakhic questions on the part of these "Qumran people."

Because the "we" group thinks it is in the right position and attempts to persuade the addressed "you" and those about him to accept these halakhot (see C28-30), the regulations can, indeed must, be expressed in C27, so to speak, more objectively as מעשי התורה מקצת, that is, without a suffix (and as a result without a preposition).⁵⁵ These are Torah regulations that ought to be clear to anyone knowledgeable in the Torah (see C28) independently from belonging to the "we" group. For the linguistic usage of the "Qumran document" — and for the Pauline parallels (cf. only Rom 4:6 [χωρὶς ἔργων] along with Rom 3:28 [χωρὶς ἔργων νόμου]) — it is especially revealing that also in the other passage which takes up the formulation "our words," namely in B2, no suffix appears in spite of the absence of a more precise qualification by "Torah."⁵⁶ Rather, it simply says מעשים. Whereas here and in C27 the subject matter is halakhot that have been and are to be judged as valid, the expression מעשיהמה in C23, which has the suffix, is obviously not to be understood in the same way, but rather has to be understood — now actually — from their, the kings', action, from their works.⁵⁷ Thus, on the basis of the difference marked by the suffix and on account of the parallel of B2 with B1 and of C27 with C30, one must distinguish between the expression in C23 on the one hand and on the other hand the expressions "'works' of the law" (in C27) and "works" (in B2) that are both related to the halakhot.⁵⁸ ⁵⁹

To consider the meaning of מעשים in B2 and C27 to be regulations of the law makes sense moreover from a diachronic point of view. This holds first insofar as the later rabbinic terminology to a great extent was not available for the author, or its use appeared to him not to be appropriate:⁶⁰ "In MMT laws are not called halakhot, מצוות and the like."⁶¹ The term מעשים can now fill in the certain semantic gap, inasmuch as "the singular מעשה, referring to law in general, is apparently found in the Bible: 'And thou shalt teach them the statutes and the laws, and shalt show them the way wherein they must walk, and the law (המעשה) that they must perform' (Exod 18:20)."⁶² This passage or a tradition developing from it has to be taken in consideration for 4QMMT quite confidently because C12 with the image of the "path (of the Torah)" could well be dependent on this text,⁶³ and because the juxtaposition מעשים and עשה, as found in C27 and C31, parallels very closely Exod 18:20⁶⁴ (especially to be considered: "the

LXX reads here the plural!").⁶⁵ Besides, in C31 the related (ultimately biblical [e.g., 2 Chr 14:1]) formulation about doing what is right and good in rabbinic literature is connected to the words from Exod 18:20, which speak of doing "works."⁶⁶ These words are applied by the rabbis to "the line of the law (i.e., the exact fulfilling of the letter of the law)" and to "performents" that "go beyond the letter of the legal demand."⁶⁷ Even aside from these types of statements, Jewish writings present "from the Second Temple period onwards . . . widespread use of the plural מעשים as a term designating specially the laws or commandments."⁶⁸

Concerning the "Qumran writings" beyond 4QMMT, this meaning is intended without question on various occasions for the expression מעשי אל.⁶⁹ Although the syntactic unit מעשי התורה is not attested outside of 4QMMT C27, the "Qumran literature" demonstrates an entire series of construct connections in which the first place is occupied by "works" — as in מעשי אל⁷⁰ — or the second place is occupied by "Torah,"⁷¹ and not infrequently this has to do with something that is set beforehand for the individual person.⁷² In CD 13:6-8 both possibilities are implemented with מעשי אל (lines 7-8) and פרוש התורה (line 6) in such a way that thereby the expression מעשי התורה is at least suggested.⁷³

In other words, the diachronic observations reinforce emphatically the conclusion that in 4QMMT B2 and C27 "works" and "'works' of the law" mean nothing other than halakhot.

2.2

Hence it appears at least conceivable that the Pauline expression ἔργα νόμου is also to be understood in this way. As νόμος stands in the genitive here, the expression could quite well reflect the construct state in Hebrew; and if this Greek expression as well as the corresponding, more extensive formulation with the article in Rom 2:15, that is, τὸ ἔργον τοῦ νόμου,⁷⁴ is a case of Greek translated from Hebrew⁷⁵ in a milieu influenced by the Septuagint, probably only מעשי (ה)תורה would come into question. For this one must take into account that as a rule the Septuagint renders תורה with νόμος and similarly stereotypically מעשׂה with ἔργον — in the especially important passage in Exod 18:20⁷⁶ more meticulously with (τὰ) ἔργα.⁷⁷ Long before the discovery of 4QMMT P. Billerbeck suspected that this Hebrew formulation lay behind ἔργα νόμου,⁷⁸ and translations of the New

4QMMT and Galatians, מעשי התורה and ΕΡΓΑ ΝΟΜΟΥ

Testament into Hebrew likewise resort to this syntactic unit that now is attested in 4QMMT C27.[79] That it ultimately lies behind Paul's expression and shapes its actual meaning would by no means be contradicted by the use of ἔργον (in Paul and) in authors close to the time of the Apostle outside of this genitive construction with another meaning.[80] If, for example, the formulation κύριος παντοκράτωρ in 2 Cor 6:18 is due to the Old Testament formulation יהוה צבאות (in 2 Sam 7:8), this in no way excludes that κύριος in other passages (e.g., Gal 4:1; 1 Pet 3:6) refers to human beings.

For the possibility that the expression ἔργα νόμου is to be understood as a translation of מעשי התורה, it suffices that the Greek vocabulary on the level of semantics does not exclude a point of contact.[81] Since it demonstrably does involve such a point of contact, as especially Exod 18:20 shows with its rendering of תורת by νόμος and of מעשה by ἔργα, where in view of the context מעשה is to be understood (in some way) legally, there can be no doubt of the possibility of a dependence of this kind. It is all the more important to look into this because Exod 18:20 does not stand isolated. Inasmuch as תורה and מעשה can be replaced by νόμος and ἔργον (or ἔργα) respectively, as is detectable from the use of language in the Septuagint, and inasmuch as thereby the pair תורה and νόμος is evidently semantically closely connected with the legal sphere,[82] one will have to draw attention to the question whether in the early Jewish and early Christian milieu ἔργον (or *opus*) is used from time to time with a legal meaning — corresponding thus, for instance, to the developing meaning of מעשה in that period in the sense of "commandment."[83] Now this is actually the case, as E. Lohmeyer supported earlier with some examples.[84] References are found in the Septuagint itself,[85] in the pseudepigrapha,[86] and in the New Testament (at least beyond the Pauline Epistles).[87]

Thus it suggests itself to try to correlate ἔργα νόμου (or τὸ ἔργον τοῦ νόμου) with a corresponding understanding. In a careful way E. Lohmeyer, as just mentioned, daringly made the attempt to do this before the discovery of the "Qumran literature."[88] In the summer of 1989, as I was struggling with the difficulties of Gal 2:15ff. and came across some brief remarks on 4QMMT,[89] I was compelled to consider this possibility.[90] Now, in the spring of 1997, a study by D. Flusser has come into my hands, which already some years earlier — and perhaps even before 4QMMT C27 had come to his attention — says: "It is difficult to get rid of the impression that the works of the law are identical with the Jewish commandments. The simple word 'works,' which Paul often uses, also means the commandments in rabbinic

Judaism of that time."[91] After consideration of the proximity that exists between 4QMMT and Galatians (see section 1 above), and after consideration of the use of מעשים in that document (see section 2.1 above), it becomes even more difficult to rid oneself of this impression. The impression could itself be something like liberation, liberation especially from the conventional understanding, associated with all sorts of difficulties, that ἔργα νόμου means action according to the Torah.[92] In any case the formulations fit well with what can be observed in 4QMMT (i) and a series of characteristics in connection with Paul's use of "work(s) of the law" can be explained better by an interpretation in the sense of halakhot (ii):

(i.a) The juxtaposition of מעשי התורה (4QMMT C27) and מעשים (B2)[93] corresponds to the coexistence of the expressions ἔργα νόμου (Rom 3:20, 28; Gal 2:16; 3:2, 5, 10; cf. Rom 9:32 variant reading) and ἔργα (Rom 4:2, 6; 9:12, 32; 11:6),[94] which the Apostle always uses without a genitive indicating a person, without a personal pronoun.[95]

(i.b) The distinction between "works (of the law)" (B2; C27) as commandments and "their works" (C23) as fulfillments of commandments in 4QMMT, evidently has its parallel in Paul, e.g., in Rom 3:20 on the one hand and Rom 2:6 on the other. And if C31-32 speaks about doing good (and about the eschatological relevance of such action), this corresponds to what Paul says about doing good, about "good work," for example in Rom 2:(6-)7.[96]

(i.c) As according to (Exod 18:20 and) 4QMMT C(27-)31 the "works (of the law)" need to be satisfied by "doing" (עשה), so this demand (for instance) is apparent also (in Rom 2:14[-15] [ποιεῖν] and) in Rom 4:(2-)4 (ἐργάζεσθαι).[97]

(i.d) If the term הלכות (as well as the word מצו[ו]ת) appears to be avoided in 4QMMT in favor of "works (of the law)," the use of "work(s) (of the law)" in Paul could be an attempt to speak about the commandments of Torah in such a way as not to exclude circumcision, but to include it, whereas in the linguistically rather analogous expressions τὰ δικαιώματα τοῦ νόμου and ἐντολαὶ θεοῦ, which he uses in Rom 2:26 and 1 Cor 7:19 respectively, he excludes circumcision.[98]

(i.e) If 4QMMT is about legal regulations which primarily concern cultic purity and in this regard also require sociologically relevant distinctions,[99] then when Romans and Galatians use "work(s) (of the law)," as just has been mentioned, one has certainly to think of the circumcision commandment, which made Judaism stand in contrast to paganism, and in the polemical (halakhic) letter to the churches in Galatia moreover questions of table fellowship (Gal 2:12-14) and considerations of the calendar (4:10) come to the fore.[100]

Thus the use of the expressions ἔργα νόμου (or τὸ ἔργον τοῦ νόμου) and ἔργα resembles the use of מעשׂי התורה und מעשׂים in 4QMMT quite considerably. Even more important for whether with this terminology Paul does not mean action(s) in accordance with Torah but lays emphasis on halakhot are of course pieces of evidence of a synchronic nature: *With this thesis one gets a lot further along with the Pauline texts in various respects!* For:[101]

(ii.a) If the expression ἔργα νόμου (and corresponding expressions) does (or do) not have to do with human action but with commandments of Torah, indeed, with God's commandments (cf. Rom 7:22, 25; 8:7; 1 Cor 7:19), then personal pronouns, which attribute "works" to human beings, of course have to be missing — otherwise they should not be missing.

(ii.b) Because the "work of the law" written in human hearts in Rom 2:15 without question does not have action in view but rather "the fundamental knowledge of God's will,"[102] this singular reference fits seamlessly into the plural references, if they are interpreted in conformity with our thesis — but only then. Moreover, the connection with the expression in the plural (and with the meaning asserted for it) loses all uncertainty as soon as one considers the use of the syntactic units τὰ τοῦ νόμου in 2:14, which without question means the prescriptions (to be fulfilled [πράσσειν]), and τὰ δικαιώματα τοῦ νόμου in 2:26 (which is employed correspondingly [φυλάσσειν]; cf. Rom 8:4 [singular] and Rom 1:32 [τὸ δικαίωμα τοῦ θεοῦ]).

(ii.c) As in Rom 2:14-15, the expressions that we wish to shed light on are used otherwise in Paul as well in parallel to the term νόμος; Rom 3:28, e.g., says "without works of the law," 3:21(-22) "without law." With the thesis defended in this essay, this is only natural — otherwise it is not natural at all.

(ii.d) With the understanding of "works of the law" in the sense of commandments of the Torah, the *crux interpretum* in Gal 3:10 (and the similar problem set up by Rom 3:20) can be dealt with easily — not laboriously as is customary. The curse for transgression is valid if one has violated only one of the biblical regulations (see Gal 3:10b). That this directive appears threatening to those who define themselves by such regulations can be comprehended quite well on the basis of our thesis (cf. Gal 5:3; Jas

2:10).¹⁰³ Why such a curse (see Gal 3:10b) should fall on those who fulfill the law (see 3:10a) is otherwise difficult to understand.

(ii.e) The coherence of the sentences linked together by γάρ in Gal 3:10, indeed of the passage in 3:10-12/13, is much more closely integrated on both a syntactical and a semantic level when ἔργα (3:10a), τὰ γεγραμμένα (3:10b), and αὐτά (3:10b [cf. (however) Deut 27:26] and 3:12b [Lev 18:5]) are directly related to each other. This is the case here (and similarly in Rom 9:32; 10:5 [Lev 18:5]) if by ἔργα one means halakhot (or τὰ κρίματά μου or τὰ προστάγματά μου [i.e., God's] as it is expressed in Lev 18:4-5 LXX) — otherwise this does not hold.

(ii.f) If for Paul the polemic against "works of the law" has to do with the disapproval of an orientation toward (certain) halakhot, it becomes easier — than with the conventional interpretation — to understand that nevertheless he regards the Torah in its entirety and its claim as a whole quite positively (e.g., Rom 3:31; Gal 5:14). This fits excellently with the fact that the Apostle in Rom 3:27 compares the νόμος πίστεως with the law τῶν ἔργων, and thereby offers an expression that finds a close parallel in Eph 2:15 with νόμος τῶν ἐντολῶν (ἐν δόγμασιν).¹⁰⁴

(ii.g) The formulation that justification is not ἐξ ἔργων νόμου (Rom 3:20; Gal 2:16; cf. Rom 4:2) is understood quite unproblematically under the assumption that ἔργα means halakhot. As the preposition allows one to recognize, halakhot are rejected as the ways or means of justification — whereas one would otherwise expect an expression such as κατὰ τὰ ἔργα τοῦ νόμου or something similar.

(ii.h) With the understanding of ἔργα νόμου suggested here, it becomes clearer — than would otherwise be the case — that Paul is thinking about this from the point of view of the Christ event. Good behavior is hardly something that is in competition with this salvation event, as, e.g., Gal 2:20 and 5:6 show. But it is very likely that upholding the halakhot, e.g., the demand to be circumcised (see again Gal 5:6), would be in such competition. To want to be "justified by the law" means for Paul to break with the Christ event (see Gal 5:4; cf. 2:18, 21b). Thus, the alternatives with respect to the sphere of *extra nos* are (reasonably) comprehensible: "by works of the law" or "through/by faith in Jesus (Christ)" (see Gal 2:16; Rom 3:20, 22, 26); "by works of the law" or "by hearing of belief" (see Gal 3:2, 5); "by works" or "by grace/faith/the one who calls" (see Rom 4:2-4; 9:12, 32; 11:6); "in the law" or "in Christ" (see Gal 2:17a, 21b; 5:4).¹⁰⁵

In summary, the passage in 4QMMT C 27 together with a concen-

4QMMT and Galatians, מעשׂי התורה *and* ΕΡΓΑ ΝΟΜΟΥ

trated attention to Paul's way of expressing himself and to his argument draws us to a specific understanding of the expression ἔργα νόμου and the shortened form ἔργα, an understanding according to which these expressions mean halakhot.

3

Where Paul places such "works" in negative light (as perhaps a pre-Pauline Christianity already did[106]), he neither stands against Torah as an expression of God's demand nor against human beings doing good[107] — a result of such importance for the relationship of Christianity to Judaism and for inner-Christian debates that it can hardly be regarded too highly.[108] The Apostle rather opposes Christian tendencies to be oriented toward certain regulations such as circumcision. According to him, the latter would mean competition with the Christ event and an offense against the inclusivity of the salvation that Christ has given. This argumentation stands out especially clear in Galatians, with which Paul, who once was an agitated persecutor and stood for exclusivity but who now had become the Apostle to the Gentiles, published, as it were, a kind of anti-document to 4QMMT, note well: a letter addressed to Christians.

Even if what has been said is only reasonably correct, one could hardly — along with J. D. G. Dunn — shut one's mind to the impression as expressed by M. Abegg:[109] "the importance of MMT for New Testament research is nothing short of revolutionary."

3. Jewish Covenantal Nomism and the Pauline Understanding of the Law, the Mosaic Floor of Beth-Alpha and Gal 3:15-29

1. On the Discussion concerning the Law

To understand *Paul* and his theology is not exactly an easy undertaking. This sad song is one that 2 Pet 3:16 starts singing, and it still applies today no less than then. In particular, the doctrine of justification, which is so important for Protestantism, is under dispute.[1] Disagreement exists already with reference to the meaning of the expression "God's righteousness," δικαιοσύνη θεοῦ, insofar as E. Käsemann, for instance and in particular, advocated understanding it as the power of the giver, that is, God, which is manifested in the gift of righteousness; against this impulse, the older position of R. Bultmann is maintained, according to which what is at stake (beyond Rom 3:5, 25-26) is the salvation granted to human beings, that is, the righteousness that counts before God. Even if one leaves this expression aside and sticks with the sentence "no one will be justified by works of the law" (Rom 3:20; Gal 2:16; cf. Ps 143:2), one does by no means come across unanimous views in the secondary literature. Again, the genitive phrase, now "works of the law" (ἔργα νόμου), is dealt with controversially: does it have to do with all possible action according to the Torah or simply or primarily with "identity and boundary markers" (so [especially] J. D. G. Dunn) between Judaism and paganism (such as circumcision and food laws)? And does it at all mean behavior that conforms to the law or rather the individual prescriptions of the law itself, the halakhot (as I suggested in 1992 and 1993)? Above all, however, disagreement exists on whether the sentence is to be understood as condemning human attempts to boast before God or should be comprehended not in such an individu-

Jewish Covenantal Nomism and the Pauline Understanding of the Law

alistic, "Lutheran" way, but in some other way, e.g., in the sense of placing emphasis on belonging to a group which is manifested (on the one hand) in works of the law and (on the other hand) in faith in Christ (so, e.g., E. P. Sanders). Thus the situation concerning Paul's understanding of justification and law is not particularly easy to survey.

It is somewhat more favorable if one inquires about how — otherwise — the law was thought about in *early Judaism*. At least on the basis of recent discussion (F. Mußner et al.), it ought to be accepted as somewhat settled that, because the sentence just mentioned from Rom 3:20 and Gal 2:16 is brought forth against erroneous Christian attitudes, it cannot simply be extended as a characterization of Jewish relationships or even of *the* Jewish relationship to the Torah. One of those who have denounced the fallacy or erroneous conclusion outlined here is E. P. Sanders, whose book *Paul and Palestinian Judaism* has determined the discussion of the last ten or fifteen years as has no other. Instead of the earlier view, which to a large extent dominated the field, that works righteousness or righteousness by achievements would be a signature of early Judaism, in the first main section of this publication Sanders sets forth the thesis that a characterization under the heading "covenantal nomism" would be more appropriate, expressing the primacy of the grace of God that elects and includes in the covenant before the demand to comply with the law.

Sanders is able to identify covenantal nomism in eight particular points (p. 422):

The "pattern" or "structure" of covenantal nomism is this: (1) God has chosen Israel and (2) given the law. The law implies both (3) God's promise to maintain the election and (4) the requirement to obey. (5) God rewards obedience and punishes transgression. (6) The law provides for means of atonement, and atonement results in (7) maintenance or re-establishment of the covenantal relationship. (8) All those who are maintained in the covenant by obedience, atonement and God's mercy belong to the group which will be saved. An important interpretation of the first and last points is that election and ultimately salvation are considered to be by God's mercy rather than human achievement.

Of course in view of Sanders's thesis — in connection with the formulation of the author himself — two things need to be asked.[2] First,to what

33

extent is it permissible to apply this "structure of religion" to the whole of Palestinian Judaism in the centuries before and after the beginning of the Christian era? Sanders (p[p]. 409[-18, 422]) describes *4 Ezra* as an exception (insofar as here "covenantal nomism has collapsed" and "does become a religion of individual self-righteousness"), and in addition one can refer to the fact that the Old Testament association of action with blessing and curse (see only Deuteronomy 27–28) persists (see only 4QMMT) and statements such as Wis 6:18b ("giving heed . . . to the laws is assurance of immortality") at least come close to what one can call righteousness by achievement. Thus the terrain of comparative history of religions is not as lucid as one possibly might like it to be. Second, which primary text after all functions to express the "structure of religion" that Sanders advocates? Sanders demonstrates it in a number of individual references (e.g. [see pp. 329-46], from Ben Sirach [see esp. Sir 7:8-9; 11:21-28; 17:12, 24-26; 24]). But with these does not he simply use the contexts as evidence for clarifying a problem brought over from the outside — from Paul — without looking into their own intentionality? This question, along with what follows below, should not be swept aside. But it seems to me that even if no single *text* gives a rather complete picture of something such as covenantal nomism, it is possible to demonstrate it from a *mosaic* in the floor of a synagogue that can be interpreted on the basis of texts (section 2 below). The interpretation of this mosaic with respect to the law, leaving aside for the moment especially the concept of *covenantal* nomism, is not particularly novel.[3] What is new, as far as I can see, is the comparison with Paul's statements in Gal 3:15-29 (section 3), which will be able to show that he is familiar with this "structure of religion." If he appeals to it here, but modifies it to a considerable degree, this perhaps could indicate that he reckons with its influence on the Galatians. The — optical — comparison of the mosaic and the paragraph of this letter may at last, especially if agreements and differences are named with some catchwords (section 4), possibly facilitate a little the struggle with Pauline themes.

2. Beth-Alpha and Covenantal Nomism

On many study trips to Israel, visits to the excavation sites of ancient synagogues are on the program. With them one is confronted with a remarkable abundance of figurative portrayals. These findings have to be regarded as astonishing, especially because at the beginning of the twentieth century such pictorial art was still categorically ruled out for Palestinian Judaism (so, e.g., E. Schürer), actually on account of the historical effects of the biblical prohibition against images, as it for instance is expressed at the beginning of the Ten Commandments (in Exod 20:4; Deut 5:8). Thus just in the rediscovery of ancient synagogues one is confronted in Israel with some sensational facts, which have, however, been known now for some decades. In the floor of the synagogue of Ḥammath-Tiberias (figure 1, p. 38), uncovered approximately 30 years ago (i.e., in the early 1960s), something sensational came to light. In the discovery, the southeast part of the mosaic that covers the surface in front of the Torah niche with the Torah shrine, pointing toward Jerusalem to a certain degree, aroused only little astonishment, because it simply shows the Torah shrine and along with it other Jewish symbols which at that time were also common: the seven-branched lampstand *(menorah)*, the palm branch *(lulab)* and citron *(etrog)*, the ram's horn *(shofar)*, and the incense brazier *(maḥta)*. These non-human forms are not inconsistent with the prohibition against images in Exod 20:4 (cf. Deut 5:8): "You shall not make for yourself an idol, whether in the form of anything that is in heaven above, or that is on the earth beneath, or that is in the waters under the earth." However, what is located under this in the square lying further toward the northwest stands in blatant contradiction of this prohibition. In the middle we see a figure that is well known to us from non-Jewish, pagan parallels, and, to be sure, as the sun god Helios or as the god Sol Invictus. Indeed Exod 20:4 and many Old Testament passages and measures in accordance with them opposed just such a thing (e.g., Deut 4:19 and 2 Kgs 23:5, 11). And now this! But that is not all. The sun god is encircled by the zodiac and by portrayals that make use of "what is in the heaven above" and of such figures that "are on the earth" and that are, even if not "under the earth," nevertheless "in the water(s)." In the upper right portion, we see, for example, Aquarius and some fish. We cannot get at the facts of this case with special pleas, above all with the plea that this is a matter of a synagogue of an atypical or marginal Jewish group. For Tiberias in the middle of the fourth century C.E., from which the mosaic dates, had been and still was the seat of the Jewish patriarch and thus the center of rabbinic Judaism in Palestine, and not only in Palestine; further, to cap it all off, an inscription at the entrance of our building names a certain "Severus" as the founder "who was raised (in the house) of the very famous patriarchs." In addition a similarly fashioned zodiac theme appears also in mosaics in the floors of at least three other synagogues (Naʿaran [at Jericho]; Beth-Alpha [on the Jezreel plain]; Ḥusifa [at Carmel]; probably also to be noted: Susiya [in Judea]),[4] and it is therefore widely attested geographically (south and north) and chronologically (ca. 350 [Ḥammath-Tiberias] and the sixth century [Beth-Alpha]) in such a way that the theses of marginal groups and/or coincidental borrowing from pagan art should be ruled out. Moreover, in at least two of these parallels (Beth-Alpha and Naʿaran and probably also Susiya) the zodiac is juxtaposed to the representation of the Torah shrine as in Ḥammath-Tiberias.

One of the parallels is now the subject of our interest, namely the one that is in the synagogue of Beth-Alpha in southern Galilee. Figure 2 (p. 39) indicates three things: First, and I will shortly return to this, another area with human figures is added to the two scenes that have been mentioned. Second, in contrast to the mosaic in the prosperous Ḥammath-Tiberias, the style of the depiction in Beth-Alpha is unsophisticated, not to say naïve; therefore and on account of its extremely well-preserved condition, the mosaic may appeal especially to us. Third, Aramaic and Greek inscriptions right at the front fit in well with this "strongly orientalizing character" (H.-P. Stähli), which enable the mosaic to be dated in the time of the reign of Justin I (518-27 C.E.) and that name the craftsmen, Marianos and his son Aninas. But now back to the first point: Three scenes are joined together here, enclosed in an ornamental frame. Since we are already familiar with the parallel at Ḥammath-Tiberias, the scene at the front hardly needs additional commentary. The one thing to be emphasized is that the Torah shrine that is portrayed not only uses — as in Ḥammath — scallop shells and indications of curtains to refer to the actual Torah niche but also with it, again facing south, refers also to the location of the Temple (by then in ruins). And it does this also by means of the "eternal light," which according to Exod 27:20 was already prescribed for the tabernacle in the wilderness. I will not bother to deal with the lions and birds. The signs of the zodiac arranged below this agree in essentials with the depiction in Ḥammath. I failed to mention the seasons of the year symbolized there by female figures in the corners and, moreover, explicitly named. From the upper left moving counter-clockwise the seasons are: spring (with a shepherd's crook), summer, fall, and winter, the last portrayed as an elderly woman. Toward the center, the signs of the zodiac that correspond to the months follow, identified as well by Hebrew letters: from the ram *(ṭl'* or *ṭālē)* on the right to the fish ([*w*]*dgym* or [*wĕ*]*dāgīm*) underneath. Then inside in the center of the medallion Helios appears again with a radiating nimbus, though he is lacking the orb of the earth here. It is clearer, however, than in the companion piece in Ḥammath, which was partially destroyed by a wall that later covered it, that Helios, in accordance with the myth, is traveling with a *quadriga*, a chariot drawn through the heavens by four horses. And in contrast to the mosaic in Ḥammath, the background of the horses and chariot is not light but is dominated by the darkness of the night which for its part is merely illuminated with stars and the moon and which must now give way to the sun. What remains to be considered is the third panel, which on a first level of understanding causes no problems because of the accompanying writing: It has to do with Abraham and Isaac, and the biblical words — which are related to a hand that comes out of an upper region — "do not stretch out [your hand]" (Gen 22:12: *'al-tišĕlaḥ*) together with the biblical reference to the ram ("and saw a ram," Gen 22:13: *wĕhinnēh-'ayil*) leave no doubt that this has to do with the story of Abraham's sacrifice (or the sacrifice of Isaac) in Genesis 22, which in Judaism (in connection with Gen 22:9) is called the "binding of Isaac" (*'ăqedat yiṣḥāq)*: the ram will have to take the place of Isaac, who is obviously bound, on the flaming stack of wood and altar. This is what the deity who acts from heaven intends.

With these hints the three panels ought to be reasonably capable of being comprehended and understood. It is, however, unsettled what together they are intended to mean as elements of a tripartite unity. To be sure, if one is permitted to depict human beings and animals, it is clear that the southern and northern panels make sense. Indeed, it is also clear that the middle panel with its pagan appearance did not slip in by chance, furthermore, nor because of some conceptions of sectarian Jewish circles. But what does it mean in context, and what does the context mean? The earlier history of our depiction in synagogues, which has already been touched on, points to the fact that we should take account of an idea that ties the scenes in the panels together, because one encounters, as we saw, the combination of the Torah shrine and the zodiac already in the fourth century in Ḥammath-Tiberias (figure 1, p. 38) and before Beth-Alpha in one or two synagogues ([Susiya and] Na'aran). Still, 100 years earlier (namely, originating before 244/245 C.E.) there are murals in a synagogue in the vicinity of the Euphrates, where since 1922 Dura-Europos has been excavated. The juxtaposition of the Torah niche and the binding of Isaac

FIGURE 1: Ḥammath-Tiberias
Mosaic floor with the zodiac and the Torah shrine
(H.-P. Stähli, 1988, 60)

FIGURE 2: Beth-Alpha Mosaic floor with sacrifice of Isaac, the zodiac, and the Torah shrine
(H.-P. Stähli, 1988, 63, 59, 57)

FIGURE 3: Dura-Europos
Torah niche and accompanying fresco
(cult symbols; façade of the temple; sacrifice of Isaac)
(H.-P. Stähli, 1988, 73)

Jewish Covenantal Nomism and the Pauline Understanding of the Law

FIGURE: Sepphoris Mosaic floor
(Weiss/Netzer, 14)

have already been found there (figure 3, p. 40), and indeed in such a way that this architectonic feature is also taken up here pictorially, that is, by placing a depiction of the entrance to the temple over it, and beside this the altar erected by Abraham, as it were, takes the place of the altar of burnt offerings in Jerusalem. Thus if both the zodiac and the offering of Isaac were pictorially tied together with the Torah niche long before the synagogue in Beth-Alpha, the combination of the three must have been intentional. The component that they have in common, the Torah niche or Torah shrine, probably also enables us to recognize the primary line of the fundamental concept; obviously it has to do with the meaning of the Torah. Not only are the sacrifice of Isaac and the zodiac already tied with the place of the Torah. Anyone who enters the synagogue through the main entrance — located in the north — is also led to the place of the Torah by the three scenes.

The comparatively late date of the mosaic should not markedly diminish the relevance of the proposed comparison with Pauline statements on the law. Therefore it is advisable to comment on the three scenes in what follows (virtually) exclusively with the help of texts from an earlier time, that is, from biblical times, although it would be at least equally possible with later documents.[5]

In the scene of the *binding of Isaac*, especially in view of the depiction in Dura-Europos (figure 3, p. 40), one will, of course, also have to recall that the site of this event, which is designated *Moriya* in Gen 22:2, is regarded as the location of the Jerusalem Temple, for example in 2 Chr 3:1,[6] and later in Judaism the binding of Isaac was the basis for every cultic sacrifice and sin offering. Naturally this connection with the Temple also refers to the Torah, which indeed in broad sections presents cultic prescriptions. But the arrangement of the scenes in Beth-Alpha is nevertheless different from that in Dura-Europos. Thus, it is striking that the hand that belongs to the heavenly realm finds its place in our mosaic floor in the middle of the panel, and as a result ultimately under the Torah shrine. Subsequently this at last gives opportunity to bring into play an understanding according to which Abraham — soon afterward also Isaac (cf. only Prayer of Manasseh 8) — is considered to be righteous, if not the paradigmatic righteous one. This links up with the fact that already Genesis 22 speaks of the testing of Abraham (see Gen 22:1) and of his obedience to God (22:18; cf. 26:5: "Because Abraham obeyed my voice and kept all my charge: my commandments, my statutes, and my laws"). Thus by no means do we read only and for the first time in the Epistle of James (2:21) that "our ancestor Abraham was justified by works when he offered his son Isaac on the altar" (similarly already Sir 44:19-21; Wis 10:5; 1 Macc 2:52; cf. CD 3:2-3). Three elements in this interpretive tradition are especially remarkable: (1) The obedience of Abraham is related not only to his willingness to sacrifice Isaac and not only to his carrying out of circumcision for himself and his sons previously (Genesis 17; see only Sir 44:20), but indeed to the entire Torah; a text that originates around the end of the first Christian century says by way of explaining this: "At that time the unwritten law was . . . common knowledge" (2 Bar. 57:2; and its commandments were fulfilled especially also by Abraham [cf. again Gen 26:5]). (2) Hope was associated with the testing and proving of Abraham in connection with this Old Testament story of sacrifice itself (see Gen 22:15-18; cf. 26:4-5), and indeed primarily for Israel as the people of the covenant that was made between God and Abraham (see Ps 105:5-11; Sir 44:19-23, esp. v. 20). (3) With this covenant as a starting point, Jews of later times were enjoined to follow the righteousness of Abraham, that is, his obedience to the Torah (see only 1 Macc 2:49-52; cf. 4 Macc 18:1). What has been said with respect to this first scene already suggests thinking about the idea of "covenantal nomism." For it does, as one comprehends Genesis 22 in early Judaism, not simply demand obedience from the individual Jew; God has rather associated himself with Israel — already in the circumcision of Abraham — and has given God's people beneficent rules that make life possible in the sphere made ready in this way and that also make it possible to return to this sheltered space. Put bold and simply: here already in Judaism God's grace precedes God's demands. Thus the first scene points to the anchoring of Jewish covenantal nomism in salvation history.

The next scene, which gives such a pagan impression, now is supposed, as it appears to me — and not to me alone — to take this picture of the meaning of the law further. Indeed since the time of Abraham and of course even more clearly, so to say, in writing, since Moses, Israel is associated with the Torah; the Torah, however, has significance not only for Israel but for the entire creation. That the zodiac has to do with the ordered world hardly requires argument. But to what extent does it have to do with the Torah? Now, in order to take note of this, one need read only two statements from the Wisdom of Solomon, one of which has to do with the "law," the other with "wisdom." One is allowed to bring the two passages together, because this book and others, which likewise come from the time before the birth of Christ, associate very closely the concepts "law" and "wisdom" (probably under the influence of Deut 4:5-6; cf. Wis 6:16-20), indeed they identify the two (see Sirach 24, esp. v. 23; Bar 3:9–4:4, esp. 4:1). First, let us cite Wis 18:4: "through whom [God's children, i.e., the Israelites] the imperishable light of the law was to be given to the world [or to the aeon]." Leaving aside that one can here be reminded of the sun in the center of the zodiac (cf. Wis 7:25ff.), according to this verse the law is also important for the world — without which the world is dark — even though at that time the law was only but nevertheless in the hands of Israel (cf. Bar 3:37; Sir 24:8, 10-12). Why the Torah can be considered as something important for the world can be recognized from the other text, which is found in Wisdom 7, here, along with other things, it says as Solomon's word that God is the one "who gave me . . . unerring knowledge of what exists, to know the structure of the world and the activity of the elements (v. 17); the beginning and end and middle of times, the alternations of the solstices and the changes of the seasons (v. 18), the cycles of the year and the constellations of the stars (v. 19) . . . what is secret and what is manifest (v. 21)" — and now comes the main point: "for wisdom, the fashioner of all things, taught me" (v. 22). Thus, wisdom was already present in the creation — as fashioner/master worker (cf. Prov 8:22ff.; Sirach 24), and it, which "for all the ages . . . shall not cease to be" (Sir 24:9), mediates the insight into the fundamental structure of the world which is necessary for successful living. Not least of all, moreover, one is to think about the structuring of time and the course of the stars (cf. also Bar 3:31–4:4). Of course the Wisdom of Solomon is totally opposed to the pagan veneration of the stars in the sense of deities. But though it rejects worship of such deities in ch. 13, nevertheless the "beauty" of the stars points to the "author of beauty who created them [all]" (v. 3). In brief, God and God's Torah stand behind the comprehensive order of creation, and our zodiac scene attempts to bring that to light. Incidentally, together with Wisdom 7, the scene can be placed in a trajectory of tradition that develops from Genesis 1, from the so-called first creation story (D. Lührmann, 1980). Also this chapter concerns the possibility of orienting oneself in the world created by God, that is, of being able to live according to it; and when there (in Gen 1:14-18) the greater and lesser light, sun and moon, serve as signs "for seasons and for days and years," our scene parallels this (and also one passage in Galatians [Gal 4:10]) rather precisely: in the corners the seasons of the year, then the months, finally the sun, which is responsible for day and night and for the succession of the years one after another. Thus the central place of the sun

Jewish Covenantal Nomism and the Pauline Understanding of the Law

makes sense also in Judaism, especially, of course, in circles that wished to replace the lunar calendar (again) with a solar calendar (cf. only the Temple Scroll; *1 Enoch* 72–82; *Jubilees*; *Damascus Document* [CD] 3; 16), but not in those circles only (cf. Psalm 19, esp. vv. 2-7; 104, esp. vv. 2-4). Of course one has to categorize astronomical phenomena appropriately: According to Wisdom 7–8, this is valid: wisdom is "a pure emanation of the glory of the Almighty, . . . a reflection of eternal light. . . . She is more beautiful than the sun and excels every constellation of the stars. . . . She reaches mightily from one end [of the earth] to the other, and she orders all things well" (7:25, 26, 29; 8:1). The Jew, and only the Jew, knows about this order by means of the Torah, and for this reason also has the responsibility of living according to it.

Corresponding to the two scenes that have been considered, this opportunity and this responsibility arise from interpreted history, salvation history, and from interpreted cosmos. And this is emphasized by the remaining panel, which now confronts observers with the *Torah shrine* (indirectly also with the Temple as the place of the Torah and wisdom [Sir 24:10-11; 45; 50; Wis 9:4ff.]) and in this respect rather directly with the Torah, which then is visible during the service in the form of the Torah scroll in and at the actual shrine. What is at stake is the responsibility, but also the opportunity — including means of atonement — which needs to be taken up with delight. In my judgment, at least also the tree bearing fruit on the right side of the shrine points to this. Certainly this is what is said in wisdom's praise of herself in Sirach 24: "I grew tall like a palm tree in Engedi and like rose bushes in Jericho; like a fair olive tree in the field and like a plane tree beside water I grew tall. . . . Come to me, you who desire me, and eat your fill of my fruits. . . . Whoever works with me will not sin" (vv. 14, 19, 22).

Paul also knows something like this. In Gal 3:12 (and Rom 10:5) he quotes from Lev 18:5: "Whoever does them [i.e., the prescriptions of the Torah] will live by them." Does he thus advocate a similar conception like the one held by the strand of Judaism that is documented in the primary message of the mosaic floor in the synagogue in Beth-Alpha? Does Paul lead us to understand that the Torah determines from the beginning and for all times the order of the whole world? The good thing about this is that the one who as a legitimate descendant of Abraham belongs to the covenant people of Israel has the opportunity to keep the Mosaic law that was already revealed to Abraham and that Abraham already obeyed, which makes it possible to live in harmony with God, the cosmos, and salvation history. Does Paul give us such information?

3. Beth-Alpha and Gal 3:15-29

To make some headway here the paragraph Gal 3:15-29 will be considered briefly. It appears to me that without being too arbitrary one can look at it through the transparency, so to speak, of the three scenes of the mosaic in Beth-Alpha. Figure 4 (p. 55) provides a corresponding arrangement. For these verses the translation and the subdivision have simply been taken from the acclaimed commentary on Galatians by H. D. Betz (1979). A certain parallel with the mosaic catches the eye at least in the first and third sections of the text; for the first, Gal 3:15-18, has to do with Abraham and the Abrahamic covenant, nothing other than the scene at the main entrance of the synagogue, and as the panel to the south with the Torah shrine in Beth-Alpha makes a claim on those who enter the synagogue, that is, with the opportunity and responsibility given to them by the Torah, so Paul from 3:26 on and — within this passage — not until this moment addresses the recipients of the letter directly, as the second person plural, the plural "you" that he now uses in these four verses, indicates. Leaving aside for the moment the more awkward middle section of the text with the vague affirmation that this section should be capable of being associated in some way with the zodiac scene, so now not only correspondences with the first and third sections at Beth-Alpha are to be established but forthrightly also differences from the views that are intended there.

As far as the *first verses* (Gal 3:15-18) are concerned, there is no talk here of associating Abraham (and likewise the Abrahamic covenant) with the Torah, which was already known to him in unwritten form and was already observed by him, the ancestor and model of the people of Israel — especially in the binding of Isaac. Quite to the contrary! Indeed Paul uses three elements given in the Old Testament in order to make a strict separation between Abraham and the Torah, or between Abraham and the people of the Torah. For one thing, he takes up the concept of "covenant" *(bĕrīt)*, which appears in the story of Abraham (see esp. Gen 15:18; 17:2, 4, 9, 10, 11, 13, 14, 19, 21), and which is rendered in the Greek translation of the Old Testament, the Septuagint (LXX), by the term διαθήκη (on this cf. also Sir 44:18, 20, 22), which is also Paul's term. Διαθήκη sounds more juridical

Jewish Covenantal Nomism and the Pauline Understanding of the Law

and specific than *bĕrīt* and often means something like a last will and testament, and this is the way the Apostle explains the covenant that was made with Abraham and the promises associated with it: by the illustration of an obviously quite special "testament," an illustration of a transaction the effective time of which is surely determined not by the death of the person whose possessions are to be transferred and which cannot be modified in any further way or even canceled by this person (probably *mattĕnat barī'* [= last will and testament of a healthy person], so E. Bammel). The conclusion is: God's "testament" with Abraham cannot be restricted by anything later. This allows reference now to be made, in the second place, to the fact that Abraham is to be ranked long before Moses, and Paul even gives, again in connection with the Greek Bible (Exod 12:40-41 LXX: 430 years in Egypt and Canaan), a concrete number: not until 430 years after Abraham's "testament" did the giving of the law at Sinai come about (on this see D. Lührmann, 1988). The conclusion from this and from the first point is that in no way can the law leverage that "testament" out: it has nothing to do with the distribution of the inheritance. A third point fits with this: In v. 16 Paul refers to the fact that with reference to the beneficiary of the covenant, of the "testament," the Abraham story speaks of "seed" in the singular, "the descendant" (see only Gen 17:8; 22:18; cf. Sir 44:21), and he interprets this expression in an extremely hair-splitting way:[7] The Scripture "does not speak (so) as (one speaks) of many . . . but as (one speaks) of one person." That this "one," this "individual" at the conclusion of the verse, is identified as Christ, is of high importance for the following explanation, and we will come back to it immediately in giving attention to the third section of the text. But it should not be overlooked that a strongly accented negation precedes this idea — i.e., "the descendant is Christ" — : "It does not say, 'And to offsprings,' as of many." After what has been said regarding the Abraham scene in Beth-Alpha, it ought to be clear what this negation must mean: The Apostle employs the singular and the negation "in order to exclude the traditional Jewish interpretation" (H. D. Betz), according to which the offspring, the descendants of Abraham, and the heirs of the covenant have to do first with the people of Israel (cf. again 4 Macc 18:1). According to Gal 3:16, with the use of the singular term "seed," "offspring," exactly this plurality is not mentioned. The conclusion is: Inasmuch as a a clean break, a hyphen between Abraham and the Mosaic Torah had been marked by the terminology of testament and by the reference to the period of 430 years, then the singular "seed," "offspring," (not only connects Abraham and Christ, but also) marks a further separation, a further hyphen, now between Abraham and the people of Israel. More precisely, both here and there Paul took what according to the customary Jewish conception was considered to be something like a hyphen that unites and made it into a hyphen that separates. On the one side each time stands Abraham, on the other side stands the law and stands the people of Israel. So much for the agreement and for the considerable differences between the first section of our text and the scene at the entrance of Beth-Alpha.

Turning now briefly to *Gal 3:26-29*, we ought not to remain on the above-mentioned point of contact with the mosaic panel of the Torah shrine, that is, that in both places concrete persons are addressed directly, the people entering the synagogue and the addressees of Galatians. First, one can state more precisely that what is at stake in Galatians is no different from Beth-Alpha: that the addressed persons understand themselves to be in the framework of the salvation history to which they belong, and the addressees of Galatians ought to understand themselves no differently from those entering the synagogue of Beth-Alpha, as descendants of Abraham. But with this the similarities more or less come to an end. What descent from Abraham actually characterizes respectively is from the stream of Jewish tradition, the Mosaic Torah that was given to Israel, whereas Paul names faith in Christ or, in order to express it with the previous verse, he names the coming (of the possibility) of this faith and thereby the Christ event. Therefore the impression arises that for Paul Christ has taken the place of the Mosaic law. The conclusion of this portion of the paragraph shows that Paul in fact aims for something that lies in this direction, because with the concept of "seed," "offspring," that we encounter here, Paul goes back to 3:16, where he has identified Christ as this singular offspring — and forthrightly not Israel, the people of the Torah. And what he has not granted to this Israel, that is, to this multitude, he now nevertheless grants to a community: those who belong to Christ. Those who — like the addressees — ought to count themselves as belonging to this community, can do so, according to Paul, because they belong to Christ, not on the basis of belonging to the people of the Torah, and as a result certainly not on the basis of adherence to the Torah. Of course Jews are not thereby excluded because in the formulation from 3:28, according to which "there is no longer Jew or Greek, there is no longer slave or free, there is no longer male and female," which is so important today in many respects for society and church, not only are those referred to who belong to the people of the

Torah, but the Jews are named right at the beginning. But when one also sees this, after this brief scrutiny of the first and third segments of the text, it remains nevertheless to establish that Paul knew the Jewish tradition that we have considered with the help of the mosaic floor of Beth-Alpha but quite radically reshaped it from the perspective of the Christ event. And as a result the meaning of the people of the Torah and, as a consequence, the significance of the Torah itself are thereby at least strongly restricted: the Torah does not have the function of the Abrahamic "testament"; rather this is redeemed in Christ and in those who belong to him — bypassing the Torah, so to speak.

When Paul asks at the beginning of the *middle section of the paragraph* (Gal 3:19-25) "Why then the law?" it is clear that this restriction of the meaning of the Torah cannot be taken back. A possible remaining doubt about this is dispelled when one reads in 3:21 that Paul touches the Jewish hope of the function of the Torah to improve life, indeed to give life, and if one realizes that he is unwilling to accept it as the contrary-to-fact condition in the conditional clause shows.

It needs to be clarified, however, whether in this passage Paul holds on to the divine origin of the Torah and in this regard to a positive role of the Torah. For in the present exegetical discussion prominent interpreters maintain that the Apostle takes the law that was given "through angels" (3:19) as demonically mediated and that he, therefore, was driving at a "disqualification of Israel's history."[8] We wish to turn to this question at least briefly, however, without being able to deal with all of the individual problems. Our closest attention will rest on 3:19-20, and there in turn primarily on probably the most difficult formulation, that is, on 3:20a. Let only this be noted first, that our entire passage, which asks about the role of the law, is determined by the polarity in the previous verses, which was introduced by the illustration of the last will and "testament" that cannot be restricted, that is, the polarity between the Abrahamic covenant and the law. To be sure, this comes about with the nuance that now Abraham himself does not stand over against the law (as in 3:18 [cf. 3:16-17]), but rather, as 3:16 anticipated, the one "seed," which — nearly bypassing Israel — was in view in the Abrahamic "testament." That is, now what is at stake is not Abraham and the law but the law and Christ or faith in Christ. This polarity, which takes up the older opposition and leads it one phase farther forward, characterizes our verses throughout, and to be sure in such a way that the time of the law is portrayed as relieved by the time of the one "seed" Christ.

Once one has recognized this, then the obscurity of 3:20a quickly clears up,[9] in any case if one is not seduced by some translations to divide the two little sentences of 3:20 only by a comma — so unfortunately also H. D. Betz (see figure 4, p. 55). Considering 3:20a, first without 3:20b, against the background of the previous context and in connection with the polarities that have been described, leaves hardly any doubt as to what is denied in the statement "the mediator is not of one": the mediator is not mediator in relation to the singular "seed" just mentioned again in 3:19; he is not mediator in relation to Christ. Even in German the negation allows one to suspect something else in that in the negation a positive idea, though unexpressed, can be implied. In the Greek this is even clearer since the numeral appears before the negative and is thereby strongly emphasized. Concerning this Theodor Zahn's commentary on Galatians correctly says: "the negation of the unity, of the singular, contains in itself the assertion of multiplicity, of the plural." Which multiplicity is meant is given as well in the previous context and in the polarity of law and Christ that determines our paragraph. This is so because a comparison that is relevant here has already met us in 3:16: "not many, but one"; this means there that the people of the Torah are not the "seed" of Abraham, i.e.: not the multiplicity of Israel, but rather the one Christ is the seed. The comparison intended in 3:20a concerning singularity and plurality should mean exactly the same, though here one starts not with the covenant promises but with the law. Therefore the negation here is not placed before the plurality but before the singularity: the mediator was to give the law not to the one, Christ, but to the plurality, Israel. Because in the commentaries interpreters interested only in the christological declaration often ignore the conflict of the negation and the positive idea already in 3:16, and because, blinded by the double reference to "one" in 3:20, they do not separate the sentences, they have produced a confusing plethora of suggestions instead of the solution that has just been given. These suggestions will not be dealt with here.

This also appears to be justified because 3:20b doggedly supports the suggested interpretation. This sentence, which obviously refers to the fundamental monotheistic confession of Israel (see Deut 6:4) and therefore also of Christianity (cf. only 1 Cor 8:4, 6), actually has to be read without question also in light of the following verse; for everywhere where Paul uses his indignant phrase "certainly not!" he thereby rejects a false thesis that does not follow logically from an earlier formulated correct statement, even though it seems to be a correct conclusion. The false thesis in this case is at the beginning of 3:21, where it is expressed in the form of the question whether "the law is contrary to the promises." In view of the polarity that stands out in the paragraph, especially in view of 3:18 and of the last part of 3:21, the following thesis therefore has to be intended: *Nevertheless* the law could determine or help determine the allocation of the Abrahamic "testament" and could restrict it in this respect. Thus, if *this* is the false thesis that Paul rejects, what is then suggested, even if not conclusively? The false thesis appears to be possible on the basis of the fundamental monotheistic confession in 3:20b, and precisely then, if it refers to an act of God both with respect to Abraham's "seed" and also with respect to those who received the law. Just these two circles of addressees (Abraham's "seed" and those who received the law) must be what 3:20a is about — and this is in line with our earlier observations (and, of course, with the Old Testament statements, which have to do with the role of Moses as mediator between God and the people). Thus, our interpretation of 3:20a is the outcome of both the preceding and the following context.

At the same time this interpretation shows — and this is of course of decisive significance for our opening question about the role of the law: on the one hand Paul agrees that one and the same God stands behind the Abrahamic promise and behind the law, and accordingly he does not reckon in any way with a demonic origin or character of the law; but on the other hand he sharply rejects (after 3:15ff., esp. v. 18) anew the view that the law has to do somewhat directly with the function that befits the Abrahamic covenant. With respect to the aspects of content of the tasks, at least this much is already clear: with the promise to Abraham what is at stake, to speak in the words of 3:21, is making alive and giving righteousness, whereas according to this verse it is precisely not this that is at stake with the law, which rather, according to 3:19 and 3:22, somehow has to do with transgressions and sin. And more formally this means — indeed we have already brought this out — : the Abrahamic covenant is aimed at one person, Christ, but the law concerns the many, Israel.

As a result the connection to the middle scene at Beth-Alpha ought finally to be obvious, certainly when we remind ourselves of 3:28, according to which in principle, in the one Christ, with those who are united with him by baptism, one is no longer to distinguish between Jew and non-Jew. Paul obviously knows that a broad stream of Jewish tradition is convinced of the universal significance of the Mosaic law to make life possible, even if this opportunity can be perceived only by the covenant people Israel. The Apostle holds onto the special relationship of Israel to the Mosaic law, which is ultimately given by God; but by the way in which he holds on to it he denies two things. First, he disputes that the goal of *improving life* can ever be attained by this law (see again 3:12, 21b); rather the law confronts Israel with transgression (see 3:19) and sin (see 3:22), and the angels very probably refer to the fact that the law is to be taken seriously in this sense (as the parallels in Acts 7:53 [cf. v. 38] and Heb 2:2 suggest). Second, he denies the function of *universal* order of the Mosaic law, which exists as such for Israel and only for Israel. To this extent the concern of the zodiac scene is criticized by Paul. Our verses show this, as we have seen. It becomes even more explicit in Gal 4:10, where Paul reproaches the Gentile Christians in Galatia who evidently seek to hold on to the Mosaic law (see Gal 4:21; 5:2-4; 6:12): "You are observing special days, and months, and seasons, and years."

On the other hand, Paul does not by any means thereby reject the legitimacy of the universal concern that aims at the whole creation. Two features make this especially clear. For one, according to the Apostle, in that Israel itself is confronted with sin by the law conferred upon it, all human beings are to be understood to be sinners, as he mentions in 3:22. The Mosaic law to this extent does not substantiate universal order, but universal disorder (cf. E. W. Stegemann). For the other, the one God who stands behind the law that condemns also stands behind the more ancient Abrahamic covenant, and this covenant drives toward the one "seed"; thus, as 3:28 shows, it drives toward a community which embraces Jews and non-Jews, indeed toward something that according to the Apostle is not yet realized but with Christ has nevertheless broken in: something where — whether now in plenty or in want — there is no longer "male and female," where thus Gen 1:27, the creation of humankind, is to be surpassed, improved, and to be sure by that which Paul at one place in our letter calls the "new creation" (Gal 6:15). According to him, with Christ the new creation is, at any rate, present to some extent. By means of the function of the disciplinarian, the "pedagogue," of demonstrating sin (see Gal 3:24), the Mosaic law, God's law, points to Christ, as well as to the "love command" (which according to Paul's interpretation [see Gal 5:14] corresponds to the ethical intention of the Torah [M. Bachmann, 1992]) that the Apostle (in Gal 6:2) obviously designates the "law of Christ."

Jewish Covenantal Nomism and the Pauline Understanding of the Law

4. Summary of Key Topics

The three stages of the mosaic floor escorted the synagogue worshiper in the sense of what one can call covenantal nomism, across the image reflecting the meaning of the righteous Abraham in redemptive history and across the emphasis on the relevance of the Torah for the order of the cosmos, in the end toward the opportunity and responsibility of one's own obedience. Paul allows his addressees with Abraham, who believed, to look at the primary covenant of God in redemptive history, then shows them the "pedagogical" function of the Mosaic law in Israel's history, and finally the Apostle points all human beings to Christ (and thereby also to the law of Christ). Paul, therefore, also instructs his addressees to perform something like three stages. Whereas, however, the mosaic led toward the Torah shrine, and whereas the covert theme in all three scenes was the Torah, for Paul it is Christ (who is hardly by chance identified by the Apostle in another text with "wisdom" [1 Cor 1:30])[10] — like the Torah in Judaism — : he is the one seed; he is the one for whom Israel waits; he is the quintessence of the new creation.

With the Agreement in the sequence of Abraham, law, and believers, which also is an agreement with respect to the priority of the gift of God's grace, thus because of the *Christ* event, Paul comes to apply to features of continuity ($\equiv$ and $\rightarrow$) and to positively slanted ideas (life, order . . .) some characteristics of discontinuity ($\mid$ and $\sqcup$) and characteristics, which are rather linked with negative associations (sin, disorder . . .). The table on page 54 attempts to capture this.

	ABRAHAM AS THE POINT OF REFERENCE FOR SALVATION HISTORY	GOD'S TORAH FOR ISRAEL	YOU AS DESCENDANTS OF ABRAHAM
	Abraham ≡ Moses / Torah Abraham → Israel / "descendants"	Torah: life Torah: establishes universal order / creation	(Hold on to the) Torah! Israel, the people of the Torah ("Jew")
	Abraham | Moses / Torah Abraham | Israel |*Christ* / "descendant"	Torah: transgressions / sin / not: life Torah: establishes universal disorder / [old creation] | *Christ* / ["new creation"]	(Hold on to) *Christ!* "Those who belong to *Christ*" ("Jew and Greek")

15 Brothers, I draw an example from common human life: likewise, nobody annuls or adds a codicil to a testament of a man, once it has been ratified. 16 Now, the promises were spoken to Abraham "and to his seed." It does not say "and to his seeds," as about many, but as about one: "and to your seed" — which is Christ. 17 But this is what I mean: the Law which came 430 years later does not make void a testament previously ratified by God, in order to nullify the promise. 18 Hence, if the inheritance comes through [the] Law, it no longer comes through [the] promise. However, by promise God has granted it to Abraham as a gift of grace.

19 What then is the Law? — Because of the transgressions it was given in addition, till the offspring should come to whom the promise had been made, ordained through angels, through a mediator. 20 But the mediator is not of one, but God is one. 21 Is the Law, then, contrary to the promises (of God)? — By no means! For if a law had been given which was capable of making alive, then righteousness would indeed come from [the] Law. 22 But Scripture has confined everything under sin, in order that the promise, by faith in Jesus Christ, might be given to those who believe. 23 Before [the] faith came, we were kept in custody under [the] Law, confined until the coming faith was to be revealed. 24 Therefore, the Law has been our guardian until Christ, in order that we might be justified by faith. 25 But since the faith has come, we are no longer under a guardian.

26 For you are all sons of God through [the] faith in Christ Jesus. 27 For as many of you as were baptized into Christ have put on Christ. 28 There is neither Jew nor Greek; there is neither slave nor freeman; there is no longer male and female. For you are all one in Christ Jesus. 29 If, however, you belong to Christ, then you are Abraham's offspring, heirs according to [the] promise.

FIGURE 4: Beth-Alpha/mosaic floor and translation of Gal 3:15-29
(E. R. Goodenough, figure 10, and H. D. Betz, 154, 161, 181)

Bibliography

(1) To 1 and 3:

M. Bachmann, "Rechtfertigung und Gesetzeswerke bei Paulus," *TZ* 49 (1993), 1-33

———, *Sünder oder Übertreter. Studien zur Argumentation in Gal 2,15ff.* (WUNT 59; Tübingen: Mohr, 1992)

E. Bammel, "Gottes ΔΙΑΘΗΚΗ (Gal. III.15-17) und das jüdische Rechtsdenken," *NTS* 6 (1959/60), 313-19

W. Bauer, *Griechisch-deutsches Wörterbuch zu den Schriften des Neuen Testaments und der frühchristlichen Literatur* (sixth ed., ed. K. Aland/B. Aland; Berlin/New York: de Gruyter, 1988)

H. D. Betz, *Galatians: A Commentary on Paul's Letter to the Churches in Galatia* (Hermeneia; Philadelphia: Fortress, 1979)

R. Bultmann, "ΔΙΚΑΙΟΣΥΝΗ ΘΕΟΥ," *JBL* 83 (1964), 12-16

J. D. G. Dunn, *Jesus, Paul, and the Law: Studies in Mark and Galatians* (London: SPCK, 1990)

R. Eisenman and M. Wise, *Jesus und die Urchristen. Die Qumran-Rollen entschlüsselt* (Munich: Bertelsmann, 1993) (orig. [English] 1992)

H. Hübner, *Das Gesetz bei Paulus. Ein Beitrag zum Werden der paulinischen Theologie* (FRLANT 119; third ed.; Göttingen: Vandenhoeck & Ruprecht, 1982); cf. ET *Law in Paul's Thought* (Edinburgh: Clark, 1984)

E. Käsemann, "Gottesgerechtigkeit bei Paulus," in *Exegetische Versuche und Besinnungen*, vol. 2 (third ed.; Göttingen: Vandenhoeck & Ruprecht, 1970), 181-93 (orig. 1961)

G. Klein, "Individualgeschichte und Weltgeschichte bei Paulus. Eine Interpretation ihres Verhältnisses im Galaterbrief," in *Rekonstruktion und Interpretation. Gesammelte Aufsätze zum Neuen Testament* (BEvT 50; Munich: Kaiser, 1969), 180-224 (orig. 1964)

J. Lambrecht, "Gesetzesverständnis bei Paulus," in *Das Gesetz im Neuen Testament* (QD 108, ed. K. Kertelge; Freiburg/Basel/Wien: Herder, 1986), 88-127

D. Lührmann, "Tage, Monate, Jahreszeiten, Jahre (Gal 4,10)," in *Werden und Wirken des Alten Testaments. Festschrift für Claus Westermann zum 70. Geburtstag* (ed. R. Albertz, et al.; Göttingen/Neukirchen-Vluyn: Vandenhoeck/Neukirchener, 1980), 428-45

———, "Die 430 Jahre zwischen den Verheißungen und dem Gesetz (Gal 3,17)," *ZAW* 100 (1988), 420-23

F. Mußner, *Die Kraft der Wurzel. Judentum — Jesus — Kirche* (Freiburg/Basel/Wien: Herder, 1987)

H.-G. von Mutius, "Ein judaistischer Beitrag zu Galater 3,16," *BN* 11 (1980), 35-37

J. Neusner, "The Use of the Later Rabbinic Evidence for the Study of Paul," in *Approaches to Ancient Judaism 2: Essays in Religion and History* (Brown Judaica Series 9, ed. W. S. Green; Missoula: Scholars, 1980), 43-63

E. P. Sanders, *Paul and Palestinian Judaism: A Comparison of Patterns of Religion* (Philadelphia: Fortress, 1977)

E. W. Stegemann, "Die umgekehrte Tora. Zum Gesetzesverständnis bei Paulus," *Jud* 43 (1987), 4-20

T. Veijola, "Das Opfer des Abraham — Paradigma des Glaubens aus dem nachexilischen Zeitalter," *ZTK* 85 (1988), 129-64

S. Westerholm, *Israel's Law and the Church's Faith: Paul and His Recent Interpreters* (Grand Rapids: Eerdmans, 1988)

T. Zahn, *Der Brief des Paulus an die Galater* (Kommentar zum Neuen Testament; second ed.; Leipzig: A. Deichert'sche Verlagsbuchhandlung Nachf., 1907)

(2) To 2 (and to nn. 3 and 10):

E. R. Goodenough, *Jewish Symbols in the Greco-Roman Period* (abridged ed., ed. J. Neusner; Princeton: Princeton University Press, 1988)

F. Hüttenmeister and G. Reeg, *Die antiken Synagogen in Israel* (Beihefte zum Tübinger Atlas des Vorderen Orients B 12; Wiesbaden: Reichert, 1977)

L. I. Levine, ed., *Ancient Synagogues Revealed* (Jerusalem/Detroit: The Israel Exploration Society/Wayne State University Press, 1982)

P. Prigent, *Le Judaïsme et l'image* (TSAJ 24; Tübingen: Mohr, 1990)

K. Schubert, "Jewish Pictorial Traditions in Early Christian Art," *CRINT* 3.2 (1992), 141-260

E. Schürer, *Geschichte des jüdischen Volkes im Zeitalter Jesu Christi* (3 vols., third/fourth ed.; Leipzig: Hinrichs, 1901-09)

H.-P. Stähli, *Antike Synagogenkunst* (Stuttgart: Calwer, 1988)

———, "'... was die Welt im Innersten zusammenhält'. Die Mosaiken von Bet Alpha — bildliche Darstellungen zentraler Aussagen jüdischen Glaubens," *Jud* 41 (1985), 79-98

G. Stemberger, "Die Bedeutung des Tierkreises auf Mosaikböden spätantiker Synagogen," in *Studien zum rabbinischen Judentum* (SBAB 10; Stuttgart: Katholisches Bibelwerk, 1990), 177-228 (orig. 1975)

Supplement

In the preceding article, the three-part mosaic floor of the Beth-Alpha synagogue (from the sixth century) was interpreted not as a simply chance phenomenon but as a singular entity produced to consciously express a theological statement. In this sense, reference was made to other examples of synagogue art in late antiquity, especially to the Torah shrine and the accompanying fresco in Dura Europos (from the third century) and to the mosaic floor in Ḥammath-Tiberias. The combination of three motifs found in Beth-Alpha — the binding of Isaac, the zodiac, and the Torah shrine — is, indeed, to be found neither on the western wall of the Dura site nor on the floor of the Ḥammath site. Yet, *together* both discoveries seem to point to precisely such a three-part composition.

Fairly conclusive proof of this inference was provided by the excavation of a further synagogue mosaic floor in the northern part of Sepphoris in the summer of 1993. This discovery has become accessible especially by means of a catalog prepared by the excavators, Ze'ev Weiss and Ehud Netzer, for a corresponding exhibition in Jerusalem's Israel Museum in 1996: *Promise and Redemption: A Synagogue Mosaic from Sepphoris* (cf. G. Stemberger, "Biblische Darstellungen auf Mosiakfußböden spätantiker Synagogen," *Jahrbuch für Biblische Theologie* 13 [1998: *Die Macht der Bilder*]). The mosaic, which probably dates from the early fifth century (Weiss/Netzer, *Promise*, p. 7, with references to coins found at the site), is divided not into three panels but into seven, with a total of fourteen sections (cf. ibid., p. 14 [or the figure presented in this volume, i.e., behind figure 3 above]). Nonetheless, the excavators (ibid., p. 34) are clearly right in asserting that "Three main foci can be distinguished in the mosaic." Proceeding from the entrance of the synagogue, the succession (first, in two panels and three sections; then, in one panel and a single section, the largest one; finally, in four panels and ten sections) is as follows: "... the Angels' Visit to Abraham and Sarah and the Binding of Isaac; ... the zodiac in the central panel; ... the architectural facade with its accompanying symbols, the consecration of Aaron and the daily offering, and the Shewbread Table and basket of first fruits" (ibid.).[11] Thus, as the excavators remark: "The mosaic carpet in the synagogue at Bet Alpha ... is organized in a similar fashion" (ibid., p. 39), proceeding from Abraham and Isaac to the Torah shrine or the architectural façade (with its allusion to the Temple) and "with a zodiac in the center" (ibid., p. 15; cf. p. 26).

Jewish Covenantal Nomism and the Pauline Understanding of the Law

Interestingly enough, the excavators even assume a unified statement (also) in the newly excavated floor: "these three foci combine to form a single message, which underlies the scheme of the entire floor" (ibid., p. 34; cf. pp. 37, 43). Weiss and Netzer sum up the intention of the entire mosaic in the title of their book as "Promise and Redemption" (cf. furthermore ibid., pp. 38-39). Already the initial section would seem to provide evidence for an eschatological interpretation in the context of salvation history. This section is not very well preserved. But the basis of the image (and perhaps of the tent related to the Binding of Isaac in Dura Europos) is surely Gen 18:1-16 — as also the corresponding Christian depiction in the Basilica of San Vitale in Ravenna strongly suggests (ibid., pp. 32-33 [esp. the figures on p. 33]) — , a scene in which the heavenly messengers announce the birth of a son to Abraham (and Sarah) (vv. 10-15). This reference to the future, which is also practically inevitable for the sections and elements related to the temple cult — long gone in the fifth century, yet still hoped for — , is of some significance for our comparison to Gal 3:15-29. For these verses are also concerned with the promise made to Abraham and its fulfillment in the last days (cf. esp. vv. 16, 17, 18, 19, 21, 28-29). Nor is the mosaic floor at Beth-Alpha fully devoid of eschatological elements, although here "unlike the Sepphoris mosaic, the depictions that symbolize the promise on one side and the building of the Temple as part of the redemptive process on the other side are much smaller" (Weiss/Netzer, *Promise*, p. 39).

Conversely, the central focus of the zodiac is even more apparent at Beth-Alpha than at Sepphoris. What Weiss and Netzer contend applies to the earlier image of the zodiac, that it symbolizes "the blessing implicit in the divine order" (ibid., p. 35), is most certainly true of the later image and can be interpreted in connection with the law's role for the structure of creation. If the inner section of the zodiac in Sepphoris, in contrast to, e.g., those in Hammath-Tiberias and Beth-Alpha, does not show an anthropomorphic figure — i.e., not the sun god Helios — but instead displays the sun on the quadriga as a disc with rays emanating from it, this would seem to support further the views expressed in the article above in light of Gal 3:19-25 (and 4:10) on the zodiac on the one hand and on the Torah and the (solar) calendar on the other (cf. Genesis 1 [esp. v. 14]; Psalm 19; Wisdom 7; cf. moreover H. Maaß, "'Du sollst dir kein Bildnis machen'. Abbildungen in frühjüdischen Synagogen," *entwurf* 2 [1998], 32-34, here p. 34 [together with] n. 32: reference to 4Q259 5:10-11; 4Q381 [1] 8).

59

4. Investigations on the Mediator: Gal 3:20 and the Character of the Mosaic Law

1

Gal 3:20, with its remarks about the (or a) mediator and about the one God, presents something like an impenetrable criminal case which cannot yet be put into a file marked "case closed." Accordingly the passage — in the first place — is often designated metaphorically as dark[1] or otherwise characterized as difficult.[2] Terrance Dennis Callan, who in 1976 submitted a dissertation (under Nils Alstrup Dahl) on this passage (more precisely, on 3:19b-20),[3] says: "This verse is one of the most obscure in the letters of Paul."[4] Almost 150 years earlier (Gottfried Constantin) Friedrich Lücke expressed his opinion even more bluntly: "For interpreters of the New Testament there is hardly any cross more irksome than this passage."[5] And a good 300 years earlier in his so-called *Short Commentary on Galatians* (from 1516-17 and 1519),[6] Luther concluded his succinct interpretive statements on the verse with the sigh which he did not repeat later:[7] *Si quid profundius latet, alii quaerant: ego mea vela colligo.*[8]

It is possible, then, to speak with Karl Wieseler about a "passage made famous by its difficulty,"[9] and one should not be surprised, particularly in view of Luther's concession, that others should endeavor to find something here possibly hidden, that — in the second place — an enormous abundance of suggested solutions has developed. Already in the nineteenth cen-

---

The English translation of the title of this chapter fails to capture the wordplay in the German original: "Investigations on the Mediator" = "Ermittlungen zum Mittler."

tury the number of them was quite high.[10] That "such assertions," as Heinrich Schlier expresses it, are based "certainly more on rumors than on examination,"[11] may make it sufficient to offer three opinions as illustrations: According to Lücke one must judge "that in the great sum of the expositions attempted up until now at each of the nine words of this short verse there appear about 30";[12] Benjamin Jowett raised the number to 430[13] (as also later Albrecht Oepke[14]) — with a no less amusing allusion to the number of years between the promise to Abraham and the giving of the law —, whereas for Friedrich Sieffert there is an "almost countless number of attempts at explanation."[15] As in a difficult criminal case, sometimes the circle of possible perpetrators, of suspects, which police or even interested citizens draw up, turns out to be rather extensive, so here the number of proposed solutions is quite considerable. Bringing a successful closure to this exegetical case appears all the more difficult than in the case of a crime; for in this case many Mafiosi could justifiably be arrested, whereas in an exegetical problem scarcely could even two clearly conflicting attempts to interpret be equally valid as reasonable answers — unless one becomes receptive to poststructuralist arbitrariness.[16]

The temptation to do so is certainly attractive, if one only casts a somewhat extended glance at the field of solutions that have been suggested. For although since 1800 some research reports have been produced — the Yale dissertation, which has been mentioned, gives the most recent of the more substantial ones[17] — this terrain remains difficult to manage, because, among other things, dazzling contrasts and fine shades of color stand side by side. For example, Ragnar Bring[18] understands the expression from 3:20a, ὁ δὲ μεσίτης ἑνὸς οὐκ ἔστιν, as a reference to the meaning of the giving of the law and of the mediator Moses for all humanity ("not of one (i.e., not only Israel's mediator)"),[19] whereas Ulrich Mauser[20] sees a description of Moses as "mediator of division" ("not mediator of the unity");[21] admittedly both understand 3:20b from the perspective of the universal sphere of the power of the one God, which also includes the Gentiles,[22] but in such a way that Bring thinks primarily of the law,[23] whereas Mauser refers exclusively to the promise to Abraham.[24] Accordingly the research reports do not make an overall view possible by which a clear makeup of the field of proposals or an objective preference for just a few interpretations could meet the eyes of the beholder. Of course some interpretations disqualify themselves almost automatically, for example the one presented by Wilhelm Siebert,[25] according to which ὁ δὲ θεὸς εἷς ἐστιν, that is, the second half of the verse, which does not even use the term, means — just as Gal 4:4 — that God is the unique mediator, the "sender"[26] of Christ: Paul would thus be speaking here of the "supernatural generation of Jesus, of his conception by the Holy Spirit."[27] But the field of the history of research, even with this kind of abstruseness cleared away, is beyond all question unlikely to evoke optimism of a quick and tidy resolution of the exegetical case. Only pessimism seems possible, if one does not blithely take advantage of the poststructuralist option or firmly take refuge, for example, in the after all somewhat conservative option from Lücke, who asserts, in spite of the unanimous textual tradition,[28] an interpolation — as he thinks, a double interpolation.[29] From Luther's readiness to reef the sails,[30] over often tentative exegetical suggestions under the rubric of an "attempt,"[31] the curve extends to Callan, who close to the end of his dissertation says with respect to 3:20a: "In any case, it may not be possible to give the clause a fully satisfactory interpretation. Paul's thought may have been unambiguous, but he has not expressed himself clearly."[32]

Therefore, to take up once again Lücke's nice phraseology, should the "interpreters," who are left feeling rather "morose" by the chaos of the history of interpretation, "unite in a general *Non liquet*"?[33] He continues shortly afterward, "Certainly if the verse stood in any other book [than in Holy Scripture or specifically in Galatians], it would have been given up long ago!"[34] At least this much is correct: for one thing, the exegetical situation appears hopeless,[35] and for another the verse is anything but a trifling matter.

Concerning the latter, the assessment of the meaning of the passage seems to have shifted, because "the church Fathers," who — under the influence of 1 Timothy (2:5) and Hebrews (8:6; 9:15; 12:24) — often and without question wrongly[36] equate the μεσίτης with Christ,[37] "still pass easily over the words,"[38] whereas only after the Reformation do the divergences of opinion increase. As Sieffert summarizes: The "doctrinal polemic . . . became . . . larger and larger from the second half of the eighteenth century on."[39] When he puts this in the context of the "gathering strength of grammatical-historical exegesis," then one should add as an important reason for the verse not being "given up" that it was taken to be relevant for determining the relationship of law and gospel in the passage, or more precisely according to the context the relationship of promise (3:14, 16, 17, 18 [2 times], 21, 22, 29; cf. 3:19) and law (3:2, 5, 10 [2 times], 11, 12, 13, 17, 18, 19, 21 [3 times], 23, 24).[40] After Auschwitz the problem proves to be even more urgent, to wit as something that concerns the sociological quantities Judaism and Christianity and their associations.[41] And yet few statements are as decisive for the self-understanding of Christianity as our verse,[42] on which essentially depends how one comprehends the succinct preceding phrases, which answer the question "τί οὖν ὁ νόμος";[43] — and which never explicitly refer to Moses. These remarks, which on their own are rather enigmatic, concern the matters that the law (1) was given "on account of transgressions" — only on account of them (?) — that it (2) plays its role until the time of the coming of the seed — and to all appearances no longer — and according to 3:16 the seed is Christ, and that in the giving of the law (3) angels and (4) a mediator, apparently Moses, were operative — possibly they alone.[44] How one should think about this last possibility and, along with that, how one should think about these remarks depends not least of all on the interpretation of 3:20. Indeed, this much is clear and undisputed, that these four points somewhat narrow the relevance of the law, the Torah.[45] But if one (first) leaves aside all subtle complexities, two alternatives emerge that rather strongly oppose each other: with what Paul states about the μεσίτης and about God, he either wants to express the indirect origin of the law from God,[46] at least to leave this open,[47] or what is at stake with the mediator is, as Hans Hübner expresses it,[48] the "withdrawal of God from the event of the giving of the law," which then is portrayed as an ungodly or demonic act.[49] 3:20 therefore is decisive for whether in Galatians[50] Paul holds on to a dignity of Judaism or, to express Günther Klein's view by quoting him, ventures "the disqualification of Israel's history in nuce"[51] and for whether a Christianity that understands itself through Paul should assume the dignity or the disqualification of the people of the Torah. Patently the exegetical problem is important.

But is this exegetical case also really hopeless, or does it merely appear to be so? When Scotland Yard, for example, is not yet able to solve an eminently significant case, it desires to pursue it further. On the one hand the possibility presents itself — as I picture it, instructed by Edgar Wallace among others — to summon all the suspects again and interrogate them. On the other hand, one could again scrutinize all the collected evidence and even seek for new clues. The first possibility makes little sense without the second, if one does not want to employ medieval methods of torture, and this is so even though the perpetrator certainly can be among a more or less large number of suspects. It may be more promising to track down and collect evidence until something like a reasonably meaningful composite profile of the perpetrator can be produced — and consequently not until then to proceed with an arrest. To translate this to our exegetical case, this means: a further attempt to survey the interpretive suggestions that are available, which would be examined according to criteria compiled more or less arbitrarily,[52] will not be made here, even though it seems likely that one could hardly find a better interpretation than one of those already presented.[53] But what will be undertaken is a listing and an orderly arrangement of the evidence, and thereby I will obviously depend heavily on the work of other exegetes who have tracked down important points, though without coming to a (genuine) integration into the above named model, which for a considerable period of time usually and until now has been treated as the best. At least this model should be outlined, to be sure, under categories, which in view of the history of the interpretation in the field did become customary, and, with the help of an outline drawn up by Franz Mußner for explaining this model, which he also recommends.[54] After that I will not take the genre of the conventional mystery novel itself as an example and prepare a profile with more or less comprehensible hints. Rather, it will be more like the conclusion of a Hercule Poirot novel: the alleged perpetrator (section 2) will be confronted with the actual perpetrator (section 3), facts that seem to exclude the guilt of the culprit will be explained differently (section 4), and the evidence that leads to conviction will be adduced (section 5). Naturally, the evidence is circumstantial. But now first the false perpetrator, that is, the interpretation that today is especially the favorite!

2

Joachim Rohde[55] in his commentary says that "the starting point is that there is an incomplete syllogism here. In it the major premise is, 'The mediator is not of one,' i.e., belongs not only to one, and the minor premise is, 'But God is one.'" With this corresponds Albrecht Oepke's attempt to paraphrase: "The concept of a mediator inevitably involves the notion that he represents not one but always a plurality. But God is one. Thus the law at least does not derive directly from God, but rather from the multiplicity of the angels."[56] This explanation has been taken over, for example, (finally) by Heinrich Schlier,[57] and it alone is cited in the *Exegetisches Wörterbuch zum Neuen Testament* and advocated there as "the apparently most probable."[58] Above all one can indeed say with Callan that in this assessment (six) decisions which have been dominant for a long time come together. This is true for the question (i) whether 3:20a is a matter of a particular (or better:[59] a concrete) proposition (e.g., exclusively about the mediator Moses) or even, as a syllogism could suggest,[60] a general (or better:[61] a universal) statement which has to do primarily "with the *concept* of the mediator."[62] [63] This holds likewise for the alternative, frequently referred to,[64] (ii) whether as the opposite of ἑνός a duality of parties or a multitudinous group is to be assumed,[65] and if the latter is the case, (iii) whether one should think about the people of Israel or rather about the angels who participated in the giving of the law according to 3:19.[66] And with respect to the grammatical function of ἑνός, (iv) is it after all the normal assessment, to presume not a genitive of quality and not an *genitivus obiectivus*, but a *genitivus subiectivus*?[67] Actually two further decisions come on top of these, which, however, as a rule are not recognized as such: the options for (v) a close correlation between ἑνός and εἷς and also (vi) between 3:20a and 3:20b as premises of an incomplete syllogism, of an enthymeme.[68] Incidentally, in the reading just outlined one should not designate the two halves of 3:20 as major and minor premises in the order in which they stand,[69] but the other way around, as minor ([*praemissa*] *minor*) and major premise ([*praemissa*] *maior*),[70] for in the presumed conclusion, which according to Hans Lietzmann runs ὁ μεσίτης οὐκ ἔστι θεοῦ,[71] something is predicated about the μεσίτης, so that this expression is the "lesser term," and therefore 3:20a would be the minor premise. This criticism concerns, however, merely the way in which the arrest warrant of the alleged perpetrator happens to be issued occasionally.[72]

The profile of the suspect drawn by Franz Mußner[73] (see p. 66) remains untouched by this, and without question it helps to clarify and is impressive.

In particular one has to observe that here, as mentioned, the host of angels is conceived of as a multiplicity, not, however, the people of Israel, which in spite of its considerable size is represented as one point only.[74] Since Mußner[75] relates the first part of the sketch not only to the Abrahamic promise of the previous context but as the attached εἷς indicates, at least in a lesser way also to 3:20b, I take the liberty of rearranging the two sides and then of drawing the arrow in question with a broken shaft. Further let illustrate with a wavy line (and a double-arrow) the asserted correspondence between ἑνός and εἷς, which presents itself by addi-

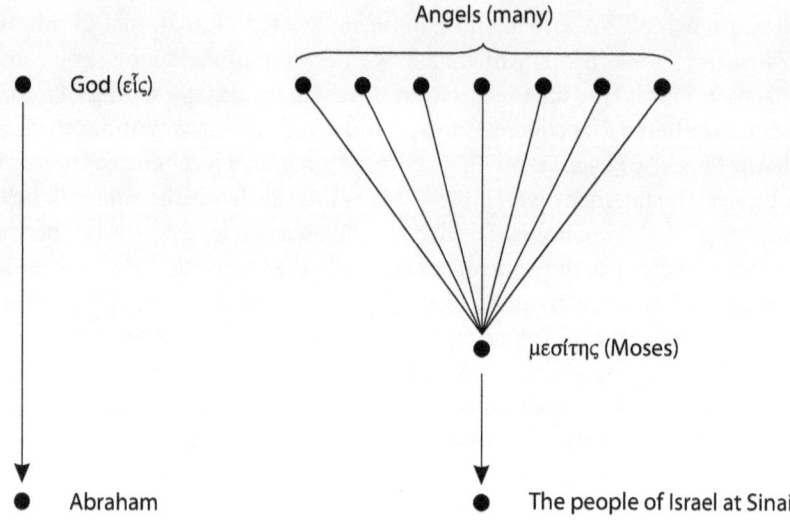

tion of the negation as a contradictory correspondence. In addition, with the use of parentheses, I would like to proceed somewhat more logically than Mußner, that is, to make a clear distinction between elements in the text and additions. The result then looks like the figure on page 67.

One of the reasons this passage has become a *crux interpretum* clearly emerges here: one feels urged, as the additions in parentheses show, to supplement an enormous amount; the text is formulated extremely succinctly.[76] To be sure, this makes partial sense if 3:20a is a "general sentence," in which Moses is simply to be subsumed under the category "mediator."[77] But only partially. For it could at least be communicated that the mediator stands in relation to a multiplicity (a), which authorized him (b). One misses such information all the more when Paul in 3:19, in connection with Jewish tradition,[78] says in the plural δι' ἀγγέλων, but without emphasizing, as would easily be possible, the large number.[79] It also seems anything but settled that the contemporary addressees were conversant with the idea of Moses as something like an agent of the angels.[80] Moreover, especially the right side of the sketch with the broken line of the arrow and with the double parentheses allows one to recognize that with the conventional thesis the problem of the succinctness of the formulation is in some respects much more intensified. To the assumed premises not only the *conclusio* that the mediator is not God's has to be added,[81] but also still a further

Investigations on the Mediator

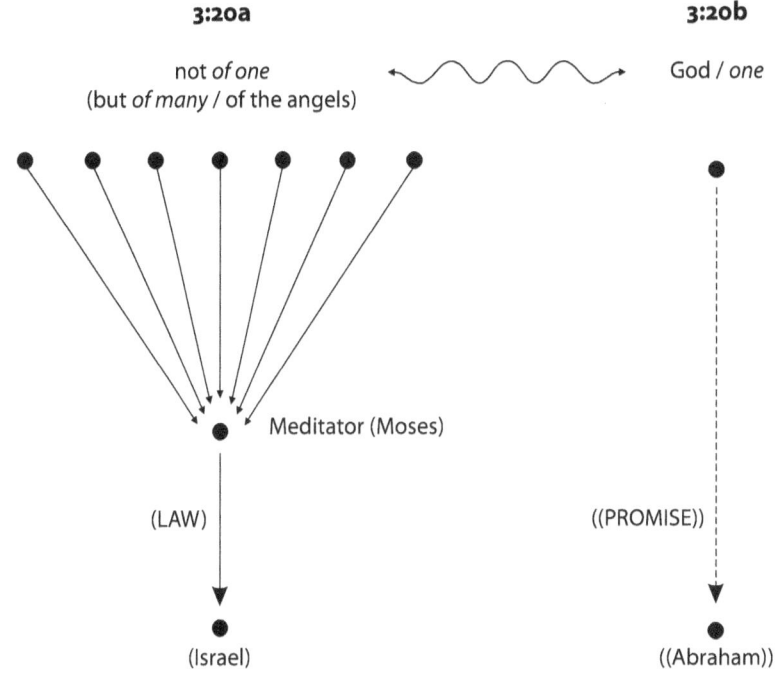

conclusion from 3:20 and the previous context. In Mußner's formulation: "Ergo the law that . . . was prescribed with the help of a mediator is not superior to the promise but inferior to it."[82] True, it is not to be contested that Paul not seldom speaks elliptically and uses enthymemes.[83] But here he surely would proceed too narrowly. If, with what I would informally call the angels-syllogism-thesis, one must first add a considerable amount of circumstantial evidence, it is presumably quite advisable to put this syllogism to disposition, that is, not to incarcerate the prime suspect on such questionable grounds. This is all the more recommended because that from which the suspicion originated, that is, "the grammatical structure" of 3:20,[84] does not lead in any way, not even somewhat indirectly, to a Pauline syllogism.[85] There is, to be precise, in Paul, as far as I can tell, (almost) no analogy to this situation that not only at the beginning of the second premise but also at the beginning of the first a δέ should occur.[86] How the Apostle is accustomed to designate such premises that follow directly one after the other[87] is shown in some passages in the third chapter of Galatians, for example in 3:18 and also in 3:28-29 (more precisely, 3:28d,

67

29a). In both places the second sentence of the syllogism presents a δέ, and by contrast the first sentence in each case offers a γάρ.[88] Let us give the one who up to this point has been the primary suspect his freedom, and instead let us attempt to come up with a new profile![89]

3

Now, this profile is easy to draw according to Mußner's instructions, if one, first, allows the arrow with the broken line, which seems somewhat to overload 3:20b, to designate clearly and unbroken 3:19 (more precisely: 3:19bβ) and therefore let it run not toward Abraham but to the seed, descendant of Abraham, and if one, second, permits the people of Israel to be symbolized "in all fairness" with more than one dot and if one in turn deletes here the angels, who in 3:20a are also not explicitly named. For the origin of the law this of course has the result that one has to insert God here, and therefore with ἑνός one can think of God only with great difficulty. Thus the expression "not of one" has to slide from above to below. This can be visualized all together as follows:

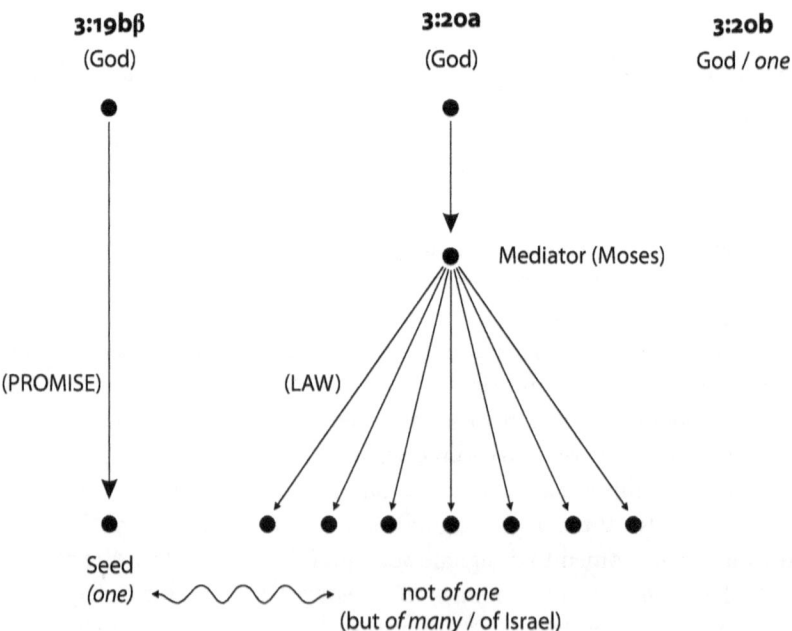

With respect to the graphics, it only remains to clarify briefly the double arrow with a wavy shaft: according to the model to be defended and substantiated, Moses did not mediate the law to the one seed, which was last mentioned in 3:19 and has already been equated with Christ in 3:16, but rather, not surprisingly, to Israel. In view of this joint relationship of God, Moses, and Israel, at least the difference from the conventional approach ought now to be in plain view: 3:20a is not about a general concept of a mediator but concretely about the mediator Moses (i);[90] here indeed a group stands over against the ἑνός (ii), though it is not the angels but rather the Israelites (iii), as then with the ἑνός itself not God is in view but the seed of Abraham, that is, Christ (v); further one should give preference to the *genitivus obiectivus* over the still possible[91] *genitivus subiectivus* (iv). It may already have been noticed, too, that the necessary additions are inserted more easily. This holds of course for 3:20a but also for the interpretation of 3:20b that is now almost unavoidable (vi): the confessional statement that touches on Deut 6:4[92] need not convey forced conclusions from a first premise that is difficult to understand;[93] rather in retrospect toward what is just said about the law and what is before said about the promise to Abraham, the confessional statement should make it all the more impressive that the one, universal God stands behind both, and this means: also behind the law. This is how Theodoret of Cyrrhus perceived this important clause.[94] Moreover, he possibly understood 3:20a in the sense of our model.[95] And in accord with quite a number of exegetes of the eighteenth and nineteenth centuries,[96] Ernst Bammel once again, more than three decades ago, interpreted both parts of the verse in this manner.[97]

4

But the model just described did not carry through, and in my view primarily for the following reasons. For one thing, one is convinced: since ἑνός and εἷς stand close together, naturally[98] this should have to do with a "unified relationship";[99] the assumption of a different reference of the numeral — here (3:20a) human, there (3:20b) God — can thus be ruled out. For another thing, three reasons seem to speak against the concept that 3:20a is a statement directly about the giving of the law: first, the article before μεσίτης could point to the concept of the mediator;[100] accordingly it would mean at best indirectly the concrete mediator of the Torah; second, the present tense ἐστίν as in 3:20b could be an indicator for "a general maxim,"[101] whereas for a formulation about Moses an ἦν would be expected;[102] third, it could seem to speak against a reference of ἑνός back to the previous context [i.e., to 3:16] that the word does not have an article before it,[103] nor does the genitive (τοῦ) σπέρματος follow it.[104] One might think that these are strong arguments. But Hercule Poirot would perhaps say that this could have to do with the rationalization of prejudices. Transferring this to exegesis would mean one could be "strongly 'controlled' by reading habits."[105]

With respect to the argument related to ἑνός and εἷς, the thesis of a "unified relationship," which is — as we have already touched on[106] — presumed but not really demonstrated, is not at all compelling. Paul could here quite well be using the rhetorical figure of a wordplay.[107] Concerning this possibility, one is reminded for example of the use of κρίνειν in Rom 14:13: "Let us therefore no longer *pass judgment* (κρίνωμεν) on one another, but *resolve* (κρίνατε) instead never to put a stumbling block or hindrance in the way of the brother." The question whether Paul also uses the concept of νόμος with the possibility of this kind of ambiguity[108] or not,[109] will not be considered here; but the fact that the genitive constructions ὁ νόμος τοῦ πνεύματος τῆς ζωῆς and ὁ νόμος τῆς ἁμαρτίας καὶ τοῦ θανάτου, which stand very close together in Rom 8:2, are not semantically identical[110] is just as indisputable as the fact that a few verses later, when the Apostle speaks about the body being dead (Rom 8:10) and about making bodies alive (Rom 8:11), the concept of the σῶμα or σώματα appears with clearly distinct nuances.[111] To assess the double use of "one" in our passage similarly is in view of the other uses of the numeral in and by Paul not far off the mark. For whereas in the quotations combined in Rom 3:10-13 pains are taken that the "one" — contrary to Eccl 7:20 — in each case occupies the position of a closing word (3:10b, 12bβ),[112] the position of the ἑνός in Gal 3:20a does not at all match the position of the εἷς in the second half of the verse. And whereas in Rom 5:12ff.[113] a typological relationship between the one Adam and the one Christ is expressed by the identical genitive ἑνός[114] and in 1 Cor 8:6 (cf. Eph 4:5-6, also 1 Tim 2:5) in addition to referring to God the Father, the nominative εἷς also occurs with reference to the Lord Jesus Christ, in the formulations under discussion the [grammatical] *casus* differs [genitive Gal 3:20a versus nominative Gal 3:20b].[115] Taken together these observations should at least permit considering the numeral in Gal 3:20 to have different referents, indeed, in view of the placement of ἑνός before the negative, this possibility ought to be given preference. Since precisely this arrangement[116] without question logically requires a mental insertion of an ἀλλὰ πολλῶν[117] to be complete,[118] thus to see here two quantities mentioned, a narrow correlation between the ἑνός, ultimately emphasizing a polarity, and the simple εἷς is much more categorically difficult than already on the basis of the deviations in position and in the forms of inflection.

In no case do the arguments for understanding 3:20a as a "universal sentence" fit better. Concerning — first — the expression ὁ δὲ μεσίτης, for "articles with appellatives" there is not only the option of a "generic" use but also another: an "individual," "anaphoric" meaning.[119] Already Johann Albrecht Bengel thought that here the latter must be taken into account.[120] He conceded *vim relativam* to the article and understood the formulation as "that mediator, Moses."[121] And in view of the δέ one will actually have to understand it roughly in this way. In Pauline writings δέ often signals a return to something said immediately before; thus in this respect it is explanatory.[122] Besides, in Paul, as Charles H. Giblin showed over twenty years ago,[123] especially the term μεσίτης in 3:19 without the article, which immediately follows (in 3:20) the expression ὁ δὲ μεσίτης, has close parallels which have to do just with explanation. Thus, as is well known, the phrase that faith comes ἐξ ἀκοῆς, ἡ δὲ ἀκοὴ διὰ ῥήματος Χριστοῦ occurs in Rom 10:17. A further example of such a sequence is present in Gal 4:24-25, where it says first with reference to one of the δύο διαθῆκαι, that it has to do with Hagar, and then (according to the probable original text):[124] τὸ δὲ Ἀγὰρ Σινᾶ ὄρος ἐστὶν ἐν τῇ Ἀραβίᾳ.

This parallel not only confirms the judgment about the beginning of Gal 3:20, which is to be taken as individual and anaphoric, but also — second — makes clear that the present tense of the copula does not stand in the way of such an understanding. For in Gal 4:24-25, where reference is made back to the Sinai event, as in 3:20, not ἦν[125] but ἐστίν is used. The use of the present in this comparable passage is, as the context allows to be clearly recognized,[126] the result of the contemporary relevance of that διαθήκη. Because in a similar way to Gal 4:21ff. (on the one hand 4:21-23, on the other hand 4:24ff. [but see 4:29a; cf. 4:24c and the citations in 4:27, 30]) Paul also in 2 Cor 3:7ff. (on the one hand 3:7-11 [but see 3:8, 9b, 11b], on the other hand 3:12ff. [but see 3:13, 14a]) switches from the past to the present,[127] the assumption naturally arises that the ἐστίν in Gal 3:20a alludes to the meaning of the giving of the law for the later time, for the time that is characterized by the Christ event. This option one must take into account all the more, as already the formulation in 3:19b, "until the offspring [Christ] would come to whom the promise had been made," indicates, so to speak, a jump from the Old Testament epoch to the New Testament epoch,[128] and as the confessional statement, according to which God *is* one, is just not confined to the past. Thus in 3:20a it is entirely possible that it concerned and concerns — also — Moses' service as Israel's mediator.

Finally — and third — the lack of the article before ἑνός and the lack of the genitive (τοῦ) σπέρματος no longer present difficulties. It is true that in this context "one" and "not-one" or "one" and ("some" or) "many" result in a clear contraposition,[129] and particularly the antithesis is clear for those in whom it recalls the picture of the giving of the law as it is described in Exodus 19ff., and who are aware of the Jews as the people of the Torah.[130] But naturally the contraposition of Christ and Israel does not make sense either logically or materially, inasmuch as according to the context Christ is not only the seed of Abraham (3:16; cf. 3:19, 29) but also belongs to Israel, indeed is "born under the law" (4:4). To fill in here the article and/or (τοῦ) σπέρματος is according to the view of 3:20a as a particular proposition thus not only unnecessary[131] but even makes matters worse. By contrast it is unproblematic to understand the bare ἑνός to mean that Moses is not assigned to one single person. Only from this is it possible to see the word as in accord with the fact that Moses also is not the mediator of the one seed, not the mediator of Christ.[132]

In toto: Prejudgments and old reading habits are to be abandoned; the one who appeared to be not guilty turns out to be the primary suspect. It remains to be shown that the evidence is actually sufficient for an arrest. In this, of course, one should pay attention above all to the time of the crime, and, beyond that, a little bit to the other activities of the person to be arrested. To look at his or her background might be interesting without, however, permitting a decision to be made about the legitimacy of the suspicion. In other words, synchrony has priority over diachrony. Nevertheless, this does not exclude observations about the history of traditions; indeed, they must not be postponed to the end.

5

I would even like to place a remarkable fact from the history of tradition at the beginning of the chain of evidence, precisely because it strengthens what has just been said about 3:20a. That what is at issue here is not a "universal sentence"¹³³ but a statement directly about Moses is supported, besides taking the phrase ὁ δὲ μεσίτης in an explanatory sense, by means of the concept itself. It is true that, outside Job 9:33, it is not found in the Old Testament,¹³⁴ and thus it does not occur where the giving of the law is involved. But it has a basis in a long list of passages, such as Deut 5:5, at the beginning of the Decalogue (as it is brought to remembrance), and Lev 26:46, at the conclusion of the so-called holiness code (Leviticus 17–26). Whereas according to Deut 5:5, Moses says that he has stood ἀνὰ μέσον κυρίου καὶ ὑμῶν,¹³⁵ in order to pass God's words on to the Israelites, who were terrified because of the phenomena of fire, the other example is even more revealing;¹³⁶ for not only are God and the addressees of the law associated together in a similar way: ἀνὰ μέσον αὐτοῦ [κυρίου] καὶ ἀνὰ μέσον τῶν υἱῶν Ἰσραήλ, but also this characterization is here still associated with the phrase ἐν χειρὶ Μωϋσῆ, in Septuagint language "almost developed to a formula,"¹³⁷ which for its part is remarkably in close harmony with the concluding formulation of Gal 3:19: ἐν χειρὶ μεσίτου. If already here the impression arises that the associations of the remarks about the μεσίτης in Gal 3:19-20 are in no way unforeseen, we must not forget that Philo¹³⁸ and the *Assumption of Moses*¹³⁹ employ the term with reference to Moses, and that Hebrews¹⁴⁰ presupposes such use of language.¹⁴¹ This corresponds to the circumstance that in rabbinic literature Moses can be designated as סרסור¹⁴² and that, in addition, here also the expression "by the hand of a mediator" (על ידי סרסור) occurs once.¹⁴³ These facts make it understandable that A. Oepke in the article on μεσίτης in Kittel's *Wörterbuch*, in spite of his thesis of the "universal sentence" in Gal 3:20a, in interpreting 3:19-20 does not go back to the use of the term as it was shaped in secular, juridical Greek (where it refers especially to the guarantor, the witness, the arbitrator).¹⁴⁴ Rather he concedes: "The use is completely Jewish Greek." And: "By μεσίτης here Paul too meant in concreto simply Moses."¹⁴⁵ In view of these judgments and in view of the material reviewed up to this point, it is hardly comprehensible how Oepke can add that Moses here "however is not designated concretely by ὁ μεσίτης, but subsumed under the concept μεσίτης."¹⁴⁶ This view is even less convincing when one adds to the parallels compiled in New Testament dictionaries the fact that μεσίτης even appears in the form of a loanword referring to Moses in the Samaritan writings.¹⁴⁷ Accordingly, one should judge that Paul with the concept of the mediator in Gal 3:19-20 refers to "a common tradition in calling Moses *mesitês*"[148] and that he therefore exclusively thinks of this mediator of the law.

This conclusion is also of interest for the most important piece of evidence, the evidence of the context, to which we now turn. Whereas reference is often made to the fact that, for the understanding of the succinct remarks of 3:20, attention to the context is decisive,[149] on several occasions the verse is nevertheless regarded as a parenthesis.[150] A view such as this might be suggested to one who thinks 3:20a is about the concept of a mediator.[151] Such an explanation is unnecessary, however, if the μεσίτης of this sentence is to be referred directly to Moses. In any case, then, the retrospective connection with the expression ἐν χειρὶ μεσίτου and along with it what goes before, especially the question "τί οὖν ὁ νόμος;" is totally unproblematic. But not only do the interpretation of the μεσίτης in 3:20a presented here and the foregoing context fit together. Above all the statements leading up to 3:20a too are what justify regarding the mediator as the representative not of the angels, as in Mußner's model, but rather of the multiplicity of Israel. It now needs to be shown that the *preceding context* speaks, so to say, for the alternative understanding that has already been presented in the sketch. Subsequent to this, I would then like to reinforce my thesis on 3:20b from 3:21ff., and from this the conclusion will be: this at the same time stands in good stead equally for 3:20a when it is understood according to the alternative concept.

That the question "τί οὖν ὁ νόμος;" in 3:19, which, as the οὖν indicates, is built on what has been said before, is much more than justified. There, in 3:15-18, Paul has categorically distinguished between the Abrahamic promise and the law, which could not mediate the effects of the promise which have just been pledged. Evidently, when the Apostle places the Torah in such a corner, he fights against a network of ideas according to which the law should have a more prominent place in the history of God with the descendants of Abraham and Isaac.[152] This impression intensifies even more if one observes that Paul uses a scriptural argument here. Three factors of the tradition are set forth for the dissociation of promise and law, more precisely for the dissociation between Abraham and Torah on the one hand and between Abraham and Israel on the other. In vv. 15 and 17 (cf. 4:24 and Rom 9:4) Paul — first — picks up the concept "covenant," ברית, which is asserted in the Abraham story (see esp. Gen 15:18; 17:2, 4, 7, 9, 10, 11, 13, 14, 19, 21). Of course he does not use the Hebrew word but its Septuagint translation, διαθήκη. This word sounds more specific and even more juridical than ברית and often means something like a testament.¹⁵³ And so the Apostle explains (in 3:16-18) the covenant established with Abraham and the promises tied to it by the image (see 3:15) of an obviously quite special testament, a transaction, namely, whose point of time is not identical with and not dependent from the death of the testator and which can in no way be modified any longer by this person and indeed cannot be canceled by him.[154] The conclusion that is thereby prepared for, that is, that God's "testament" with Abraham could not be diminished by anything later is now — in the second place — linked with the fact that according to the Old Testament description Abraham takes his place long before Moses. Incidentally, Paul even names in 3:17, again in connection with the Greek Bible (Exod 12:40-41 LXX), a concrete number: not until 430 years after the "testament" with Abraham did the giving of the law (on Sinai) take place.[155] With these two biblical elements, which are combined in a juridical-chronological argument, there is a clear division of Abraham from Torah: the Torah cannot in any way abolish the "testament" with Abraham; the law has nothing to do with the allocation of the inheritance (see 3:17-18). A sociological argument joins the juridical-chronological argument. To be exact, Paul — in the third place — refers in 3:16 to the fact that the Abraham story speaks with respect to the benefit of the covenant in the *singular* about "the seed," "the posterity" (τῷ σπέρματι; see, on the one hand, esp. Gen 13:15; 17:8; 24:7 LXX ["to the seed"], on the other hand, Gen 22:18 ["in the seed"]),[156] and he interprets this expression — contrary to the intended collective meaning there (see only Gen 13:16; 15:5; yet cf. nevertheless 17:21; 21:12; 22:16ff.; 24:7; also 12:7; 13:15) and incidentally also contrary to what he later says in Romans 4 (vv. 9ff., esp. vv. 11-14, 16, 18; yet cf. Rom 9:6-13) — (first) splitting hairs to the extreme:[157] the Scripture "does not speak (so) as (one speaks) of many . . . but as (one speaks) of one person."[158] When at the end of the verse this "one," "single person" is identified as Christ, as already mentioned,[159] this is of course of high importance for the following remarks. But with respect to this important point, it ought not to be ignored, as often happens,[160] that the statement ("the offspring is Christ") is preceded by a strongly accentuated negation,[161] which names and interprets the absence of the plural: "It does *not* say 'and to the offsprings,' as of many." How (and because) the juridical-chronological argument, so to say, is used against a hyphen that unites Abraham and Torah and casts a vote for a hyphen that separates the two, the sociological argument — in the words of H. D. Betz[162] — has to do with fending off the "traditional Jewish interpretation," according to which the descendant or descendants of Abraham, the heir(s) of the covenant, refer(s) (first of all) to the people of Israel (cf. esp. Ps 105:5-11; Sir 44:19-21; 4 Macc 18:1). This is to say — to express it thus once more — that the hyphen that unites Abraham and Israel becomes also a hyphen that separates, and it cannot or should not be said that one might have, as V. Stolle[163] thinks, "to understand the phrase ὡς ἐπὶ πολλῶν . . . as a matter of the language *(sprachlogisch)*, not as a reference to a concrete opposite." Quite the reverse! The one seed, Christ, stands directly in contraposition to the multiplicity of Israel. Or the other way around: the multiplicity of the people of Israel stands directly in contraposition to the one seed, Christ. According to Mußner's sketch, if again the double arrow with a wavy line marks the opposition, this can be captured graphically as follows:

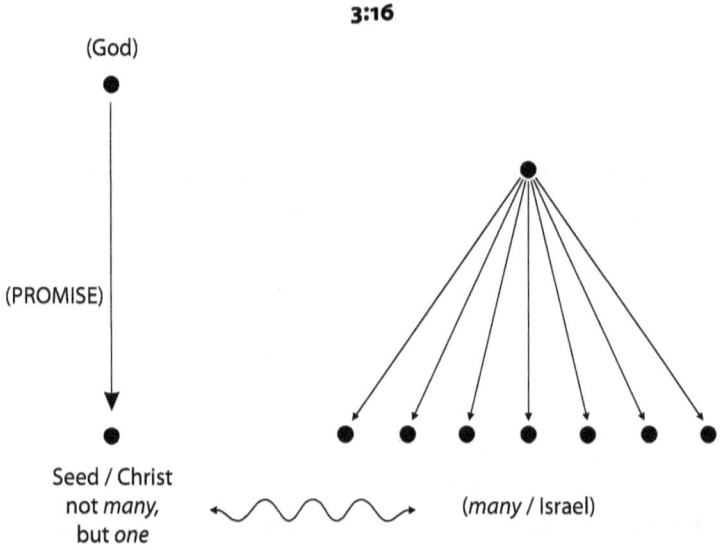

Before this diagram can and should be related to 3:20a, two additional comments need to be made about how the text from 3:19 onward refers back to the preceding passage in 3:15-18, the conclusion of which — 3:18 — incidentally in the form of a (non-Aristotelian) syllogism draws the summation from the arguments that are outlined, the summation namely, that the Torah has nothing to do with the allocation of the inheritance.[164]

Investigations on the Mediator

For one thing, of course with good reason such a conclusion provokes (as already indicated) the question "τί οὖν ὁ νόμος;". And the answer must be about whether the Torah, if its task is not identical with that of the Abrahamic "testament," still has a role at all, or whether it is purely a *negativum* (or *nullum*). The fact that Paul then immediately makes reference to the giving of the law with the formulation τῶν παραβάσεων χάριν προσετέθη shows that he views this problem as one that concerns the history of Israel, and the passive, which does not just exclude God's participation in it, could thereby indicate that no antinomistic answer is intended, especially since 3:21 says analogously ἐδόθη about the νόμος and since in 3:22 it is said that the promise "has been given."[165]

For another thing, it is hardly by chance that the syllogism in 3:18 speaks no longer just about the promise (or the promises) but about what was pledged "through promise" and what will be obtained "from promise"; indeed it is expressly about the κληρονομία. Thereby a shift in accent or in phases must be indicated, a shift that has already been prepared for in 3:16, when it says there that the ἐπαγγελίαι were given to Abraham *and* to his seed. In any case, subsequent to 3:18 the theme of the promise develops further (3:19, 21, 22, 29), starting from a situation where both addressees of the promise are in view, Abraham and his seed. But Abraham now fades completely away (but see at any rate 3:29), whereas τὸ σπέρμα immediately appears in 3:19 (cf. 3:29). This is to say that the juxtaposition of Abraham and the law is now taken over by another that has to do no longer with the announcement or the definition but rather with the fulfillment of the "testament" with Abraham:[166] by the juxtaposition of law and the seed Christ or of law and faith in Christ.

After these two comments, as a result of which in 3:19ff. the question about the role of the Torah is dealt with in view of the fulfillment of the Abrahamic promise, we can now easily make the observations about the argument in 3:15-18 that are beneficial for 3:19-20a. For now it is quickly seen that here the juridical-chronological as well as the sociological argument is taken up. The first of them, by Paul, certainly still playing on the notion that the Torah was *added on* (προσετέθη, 3:19bα), then — according to the shift in phases that has been mentioned — laying emphasis on the span of time up until (ἄχρις οὗ) the coming of the seed (3:19bβ), during which time the Torah receives its role, indicated (among other things) through τῶν παραβάσεων χάριν.[167] And the second, the sociological argument, is established, if not already with the hints δι' ἀγγέλων and ἐν χειρὶ μεσίτου, so certainly at least with the explanation in 3:20a concerning the mediator, in which the ἑνὸς οὐκ ἔστιν, even according to the currently common interpretation, points to a group which took part in the giving of the law. Of course 3:20a fits still better with the foregoing when one understands the position implied by the negation ἑνὸς οὐκ ἔστιν not as referring to the circle of angels but to that of the people of Israel. For just a contraposition relating to this was already encountered in 3:16 in the sociological argument: not many but one, not Israel but the one seed Christ. According to our thesis, the comparison intended in 3:20a means by unity and multiplicity precisely the same, only that here — again in accordance with the earlier described shift in phases — the comparison begins not with the promises but with the law. Therefore, the negation has its place here not before the multiplicity but rather before the unity: Moses did not give the law to one — therefore: also not to Christ[168] — but to Israel. Perhaps it would be helpful to combine the two diagrams of 3:16 and 3:19-20 and to consider them again (see p. 79).

As it appears to me, the obvious correspondence between 3:16 and 3:19-20a, particularly between the ἑνός in each text, has been in most cases insufficiently noticed because in 3:16 interpreters have not taken the conflict between the positive statement and the negation seriously enough and have rather almost exclusively been occupied with the indication about the one seed, ὅς ἐστιν Χριστός, and because, in addition, they were spellbound by the εἷς in 3:20 so quickly following the ἑνός.[169] This has just been corrected for 3:16, and the justification of this correction was and is particularly supported by the taking up of the concept of σπέρμα in the singular in 3:19.

As far as the εἷς in 3:20b is concerned, the *following context* speaks definitively for not understanding it as referring to the one God as if one is to think about him also in the ἑνός of the preceding clause. Before I give reasons for this especially with the μὴ γένοιτο in 3:21 on the one hand and on the other hand with the goal of the passage in 3:21-29, one point — to be sure not undisputed — should be addressed in anticipation, which in my opinion makes it possible to strengthen what is said on the sociological argument and its adoption in 3:20a.

As I have attempted to show elsewhere[170] — in connection among other things with an essay by T. L. Donaldson[171] — quite a lot speaks for understanding the use of the first person plural in 3:1–4:7, where the "we"[172] alternates primarily with a "you" (plural),[173] in the sense that Paul here (except in 3:14b; 4:6b) distinguishes Jews or Jewish Christians from

Investigations on the Mediator

3:16

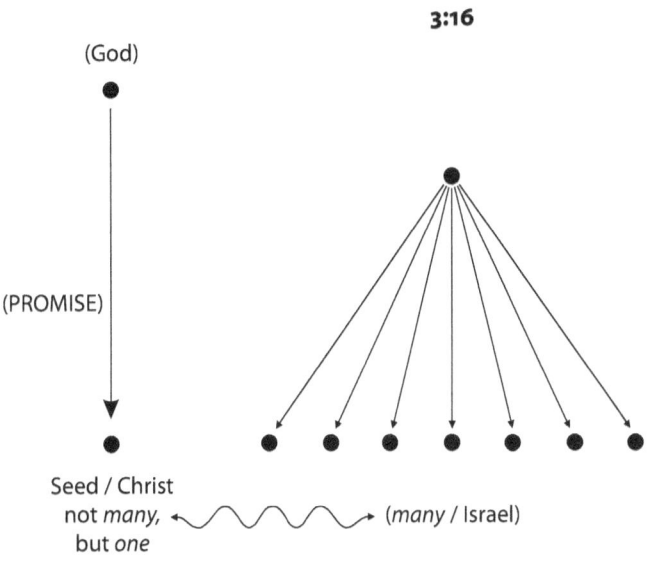

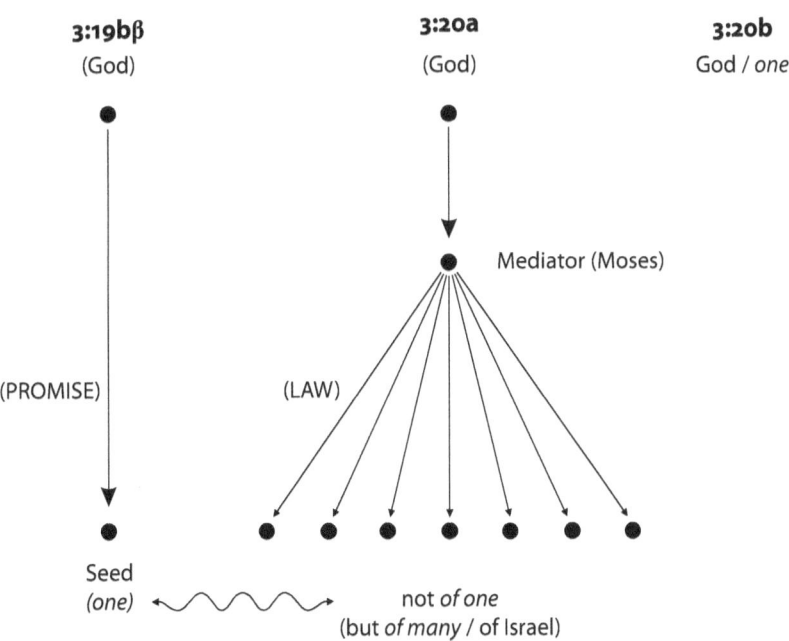

Gentile Christians by means of this linguistic device. If this thesis is correct, for which *inter alia* the use of the first person plural in 2:15-17a, which without question is aimed exclusively at Jewish Christians, can be adduced, then also those verses in which the metaphor of the pedagogue (3:24-25) is decisive (3:23-25; cf. 4:1ff.) must also deal with the former existence specifically of the Jews or Jewish Christians under the law. This is to say that with the "we" of 3:23-25 Paul then makes reference quite similarly to the sociological point, that the Torah is assigned to Israel, as it became unavoidable for us in view of the ἑνὸς οὐκ ἔστιν in 3:20a.

But now — first — to the μὴ γένοιτο in 3:21b![174] Here also I can be brief, and admittedly again, because in my book on Gal 2:15ff. I was not. There I showed,[175] subsequent to some predecessors, once more that wherever Paul formulates this expression of indignation — and in his writings this is the case in no fewer than thirteen passages — he is rejecting a false thesis expressed in the form of a rhetorical question, a false thesis which is not, though it appears to be, the conclusion from a correctly formulated statement. The false thesis occurs in our case at the beginning of 3:21, where what is under consideration is whether "the law is against the promises." Admittedly this question is occasionally[176] understood as if with it the Apostle reflects the distinct tasks of law and promise, sharpening the actual relationship into a contradiction. But such a sharpening would in view of the "opponents," who in all probability were Judaists,[177] not be particularly plausible, whose own position of course could not be so paraphrased; moreover, they would characterize also Paul's concept indeed more likely as the conflict of law and faith (see only Rom 3:31) or grace (see only Rom 6:2-3, 15) than as the conflict of law and promise (cf. esp. Rom 9:4). If one tries, therefore, to understand the question differently, namely, whether law and promise had the same intention and therefore as if they — let us say, like a Mercedes dealer and a BMW dealer — stood in competition with one another,[178] this succeeds very well. So the danger for the addressees according to Paul appears to consist in equating the task of the law with that of the promise (cf. esp. 2:21b; 5:4); indeed, he has named and criticized precisely this thought with the syllogism of 3:18.[179] Also the contrary-to-fact condition — which in regard to content goes back behind the μὴ γένοιτο[180] —, the condition in 3:21c,[181] supports this interpretation; for the protasis considers — and rejects — just this possibility that the law could give life and thereby guarantee what according to the Apostle comes about through Christ (Rom 5:18), through the πνεῦμα (Gal 6:8), and what therefore lies in

Investigations on the Mediator

the line of the ἐπαγγελία ([τοῦ πνεύματος], 3:14b). If accordingly this is the false thesis rejected by the Apostle, that the Torah could possibly determine or participate in determining the allocation of the "testament" pledged to Abraham, it remains to explain what the correct message is from which the false one has been deduced or seemingly deduced. Now, from 3:20b, and precisely then, if one understands this sentence in the way that was earlier characterized (namely in section 3 above), that is, if it is related to an acting of the one God in promise as well as in law.[182] The following context and the way in which Paul is wont to use the interjection μὴ γένοιτο thus lead just to that understanding of 3:20b that we wished to substantiate. What is more, the interpretation of 3:20a also undergoes a further confirmation; for if God stands behind both the law and the promise, it fits naturally the best that, according to 3:20a, the mediator Moses has the law not to give it to an individual, thus[183] also not to the one seed, to whom according to 3:16 and 3:19 God's promise holds, but to a plurality, Israel. Let us look one last time at the diagram of 3:19-20 (below) in this connection!

The curved bracket that has been added on the left is intended to signal that already in 3:19-20a emphasis is laid on promise as well as on law.

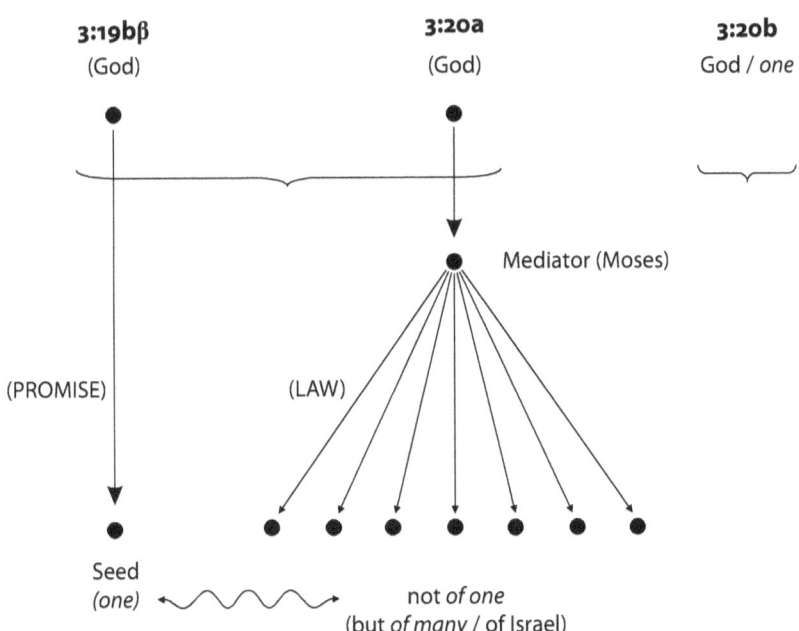

Accordingly with the similar bracket on the right I wish to indicate that according to — 3:21 and therefore also according to — 3:20b, the one God stands behind just these two elements. However, not only in 3:19-20a do the different addressees of God's acting in promise and law, that is, the one seed Christ and the plurality of Israel, come into play but they are alluded to even in the brief sentence in 3:20a: ὁ δὲ μεσίτης ἑνὸς οὐκ ἔστιν.

Concerning the following context one has not only to take into account the μὴ γένοιτο, but further — in the second place — the goal of 3:15-29. Already in 3:22 the idea of a certain universality of humanity surfaces: "the Scripture has joined together τὰ πάντα under sin, so that the promise through faith in Jesus Christ might be given to those who believe." The formulation allows one to imagine that the Scripture does not only effect the inclusion of all under sin; rather, it also has the purpose of bonding believers together, and this is exactly what was foreseen in the Abrahamic promise in 3:8: God justifies by faith, and to be sure (πάντα) τὰ ἔθνη. This expressed goal, which comes into view again in 3:22, is now, however, by means of argumentation not reached directly, but — and this is hardly by chance — with the παιδαγωγός metaphor in the passage immediately following, which with its "we," as indicated,[184] lays emphasis on Jews or Jewish Christians. As in these verses the sociological component of 3:19-20a obviously returns, so also in each of the three sentences in 3:23-25 the chronological component reappears:[185] What is indeed at stake in them has to do with the law until the coming of Christ or of the faith. When as a result the terse sketch in 3:19-20a on the giving of the law is now explained, those remarks of the Apostle, which have not been discussed until now — also not by us[186] — may find their interpretation, that is, the remarks in 3:19bγ concerning the transgressions,[187] and indeed also the other about the involvement of the angels. Especially this speaks for connecting the angels with the νόμος as παιδαγωγός, as in Stephen's speech (Acts 7:2ff.; here v[v]. [38,] 53) and Heb 2:2 (cf. 12:18-21)[188] they certainly stand for the urgency of the keeping of the regulations of the law and for culpability for not keeping them.[189] How this may be and independent of the problem whether the παιδαγωγός metaphor[190] alludes only to punishment of disobedience or also to protection[191] from wrong conduct: without question the passage in 3:23-25 makes certain that also those who are under the pedagogue are not without sin and that in this regard they need justification through Christ. So the precondition is given for taking up the πᾶς of 3:22 again (3:26, 28) and for speaking of the joining of all believers in Christ, in the seed of Abraham, that is to formulate that now indeed[192] a collective body, namely, this collective of all believers, is the seed of Abraham — and correspondingly succeeds to the inheritance according to the promise (3:26-29). This universal community is dealt with in Gal 3:28, which is also so important for the church in our time: when according to this verse in Christ not only the distinctions between "slave" and "free" and "male" and "female" are abolished in principle but first of all of "Jew" and "Greek" coming together; so precisely this goal of the passage supports our interpretation of 3:20b. The fact that believers are εἷς in 3:28 corresponds to the fact that God is εἷς in 3:20b. In other words, that God is one corresponds with the fact, to say it in the words of 3:26, that "all" are able to be "sons of God," with the fact that Jews and Gentiles are able to share in salvation.

Briefly, promise and law do not contradict each other according to Paul; rather, although they are chronologically, sociologically, and functionally different,[193] they belong together equally as works of God — of the God who as the universal God did join just to the people of Israel (especially) in the giving of the law under the mediator Moses. In view of our text one thus ought not to speak about a demonic character of the Torah, and this result is all the more important in that the Apostle actually "nowhere else makes remarks pointing in this direction."[194]

With these emphatic formulations the investigations on the mediator could quite well be closed — the investigation on the mediator about whom the text says: ἑνὸς οὐκ ἔστιν. Regarding the synchrony, the time of the crime, one may nevertheless still add that as an outcome of this investigations in our passage first ἑνός and ἑνός (3:16, 20a) as well as εἷς and εἷς (3:20b, 28) can be linked together, but that this is then true of all four passages inasmuch as the first and last (3:16, 28[-29]) are concerned with the one seed of Abraham, Christ.

But in order to let some remaining resistance against the arrest of his suspect melt away, Hercule Poirot would perhaps draw attention to the suspect's other behavior. In our case it would be appropriate to cast at least a brief glance at how Paul speaks about the one God in other passages. Now, in 1 Cor 8:4-6 not only is this one God set over against other "so-called gods" (8:5), but as already mentioned[195] is also set in parallel to the one Lord Jesus Christ (8:6a, b) and (no differently than Christ) to that which here is called τὰ πάντα (cf. Gal 3:22), and to the community as well.[196] And in Rom 3:29-30 the one God is characterized as the God of the

"Jews" and the "Gentiles" (3:29), of the "circumcision" and of the "uncircumcision" (3:30), who justifies both groups "through (or 'out of the') faith" (3:30) and in this regard unites them, and to be sure, as the subsequent verse makes clear, precisely without Paul thereby discrediting the Torah.

This fits the context of Gal 3:20, and it fits the interpretation of this verse that has been suggested and substantiated above. Of course the collection of evidence in a difficult case is one thing, its conclusion another. Also with regard to such an end, as for example with regard to the capture of one whose arrest is not easy to manage, the following clause is usually valid — if I here am permitted, just for fun, to shift to a universal sentence and to a *genitivus subiectivus*: — ἑνὸς οὐκ ἔστιν.

5. The Other Woman: Synchronic and Diachronic Observations on Gal 4:21–5:1

1

In the famous-infamous and difficult[1] passage Gal 4:21–5:1 at least four things are clear. *First,* when Paul speaks about Abraham, his two sons, and the two women who gave them birth, he has his sights set on two communities, two *corporations.* Indeed in the end more than the one offspring actually born to each of the two women belongs to them: According to 4:25 and 4:28 (cf. 4:27, 31) what is at stake is children, τέκνα — in the plural. *Second,* in 4:24 the Apostle brings these two corporate entities together under the concept of the covenant, the διαθήκη: he relates the two women who gave birth or the two communities to two covenants, to δύο διαθῆκαι. From there, however, a sharp *opposition* develops immediately,[2] which from then on determines the structure of the pericope. *Third,* the Sinai covenant appears in 4:24-25, and along with it the woman named *Hagar is given precedence,* and the other woman simply follows after her. The latter is never introduced by name, and not until 4:26 does she move to the center of interest (cf. already 4:22-23). Nevertheless, when I speak of "the other woman" in the title of this study, I do not mean the postpositive but the preceding one. With this I would like to mention *in the fourth place* another indisputable

---

The material in this chapter was previously presented in the form of a short paper at the Prague meeting of SNTS on August 3, 1995. It appears here in a slightly reworked and expanded form with notes. With this contribution I continue the interpretative approach that I briefly outlined in my postdoctoral thesis *Sünder oder Übertreter. Studien zur Argumentation in Gal 2,15ff.* (WUNT 59; Tübingen: Mohr, 1992), pp. 130-33.

fact, namely, that — in a way similar to the story in Genesis (esp. Gen 16:1-7, 27; 21:1-21) — *the second one to give birth*, that is, Sarah, and with her Isaac, who is named in Gal 4:28, is *positively* accentuated, while the first to give birth, Hagar, and with her Ishmael her son, who in Galatians 4 is not named, stands, so to speak, in the shadows. Whereas in 4:26 and 4:31 Paul ultimately connects himself and his addressees as children with the second mother to give birth and assigns to her the positive attributes "free (woman)" (ἐλευθέρα [4:22, 23, 26, 30, 31]), "promise" (ἐπαγγελία [4:23, 28; cf. 3:14-19]), and "Spirit" (πνεῦμα [4:29; cf. 3:2-14; 4:6; 5:5–6:18]), in 4:31 he simultaneously excludes a corresponding relationship with Hagar. In view of this figure and corporate entity, thus so strictly separated from the legitimate Christian community, he uses by way of contrast the concepts "slave (woman)" (παιδίσκη [4:22, 23, 30 (2X), 31]) and "flesh" (σάρξ [4:23, 29; cf. 3:3; 4:13–6:13]). Accordingly "freedom" (ἐλευθερία [5:1; cf. 2:4; 5:13]) is attributed to the children of the "free woman" and "slavery" (δουλεία [4:24; 5:1; cf. 4:25 (verb) and Rom 8:15, 21]) is attributed to those of the "slave woman." Without question, the second woman to give birth stands in the limelight, while the first to give birth stands in the dark. As seen by Paul and his addressees, she is the other woman.

2

Something comparable is true also for an interesting portrayal of two women which is found in the Freiburg Cathedral, specifically in two stained glass medallions that match each other in the so-called *Tucherfenster*. They were created at the end of the thirteenth or the beginning of the fourteenth century.[3]

The Other Woman

That a similar evaluation occurs here as in Galatians 4 is no accident; for to the statements which are taken up in this portrayal as in similar examples in the history of art[4] not least our text belongs.[5] Of course, in addition other biblical contexts enter in here: thus on the left side, the mount bears features on the head and on the legs of a bull, a man, a lion, and an eagle and therefore is called tetramorph, drawing on Rev 4:6-7 and Ezekiel 1 (esp. 1:10) or chapter 10 (esp. 10:14) respectively; and on the right side, the scarf that virtually hinders the vision of the woman who is riding an ass draws on 2 Corinthians 3 (esp. 3:14) — indeed according to this passage "to this very day, when they hear the reading of the old covenant, of the παλαιὰ διαθήκη, that same veil is still there," which, according to Exod 34:34, Moses had placed on his glowing face after the revelation at Sinai (see 2 Cor 3:7, 13). With this feature and, for instance, also with the other, that the woman on the right wears a yellow dress, it is completely obvious that she is meant to be the synagogue[6] and the woman positioned opposite, who is dressed in blue, is meant to be the church, which then, so to speak, comes along riding on the four Evangelists.[7] Of course we really ought not to be concerned here with the iconography of the motif. But the portrayal with its conspicuous allusions to Galatians 4, along with the interpretation of this passage that comes to expression with this visual representation, can serve to indicate two habits of interpretation, two problems of interpretation.

To begin with, as far as the clear allusions are concerned, so here too — following the four points named above — *first*, by means of the two female figures, corporate entities are emphasized. *Second*, they belong together under the concept of covenant. Whereas the ram's head in the window on the right symbolizes the temple cult,[8] on the left there is the cup with the blood of the new covenant (see Luke 22:20; 1 Cor 11:25). Thus, we are confronted with the juxtaposition of the old and new covenant or testament,[9] and especially the arrangement with its, so to speak, symmetrical axis running between the two medallions drives even at a contraposition. *In the third place*, of course one cannot speak of a precedence of the woman who is associated with the Sinai covenant, e.g., by means of the scarf and the ram's head, since we happen to have symmetry here. But if this figure has its place on the right from the observer's sight, and if the one with the chalice is on the left, it fits well again, *in the fourth place*, with the evaluation of the two figures that is expressed in Galatians 4. For in this way the woman on the tetramorph, as a crucifix medallion arranged higher in the same window allows one to perceive,[10] (at least in the end) occupies the place on the right hand of Christ.[11] And how positive stands against negative here is also detectable from this,[12] that the figure of the *ecclesia* wears a crown and holds a spear-flag with an upright staff, whereas the sign of majesty is slipping off the head of the woman riding on the ass (cf. Lam 5:16) and in her case the flagstaff is broken in two places. This woman is portrayed negatively: She is the other woman.

But not only is Galatians 4 taken up here in such a manner, but in addition decisively interpreted in a *doubled* way, and in both respects, at last now in view of the Holocaust, but as it seems to me also already on account of the Pauline expressions, one must speak of a delicate interpretation. *For one thing*, on the basis of the symmetrical juxtaposition as well as on the basis of the crown that is slipping down, of the broken flagstaff, and of the body, falling over backward, one gets the impression of the woman on the right that this has to do with something very close to a combat scene,[13] and the contraposition is then, for example, portrayed just as tournament combat in a variant on the motif in the choir stalls in the Cathedral in Erfurt.[14] Is Galatians 4 supposed to have this pragmatic function: A battle against enemies? *For another thing*, not only is the positive figure who rides on the tetramorph animal — as we have seen — unambiguously identified, but notably also the other woman. She symbolizes — we already had to establish this — Judaism. Whereas the association of the positive figure of Galatians 4 with the church seems in fact reasonable in so far as in 4:26 and 4:31 Paul, as we likewise already established, produces a relation between this woman and himself as well as the Christians who are addressed, the equating of the other corporate entity with Judaism appears certainly logical to some extent,[15] without, however, to be forced by such a feature of the text as the "we" in 4:26 and 4:31 (cf. 5:1a). *If* it should be understood in this way, *then* Paul would have — nearly — turned the Jewish view of redemptive history "upside down" and would have completely removed Judaism from the lineage "Abraham, Sarah, Isaac" that from its own tradition precisely leads to Judaism itself, after all, and he would have transposed it to the lineage "Abraham, Hagar, Ishmael" that actually leads away from Israel.[16] One could understand, then, why with respect to our verses Friedrich Nietzsche's harsh saying from "Morgenröte"[17] is readily quoted: He speaks of an "outrageous philological prank on the Old Testament."[18] Such an opinion is to be taken lightly all the less as both interpretive approaches — the one on the pragmatic function of the passage and the one on the identification of the other woman — not only belong to the medieval artistic tradition but also play a prominent role in exegesis today.[19] So, for instance, the recent major German portrayal of Paul, which Jürgen Becker — first — presented in 1989, says the following with regard to Galatians 4: "Israel is classified as belonging to the female slave of Abraham and its covenant with God is identified as slavery." "The Jewish religion is slavery and service of the law (Gal 4:24-25). In the law (Gen 21:10, 12 = Gal 4:30) none other than God commands 'to drive out' these descendants of Abraham."[20] Each of these two interpretive approaches will now be investigated (section 3; sections 4 and 5).

3

I would like to begin with what concerns the intention of the passage. Can it be grasped with J. Becker or Alfred Suhl,[21] so to say, in 4:30, where reference is made to Gen 21:10, and where it speaks of the driving out of the slave and her son? Now, it seems to me that this thesis with its fixation on Jewish or Jewish-Christian or Judaizing *opponents*[22] might affect these persons, but not what is given in the text.

This holds first for the citation and the way in which it is introduced. What is cited is not only, as the Apostle phrases it, a word of "Scripture," but specifically a word of Sarah.[23] Since Paul does not show interest in this detail,[24] it is no wonder that he does not simply take over the concluding expression of the Old Testament statement in which this feature appears.[25] It says there: "not (together) with my [Sarah's] son (, with) Isaac."[26] It would have sufficed if the reference to "*my* [i.e., Sarah's] son" had been deleted and reference had only been made to Isaac, and such a deletion, or else the further deletion of every reference to Sarah and Isaac, would have served best to fit the alleged intention to support an argument with opponents. But Paul simply does not proceed in this way. Rather, he alters the phrase "with my son (, with) Isaac" to the more pronounced phrase "with the son *of the free woman.*" The contrast between "slave woman" and "free woman" that is achieved and carried forward thereby does not in any way support the concentration on merely *one* corporate group, i.e., on the "slave woman." And that Paul indeed does not have this concentration in mind is shown in the following verse in which just that contrast, achieved by means of the alteration of Gen 21:10, is taken up: between "the slave woman" and "the free woman," between παιδίσκης and ἐλευθέρας. With this verse it is then clear what the goal of the modification of the Septuagint is.[27] It has to do with the place of Paul and above all of his addressees in this juxtaposition of "slave woman" and "free woman": "So then, brothers" — the writer concludes in 4:31 — "we are not children of the slave but of the free woman."[28] With this, the picture of what is said from 4:26 onward with respect to this positive community is filled out at the same time. The thesis established there about "our mother" is now substantiated, after 4:27 had to do with motherhood and the status of being children and after in 4:28 the "brothers" (ἀδελφοί) who are addressed had for the first time been designated "children" (τέκνα). Thus, 4:31 does not hark back to the pair "slave/free" in 4:30 alone, but is, with the reference to "we" and to "brothers," also related to 4:26 and 4:28 respectively.[29] This contradicts emphatically A. Suhl's view, according to which Paul in 4:31 certainly operates still "with the terminology of the proof from Scripture in 4:22ff, but has meanwhile abandoned its concrete point of argument," which has already been reached in 4:30.[30]

In addition, Suhl's view is hardly viable, because then Paul would have to give the last and most important statement of the argument as a quotation from Scripture. As far as I can tell, this is without any analogy for the Apostle. Elsewhere, however, when he, similar to the case of 4:30, introduces a citation with the remark that, or the question if, the Scripture or a divine oracle says something (τί [. . .] λέγει), it has to do with an authoritative validation of a statement formulated with his own words. Such is the case in Rom 4:3 (see 4:2, 5), and thus also twice at the beginning of Romans 11 (vv. 2b, 4; see vv. 1-2a, 5).[31] The context 10:4-5 is especially informative there. For the statement quoted from 1 Kings 19:18, that God has kept for himself 7,000 who have not bowed the knee to Baal (see Rom 11:4), is made beneficial in the following way: "Even so at the present time there is a remnant, which is chosen by grace" (11:5): οὕτως οὖν καὶ ἐν τῷ νῦν καιρῷ (λεῖμμα κατ' ἐκλογὴν χάριτος γέγονεν). This kind of use of Scripture, interpreted with reference to the present situation, also determines the context of Gal 4:30. Indeed it says precisely analogously in 4:29: οὕτως καὶ νῦν, "so also now." With this the statement from Gen 21:9 about Ishmael's "joking" (צחק [LXX: παίζειν]) (with Isaac [LXX]), which Paul understands with a number of Jewish traditions with a hostile meaning[32] and which he interprets as "persecution" (διώκειν; cf. 1 Cor 10:7 [in addition to Exod 32:6]), is related to the situation of Paul and the Galatians. This situation is, after all, characterized according to some comments of the letter (5:11 and 6:12) among other things also by such a διώκειν (cf. 1:13, 23). That the addressees thereby belong precisely not on the side of the persecutor, but rather on the side of the persecuted Isaac is as good as certain with 4:29[33] — although of course being persecuted, as is indicated by the ἀλλά at the beginning of the verse, does not fit even well with the positive tenor of the preceding verse. Starting anew with ἀλλά,[34] Paul therefore strengthens his proof from Scripture even more, before he explicates this consequence, by the inclusion of the subsequent statement in Genesis 21 about driving out the slave woman and her son as well as about the no inheritance on the part of this boy and about the inheritance on the part of Sarah's offspring. With the citation given in 4:30, the first part of which could hardly be given up on account of this (or these) opposition(s) as well as in view of the context set in advance just by Gen 21:9-10, the conclusion in 4:31 is now in fact completely assured. For with the catchword of the inheritance the argument about Abraham in chapter 3 (esp. 3:15-29; cf. 4:1-7) is picked up,[35] which there — in 3:29 — leads to the conclusion: "You are Abraham's descendant" and "heirs according to the promise" (3:29b). What this means, applied to the corporate entities determined by the two *women*, is formulated in 4:31 as the logical conclusion from Genesis 21. Accordingly, this has to do here not with an appeal to a clash with the opponents, but with a kind of instruction about place[36] in the juxtaposition of the two communities which are characterized: Paul and his addressees belong on the side of the free woman!

This outcome (achieved on the basis of the modification of the citation and its use in the argument) will be confirmed still further by two additional considerations. One has to do with the structure of our passage, the other with its context.

With respect to the internal structure, I can be brief, since I have made preliminary reference, among other things, to the contraposition of the two women and the postposition of the free woman combined with it. If one looks more closely — and more than anyone else[37] Gijs Bouwman has taken the initiative here[38] — one sees that, so to speak, an axis of symmetry develops between 4:25 and 4:26, very similar to that between the two medallions of the Freiburg Cathedral. I illustrate the ring composition with a diagram, which simplistically displays some features of the text (see p. 92).[39]

What should interest us at the moment in this small structural dia-

Gal 4:21–5:1

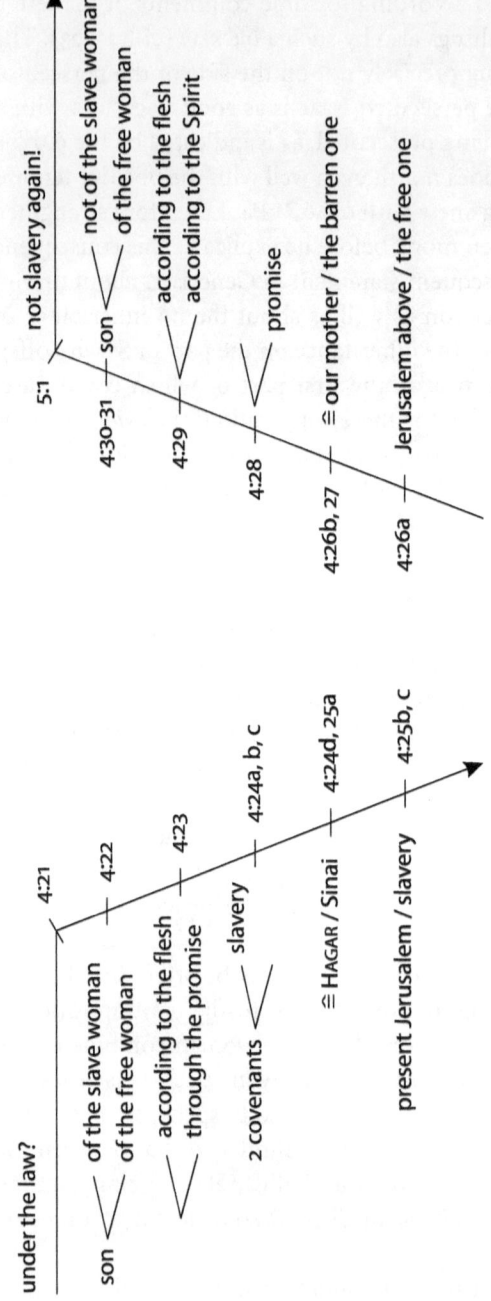

gram is the correspondence between the beginning and the end of the pericope.[40] These two phrases are not actually formulated on the level of the proof from Scripture; rather they determine its function. According to 4:21, this function has to do with an endeavor of the addressees — their willingness to be circumcised is well known (5:2-3; cf. 5:11; 6:12-13, 15, also 2:3, 7) — to be under the law (ὑπὸ νόμον), and Paul emphatically rejects this endeavor in 5:1:[41] "For freedom Christ has set us free; now stand firm and do not be burdened again by a yoke of slavery!" This exhortation, therefore, which concerns only the addressees and not some kind of opponents,[42] is the focal point of the proof from Scripture, and it takes yet another step beyond 4:30-31, while at the same time it shows that there no argument with others was intended. If in view of 4:30-31 we spoke of a kind of instruction about place in the juxtaposition of two communities, so it is now clear that the thereby intended orientation concerns, more precisely, a reorientation: a reorientation[43] that was considered necessary because according to the Apostle a mistaken orientation among the Galatians toward the law, toward the Torah, is threatening.

With this we have arrived at the context. For in my book on Galatians I set forth in more detail that in chapters 3 to 6, which are related directly to the Gentile Christian addressees, the temporal adverbs οὐκέτι (3:18, 25; 4:7; cf. 2:20) and πάλιν (4:9b; 5:1; cf. 1:17; 2:18, also 1:9; 2:1; 4:9c, 19; 5:3) can be taken as signals for the orientation of the first two large sections.[44] Galatians 3:1–4:7 takes a look back toward the turning point of conversion, and in this respect the οὐκέτι is made the theme, i.e., that the sphere which with baptism has been left behind is now no longer the determining factor. And so it says at the conclusion of this section, in 4:7: "so you are *no longer* a slave but a son, and if a son, then also an heir, through God." The following passages from there to the end of our pericope then stand under the designation πάλιν, again, back-again. When this restitutive πάλιν is used also toward the conclusion of the passage, in 5:1,[45] that is, in the demand not to burden oneself *again* by the yoke of slavery, then it is completely clear that this has nothing to do with an attack on opponents but with a warning against falling behind baptism, with a reorientation. So much for the first of the two interpretive approaches, illustrated by the medallions in the Freiburg Cathedral. The result runs: Not an attack against opponents, but a reorientation in the juxtaposition of two corporate entities!

4

A glance at the context makes it possible as well to approach the second question raised by the stained glass windows with some prospect of success, the question about which corporate entity is in view with the other woman, whether the entity ultimately symbolized by the slave woman possibly has to be identified with Judaism.[46] With this special approach to a solution, the context actually presents problems, and this is true in two respects.

For one thing one wonders how Paul can speak of a return of the addressees to the realm of slavery identified with Judaism in our pericope given that in 4:8 the Galatians had been designated as non-Jews in that they once had rendered service not to God but to the gods. Turning to the Torah for the first time cannot be a return to Judaism, after all![47] The problem would at least be considerably reduced, if the other woman indeed meant a corporate entity characterized by the feature of slavery, which as such, however, alongside Jews contained especially Gentiles. Then turning to Judaism for the first time could in fact be conceived of as a return to the realm of slavery. One should reckon with such a concept of the other woman all the more in that in the comments that concern this figure Paul consistently, and still in 5:1, avoids the term νόμος (possibly circumventing the word with the naming of Sinai in 4:24), although the situation to be dealt with according to the introduction in 4:21 appears to be defined simply by the desire to be under the νόμος. This fits in with the fact that at the beginning of chapter 4 the Apostle (vv. 3, 9) expresses a certain correspondence between Judaism and paganism by applying the term "elements/powers of nature (of the world)," στοιχεῖα (τοῦ κόσμου),[48] to both groups, and in this connection in 4:9 he had spoken of the return of the addressees to the "elements" or "powers of nature" very similarly as then in 5:1 of the return to the yoke of slavery.[49] Incidentally, in spite of this parallelism the distinctions are not eliminated in 4:1-7, 8-11: Of the Jews it says in 4:3, by means of the passive of δουλοῦν, that they have *been made* slaves, whereas in 4:8-9 for the Gentiles an *active* subservience is expressed by employing the verb δουλεύειν.[50] Therefore according to Galatians slavery is even more characteristic for Gentiles than for Jews. For our pericope, which remarkably offers δουλεύειν in 4:25 too (and, as emphasized, with the exception of the introduction 4:21, nowhere νόμος), the considerations can be summarized in the following diagram, which looks like a piece of "set theory."

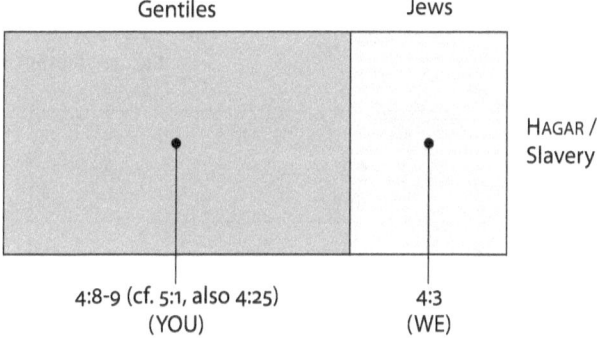

The *second* problem that the context raises when the Hagar corporate identity is equated with Judaism is that within our pericope Paul would then have to have evaluated Judaism strictly negatively, whereas indeed previously he was able to highlight God's action with Jews in the history of salvation straightforwardly as positive, whether one thinks about the Son of God who according to 4:4 was made "under the law" or thinks about the Jewish writer himself, whose way was expressed in chapter 1[51] (cf. the "we" in 2:15-17; 3:13–4:6[52]). And thus, then, in our passage itself there can be no doubt that with the "we" in 4:26, 31 and 5:1a Paul not only, as is the case with "you" (plural) in 4:21, 28 and 5:1b, thinks about Gentile Christians (at least primarily), but also includes himself (and possibly others in addition),[53] that is, he includes at least *one* Jewish Christian. Our "set theory" diagram needs to be appropriately enlarged (see p. 96).

As a result here also we have come to a rejection of the interpretive approach illustrated by the medallions in the Freiburg Cathedral. Bouwman, who has already been mentioned, gives a similar opinion: "The two women . . . are here not two groups of people who lived one after the other."[54] However, of course, in my opinion when he continues: They are "two ways of living . . . that . . . exist side by side and have always existed since Abraham,"[55] he has not really done justice to an important feature of the text, which up to this point I have almost circumvented, but now — as the marginal annotations in the expanded "set theory" diagram may enable one to expect — in conclusion I would like to elucidate briefly both synchronically and diachronically. This has to do with the notion of the present Jerusalem and the Jerusalem above that is associated with the two women and which is found in the center of our passage, in 4:25 and 4:26.[56]

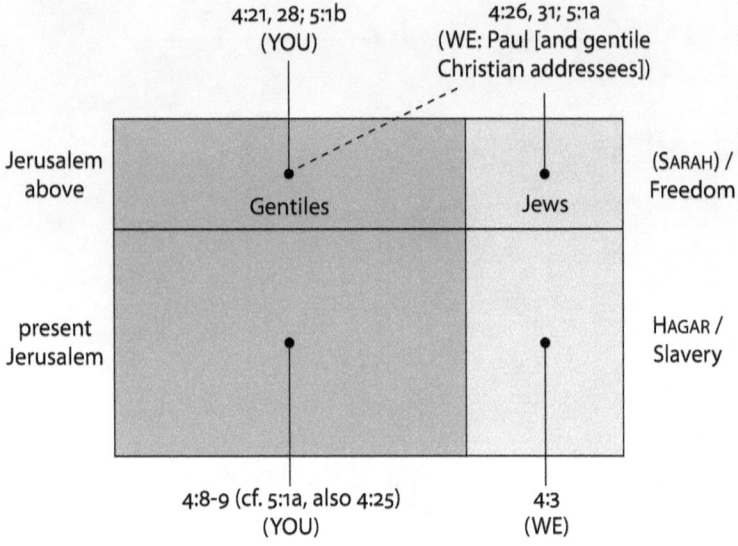

Here also the adverbs are of great interest.[57] First, according to the intention of Bouwman,[58] the facts should be stressed, that in spite of the reference to two covenants (4:24) our passage, differently from 2 Corinthians 3 (and Hebrews 8-9 [cf. 10:16-17]: first [8:7, 13; 9:15, 18; cf. 8:9] and new [8:8, 13; 9:15; cf. 12:24] or second [8:7] covenant), not only does not speak about old (2 Cor 3:14) and new (2 Cor 3:6; cf. 1 Cor 11:25, further Luke 22:20) covenants,[59] but not even about old and new Jerusalem.

Instead of the expression "the new Jerusalem," used, e.g., in Rev 21:2 (ἡ πόλις ἡ ἁγία Ἰερουσαλὴμ καινή [cf. 3:12]),[60] Paul applies the expression "the Jerusalem above,"[61] and in fact this ought to mean that he does not have in mind the idea of a replacement of the old by the new,[62] which for example characterizes the stained glass medallions in the Freiburg Cathedral.[63] For this reason in the enlarged "set theory" diagram, I have not arranged the two corporate entities beside each other but one above the other.

Strangely enough, however, it is not the Jerusalem below (ἡ κάτω Ἰερουσαλήμ)[64] but the present Jerusalem, ἡ νῦν Ἰερουσαλήμ, that stands opposite the Jerusalem above (ἡ ἄνω Ἰερουσαλήμ).[65] This is also hardly by chance. Indeed the present, the νῦν, is also emphasized in 4:29, where the former (τότε, with verbs in the past tense) connection between Ishmael and Isaac (4:29a) is related (4:29b) just to the present (νῦν).[66] This point and no differently the conspicuous feature that from 4:24 on until 4:31[67] the present tense is used[68] speak against Bouwman's view that Paul thinks of a thoroughgoing juxtaposition of two corporate entities since the time of Abraham.[69] No, whereas the Abraham argument in chapter 3 was an argument of salvation history and as a result an argument focused also on the past,[70] now in our passage a statement is made about a contemporary contraposition,[71] in which the addressees should reorient themselves in order to find the correct position. Since their positioning stands in question particularly on the basis of the desire to be circumcised, that is, on the basis of Judaizing tendencies, it makes sense also that in 4:25 Paul employs especially Jewish symbols for the other woman, that is, "Sinai" and "present Jerusalem"[72] — although as we saw with the other woman, a broader horizon is outlined for the endangered Gentile Christians in view: the horizon of slavery in general.

5

For both, that is, a contemporaneous contraposition and the employment particularly of Jewish symbols, it is interesting to take notice of some facts of the history of tradition. These deserve at least to be mentioned. For instance, the fact that in chapter 4, differently from chapters 1 and 2 (1:17, 18; 2:1), Paul does not use the neuter (τὰ) Ἱεροσόλυμα to designate the city but the feminine form (ἡ) Ἱερουσαλήμ,[73] causes one's view to shift back to the Old Testament state of affairs, to which some years earlier Odil Hannes Steck dedicated a splendid essay entitled "Zion als Gelände und Gestalt. Überlegungen zur Wahrnehmung Jerusalems als Stadt und Frau im Alten Testament."[74] Given that in Hebrew substantives for what is embracing and life-producing are often feminine, cities are conceived of accordingly.[75] The personal idea is especially employed with respect to Jerusalem in a quite restricted textual sphere, but yet one that in manifold ways is far-reaching.[76] In view of the focus on those who belong to this corporate entity the city thus conceived of as a woman can thereby — as in Gal 4:26 (cf. 4:27, 28, 31 [also in 4:25]: τέκνα)[77] — be characterized as "mother" (Isa 50:1; Jer 50:12) and with respect to its relationship with God it can particularly be characterized as "daughter Zion" (e.g., Isa 52:2) and as "wife" (e.g., Isa 62:4-5). Insofar as the relationship with God is (culpably) disturbed (see esp. Ezekiel 16), Jerusalem can be spoken of as the "forsaken wife" (e.g., Isa

54:6-7), the "widow" (e.g., Lam 1:1),[78] and the "whore" (e.g., Ezek 16:30-31), a conceptuality and view which moreover can be related to foreign cities (e.g., Nineveh [Nah. 3:4]),[79] in Isaiah 47 also to Babel, Babylon, which suddenly becomes a "widow" (vv. 8-9) — though in this chapter without using the term "whore" (זונה), which nevertheless is suggested by the context (see vv. 1-3 [and cf. on this Ezek 16:35-37; Nah. 3:4-5]). This use of language directed, so to speak, outwardly does not, however, dominate the usage with respect to Jerusalem. Furthermore, genetically "the emergence of the idea of Jerusalem as a person in the Old Testament only from the period of the exile onward" ought to be "causally connected with the experience of Jerusalem's catastrophe" and the corresponding negative formulations, like the "prostitute metaphor" from Isa 1:21-26 — prepared for, among other things, by the remarks in Hos 2:1-4 related to the land — are carried over from Jerusalem to foreign cities where therefore "counter-statements" turn up.[80] "A second phase of development" will then have led to "prophecies with a salubrious portrayal of the woman Zion."[81] According to this, as a result — as in the saying from Isa 54:1 (here, among other things: "desolate woman" *vs.* married woman ["who has a man"]) taken up in Gal 4:27[82] — two female figures, who are assessed differently, stand in contrast: Jerusalem/Babel as a negative entity on the one hand and Jerusalem as a positive unit on the other. And for these considered corporate entities it is thereby essential that now — not least of all on account of Babel's extensive pretensions to power (see only Isa 47:5-8, 11)[83] — "the idea of Zion as a person is connected with her position as queen with regard to the world of nations."[84]

In the sense of a current, indeed apocalyptic, contraposition one encounters the ideas which thus were at hand — and which were incidentally already in Ezekiel 16[85] (cf. Isa 54:4[-5], 6[-7]; 61:8) emphatically associated with the notion of the (broken and to be renewed) covenant (Ezek 16:8, 59-62) — then, as is well known, in the Revelation to John.[86] There in chapters 17–18 the whore Babylon is first depicted, then in chapters 21–22 (and chapter 19 [vv. 7-9; cf. also 20:9]), the pure "bride,"[87] the "new Jerusalem."[88]

With this, of course, corporate entities are in mind and the negative entity stands in front, just as in Galatians 4. As in Galatians 4, persecution goes out from the negative entity (see only Rev 17:6, 13-14; 18:24) and the author intends to provide orientation in a confused situation (see only Rev 17:2, 7). Above all, as in Galatians 4, Judaism is not specifically in view in the figure of the other woman — definitely not Judaism only.

For, in the first place, according to the Old Testament tradition this "Babylon the great" (Rev 17:5; 18:2 and *passim;* cf. Dan 4:27), no different from the "new Jerusalem," is related to the whole earth (see esp. Rev 17:2; 19:2; 21:24) and to all nations (see esp. Rev 17:15; 18:3; 21:24, 26; 22:2),[89] and, secondly, Revelation 17 (see esp. vv. 8-12) points — and at about the end of the first century the name "Babylon" points (see 1 Peter 5:13; 2 *Bar.* 67:7) — sufficiently clearly to Rome and the Roman Empire.[90] In view of the history of the motif mentioned briefly by us one should not, however, be surprised that, in spite of the Babylon terminology, occasionally an interpretation of the "great whore" can be held that thinks of Jerusalem.[91] As little as this corresponds to the results concerning the Apocalypse, it deserves to be stressed all the more: ultimately, according to the history of tradition, Jerusalem motifs stand in the background of the "whore Babylon," and the seer John takes this into consideration in some respects.

John, to be precise, uses Jewish ideas, or ideas influenced by Judaism, not only for the positive corporate entity — beside the new Jerusalem conceived of as a bride, one needs to remember above all the woman clothed with the sun in chapter 12 with the crown made up of twelve stars on her head (Rev 12:1)[92] and the direct references to the twelve tribes of Israel (see only Rev 7:3-8 [cf. 14:1]; 21:12-13 [cf. 22:3]).[93] Rather, he proceeds analogously also with respect to the negative corporate entity standing opposite. This may be indirectly the case for Rev 7:3-8 insofar as mentioning the tribe of Dan appears to be avoided here (by means of naming Manasseh *and* Joseph), due to the fact that it is assessed as a comprehensive negative entity.[94] With respect to the "synagogue of Satan,"[95] the manner of speaking, which is used in the letters to Smyrna and Sardis, is directly and aggressively related to the negative, Satanic sphere, though merely to segments of it (Rev 2:9; 3:9).[96] It is still more remarkable, however, that and how in Revelation 11 the expression "great city" occurs, which appears also in chapters 17 and 18 (Rev 17:18; 18:16, 18, 19; cf. 16:19; 18:10, 21, also Jer 22:8[97]).[98] In Rev 11:8 an expression occurs in reference to this town to the effect that it is "spiritually called Sodom and Egypt, where also their Lord was crucified." This universal[99] πόλις, which according to 11:9(-10) is connected with the λαοί, φυλαί, γλῶσσαι, and ἔθνη, of course alludes to that entity which in 11:2 was still called the "holy city" and which is, as a city given over to the ἔθνη for a certain span of time[100] and as such not to be measured, distinguished from the heavenly "temple of God" in 11:1, which in contrast is to be measured.[101] Thus, in certain respects already within chapter 11 itself, namely, with 11:2-10 on the one hand and 11:1 on the other, in any case, however, with chapter 11 (vv. 2-10) (and chapters 17–18) on the one hand and chapters 21–22 on the other, precisely Jerusalem and Jerusalem — assessed negatively and positively — stand opposed to each other, and, to be sure, in such a manner that here the negative symbol (no other than the positive one) refers in the end not to Judaism, in any case not to Judaism only.[102]

6

The history of tradition, therefore, as well as the situation that Paul has to cope with, makes the figurative language understandable which the Apostle uses. And both diachrony and synchrony give counsel to take leave of a tradition of interpretation *("Rezeption")* that in any respect takes place according to the stained glass medallions in the Freiburg Cathedral.[103] Not until the absence of a battle command is noted and a careless identification of the threatening other is avoided, can Paul's demand for a reorientation be grasped and be made beneficial for our situation.

6. The Church and the Israel of God: On the Meaning and Ecclesiastical Relevance of the Benediction at the End of Galatians

1

The difficulty of grasping the meaning of the expression "the Israel of God" (ὁ Ἰσραὴλ τοῦ θεοῦ), which occurs close to the end of Galatians in 6:16, becomes clear by looking at F. Mußner's comments on the passage. In 1963 he still confidently falls in with what at least in the twentieth century has to be accepted as the majority opinion[1] — and at the same time he dismisses the view that the phrase has simply Jewish Christians in mind: "Very probably . . . the entire community of Christians is meant," which — so to speak as ὁ Ἰσραὴλ κατὰ πνεῦμα — stands in opposition to ὁ Ἰσραὴλ κατὰ σάρκα (in 1 Cor 10:18).[2] And "the nineteenth benediction of the Shemone Esre probably represents the late Jewish background: 'Let peace, (salvation) and blessing, (favor and love and mercy) be upon us and *upon all Israel, your people.*'"[3] In the context of his work on his substantial commentary on Galatians, the Catholic exegete then comes to something of a different assessment: In comparison with the preceding ἐπ' αὐτούς, which according to him appeals to "the Gentile Christians and those Jewish Christians who do not expect salvation from the law and who ignore the arguments of the opponents of the Apostle," "the merely complementary 'and on the Israel of God' must have another meaning, for which then Israel, more clearly the Jews, is worthy of consideration."[4] To strengthen this, he adds not only a reference to Rom 11:26[5] but also the assumption that in analogy with the parable of the olive tree "in Romans 11 . . . with 'the Israel of God' the entire people of God, consisting of Jews and Gentiles, could be meant."[6] And he concludes with the rather resigned statement: "Exegesis will never arrive at a unanimous opinion about whom Paul had in mind with 'the Israel of God.'"[7]

This final statement at least enables one to sense that with "the Israel of God" in Gal 6:16 we are dealing with a *crux interpretum*.[8] And with what has been brought up just before, on the one hand the spectrum of interpretations which has been and is suggested in older and more recent exegesis and which goes from Jewish Christianity to the Christian community made up of Jews and Gentiles and to Judaism is indicated.[9] But on the other hand, at the same time it also shows how the field of the arguments is roughly structured — of those arguments which of course are again thoroughly debated with respect to their relevance. Four areas may be distinguished.

In the first place, the context of the expression "the Israel of God" is referred to: it is, above all — but not only — the larger context, that is, Galatians in its entirety. So J. Roloff, not least of all with Gal 4:21ff. in view, thinks that he is able to detect a "consistent disinheritance theory in Galatians."[10] In view of the "disinheritance of the Jews remaining under the Torah" and in view of the opinion that "thereby the representatives of the true Israel . . . are only those who are free, because they are believers apart from the law," the "wish for peace for 'the Israel of God,' with which Paul concludes Galatians (Gal 6:16), can hardly" be understood "in any other way than as the summary of this general line of the letter: 'The Israel of God' is the church that stands beyond the slavery of the law and that lives from the freedom given in Christ."[11]

However, in comparison with such a way of arguing, which here is accepted as "the customary interpretation,"[12] G. Schrenk — to quote here again only one of several authors — insists that an "overall concept of the letter" can be seen, e.g., in Gal 2:1, 8-9; 3:24; 4:4, and above all in 2:15-21, in which "the authentic Jewish Christianity" is emphasized, and precisely for this the "conclusion" constitutes "the final chord."[13]

In the second place, in looking at the syntagm "the Israel of God" the Pauline Israel terminology is asserted. So against the conventional interpretation, i.e., "the community of Christ as a whole," Schrenk puts forward the following argument: "If this were . . . the case, this use of 'Israel' would be completely unique in Paul. In all the other cases, without exception . . . he has reserved the name Israel for the Jews," "for the concrete Israel."[14] Even the phrase ὁ Ἰσραὴλ κατὰ σάρκα does not lead to an exception to the rule: "The expression does not in any way require a tacit completion by an *Israel kata pneuma,* which indeed is not explicitly mentioned."[15] For this

The Church and the Israel of God

reason, with "the Israel of God" one should think "of the concrete Israel and not of the Christian church"[16] — more precisely "the Jews who believe in Christ"[17] are meant.

However, although the gist of the argument, "Schrenk's main argument,"[18] cannot be denied, N. A. Dahl, who indeed sees this very well,[19] at least thinks he is allowed to say: "1 Cor 10 shows . . . the *possibility* that from his point of view Paul was able to describe the church [as] 'Israel according to the Spirit', or correspondingly as 'Israel of God.'"[20] He attempts to back up this view by referring to the sphere of the Apostle's ecclesiological terms and ideas.[21]

In the third place, even this sphere comes into the process of appraisal. Thus Dahl names as "indicators for thinking" that Paul could have "transferred" the term "Israel" "to the Christian church," "the transfer of the terms 'children of Abraham,' 'circumcision,' 'people of God' (2 Cor 6:16; Rom 9:25), etc.," further the Pauline "view of the church in general," as it finds expression especially in 1 Cor 10:18 and Gal 4:29 (cf. Eph 2:11ff.).[22]

However, against such a conclusion from the other terms, which are applied to the Christian community, to the expression "the Israel of God," it is possible to raise objections on the basis of the history of tradition, namely that just this term "Israel" was apparently not used with regard to the church for quite a long time. In this context, P. Richardson speaks of "the total absence of an identification of the Church with Israel until A.D. 160,"[23] i.e., until the time of Justin's *Dialogue with Trypho* (see esp. *Dial.* 11:5; 123:7-8).[24]

In the fourth place, Jewish parallels to the benediction at the end of Galatians are also put forward, especially the nineteenth petition of the Eighteen Benedictions. Richardson judges like this: "The Galatians sentence conveys the impression of being an interpreted reflection of the benediction."[25] Namely, in view of the correspondence with that prayer containing the sequence of "us" and "all Israel," it must hold for Paul and "the Israel of God," which follows "them" in Gal 6:16: "Israel is not yet the Christ-believing Jews, it is those [Jews] who are still to believe."[26]

However, Schrenk, against whom the negation is directed[27] and for whose argumentation the Jewish comparative material is of considerable importance,[28] supposes that precisely the more detailed determination "the Israel *of God,*" which is elsewhere not attested with "Israel," indicates the Pauline *proprium:* the Apostle is driving at a "separation in Israel" and he precisely means the Jewish Christians.[29]

If one surveys the four areas of argumentation outlined here which engage with each other in the interpretation of Gal 6:16, the impression is confirmed that we are dealing with a *crux interpretum,* precisely insofar as each of these areas can be used in different ways. Mußner's resigned comment quoted above is quite understandable, but in my opinion such an assessment need not remain. There is no lack of quite unambiguous results, as the example of the Pauline use of Ἰσραήλ (and Ἰσραηλίτης) shows. And with a little more thorough study with the individual areas of argumentation, to which we now turn (in section 2.1-4), at least the synchronic reading (2.1), which is considered first for methodological reasons, promises in view of recent exegesis of Galatians to lead out of established aporias. Since these observations and those following them (2.2-4), in which one's view should go beyond the writing directed to the Galatian communities (see Gal 1:2), will lead to a statement "against today's dogmatization of the interpretation"[30] of ὁ Ἰσραὴλ τοῦ θεοῦ as referring to the church, it seems sensible to deal a bit more closely with the relevance of Gal 6:16 for the ecclesiastical profile of this epistle in a concluding section (section 3 below).

2

2.1

If we begin with the *wider context* of Gal 6:16, the question arises, according to what has been presented, whether a "consistent disinheritance theory" (J. Roloff) actually determines Galatians. However, someone committed to this or a similar view does not necessarily have to reject an emphatic reference of "the Israel of God" to Jews (or Jewish Christians). This can be demonstrated by the explanation of G. Schrenk, who, remarkably, is able to judge as follows: "It cannot be denied that, according to Paul, the law-free, believing Christianity is the 'heir' to the Jewish national identity. Those who belong to Christ are the seed of Abraham and heirs according to the promise: Gal 3:29; cf. Rom 4:13. This opposition can also be found in Gal 4:22-29: Jewish national identity on the one hand and law-free Christianity as the universal community consisting of all peoples."[31] But whereas from such a reading of the letter, that is, from "the christocentric narrowing of the descendants of Abraham and the allegory of Hagar and Sarah," the usual conclusion is: "'The Israel of God' includes Christ-believing Gentiles and Jews, and not the Jewish Christians or a part of Israel and certainly not past and present Israel in toto,"[32] additionally and especially in Gal 2:15-21 Schrenk discovers "another line of the epistolary corpus" in view of which "a wish for a blessing for Christ-believing Israel in Galatians is nothing odd at all."[33]

The fact that in the structure of Galatians a decisive role has to be attached to 2:15-21 is something that I have tried to give reasons for with recourse to T. Zahn's interpretation of the text[34] in my *Habilitationschrift*:[35] Here Paul places before the eyes of the addressees, the majority of whom are Gentiles (see only 4:8-9; 5:2), the example of Jews by birth, the example of conversion (2:15-17a), of threat (2:17b-18; cf. v. 21), and of Jewish Christians whose life is in accordance with Christ and orientated toward God (vv. 19-20); and going on from there, in 3:1–6:17 the Apostle can demonstrate to the Galatians what their own turning to Christ is all about (3:1–4:7), that also for them an orientation toward certain ritual prescriptions has the effect of a fundamental threat (4:8–5:1), and what *vita Christiana* means with respect to its content (5:2–6:17).[36] This preceding position of Jewish and Jewish Christian life in the corpus of the Epistle — and particularly the connection to the distinction between "Jews" and "Gentile sinners" in 2:15(-17a) — allows one to recognize the author's orientation toward the history of redemption, which maintains the priority of Judaism, even while he emphasizes the dependence also of Jews (or Jewish Christians) on Christ and on the forgiveness of sins (esp. 2:16-17, 20d, 21b). This priority also remains decisive in 3:1–4:7, because here also (with the exception only of 3:14b and 4:6b), as in 2:15-17a, the first person plural is used of Jews (or Jewish Christians), so that in 3:1-14, in 3:15-29, and in 4:1-7 the salvation event asserted for the Jews is expressed as the prerequisite for what — for this reason — can also be effective for the Gentiles (see esp. 3:14, 26-29; 4:6-7).[37] It fits in seamlessly with this that with respect to the way leading from Abraham to the Gentiles (see esp. 3:8), for which in this writing one could actually speak of a "christocentric narrowing" (see esp. 3:16, 19, 22, 26, 28-29; 4:6), Christ is characterized as γενόμενος ὑπὸ νόμον (4:4) and that thereby he is precisely characterized as a Jew (see esp. 2:14-15 [cf. 2:16-19, 21b]; 3:23-24; cf. 1 Cor 9:20), and it seems to be necessary to do so.

The following passages do not deviate from this redemptive history perspective either. For here the Galatians are first warned (4:8–5:1) not to fall short of the understanding of God which they had attained and which had been documented by their conversion, the understanding of *the* God in whom Abraham believed and who both sent Christ and also raised him (see only 1:1; 3:6; 4:4). Then they are made aware (5:2–6:17) of a life which is determined by love (see 5:6, 13, 22) and by the Spirit (see 5:16-18, 22, 25; 6:8) and which is, precisely in this way, in harmony with the law (see 5:14, 23; cf. 6:2) — given to the Jews (see esp. 3:20a, 23-25; 4:5).[38] Taking this context into consideration (see esp. 4:8-9; cf. 4:1, 7, 10), the section in 4:21–5:1 in particular, which is difficult and is often interpreted as anti-Jewish, can hardly be assessed as evidence for a "consistent disinheritance theory." If one looks at it more closely,[39] it cannot be understood as a demand to "drive out" either Judaizers or even Jews (cf. 4:30) nor in the sense of discrediting a Judaism defining itself by the Sinai event (cf. 4:24-25). Rather, here there is an urgent exhortation in the current dispute (see 4:29; cf. 5:11; 6:12) to remain, in concert with the Jewish writer (see 4:26, 31; 5:1a), on the side that is characterized by freedom (4:28–5:1) — and that is referred to in catchwords of redemptive history such as "the free woman" (that is, Sarah), "Isaac," and "Jerusalem above" (4:22-23, 26, 28, 30-31) — and not to return to the status of slavery, which is primarily characteristic of the Gentiles (see 5:1) and in which they were before their conversion (see 4:8-9), which, however, is now particularly threatening with the (first) adoption of the regulations of the Torah (see 4:21, 25; cf. 4:10; 5:2-4; 6:12-13).

Thus, in the corpus of the letter — with its unquestionably limiting remarks on the law (see again esp. 3:13, 17-19), with its reference to sin and aberrant behavior of Jews also (see esp. 2:16-17a; 3:19) and with its "christocentric narrowing of the descendants of Abraham" (see esp. 3:29) — the priority of Judaism in redemptive history is definitely respected. In certain respects even the preceding, more narrative part of the writing (1:11–2:14) corresponds to this. For in 2:7-9 (cf. 1:17, also 1:13, 22-23), notwithstanding his own christophany and his orientation toward non-Jews which is immediately associated with it, Paul presupposes the temporal priority and the indisputability of the ἀποστολὴ τῆς περιτομῆς (2:8) over against his own commission, which includes the Gentiles; moreover, he does not conceal here that the Jerusalem "pillars" offered him and Barnabas κοινωνία (2:9) and that it was not the other way around (nor could it have been).[40]

From the wider context it thus appears quite possible that with "the Israel of God" in 6:16 real Jews are in view without exception. For this reason, the opinion that the character of Galatians requires the interpretation that the church made up of Jews and Gentiles is meant by the syntagm

The Church and the Israel of God

must be rejected — although this interpretation is not to be simply excluded by the evidence considered.

For this reason let us now consult the *nearer context!* Here it first deserves attention that 5:2-12 and 6:11-17, which begin with ἴδε and ἴδετε and the "I" of the author, are clearly in contact (cf. only 5:2b-4 with 6:16-17, and 5:6 with 6:15), but deal with the "opponents" in different ways:[41] whereas in the earlier passage their vehement condemnation and particularly the sarcastic recommendation of their castration constitutes the conclusion (5:7-10, esp. 5:12), in the later passage the reference to these people precedes (6:12-13) without reaching a severity similar to that of the earlier passage — in spite of naming or insinuating dubious motives. It corresponds to this somewhat milder tone that although 6:17, which stands immediately before the *Eschatokoll,* begins with a dismissive expression (6:17a), it does not end in polemics but with a positive word that characterizes the connection of the writer — who is Jewish and who according to 6:14 nevertheless boasts only about the cross — with Christ: "I bear the marks of Jesus on my body" (6:17b).

Apart from the less aggressive formulation of 6:12-17 it is striking that here for the first time in the letter a somewhat clear connection of the "opponents" with Judaism is brought up. The connection can be seen in the catchword "boast" (6:13, 14; cf. [Rom 2:23; 3:27; and] 6:12) and also in the fact that according to 6:13b (cf. 5:2) these people not only work toward the circumcision of the Galatian Christians but in 6:13a are themselves characterized as περιτεμνόμενοι.

If one considers both the manner of speaking in 6:12-17, that it is a little more gentle, and the rather clear references, given not until now, to a Jewish background, defined by περιτεμνόμενοι, for the crisis in Galatia, one will have to take into serious consideration a concluding and positive reference to real Jews for the first and only use of the term "Israel" in 6:16. The fact that the two ὅσοι sentences in 6:12 and 6:16 correspond to each other at least formally could particularly speak for such an understanding.[42] If the term Ἰσραήλ were not understood in a figurative sense, the polemic of 6:12-13 could not be adhered to. Rather, the tone toward those who are circumcised would be more conciliatory, particularly since Jews in 6:15 — by the relativizing of "circumcision" and "the state of not being circumcised" — are just as little excluded from salvation at the end of time as Gentiles (cf. 3:27-28; 5:6).

If "the Israel of God" in 6:16 does not mean the Christian community made up of Jews and Gentiles — and if accordingly μηδείς in 6:17 is not restricted exclusively to Christians[43] — it will be rather simple to explain why Paul in the concluding sentence of Galatians (6:18), differently than elsewhere in his letters,[44] mentions the addressees once more specifically as ἀδελφοί:[45] their circle is then not identical with those who are in mind earlier, particularly not with ὁ Ἰσραὴλ τοῦ θεοῦ; therefore especially in this case this circle must be named.

Finally, the, so to speak, *immediate context* also provides evidence against the usual interpretation of 6:16. One has to consider how the expression "the Israel of God," which is placed at the end of the benediction, is connected with what precedes, that is, with εἰρήνη ἐπ' αὐτοὺς καὶ ἔλεος (6:16b) and with the characterization of those who (at least) are meant here by ὅσοι τῷ κανόνι τούτῳ στοιχήσουσιν (6:16a) — a description which for its part harks back to the interpretation of the Christ event in the sense of the "new creation" that goes beyond the distinction between "circumcision" and "the state of not being circumcised" (6:14-15).

Like "most exegetes"[46] W. Kraus, for instance, understands the connection: "A . . . natural solution results if the last καί in 6:16 is understood epexegetically: Then Ἰσραὴλ τοῦ θεοῦ refers back to αὐτούς, i.e., to those who live according to the guiding principle of the new creation. They, who are identical with those who are ἐν Χριστῷ, constitute the Israel of God."[47] However, it would be better not to speak of a natural solution in this connection. It is not only the case that here the factors pointing toward the nearer or more distant future, that is, at least the future tense στοιχήσουσιν and the term ἔλεος (cf. only Rom 11:31-32), are hardly given due attention![48] Furthermore, there is even a lack of Pauline parallels which would permit us to classify the καί in καὶ ἐπὶ τὸν Ἰσραὴλ τοῦ θεοῦ as epexegetical.[49] Moreover, T. Zahn rightly raises the following objection against such a view: "Only without the καί, which in order to produce this meaning has been occasionally deleted, could this if necessary be an apposition to ἐπ' αὐτούς, although a reference by οἵτινές εἰσιν or τουτέστιν would be more natural and the lagging behind of the apposition would be completely without cause."[50] Therefore, with ἐπ' αὐτούς and with ἐπὶ τὸν Ἰσραὴλ τοῦ θεοῦ two distinct circles are in mind and by no means does one have to include the other.[51]

If one pays attention to the fact that both connected prepositional phrases in 6:16 use ἐπί with the accusative, then the impression which has been gained is confirmed. For "that figure of speech in which the second ἐπί adds a new factor is the predominant one by far,"[52] to say it with Schrenk's words. Among the examples that he has collected,[53] this holds in any case for Matt 27:25 ("on us and on our children"); Acts 5:11 ("on the whole church and on all who heard these things"); 11:15 ("upon them just as it had [ὥσπερ καί] upon us at the beginning"); Heb 8:8 ("with the house of Israel and with the house of Judah"); and Rev 20:4 ("on their foreheads and on their hands"). Although in Paul, as far as I can see, with the exception of Gal 6:16 a linking of two prepositional phrases in this way by a simple καί is missing, he does suggest from time to time a corresponding wording. So, for the sake of completeness, one could place a statement in which the negation is omitted in front of the formulation καὶ ἐπὶ τοὺς μὴ ἁμαρτήσαντας ἐπὶ τῷ ὁμοιώματι τῆς παραβάσεως Ἀδάμ, which can be found in Rom 5:14. Even more interesting for the connection that has to be clarified is Rom 4:9, including its context. For if it is asked whether the μακαρισμός in Rom 4:7-8 (and in Ps 31[32]:1-2) is enacted ἐπὶ τὴν περιτομὴν ἢ καὶ ἐπὶ τὴν ἀκροβυστίαν, there is, at least with the motives of the benediction and of the "circumcision"/"state of not being circumcised," moreover with the expression found in 4:12 concerning those who "walk" (στοιχεῖν) in Abraham's footprints, a considerable linguistic and thematic resemblance to Gal 6:15-16. Additionally, Rom 4:11-12, with its manner of speaking about Abraham as "father of all the uncircumcised [δι' ἀκροβυστίας] who believe" and as "father of the circumcision," suggests the answer for the question in 4:9, which is that the blessing extends ἐπὶ τὴν ἀκροβυστίαν καὶ ἐπὶ τὴν περιτομήν!

The observations of the larger, nearer, and immediate context have made it probable that Gal 6:16 can be understood in a similar way. The first complement, that is, καὶ ἔλεος,[54] which follows immediately after εἰρήνη ἐπ' αὐτούς and precedes καὶ ἐπὶ τὸν Ἰσραὴλ τοῦ θεοῦ, has hardly been included in the considerations until now. First, this complement underlines the future character already marked by στοιχήσουσιν. The striking postposition in relation to the term εἰρήνη[55] — in contrast to, e.g., 1 Tim 1:2 — already suggests this, and to support it, with ἔλεος (and ἐλεεῖν) "eschatological" connotations, combined with it in Paul, are added, which also appear outside the Pauline Epistles.[56] Second, for the Apostle, and not for him only, ἔλεος and ἐλεεῖν deal with the problem of Israel.[57] Both points together strengthen what has already been said about the correspondence of Gal 5:2-12 and 6:11-17,[58] inasmuch as it is so thoroughly clear that the reference to the — future — divine mercy now at least in the friendliness of the formulation goes beyond the sharpness of 5:10-12 and especially beyond the threat of judgment hurled against every troublemaker in 5:10.[59] At the same time, with what has just been noted about the term "mercy," the view already goes beyond Galatians. The Pauline terminology of Israel, to which we now turn, is also found primarily outside this letter.

2.2

That the terminology of Israel in the Pauline corpus emphatically supports the interpretation of the expression "the Israel of God" in Gal 6:16 as a reference to real Jews, has already been mentioned[60] and can be shown quite quickly. This first holds for the gentilic *(Gentilium)* Ἰσραηλίτης, which Paul uses three times (Rom 9:4; 11:1; 2 Cor 11:22), in each case establishing thereby a connection to his own person. By writing καὶ γὰρ ἐγὼ Ἰσραηλίτης εἰμί in Rom 11:1 and by in support of this referring to his descent from Abraham and to his membership in the tribe of Benjamin, he demonstrates that ὁ θεός has not rejected (11:2; cf. 11:1 and 1 Kgdms [1 Sam] 12:22; Ps 93[94]:14) τὸν λαὸν αὐτοῦ (11:1-2), in spite of all evidence to the contrary (see only 9:31; 10:18-21), but rather adheres to it, to — his — Israel (see only 10:21; 11:2). With the features in Rom 9:4-5, where Paul refers to "the 'adoption' (cf. Gal 4:[1-]5), the 'glory,' the covenants, the giving of the law, and the promises," and further to "the patriarchs" and the descent of Christ, the Apostle accordingly emphasizes the redemptive historical distinction of those whom he calls "Israelites" and whom he (in 11:3) describes as his "brothers" and his "kindred" (cf. Rom 16:7, 11, 21).[61] Whereas in Rom 9:1-5 (see esp. 9:1-2 and the "amen" in 9:5) he directs to them his "sympathy that is expressed with great emotion,"[62] 2 Cor 11:22 has to do with a debate with "opponents." It is remarkable that in his "fool's speech" he does not declare their "reference . . . to participation in the privileges of the people of God,"[63] that is, to be "Hebrews," "Israelites," and "seed of Abraham," to be simply irrelevant. He rather uses these predicates, which belong together,[64] particularly that of being an Israelite, also for himself: although this descent can be asserted in a questionable way by questionable people, for Paul the physical and "full membership in the people of Israel"[65] is by no means something to be disregarded.

Things are similar with the ethnic term *(Ethnikon)* Ἰσραήλ, even if in the context of Phil 3:2ff., which is reminiscent of 2 Cor 11:18ff., physical membership in the people of Israel, which is again unambiguously emphasized (Phil 3:5: περιτομῇ ὀκταήμερος, ἐκ γένους Ἰσραήλ, φυλῆς Βενιαμίν, Ἑβραῖος ἐξ Ἑβραίων . . .), is with regard to its relevance more clearly limited and christologically relativized (3:7-8: ζημία, σκύβαλα). Apart from Phil 3:5 the term appears in at least thirteen verses (cf. further Rom 10:1 [variant reading] as well as Eph 2:12) in the Pauline Epistles (Rom 9:6, 27, 31; 10:19, 21; 11:2, 7, 25, 26; 1 Cor 10:18; 2 Cor 3:7, 13; Gal 6:16). Here the term Ἰσραηλῖται, which refers to present membership in the people of God, is, so to speak, replaced for the past by the expression οἱ υἱοὶ Ἰσραήλ, as it is used in 2 Cor 3:7, 13 in dependence on Exod 34:35 and as it is taken up from Hos 2:1 in Rom 9:27, of course without the absence of an "eschatological" perspective in either of these (see only Rom 9:27b [Isa 10:22]; 2 Cor 3:13b-16)[66] — and this is not different in Phil 3:2ff. (see esp. 3:9-11, 20-21). Since the reference to the future is furthermore decisive for Romans 9–11 altogether (see esp. 11:11-32) — thus for those chapters which provide the majority of the Pauline references to Ἰσραήλ — and since, moreover, in 1 Corinthians 10 the desert generation and the Ἰσραήλ κατὰ σάρκα (10:18) are regarded typologically (see 10:6, 11) in view of the Christian community and of the "eschaton" (see 10:11-13), one will first have to note: the future dimension, which we already came across in Gal 6:16, is a feature that joins all contexts that have to be considered here. Furthermore the term Ἰσραήλ — as was already the case with Ἰσραηλίτης and Ἰσραηλῖται — exceptionally has to do with real Jews. The following groups are taken into consideration (beyond Gal 6:16): the desert generation (1 Cor 10:18 [cf. 10:1-11]) and this not least of all (2 Cor 3:7, 13), the addressees of Elijah (Rom 11:2) and Isaiah (Rom 9:27; 10:21) — as well as comparable people (cf. Rom 11:5) — , Paul himself (Phil 3:5), a Judaism embracing all periods of time (Rom 9:31; 10:19; 11:17), the Judaism of the Pauline present (Rom 11:25), and the "eschatological" Judaism (Rom 11:26). If one disregards the formulation πᾶς Ἰσραήλ in Rom 11:26, whose precise meaning is not undisputed[67] and which somehow is "to be understood collectively,"[68] then it is finally characteristic for 1 Cor 10:18 and for the examples in Romans 9–11 that distinctions are made within Judaism: whereas the paradoxical way of speaking in Rom 9:6 (οὐ . . . πάντες οἱ ἐξ Ἰσραὴλ οὗτοι Ἰσραήλ) at least suggests the idea of a smaller corporate entity, compared to which the all-embracing community, in spite of the name used for it, should really not be called Ἰσραήλ, the statement about the "remnant" in Rom 9:27 does not constitute a limitation of the term "Israel" to a core group, and this is also not the case in Rom 10:19–11:10 with its distinction in 11:7 between the "chosen" and the obstinate "others," and not in the reference in Rom 11:25 to a "partial obstinacy" in Israel.[69] The formulation ὁ Ἰσραὴλ κατὰ σάρκα in 1 Cor 10:18 fits in with this and also with the use of σάρξ in Rom 9:3 (cf. 11:14; somewhat different: 9:5) and 9:8 (cf. Phil 3:3-4; Gal 6:12-13). For what these passages in Romans 9–11 enable one to presume, namely that here the complement of such a core group (in other words, of the "remnant") is in view, i.e., rather negatively qualified Jews, is confirmed by the context (cf. esp. 1 Cor 10:14, 19 with 10:7, and 10:22 with 10:9). In contrast to other interpretations, W. Schrage thinks that it is quite probable[70] that one should think of "Israel, insofar as it does not offer sacrifice to God but to the idols."[71] If one boldly wished to bring in the counterpart term ὁ Ἰσραὴλ κατὰ πνεῦμα (cf. Rom 1:4; Gal 4:29), particularly as the desert generation according to 1 Cor 10:3-4 received "spiritual food" and "spiritual drink," this expression could be understood "as an *oppositum*" and it would not mean "another Israel in the form of the new people of God, but those in whom God delighted because they did not belong to the people who pursued idolatry."[72]

To sum up, one will have to say that the Pauline terminology for Israel beyond Gal 6:16 almost excludes the possibility that "the Israel of God" in this passage means the church made up of Jews and Gentiles.[73] In view of this comparative material it is rather very probable that real Jews are meant here, especially because the relationship of God to his people, the Israel *of God*, and the reference to the future, which are characteristic for Gal 6:16, find their equivalents in the context of the Apostle's other statements about Israel.[74]

2.3

Against the data just considered and against the overall fact mentioned at the beginning[75] that also outside the Pauline writings the term "Israel" is not applied to the church made up of Jews and Gentiles before the middle of the second century, references[76] to those ecclesiologically relevant terms for which such a process of transfer of meaning is given do not get the better. This opinion can be defended more confidently because the facts of the matter in the history of tradition are to a large extent different: already in Jewish writing it is possible to speak of being children of God (see esp.

Rom 8:14, 15, 19, 23; 9:8, 26; Gal 3:26; 4:6-7) and about a connection to Abraham as father (see esp. Rom 4:1, 11-12, 16-17; 9:7; Gal 3:7, 9, 29; cf. 4:28) in such a way that not only those who are born Jews are in view (see esp. *Joseph and Aseneth* 19:[5-]8; Sir 44:19[-21]); a spiritualizing speaking about circumcision (see esp. Rom 2:25-29; Phil 3:3) already occurs in the Old Testament (see only Jer 4:4; cf. Ezek 44:7, further *Jub.* 1:23), as well as the — limited — challenge of the title "people of God" for Judaism (of the Northern Kingdom), and in passages in which Paul does not limit this expression to Jews (see Rom 9:25-26; 2 Cor 6:16[77]), he precisely refers to this (namely to Hos [1:9–]2:1) and to statements of the Scriptures (Ezek 37:27 [cf. Lev 26:12]; Hos 2:25) which can be interpreted "eschatologically."[78]

Moreover, especially Romans, in which, for instance, circumcision and with it Jewish existence in a figurative sense are encountered (see again 2:25-29), and in addition corresponding references to Abraham's descendants (see again 4:11-12, 16-17), shows that a general expansion of the sphere of meaning attached to the terms in question is by no means connected with this. Whenever the Apostle means physical circumcision, real Jews, and real descendants of Abraham, he is able to express that unambiguously (see only Rom 3:1, 29-30; 11:1). And the special position which the term Ἰσραήλ (and analogously the designation Ἰσραηλίτης) takes in Paul particularly in comparison with Ἰουδαῖος, "becomes esp. clear by the distribution of both words in Romans, where in chapters 1–8 Ἰουδαῖος is used exclusively and where from chapter 9 on consistently Ἰ. [i.e., Ἰσραήλ] can be found"[79] — in addition in the context of the distinction from non-Jews (as previously [see only 1:16; 3:9]) furthermore also Ἰουδαῖος (9:24; 10:12; cf. further again: 9:3; 16:7, 11, 21 [συγγενής]).

The clear division in terminology is difficult to ignore for Galatians. This seems to be even less permitted because here also Ἰσραήλ (6:16) is not used until after other concepts referring to Jews and because at least Ἰουδαῖος (2:13, 14, 15; 3:28) is used in a "physical" or ethnic sense without exception (see esp. 2:15; 3:28), to which the use of Ἰουδαϊσμός (1:13, 14) corresponds; furthermore the basis of the employment of Ἰουδαϊκῶς and ἰουδαΐζειν (2:14) is formed by an image of a "Jewish way of life according to the law."[80] This way of life, however, should actually be expected only precisely from Jews.[81] In this context it is obvious that also real circumcision is in mind (cf. 2:14 with 2:3; 6:12), and precisely also περιτέμνειν (2:3; 5:2-3; 6:12-13) and περιτομή (2:7-9, 12; 5:6, 11; 6:15) are encountered in Galatians exclusively in the "physical" meaning or as metonyms for characterizing Jews.

ANTI-JUDAISM IN GALATIANS?

For the claim that with "the Israel of God" nevertheless Jewish and Gentile Christians are in mind, at the most those statements and passages of the writing which — in quite distinct ways — make use of the idea of the seed of Abraham (and of being children of God), namely 3:6–4:7 and 4:21–5:1, can be used against the numerous pieces of evidence that point in another direction. However, these sections hardly bear the burden that they are saddled with by such an argument. Besides what has already been dealt with (in section 2) above — concerning the preservation of a redemptive-historical priority of Judaism that can be observed in this letter and especially in 3:1–4:7 — only a few points will be put forward here.

"The christocentric narrowing of the seed of Abraham,"[82] as it occurs in 3:1-29 (see esp. 3:16, 19, 26-29), means especially that Paul here emphasizes the singular σπέρμα (e.g., in Gen 17:8) and relates it to Christ (3:16, 29; cf. 3:19), whereas he precludes an association of the Abrahamic promise(s) with a Jewish corporate entity (differently than in Romans 4 [see esp. 4:12, 16]), which for instance comes to mind with the plural σπέρματα (Gal 3:16; cf. 4 Macc 18:1) and which is somewhat vaguely characterized by πολλοί (Gal 3:16; cf. 3:19). Thereby the meaning, e.g., of the law (see 3:17-25) and of Christ's belonging to this domain (see 4:4) is by no means denied, but it nevertheless becomes clear that here the Apostle refuses the traditional[83] connection of the topics of Abraham and Israel,[84] found for instance in 4 Macc 18:1 and put forward by Paul himself in Rom 9:3-8; 11:1-4; and 2 Cor 11:22. Therefore, by the retrospective view, which has not least of all to do with the past of the Jewish people, the idea of such a community which is composed of a Jewish "remnant" of Israel and of Gentiles is not prepared.

When particularly in 3:26-29 and 4:6-7 light falls on the present, then the collective entity of the saved, to which Jews now belong as well as non-Jews (see esp. 3:28; cf. 3:8-9), is held together only indirectly by Abraham (see 3:29), whereas by contrast it is held together directly by Christ (see esp. 3:28), behind whom stands the *one* God of Jews and Gentiles (see esp. 3:20b; cf. Rom 3:29-30),[85] so that in the end this group can be conceived of as the totality of the "sons of God" (3:26) or the "sons" (4:6; cf. 4:7) — but not as "the Israel of God."

4:21–5:1 deals also and now quite emphatically with present matters, particularly with the threatened Christian community (see esp. 4:29: οὕτως καὶ νῦν [cf. 4:25]),[86] which also according to this passage is held together by the Christ event, i.e., by the liberation effected by Christ (see

The Church and the Israel of God

5:1). Insofar as this corporate entity, which is linked among other things with Abraham (4:21) and Isaac (4:28) and "Jerusalem above" as "mother" (4:26), thereby stands opposite another entity, which is likewise connected with Abraham (4:21) and beyond that with central issues of Judaism such as "covenant(s)" (4:24), "(Mount) Sinai" (4:24-25), and "(present) Jerusalem" (4:25), the result is a picture of a current opposition of two communities[87] characterized by Jewish symbolism and represented by two women (see only 4:22, 25-26), but not by the — so to speak — masculine idea ὁ Ἰσραήλ (κατὰ πνεῦμα/κατὰ σάρκα). In spite of a positive or negative judgment (see only 4:23 [cf. 4:28-29]: κατὰ σάρκα or δι' ἐπαγγελίας) about the two entities, in contrast to Rom 9:6-9 a connection to the conceptualism of Israel is missing.

Moreover, differently from Rom 9:6-7 (cf. 9:4-5),[88] in Gal 4:21–5:1 there is no reference to the future pointing beyond the current situation of the community. This also holds, at least essentially, for Gal 3:1–4:7,[89] and it distinguishes both passages from the benediction in 6:16. The not insignificant independence of this verse in the context of Galatians will thus have to be respected.

2.4

The fact that in Gal 6:16 ἔλεος follows εἰρήνη, whereas in 1:3 and in other prescripts to Paul's letters (cf. further 1 Pet 1:2; 2 Pet 1:2; Rev 1:4; *2 Bar.* 78:2) εἰρήνη occupies the second place after χάρις (see esp. Rom 1:7; 1 Cor 1:3; 2 Cor 1:2; Phil 1:2; 1 Thess 1:1; Phlm 3), also fits in with a certain independence of this verse. When, moreover, at the beginning of the Pastoral Epistles (1 Tim 1:2; 2 Tim 1:2; Tit 1:4; cf. 2 John 3 as well as Jude 2) also ἔλεος comes before εἰρήνη, then the sequence in Gal 6:16 can appear to be "illogical."[90] However, in contrast to this one can refer to the fact that in Romans 5 εἰρήνη emphatically marks the beginning of the argument (see 5:1) and to the fact that thereafter the subject of "eschatological" salvation (see 5:9-10) is brought up.[91] Furthermore, Gal 6:16 is not an exception insofar as in Paul with respect to the conclusions of the letters[92] at least "a quite large regularity" can be detected and insofar as in these conclusions often "another benediction occurs before the concluding wish for grace,"[93] which for the most part speaks of "the God . . . of peace" (see Rom [15:33 and] 16:20; 2 Cor 13:11; Phil 4:7, 9 [and 4:19]; 1 Thess 5:23; cf. Eph 6:23; 2 Thess

ANTI-JUDAISM IN GALATIANS?

3:16 [as well as the ἀνάθεμα in 1 Cor 16:22], further Heb 13:20, also 1 Pet 5:14; 3 John 15)[94] — so that in these cases εἰρήνη stands before χάρις.

In view of the comparable Pauline benedictions it is, however, unquestionably striking that Gal 6:16 speaks of ἔλεος and also of Ἰσραήλ — however little the juxtaposition of these two terms takes the readers by surprise when one compares this to Romans (and 1 Pet 2:10).[95] Hence, this suggests that we investigate Jewish parallels in epistolary conclusions and beyond.

The concluding formulas of two Hebrew pieces of writing show that Gal 6:16 makes sense in such a context. Close to the end of 4QMMT, which is documented by several "Qumran fragments" (and reconstructed from them) and which is possibly a letter, perhaps even composed by the "Teacher of Righteousness," that person who is referred to in this document by the second person singular ("you") is again approached in summary about the "precepts of the Torah" (C27) which have been explained earlier in detail[96] and which are valid in the group represented by the author. These precepts are thereby considered to be important "for your welfare [לטוב] and the welfare of your people" (C27). Then the eschatological relevance of these precepts and the contraposition between God and Belial (cf. Rom 16:20 [and 1 Cor 16:22]) are emphasized (see C28-30, esp. line 30: "at the end of time"). In view of the practical implementation of the precepts, it says subsequently: "And this will be counted as a virtuous deed of yours [cf. Gen 15:6, further Gal 3:6], since you will be doing what is righteous and good in His eyes, for your own welfare [לטוב] and for the welfare of Israel" (C 31-32). Although in Gal 6:11-18 Paul distances himself especially from the obligation of circumcision, which here is connected with the observing of the law, the points of contact of these passages, particularly Gal 6:16, with the final lines of 4QMMT are indeed astonishing.[97] For the Apostle also presents an eschatological contraposition (among other things of κόσμος and καινὴ κτίσις [see Gal 6:14-15]), and he also attempts to tie the circle of addressees down to a guiding principle and a behavior corresponding to it (see 6:16: κανών, στοιχεῖν). Furthermore, in 4QMMT the "you" (singular) is differentiated from "his people" with respect to "well-being," and finally instead of this people it is spoken of Israel — without a suffix in the Hebrew — and likewise also Paul begins with a greeting of peace, which refers directly to those who will "walk" according to this rule in the future, and then he goes over to using the term "Israel," more precisely "the Israel of God."

Similarly, at the end of a far less religious letter composed during the

Bar Kochba revolt, which is concerned with a property issue — the right of possession of a certain cow — it says: "Best wishes [שלום] to you and all Beth-Israel" (pap Mur 42:7).[98] When there not only the addressee, Yeshua son of Galgula (line 2), but also Israel, precisely the entire house of Israel, is mentioned, then it is here completely clear what is also indicated in 4QMMT C 27, 30-32: At the conclusion the perspective widens; connected by means of the word "and," the Jewish people as a corporate entity comes into view.[99]

The background of such wishes, and also of similar later synagogue inscriptions,[100] is of course the Hebrew Old Testament or (correspondingly) the Septuagint. From this sphere, one naturally has to compare the concluding expression שלום על ישראל or εἰρήνη ἐπὶ τὸν Ἰσραήλ, which is encountered in two psalms, that is, in Ps 125:5 (LXX 124:5) and Ps 128:6 (LXX 127:6).[101] Taking Gal 6:11-18 into consideration, three things deserve to be emphasized here. First, the benediction has in mind especially the righteous (see only Ps 124[125]:3), those who fear the Lord, and those who walk in the ways of the Lord (see esp. Ps 127[128]:1; cf. Gal 6:16) — who in Ps 124(125):5 are confronted with other people who are judged less positively (cf. Gal 6:11-13, 17).[102] Second, there is (also beyond that) no lack of quite synonymous expressions for "Israel." Inasmuch as among them ὁ λαὸς αὐτοῦ, that is, κυρίου, is found (Ps 124[125]:2; cf. v. 1 and Ps 127[128]:5: Ἰερουσαλήμ), the expression ὁ Ἰσραὴλ τοῦ θεοῦ,[103] which outside of Gal 6:16 is not documented anywhere in antiquity, cannot be considered to be unprepared. Third, the future reference of both benedictions is particularly accented by their preceding context (see esp. Ps 124[125]:1-2; 127[128]:2) (cf. Gal 6:15).

In those passages of the Septuagint where, instead of peace, God's mercy with respect to the Jews or in reference to Israel[104] is mentioned, the future component plays a completely obvious role (differently for instance Ps 97[98]:3), so, e.g., in Hos 1:6, 7, 25 (cf. Rom 9:25; 1 Pet 2:10); Amos 5:15; Zech 1:12, 17; Isa 14:1; and Ezek 39:25.[105] Here it is particularly striking that such sometimes "eschatological" formulations not infrequently have their place in prayers (see esp. Jdt 6:19; Tob 13:10; Sir 36:11;[106] cf. Neh 1:5; 9:32; Tob 8:4), and also at the end of a psalm (Ps 32[33]:22; cf. Mic 7:20, the conclusion of this prophetic book) — just as the wish for peace of Ps 124(125):5 or Ps 127(128):6.

The intertestamental writings impressively continue this use of ἔλεος and ἐλεεῖν (e.g., 1 En. 27:4; T. Zeb. 8:1-2). Above all the *Psalms of Solomon*[107] provide numerous examples (see esp. *Pss. Sol.* 2:35; 4:25; 7:6; 10:3, 6[-7]; 9:8[-9]; 11:1; 17:45; 18:3). Also here, often close to the conclusion of the hymn or prayer in question, God's mercy is invoked (see *Pss. Sol.* 2:35-37; 6:6; 7:10; 10:6-8; 11:9; 15:13; 16:15; cf. 9:11, further Prayer of Manasseh 14–15). Furthermore, the Greek version of *1 En.* 1:8 requires attention, particularly as the context containing elements of judgment (see esp. v. 7) and of theophany (see esp. vv. 4-7, 9) allows readers to recognize a decidedly "eschatological" orientation.[108] It is worthwhile to quote nearly the whole verse, which has to do with God's future care:

(a) καὶ μετὰ τῶν δικαίων τὴν εἰρήνην ποιήσει,
(b) καὶ ἐπὶ τοὺς ἐκλεκτοὺς ἔσται συντήρησις καὶ εἰρήνη,
(c) καὶ ἐπ' αὐτοὺς γενήσεται ἔλεος,
(d) καὶ ἔσονται πάντες τοῦ θεοῦ,
...
(i) καὶ φανήσεται αὐτοῖς φῶς
(j) καὶ ποιήσει ἐπ' αὐτοὺς εἰρήνην.

The points of contact with Gal 6:16 are striking and ought to help in understanding the disputed Pauline formulation better. It is of particular importance that in *1 En.* 1:8b, c we have unquestionably before us a close parallel for the "illogical" sequence of εἰρήνη and ἔλεος. More exactly the word ἔλεος in v. 8c is obviously to go beyond the term εἰρήνη in v. 8a and v. 8b (and beyond the term συντήρησις in v. 8b), with the pronoun αὐτοί probably referring both to the "righteous" (v. 8a) and to the "chosen" (v. 8b) — as does the πάντες in v. 8d at the latest. Moreover, here (in v. 8d) the genitive τοῦ θεοῦ of the expression ὁ Ἰσραὴλ τοῦ θεοῦ in Galatians finds a certain kind of equivalent, and the postpositive καὶ εἰρήνη in v. 8b supports the older supposition for the similarly placed καὶ ἔλεος in Gal 6:16: "καὶ ἔλεος becomes . . . an afterthought, to which καὶ ἐπὶ τὸν Ἰσραὴλ τοῦ θεοῦ appends a second afterthought."[109] If one adds *1 En.* 1:4 (ὁ θεὸς . . . ἐπὶ γῆν πατήσει . . . ἀπὸ τοῦ οὐρανοῦ τῶν οὐρανῶν) to the repeated ἐπί with the accusative in v. 8, the consideration, which is not new either, should finally be confirmed: "The idea is present in ἐπ' αὐτούς [Gal 6:16] that salvation . . . will come down upon them."[110]

In spite of the difficulty in dating traditional liturgical formulations exactly, the passage that has just been considered should allow us to look at those prayer texts which have long been used for comparison especially for the succession of "peace" and "mercy" in Gal 6:16,[111] and among these (particularly) the so-called Babylonian version of the Eighteen Benedictions and the Kaddish de Rabbanan.[112] When in the first formula the "light (of the divine countenance)" is mentioned, and when according to the other formula peace comes down upon different groups "from heaven," and when in both at the end one encounters once more the concept of peace, then this of course reminds one of *1 Enoch* 1. In the entire context of our diachronic observations it is, however, of even greater importance that in both cases the corporate entity Israel is mentioned as the last (and largest) of those groups referred to in the benediction: "thy people Israel" and "all congregations of the entire house of Israel" respectively. In each case this has to do again with a formulation at the conclusion of a prayer — which moreover, just as Galatians, comes to an end with an "amen."

In summary, it fits extremely well into the parallel Jewish material which has been investigated, especially into the conclusion of letters (or documents intended for dispatch) and of prayers, that shortly before the conclusion of his writing to the communities in Galatia Paul speaks of "peace" and "mercy" in a benediction and thereby has in mind two circles of people, and the second to be mentioned is ὁ Ἰσραὴλ τοῦ θεοῦ. In view of this background, it seems reasonable to think that "the Israel of God" means real Jews. Although such concluding formulas can be preceded by demarcations against certain people,[113] this kind of opposition mostly recedes with the mentioning of the corporate entity Israel (see, however, *Pss. Sol.* 17:45 and on this cf. Gal [6:11-13 and] 6:17).

3

The evidence that has been amassed above and that arises from Galatians as the context of the expression "the Israel of God" (section 2.1; cf. 2.3), from Paul's use of Israel terminology (2.2), from the terminology with which the Apostle elsewhere characterizes Gentiles as belonging to the people of God (2.3), and from Jewish parallels to the benediction in Gal 6:16 (2.4) points in one and the same direction, that is, that the expression ὁ Ἰσραὴλ τοῦ θεοῦ does not include Gentile Christians but only Jews — and hardly merely Jewish Christians. The view of the majority should therefore be given up, and this without holding back (cf. section 1). This has of course considerable consequences.

ANTI-JUDAISM IN GALATIANS?

With respect to the question of a development of Pauline theology for example, one will have to form more cautious opinions from here[114] and will hardly be able to continue to say that "concerning the topic of Israel, the differences between . . . Galatians and Romans" are "perceptible only as a radical change";[115] for the presupposition of a considerable difference between the concepts of the people of God that are supported here and there should not hold true, particularly not the following opinion: "The only instance in which Paul explicitly challenges the position of the Old Testament people of God can be found in Gal 6:16."[116] It is more likely that the following statement is true: "the letter to the Galatians, while strongly pleading the right of the non-Jewish Christians to stay in their non-Jewish state . . . , concludes with the prayer" in Gal 6:16, and so Galatians, just as Romans, arrives at the point: "Gentiles are invited to call the Jews by the cherished, inner-Jewish name of the Covenant People: Israel."[117]

Of course this also affects the ecclesiological profile of Galatians, insofar as it is no longer the case, or to say it correctly, as it was never the case, that in this writing, and "only here," more exactly: "in Gal 6:16," the Apostle develops "a new understanding of 'Israel'": "As Ἰσραὴλ τοῦ θεοῦ the church made up of Jews and Gentiles comes into the inheritance of the previous people of God."[118] If the benediction does not intend such a "polemical exaggeration"[119] but rather reminds the addressees, who are primarily Gentile Christians, that their salvation is tied up with the fate and the salvation of Jews, with the destiny of the corporate entity "the Israel of God," then the conclusion of the letter additionally casts light on what was previously said with respect to the "church."

First, it becomes especially clear from the benediction in 6:16 and from the *Eschatokoll* in 6:18, which comes to an end with "amen," that the conclusion and the prescript in 1:1-5, which also ends with "amen" and likewise includes the naming of χάρις (see 6:18) as well as of εἰρήνη (see 6:16), correspond with each other.[120] This can be denied even less because the introductory passage does not lack an "eschatological" perspective, which is documented primarily by the reference to the resurrection (1:1), by the manner of speaking about being set free "from the present evil eon" (1:4), and by the expression "in the eons of the eons" (1:5; cf. esp. Rom 16:27; Phil 4:20), which is unique in this position in Paul. Although in the apocalyptic and "eschatological" horizon which is characteristic of Galatians as a whole,[121] Paul differentiates more precisely with regard to time, and we immediately will have to distinguish according to this fact,[122] it needs to be pointed out beforehand that in this context — especially also in view of the material compared with Gal 6:16 and particularly of the *Psalms of Solomon* — two factors can be understood better: on the one hand, the concluding remark on the agreement made in Jerusalem, particularly between the "pillars" — James, Cephas (Peter), John — and Paul as well as Barnabas (Gal 2:9-10), on the other hand, the syntagma ἡ ἐκκλησία τοῦ θεοῦ used in reference to the Jerusalem community (1:13). This is obvious, as soon as one takes into account how in *Pss. Sol.* 10 the eternal mercy of God (10:6) and God's salvation ἐπὶ οἶκον Ἰσραήλ (10:8) are tied together with God's merciful action to the πτωχοί (10:6) and with the praise ἐν ἐκκλησίᾳ λαοῦ (10:6) and on the part of the συναγωγαὶ Ἰσραήλ (10:7), and as soon as one also takes into consideration the extensively comparable concluding formulations of *Pss. Sol.* 17 (esp. 17:42-46),[123] a "messianic" text that accents the centrality of Jerusalem (see only 17:21-22, 30-31) in the "eschatological" events. The explanations concerning the "collection" for the "poor . . . in Jerusalem" in Romans 15 (see only 15:7-12, 16-21, 25-27, 31), although here the term ἐκκλησία is missing, confirm the impression that in Gal 2:10 and also in 1:13 Paul alludes to the priority of Jerusalem and of Judaism in redemptive history, which in the case of the "collection," as he especially emphasizes, he "deliberately" respected, but which he first had ignored by his persecution of the Christians.

Considered chronologically, regarding the remarks about the actions against the ἐκκλησία τοῦ θεοῦ (1:13[-14]) that will allude (primarily) to events that happened in Jerusalem, and regarding the statements about the persecution of the ἐκκλησίαι τῆς Ἰουδαίας (1:22-23) that are connected to these remarks, we are dealing with the earliest ecclesiastical stage, which Paul — at the same time as the first — considers more closely in Galatians. With this, as the parallel referring to the same events in 1 Cor 15:9 (cf. Phil 3:6) probably confirms, the Apostle is falling back on a self-designation of early Christianity in Jerusalem.[124] Yet "this means, however, that in the concept ἐκκλησία not the contrast to Judaism is accentuated but the continuity with it."[125] Together with tradition-historical reasons — not only the expression קהל אל documented in "Qumran" (1QM 4:10; cf. 1QSa 1:25)[126] can be referred to here[127] — and above all together with the phrase "the Israel of God" in Gal 6:16 the result therefore is: Paul in principle places the Christian community that originated on a Jewish basis in an insoluble connection with the Jewish people. Their (already "eschatological") *nucleus* is Jews and Jewish-Christians, and for the Apostle the future of Christianity is not conceivable without God's "eschatological" loving care for Israel, for "the Israel of God."

In 1:15-17 the proclamation of the gospel ἐν τοῖς ἔθνεσιν (1:16; cf. 2:3) is attributed to God's initiative, and in 2:9-10 by the commitment to the "collection," the Gentile mission and therefore the Gentile Christians are linked back to the Jewish *nucleus* of Christianity, before — prepared by the account of the conflict in Antioch (2:11-14) and by statements about a justification which not even for Jews occurs ἐξ ἔργων νόμου (2:15-21) — in 3:1–4:7 the Christian community made up of Jews and non-Jews comes into view, and that is especially under the aspect of the former conversion of Gentile Christians. The concentration on the Christ event is obvious here (see 3:13-14, 26-29; 4:4-5); but although with this, as it has already been presented,[128] for the moment a narrowing of the descendants of Abraham to the *one* seed Christ (see 3:16; cf. 3:19-20) takes place, which is a separation from traditional Jewish ideas, and although the Sinai-revelation is emphatically related to the Jewish people and the importance of these events is, not least for this reason, limited too (see esp. 3:17-19, 23-24), the component of redemptive history is, along with the christological component, not missing at all — just as in Romans.[129] Also this only needs to be remembered:[130] with references to the motif of Abraham and the universal promise associated with this man (see esp. 3:6-7, 16, 18, 29), to the remark on Christ's earthly origin (4:4), and to the priority of the order of Jewish experience and salvation, as they are expressed in the order of 2:15-21 before 3:1–6:17 and in the use of the first person plural in 3:13-14a; 3:23-25 and in 4:3-6a. In brief: The picture of a Christianity made up of Jews and Gentiles, in which the priority of Judaism in redemptive history is held on to, arises here, and to be precise with completely equal rights of membership in this community of Jews and of non-Jews who do not define themselves by the Torah (see esp. 3:2-3, 28). The fact that for this corporate entity the expressions "sons of God" and "sons of Abraham," which are grounded in Judaism,[131] are used (3:7, 27; cf. 4:6-7, also 3:29), can be regarded as the summary of this ecclesiological concept, particularly since according to 3:20 this has to do with the *one*, universal God,[132] and particularly since the status of sonship of Christians is linked with God's sending of the "Spirit of his son" in 4:6 (cf. 3:2-5).

After the Jewish *nucleus* of the Christian community and after the community of the "sons," which comprises Jews as well as non-Jews and which the Galatian Gentile Christians have joined in their baptism and in

The Church and the Israel of God

which they now live, in 4:21–5:1 the present situation of this corporate entity comes into view from the aspect of a current endangering. More exactly, here two corporate entities stand opposite one another — which has already been explained:[133] the group consisting of Jews as well as non-Jews, which is connected with the "free woman," i.e., Sarah, and with ἡ ἄνω Ἰερουσαλήμ, and another corporate entity, whose principal characteristic is "slavery," an attribute that especially holds for non-Jews (see 4:8) and which is symbolized by Hagar and by ἡ νῦν Ἰερουσαλήμ. In other words: A community made up primarily of non-Jews is opposed with the church made up of Jews and Gentiles, in which the Gentile Christians are threatened — again — by the loss of their freedom, now by an orientation toward the Torah and its precepts (see 4:21; 5:1).

Insofar as positive Jewish symbols — Abraham, "the free woman" (i.e., Sarah), Isaac, and "Jerusalem above" — characterize the community that is thus endangered and insofar as the circumcision of Gentile Christians is thought to be the most important factor among these threats (see only 5:2), the last ecclesiological picture, which is invoked in 6:16 and which has to do with the future, which will replace the apocalyptic contraposition, follows immediately with regard to the contents.[134] On the one hand, this picture still concerns Christians, primarily probably the Galatian Gentile Christians, if they will allow themselves to be determined by the "new creation" and thus by the "relativizing" especially of the "circumcision" (6:16a; cf. 6:15). On the other hand — hardly any different from Romans 11 — it has in view that corporate entity which provides (and provided) the *nucleus* of Christianity, ἡ ἐκκλησία τοῦ θεοῦ, and which in a particular way is assigned to God, to the *one* God; this corporate entity is here included in the benediction from an eschatological perspective[135] as ὁ Ἰσραὴλ τοῦ θεοῦ.[136] While, according to the author of Galatians, the Christ event, which is mentioned once again in 6:17 and 6:18, means at any rate for *Gentile* Christians that the orientation toward precepts like the rule of circumcision is a self-contradiction, an offense against the "new creation" (see esp. 5:2, 4; 6:12-15; cf. 2:18, 21b), nonetheless there can be no talk here of a disinheritance of *Judaism*. Rather, the Pauline benediction is directed precisely also to the Jews, to "the Israel of God" — and for this reason, the hope of the Gentile Christians, at least the hope of the Galatian Christians, should also be meant for this corporate entity.[137]

Notes

Notes to the Preface

1. In a review, P. J. Tomson remarks (*De stem van het boek* 11 [2000], no. 1, 10): "Dit alles impliceert een radikale herlezing van Paulus met het oog op zijn joodse achtergrond. Dat is zeker in de Duitse literatuur nog lang geen gangbaar streven."

2. Cf. the reviews by I. Maisch (*Freiburger Rundbrief*, Neue Folge 8 [2001], 59-62), F. W. Horn (*Theologische Zeitschrift* 59 [2003], 88-89), and R. Kampling (*Theologische Revue* 100 [2004], 200-202).

3. Cf. the review by G. Stanton (*Journal of Theological Studies* 56 [2005], 573-75).

4. For the most part, abbreviations are used in accordance with the guidelines in *The SBL Handbook of Style* (Peabody: Hendrickson, 1999); additionally, in a few cases, the list compiled by S. M. Schwertner for *TRE* (1993 [second ed.]) provides the standard.

5. Relevant publications are listed below in the "Bibliographical Appendix."

Notes to the Preface to the 1999 Edition

1. See Lambrecht, *Studies*, 303 together with n. 4 (cf. ibid., 211-30, and on this Bachmann, *Sünder*, VII), and A. Wechsler, *Geschichtsbild und Apostelstreit. Eine forschungsgeschichtliche und exegetische Studie über den antiochenischen Zwischenfall (Gal 2,11-14)*, BZNW 62 (Berlin/New York: de Gruyter, 1991), esp. 390-93. For short titles used in this preface, see chapter 5, nn. 1, 4, 20, 43, and chapter 6, n. 9. But here, unlike chapter 5, n. 20, the German translation of Ruether, *Faith*, is used, i.e., R. Ruether, *Nächstenliebe und Brudermord. Die theologischen Wurzeln des Antisemitismus*, Abhandlungen zum christlich-jüdischen Dialog 7 (Munich: Chr. Kaiser, 1978).

2. On "New Testament and anti-Judaism," cf. I. Broer, "Die Juden im Urteil der Autoren des Neuen Testaments. Anmerkungen zum Problem historischer Gerechtigkeit im Angesicht einer verheerenden Wirkungsgeschichte," *TGl* 82 (1992), 2-33, and G. G. Stroumsa, "From Anti-Judaism to Antisemitism in Early Christianity?" in *Contra Judaeos — Ancient*

and Medieval Polemics between Christians and Jews, ed. O. Limor and G. G. Stroumsa, Texts and Studies in Medieval and Early Modern Judaism 10 (Tübingen: Mohr, 1996), 1-26, and the references listed there.

3. It was not until the present collection of essays had been sent to print that I discovered an article dealing with precisely this phrase: J. A. Fitzmyer, "Paul's Jewish Background and the Deeds of the Law," in *According to Paul: Studies in the Theology of the Apostle* (New York/Mahwah, NJ: Paulist, 1993), 18-35 (and pp. 125-30). According to this scholar, the phrase (and its "abbreviated form" without the genitive) sounds "like a slogan derived from his [Paul's] Jewish theological background, summing up the deeds prescribed or proscribed in the Mosaic Law, its 'precepts'" (p. 20). Fitzmyer finds confirmation of this position in the Dead Sea Scrolls, esp. in 4QMMT (C27); for this document, the author says: "It is clear ... that *m'śym* is to be understood as 'precepts'" (p. 22, with reference to Exod 18:20). Cf. another important study which has also just become available to me: R. Penna, "Le 'opere della Legge' in s. Paolo e 4QMMT," *Ricerche storico-bibliche* 9/2 (1997), 155-76, esp. 159, 173-76.

4. Cf. the Table of Contents of this volume for the bibliographical data of the original publications.

5. The close orientation to the Pauline letters and, in particular, to Galatians resulted in some consideration of the relationship between Paul's writings and 4QMMT, but without discussion of (e.g.) the relationship between the latter and the more or less halakhic writing in Acts 15:23-29 (and its three-party constellation).

Notes to Chapter 1

1. On this see A. E. McGrath, Iustitia Dei: *A History of the Christian Doctrine of Justification,* 2 vols. (Cambridge: Cambridge University Press, 1986), esp. 1.1-4; however, here it is also noted by way of restriction (1.3-4) that the actual history of the doctrine of justification has "its sphere within the western church alone" (1.3). On the present state of the rather encouraging efforts to review and overcome the pertinent doctrinal condemnations of the time of the Reformation and the Counter-Reformation, see W. Pannenberg, "Die Rechtfertigungslehre im ökumenischen Gespräch," *ZTK* 88 (1991), 232-46 (who debates especially J. Baur, *Einig in Sachen Rechtfertigung? Zur Prüfung des Rechtfertigungskapitels der Studie des ökumenischen Arbeitskreises evangelischer und katholischer Theologen: "Lehrverurteilungen — kirchentrennend?"* (Tübingen: Mohr, 1989).

2. *Martin Luther: Werke. Kritische Gesamtausgabe (Weimarer Ausgabe,* hereafter *WA),* 54, 179-87 (in O. Scheel, ed., *Dokumente zu Luthers Entwicklung <bis 1519>,* SAQ: Neue Folge 2; second ed.; Tübingen: Mohr, 1929], 186-93). Citations: 185,19 (Scheel: 191,35-36); 186,7,20 (192,13-14,27). Cf. McGrath, Iustitia, 2.3-10, esp. 4.

3. On this see E. Hirsch, *Hilfsbuch zum Studium der Dogmatik. Die Dogmatik der Reformatoren und der altevangelischen Lehre quellenmässig belegt und verdeutscht* (fourth ed.; Berlin: de Gruyter, 1964), 130(-33).

4. As is well known, Luther also translates Rom 1:17 with this meaning (cf., e.g., D. Martin Luther, Biblia. *Das ist die gantze Heilige Schrifft. Deudsch auffs new zugericht,* Wittenberg 1545 [ed. H. Volz, 3 vols.; Munich: Deutscher Taschenbuch Verlag, 1974], 3.2270: "Gerechtigkeit/die für Gott gilt" [cf. *WA.DB* 7, 30, or 31 respectively]).

5. E. Käsemann ("Gottesgerechtigkeit bei Paulus," in *Exegetische Versuche und Besinnungen*, vol. 2 [third ed.; Göttingen: Vandenhoeck & Ruprecht, 1970], 181-93 [orig. 1961]), whose basic starting point, as, e.g., the reviews of research by J. A. Ziesler (*The Meaning of Righteousness in Paul: A Linguistic and Theological Inquiry* [SNTSMS 20; Cambridge: Cambridge University Press, 1972], 9-14) and H. Hübner ("Paulusforschung seit 1945. Ein kritischer Literaturbericht," *ANRW* 2.25.4 [1987], 2649-2840, here 2694-2709) show, C. Müller, P. Stuhlmacher, and K. Kertelge among others followed, against whom stand R. Bultmann ("ΔΙΚΑΙΟΣΥΝΗ ΘΕΟΥ," *JBL* 83 [1964], 12-16) and G. Klein ("Gottesgerechtigkeit als Thema der neuesten Paulus-Forschung," in *Rekonstruktion und Interpretation. Gesammelte Aufsätze zum Neuen Testament* [BEvT 50; Munich: Kaiser, 1969], 225-36 [orig. 1976]).

6. On this see esp. E. Lohse, "Die Gerechtigkeit Gottes in der paulinischen Theologie," in *Die Einheit des Neuen Testaments. Exegetische Studien zur Theologie des Neuen Testaments* (second ed.; Göttingen: Vandenhoeck & Ruprecht, 1973), 209-27, 210-13, 227. Cf. below (at) n. 49.

7. I have recently examined this expression in a concisely formulated excursus and from a somewhat different angle: M. Bachmann, *Sünder oder Übertreter. Studien zur Argumentation in Gal 2,15ff.* (WUNT 59; Tübingen: Mohr, 1992), 91-100 (cf. further pp. 9-11, 90-91, 100-101, 162). Contacts with this exposition will not be stated in each case. Cf. n. 11 below.

8. Cf. (e.g.) the similar listing by O. Hofius, "'Rechtfertigung des Gottlosen' als Thema biblischer Theologie," in *Paulusstudien* (WUNT 51; Tübingen: Mohr, 1989), 121-47 (orig. 1987), here 127 n. 35, and also the tabular overview on ἔργον in the Corpus Paulinum by D. J. Moo, "'Law,' 'Works of the Law' and Legalism in Paul," *WTJ* 45 (1983), 73-100, here p. 93. According to this chart one should parallel the following passages to the above named verses: Eph 2:9 ("by/from works"); Tit 3:5 ("by/from works in the righteousness"); Rom 2:15 ("the work of the law"; on this see below [at] nn. 109-21, and on Eph 2:9 and Tit 3:5 below n. 96 [and n. 97]).

9. This goes without question for the ἔργα linked (in the end) to Abraham (Rom 4:2, 6) and to Jacob and Esau (Rom 9:12) (so correctly Moo, "Law," 81, 94-95). It is quite possible that in view of the retrospective context and especially in view of the ongoing effects of the theme of Abraham (see Rom 9:12; 11:1) one should also understand Rom 11:6 in a corresponding fashion, whereas this is less likely for Rom 9:32 (where the expression "by/from works" after 9:31 and before 10:5 should rather be understood as an abbreviation, which permits a concise comparison with "by/from faith") — if here in any case according to the majority text it should not read ἔργα νόμου. Provided that the ἔργα from 4:2ff. are to be understood from the background of 3:20ff., it is probable that in chs. 4ff. one must think — if not about Torah itself — about an analogy with the works of the law (cf. [however] John 8:39 and on this [H. L. Strack and] P. Billerbeck, *Kommentar zum Neuen Testament aus Talmud und Midrasch* [4 vols.; Munich: Beck, 1922-28], 2.524 and 3.186-87). It is difficult to see, therefore, why Moo ("Law," 94-96) does not interpret the prepositional expressions in 4:2, 6; 9:12, 32; and 11:6 in view of the longer expressions (with the genitive τοῦ νόμου) in 3:20, 28 as a foil, but rather explains them (and even the more complete formulations) from the use of the absolute term ἔργον or ἔργα respectively, and correspondingly why J. Lambrecht ("Gesetzesverständnis bei Paulus," in *Das Gesetz im Neuen Testament* [QD 108, ed. K. Kertelge; Freiburg: Herder, 1986], 88-127, here pp. 126-27) says: "In Rom 4:2-5 and 9:10-13,

16 Paul clearly says that God's justifying and electing grace is set above *all* human 'works,' thus not only above the works of the law" (cf. S. Westerholm, *Israel's Law and the Church's Faith: Paul and His Recent Interpreters* [Grand Rapids: Eerdmans, 1988], esp. 119, and on this the inquiries of J. D. G. Dunn, *Jesus, Paul and the Law: Studies in Mark and Galatians* [London: SPCK, 1990], 238-39). (As far as the running and willing in Rom 9:16 are concerned, incidentally a certain counterpart is found precisely in Psalm 119[118], namely in 119:32, 35.) Cf. (at) nn. 106, 123 below.

10. Cf. with respect to chronological order, e.g., Rom 5:13, 14a, 20 and Gal 3:17, 19, but also Rom (5:14b and) 7:7ff. (and on this see O. Hofius, "Das Gesetz des Mose und das Gesetz Christi," in *Paulusstudien*, 50-74 [orig. 1983], here 57-58 n. 26, and Bachmann, *Sünder* [1992], 76 together with n. 253).

11. Studies in which the expression ἔργα νόμου is more or less the center of attention: E. Lohmeyer, "Probleme paulinischer Theologie 2: Gesetzeswerke," in *Probleme paulinischer Theologie* (Stuttgart: Kohlhammer, 1954), 31-74 (orig. 1929); J. Blank, "Warum sagt Paulus: 'Aus Werken des Gesetzes wird niemand gerecht?'" *EKKNT: Vorarbeiten* 1 (1969), 79-95; U. Wilckens, "Was heisst bei Paulus: 'Aus Werken des Gesetzes wird kein Mensch gerecht'?" in *Rechtfertigung als Freiheit. Paulusstudien* (Neukirchen-Vluyn: Neukirchener, 1974), 77-109 (orig. 1969); J. B. Tyson, "'Works of Law' in Galatians," *JBL* 92 (1973), 423-31; R. Fuller, "Paul and 'the Works of the Law,'" *WTJ* 38 (1975), 28-42; Moo, "Law"; L. Gaston, "Works of Law as a Subjective Genitive," in *Paul and the Torah* (Vancouver: University of British Columbia Press, 1987), 100-106 (orig. 1984); R. Heiligenthal, "Soziologische Implikationen der paulinischen Rechtfertigungslehre im Galaterbrief am Beispiel der 'Werke des Gesetzes.' Bemerkungen zur Identitätsfindung einer frühchristlichen Gemeinde," *Kairos* 26 (1984), 38-53; J. D. G. Dunn, "Works of the Law and the Curse of the Law (Galatians 3:10-14)," in *Jesus, Paul, and the Law*, 215-36 (orig. 1984) (cf. 237-41) (cf. "Yet Once More — 'The Works of the Law': A Response," *JSNT* 46 [1992], 99-117); H. Hübner, "Was heisst bei Paulus 'Werke des Gesetzes'?" in *Glaube und Eschatologie. Festschrift für Werner Georg Kümmel* (ed. E. Grässer and O. Merk; Tübingen: Mohr, 1985), 123-33; R. H. Gundry, "Grace, Works, and Staying Saved in Paul," *Bib* 66 (1985), 1-38; G. Klein, "Werkruhm und Christusruhm im Galaterbrief und die Frage nach einer Entwicklung des Paulus. Ein hermeneutischer und exegetischer Zwischenruf," in *Studien zum Text und zur Ethik des Neuen Testaments. Festschrift zum 80. Geburtstag von Heinrich Greeven* (BZNW 47, ed. W. Schrage; Berlin: de Gruyter, 1986), 196-211; P. Trummer, "Wieso 'aus Werken des Gesetzes kein Mensch gerechtfertigt wird' (Gal 2:16) und welche Konsequenzen das für uns hat. Ein Essay," in *Aufsätze zum Neuen Testament* (Grazer Theologische Studien 12; Graz: Universität Graz, 1987), 81-94; Westerholm, *Israel's Law*, 116-21; W. Stegemann, "Christliche Judenfeindschaft und Neues Testament," in *Kirche und Nationalsozialismus* (ed. W. Stegemann; Stuttgart: Kohlhammer, 1990), 153-67; C. E. B. Cranfield, "'The Works of the Law' in the Epistle to the Romans," *JSNT* 43 (1991), 89-101; T. R. Schreiner, "'Works of Law' in Paul," *NovT* 33 (1991), 217-44 (contains further bibliography). Cf. n. 7 above.

12. On this cf. particularly Lohmeyer, "Probleme," esp. 73-74 ("the kind of genitive remains unclear grammatically" [p. 73]), and W. Stegemann, "Christliche Judenfeindschaft," 160-61, also P. C. Böttger, "Paulus und Petrus in Antiochien. Zum Verständnis von Galater 2.11-21," *NTS* 37 (1991), 77-100, here p. 87, further R. Liebers, *Das Gesetz als Evangelium.*

Untersuchungen zur Gesetzeskritik des Paulus (ATANT 75; Zurich: Theologischer Verlag, 1989), 41.

13. According to Schreiner, "Works," 225, 228-35, the judgment in the research is unanimous (see esp. p. 225): The syntagm "simply designates the deeds or actions commanded by the law" (p. 235), more specifically, on the part of the Mosaic law (see p. 225; cf. Moo, "Law," 92 together with n. 68; Heiligenthal, "Soziologische Implikationen," 41, and n. 112 below). Leaving this aside, however, there is, as it will immediately become clear, no consensus with respect to what Paul intends with this expression (see Schreiner, "Works," 217).

14. Billerbeck, *Kommentar*, 3.160-61, 199, quoting 199; Lohmeyer, "Probleme," 67 (and *passim*) (cf. Tyson, "Works," 426 [and *passim*]); and Hofius, "Rechtfertigung," 127 n. 35 — who distances himself emphatically from understanding ἔργα νόμου as "individual fulfillments of commands" (p. 127 n. 35) with Billerbeck and the commentators who "as a rule" (p. 127 n. 35) follow Billerbeck, as then Lohmeyer ("Probleme," 69) also understands in an integrated way and means by "'duty *(Dienst)* of the law' a permanent determination of human existence" (cf. nn. 69, 136 below).

15. On this cf. (at) nn. 13 and 14 above.

16. Lohmeyer, "Probleme," 68.

17. G. Ebeling, "Die Rechtfertigung vor Gott und den Menschen. Zum Aufbau der dritten Thesenreihe über Röm 3,28," in *Lutheriana. Zum 500. Geburtstag Martin Luthers von den Mitarbeitern der Weimarer Ausgabe* (Archiv zur *WA* 5, ed. G. Hammer and K.-H. zur Mühlen; Cologne/Vienna: Böhlau, 1984), 103-30, here p. 105. Cf. *WA* 39 I, 44 n. 2, which speaks of "five series of theses on Rom 3:28," which "in the editions since 1538" are "united" (H. Hermelink).

18. *WA* 30 II, (627-)632-46 (also in *Luthers Werke in Auswahl* 4 [ed. O. Clemen, sixth ed.; Berlin: de Gruyter, 1967], 179-93).

19. *WA* 30 II, 633, 29-30 (Clemen 4:180.7-8). Incidentally: "The particula exclusiva is . . . , one might say 'ironically,' a creation of James" (U. Luck, "Die Theologie des Jakobusbriefes," *ZTK* 81 [1984], 1-30, here p. 2); in any case it is found in Jas 2:24.

20. *WA* 30 II, 633.7–640.32 (Clemen 4:180.15–187, 34).

21. *WA* 30 II, 637.21-22 (Clemen 4:184.27).

22. *WA* 30 II, 640.33–643.13 (Clemen 4:187.35–190, 15).

23. *WA* 30 II, 640.37–641.1 (Clemen 4:188.1-3).

24. Similarly, e.g., A. Peters, "Glaube und Werke. Luthers Rechtfertigungslehre im Lichte der heiligen Schrift," *AGTL* 8 (1962), 261-62 (cf. also: "Werkgerechtigkeit," in *Deutsches Wörterbuch von Jacob Grimm und Wilhelm Grimm*, XIV, I, 2 [ed. Deutsche Akademie der Wissenschaften zu Berlin; Leipzig: Hirzel, 1960], 368). Cf. (at) nn. 29, 46 below.

25. *WA* 30 II, 643.5-6 (Clemen 4:190.7-8).

26. *WA* 8, (313-)323-35. H. Junghans offers a translation: *Martin Luther, Glaube und Kirchenreform* (Martin Luther Taschenausgabe 2, ed. H. Beintker et al.; Berlin: EVA, 1984), (153-)154-70.

27. *WA* 8, 324 (Junghans, 155).

28. *WA* 8, 324 (Junghans, 155). Cf. n. 46 below.

29. This fact is known and has led to inquiries with respect to the appropriateness of such parallelism and with respect to an exegesis of Paul that takes place, so to say, with Lutheran spectacles (on this see primarily K. Stendahl, "The Apostle Paul and the Introspective

Conscience of the West," in *Paul among Jews and Gentiles and Other Essays* [Philadelphia: Fortress, 1976], 78-96 [orig. 1960, respectively 1961/63], esp. 85-87; J. D. G. Dunn, "The New Perspective on Paul," in *Jesus, Paul, and the Law*, 183-206 [orig. 1983] [cf. 206-14], esp. 185, 194-95, 202; also Bachmann, *Sünder*, 3-4; see, however, Moo, "Law," 98-99, and Schreiner, "Works," 241-43; cf. further at nn. 34-37 below).

30. *WA* 2, (436-)451-618. I. Mann offers a translation: *Martin Luther, Kommentar zum Galaterbrief 1519* (Calwer Luther-Ausgabe 10, ed. W. Metzger; Munich/Hamburg: Siebenstern Taschenbuch Verlag, 1968).

31. *WA* 2, 491.33-34 (Mann, 87).

32. *WA* 2, 489.31-34 (Mann, 83-84).

33. *WA* 2, 489.30-31 (Mann, 83 [in n. 52 Mann refers to *"speciosa"* in the text of the Vulgate in Matt 23:27, and correctly, as is apparent in *WA* 1, 356.18-19]).

34. In volumes 49 and 50 of the series (Munich: Kaiser).

35. Citation(s): vol. 50, 15 (cf. p. 17).

36. Vol. 50, 15.

37. Vol. 50, 16-17 (and *passim*).

38. On this cf., e.g., W. Joest, *Gesetz und Freiheit. Das Problem des* Tertius usus legis *bei Luther und die neutestamentliche Parainese* (Göttingen: Vandenhoeck & Ruprecht, 1951), 45-55; McGrath, Iustitia, 2.26-32.

39. So Melanchthon in a letter looking back on the meeting and originating a good two weeks after the event (R. Stupperich, ed., *Melanchthons Werke in Auswahl*, vol. 7.2: *Ausgewählte Briefe 1527-1530* [ed. H. Volz; Gütersloh: Mohn, 1975], 112-19 [or *Corpus Reformatorum* 1, 1098-1102], here 114, 29-33; McGrath, Iustitia, 2.33 [together with n. 13], cites the passage oddly enough from a Latin translation of the German). On the differences between the Lutheran and the Swiss Reformations with respect to the *tertius usus legis* see, e.g., Moo, "Law," 73-74 (bibliography).

40. The fact is interrelated with the other point, that for Luther "the term 'works' [is] not an unambiguous term" (R. Bring, "Das Verhältnis von Glauben und Werken in der lutherischen Theologie," *FGLP* 10.7 [1955] [orig. 1933 in Swedish], 14; on this see pp. 14-15, and cf. p. 116).

41. On this cf. above (at) n(n). 18(-25). It is possible also to refer to other writings of Luther, such as, e.g., the Heidelberg Disputation (*WA* 1, [350-]353-74; see here esp. the support for theses XXI and XXV [pp. 362, 364]). Indeed even more informative is the Preface to Romans: D. Martin Luther, Biblia . . . (see n. 4 above), 3.2254-68 (cf. *WA.DB* 7, 2-26 or 3-27 respectively), here especially 2256-57, 2263 (cf. *WA.DB* 7, 6, 8 or 7, 9 and 7, 16, 18 or 17, 19).

42. So, e.g., *WA* 30 II, 642.33-34, 13 (Clemen 4:189.37-38, 15).

43. So, e.g., *WA* 30 II, 641.36-37; 642.2 (Clemen 4:189.1, 4).

44. Cf. above (at) nn. 30-33.

45. *WA* 2, 492.37-39 (Mann, 90). Cf. above (at) nn. 28, 32-33 and below (at) n. 128.

46. On the expression *opus bonum*, as it appears in thesis xiii of the *Themata de Votis* cited above at n. 28, Junghans (155 n. 6) adds the explanation: "In the sense of the piety of the late Middle Ages." On this cf. further "Werk," in *Deutsches Wörterbuch* . . . , XIV.I.2 (see n. 24 above), 327-47, here p. 336: *"from the early German time there exists — supported by the Catholic doctrine — the stereotypical combination* gute Werke *(opera bona)."* Cf. (at) nn. 24, 29 above.

47. On this see especially (at) nn. 61-65 below.

48. Lambrecht, "Gesetzesverständnis," 99-104; Lambrecht starts, in distinction from what follows (cf. W. Stegemann, "Christliche Judenfeindschaft," 156-59), with the position of U. Wilckens and takes up also that of J. D. G. Dunn (in the third place), which — dependent on E. P. Sanders — relates the expression ἔργα νόμου primarily to particular sociologically relevant characteristics of Judaism such as circumcision and food laws (cf., e.g., Dunn, "Perspective," 191, or idem, "Works," 219-20; particularly on Dunn's view see Cranfield, "Works," esp. 89-90, 99-100 [see in turn Dunn, "Response"], Westerholm, *Israel's Law*, esp. 117-19 [see in turn Dunn, *Jesus, Paul, and the Law*, 237-41], and Bachmann, *Sünder*, 11, 91-93[-100]). Schreiner differentiates not three or four but five views, "Works," 218-24 (as does R. B. Sloan, "Paul and the Law: Why the Law Cannot Save," *NovT* 33 [1991], 35-60, who, however, distinguishes other ways). He grants ("Works," 220-21) L. Gaston's thesis on ἔργα νόμου as a *genitivus subiectivus* a special entry (on this see [at] n. 120 below, at n. 4 above); moreover, Schreiner cites, like Lambrecht and in distinction to the present chapter, where possible, several representatives of recent exegetical discussion with respect to individual positions.

49. Meanwhile Catholic exegetes make a similar judgment (on this see, e.g., Lambrecht, "Gesetzesverständnis," 100-101 [together with n. 41] and 126-27 [together with n. 123], as well as Schreiner, "Works," 218-20 [together with nn. 6, 9]). Cf. (at) n. 6 above.

50. R. Bultmann, *Theologie des Neuen Testaments* (sixth ed.; Tübingen: Mohr, 1968), 264; see generally pp. 260-70, 341-46 (cf. ET *Theology of the New Testament* 1 [New York: Scribner, 1951], 259-69, 340-45), further R. Bultmann, "Christus des Gesetzes Ende," in *Glauben und Verstehen. Gesammelte Aufsätze*, vol. 2 (fifth ed.; Tübingen: Mohr, 1968), 32-58 (orig. 1940).

51. Bultmann, *Theologie*, 265.

52. Bultmann, *Theologie*, 264-65. Cf. R. Bultmann, "Römer 7 und die Anthropologie des Paulus," in *Exegetica. Aufsätze zur Erforschung des Neuen Testaments*, ed. E. Dinkler (Tübingen: Mohr, 1967), 198-209 (orig. 1932; cf. ET "Romans 7 and the Anthropology of Paul," in *Existence and Faith: Shorter Writings of Rudolf Bultmann* [Cleveland: World, 1960], 147-57, 307-9), 200: "It is not foremost *('erst')* the evil deeds, the transgressions of the law, that render the Jew objectionable before God, but already the intent to become righteous before God by fulfilling the law is the sin that comes only to light in the transgressions" (cf. [at] nn. 62-63 below).

53. Bultmann, "Christus," 41.

54. H. Räisänen, "Legalism and Salvation by the Law: Paul's Portrayal of the Jewish Religion as a Historical and Theological Problem," in *The Torah and Christ: Essays in German and English on the Problem of the Law in Early Christianity* (Publications of the Finnish Exegetical Society, 45; Helsinki, 1986), 25-54 (orig. 1980), 33: "One gets the impression that zeal for the law is more damaging than transgression."

55. Wilckens, "Was heisst bei Paulus?" 107 (who understands himself to be in agreement with A. Schlatter [see pp. 103-6] in rejecting the view of Bultmann [and of Luther]); cf. further, e.g., p. 94: It is "not as if the works of the law themselves, the intention in general to fulfill the law by works and thereby to qualify oneself before God as righteous, are fundamentally disputed by Paul with regard to the justification of human beings. . . . Rather, Paul simply says that *sinners* cannot be justified on the basis of works of the law." The actual transgression of the law, which in Bultmann, besides self-glorification, takes place secondly

on the grounds of not being justified, moves to the top for Wilckens. However, not "craving for recognition" (p. 107) — which is evaluated indeed simply as an important element of "the catalog of sins" (p. 107) — really takes second place here; rather this position is given to the following factor (which is only vaguely associated with the element of actual sin): "the persistent holding on to justification by the law over against the justification by faith through the grace of God that is now opened after Christ" (p. 102; cf. the immediately following position in the text, esp. [at] n. 58 below). In my view, the allocation of emphasis by W. Stegemann, "Christliche Judenfeindschaft," 157-59, is not completely fortunately portrayed, for instance, when he notes with respect to Wilckens's view: "The Torah was theoretically a means of salvation" (p. 158), that is, before Christ.

56. E. P. Sanders, *Paul and Palestinian Judaism: A Comparison of Patterns of Religion* (Philadelphia: Fortress, 1977), 552.

57. Sanders, *Paul and Palestinian Judaism*, 475 (cf. idem, *Paul, the Law, and the Jewish People* [Philadelphia: Fortress, 1983], 150 [together with n. 26]) — where Sanders already has the position of Bultmann (and that of A. Schweitzer) in view. I have earlier noted (Bachmann, *Sünder*, 11 [together with n. 75]) that W. Bousset, *Der Brief an die Galater* (SNT 2, third ed.; Göttingen: Vandenhoeck & Ruprecht, 1917), 31-74, here 49-50 (on Gal 2:21 [see the following note]), saw things similarly; Sanders himself (*Paul*, 6 together with n. 14) refers to G. F. Moore, *Judaism in the First Centuries of the Christian Era: The Age of the Tannaim* (3 vols.; Cambridge: Harvard University Press, 1927-30), 3.151 (with n. 209 on 1.495) as a predecessor.

58. Sanders, *Paul and Palestinian Judaism*, 482, who appeals here to Rom 10:2-4, whereas shortly before (pp. 481-82) he refers to his standard evidence (cf. the previous note [Bousset]): Bultmann's position "is wrong by being backwards. It is not Paul's analysis of the nature of sin which determines his view, but his analysis of the way of salvation; not his anthropology, but his Christology and soteriology. Paul's own reason for maintaining that 'man shall not, must not, be "rightwised" by works of the Law' is not that man must not think of procuring his own salvation, but that if the law could save, Christ died in vain (Gal. 2.21)." Cf. on the one hand n. 55 above, on the other hand on (possible) sociological implications of Sanders, at n. 48 above. Cf. further (at) nn. 164-66 below.

59. On the history (and the questionableness) of this expression see McGrath, *Iustitia*, 2.1 together with n(n). (1 and) 3.

60. See (at) nn. 12-14 above.

61. See (at) nn. 40-43(-47) above.

62. Wilckens, "Was heisst bei Paulus?" 107 (where only the final occurrence of "work" is italicized). Cf. further pp. 78 and 102 ("Works of the law, that is, fulfilling the commands") as well as p. 108 (where also the expression "one's own work" appears), further the statement of Bultmann cited above in n. 52. Cf. (at) n. 74 below.

63. Bultmann, *Theologie*, 78 (cf. ET, 75).

64. Sanders, *Paul and Palestinian Judaism*, 516-17.

65. That certainly the two prepositions must be distinguished is made quite clear by C. H. Cosgrove, "Justification in Paul: A Linguistic and Theological Reflection," *JBL* 106 (1987), 653-70, here 657-60, esp. 659-60. On the abbreviations "apart from works" and "by/from works" see (at) n(n). (8-)9 above.

66. Namely, immediately in section 3, whereas the concluding section 4 comes back to

the exegetical dispute with respect to "the key statement of the Pauline doctrine of justification" and to the burden tied to it in church history.

67. Cf. (however) nn. 83, 156 below.

68. The thesis is touched on jokingly by Liebers, *Gesetz als Evangelium,* 41 n. 3.

69. The thesis is available *in nuce* in Lohmeyer, "Probleme," 38-41, 46, 64, 66-68, 70-71, who was led above all by the multilayered concept of "work" beyond the syntagm "works of the law" to paraphrase it not as "commands" (or something similar) but as "duty *('Dienst')* of the law" (p. 67 [and *passim*]). Correspondingly Tyson, "Works," 426 (and *passim*), who follows Lohmeyer's study very closely (see p. 424-25; on this cf. Gaston, "Works," 219-20 [with n. 6 on 101]). Cf. (at) n. 14 above and (at) nn. 106, 136 below.

70. G. Bertram, "ἔργον," *TWNT* 2 (1935), 631-53 (cf. ET *TDNT* 2, 635-55), here 635. Cf. "Werk," in *Deutsches Wörterbuch* . . . , XIV, I, 2 (see n. 24 above), 328: "werk *proves to be an Indo-Germanic word by identity with Greek* . . . ἔργον."

71. See ibid. Cf., however, (at) nn. 144-45 below.

72. Thus the translation of H. Kraft, *Offenbarung des Johannes* (HNT 16a; Tübingen: Mohr, 1974), 68.

73. According to Kraft, *Offenbarung,* 68.

74. On this cf. (at) n. 62 above.

75. On this see T. Zahn, *Die Offenbarung des Johannes* (2 vols., KNT 18, first-third ed.; Leipzig: Deichertsche Verlagsbuchhandlung, 1924-26), 1.294 ("It is difficult to understand these works of Jesus in analogy to . . . v. 19, as Jesus' good conduct, but instead [what is meant is] what Jesus taught and commanded his disciples to do and not to do"), and Lohmeyer, "Probleme," 60 (together with n. 2). Cf. Kraft, *Offenbarung,* 71 ("Typical example for a pregnant expression"). Unfortunately reference to just this use of ἔργον by T. Holtz, "Die 'Werke' in der Johannesapokalypse," in *Neues Testament und Ethik. Für Rudolf Schnackenburg* (ed. H. Merklein; Freiburg: Herder, 1989), 426-41, has not been taken into consideration.

76. On this cf. Lohmeyer, "Probleme," 60 together with n. 3 (he refers also to Rev 1:3; 3:8; 22:7, 9). Moreover, according to Zahn, *Offenbarung,* 1.294, the expression τὰ ἔργα αὐτῆς in Rev 2:22 means "the immorality taught by the false prophetess" (cf., however, his translation, p. 282). Cf. further the Textus Receptus reading at Rev 22:14: ποιοῦντες τὰς ἐντολὰς αὐτοῦ (and on it, for instance, Holtz, "'Werke,'" 428 together with n. 12).

77. On this cf., e.g., (at) n. 70 above.

78. According to Lohmeyer, "Probleme," 80 (together with n. 5), an additional denotation occurs in Revelation in 14:13, where it means "reward."

79. As is normally the case with a personal genitive (cf., e.g., Gen 2:2; Ps 76[77]:12; Jer 27[50]:29; John 3:20; Rom 2:6; 2 Tim 1:9, further Rev 2:19, 23 once more). Cf. (at) nn. 94-98 below and also the following note.

80. Cf. from the rest of the New Testament on the one hand 1 Cor 15:58; 16:10; and Phil 2:30 ("work of the Lord [or of Christ]," "in which the genitive designates the person instructing" [R. Heiligenthal, "ἔργον," *Exegetisches Wörterbuch zum Neuen Testament* 2 (1981), 123-27 (cf. ET *EDNT* 2, 49-51), 124; cf. (at) n. 98 below], and on the other hand Acts 13:2; 14:26; and 15:38 (εἰς τὸ ἔργον with respect to the "mandate of mission" [Heiligenthal, p. 124; cf. Lohmeyer, "Probleme," 61 together with n. 6]); finally also Jas 1:25, where "(hearer of the law and) doer of the work" refers back to the "perfect law of liberty." Cf. (at) n. 145 below.

81. On this see Lohmeyer, "Probleme," 60 together with n. 4 (and, less satisfactory,

Bertram, "ἔργον," 639, Heiligenthal, "ἔργον," 124-25, as well as Westerholm, *Israel's Law*, 116 together with n. 19).

82. Cf. further John 14:10(-15:10); 14:12(-15:12) and also Rev 15:3(-4) — and on the Septuagint cf. (at) n. 143 below.

83. On this cf. (at) n. 121 below. It is interesting that parallels from Qumran are not lacking; for instance, the expressions *m'śy 'l* and *mṣwt 'l* in CD 2:14-15, 18 are comparable and correspond to each other.

84. On this see, for instance, M. Hengel, "Der Jakobusbrief als antipaulinische Polemik," in *Tradition and Interpretation in the New Testament: Essays in Honor of E. Earle Ellis for his 60th Birthday* (ed. G. F. Hawthorne and O. Betz; Grand Rapids: Eerdmans, 1987), 248-78, esp. 253-55, further the more cautious statements in R. Heiligenthal, *Werke als Zeichen. Untersuchungen zur Bedeutung der menschlichen Taten im Frühjudentum* (WUNT 2.9; Tübingen: Mohr, 1983), 49-52.

85. According to Heiligenthal, *Werke als Zeichen*, 50, it holds true that "some arguments based on the contents . . . speak against an explicit controversy of James with Pauline thought."

86. It is on the one hand striking that this opposition finds a certain correspondence in James in the similarly sounding "works" and "faith" (cf. Heiligenthal, *Werke als Zeichen*, 49, further [at] n. 89 below), and on the other hand Lohmeyer, "Probleme," 59 together with n. 2, correctly states for the New Testament (cf. [at] nn. 92, 94, 99 below): "An absolute use of the word 'works' as in Paul is hardly found in any passage" (p. 59); "only James 2:14-20 is an exception" (n. 2). See, however, (at) n. 90 below.

87. On this cf. Heiligenthal, *Werke als Zeichen*, 50 together with n. 113, and H. Frankemölle, "Gesetz im Jakobusbrief. Zur Tradition, kontextuellen Verwendung und Rezeption eines belasteten Begriffes," QD 108 (see n. 9 above), 175-221, here 202 and 216 (cf. p. 197).

88. On this cf., e.g., Wilckens, "Was heisst bei Paulus?" 108, and Bachmann, *Sünder*, 91 (together with nn. 335, 338 [bibliography]).

89. On this cf. (at) n(n). 8 (and 86) above, also Lohmeyer, "Probleme," 64.

90. Correctly emphasized by Lohmeyer, "Probleme," 59 together with n. 5, who (in n. 5) also refers to Jas 2:14, 22 in addition to 2:18. Cf. (against this) n. 86 above.

91. The study mentioned in n. 11 above was first published in *ZNW* 28, 177-207.

92. Lohmeyer, "Probleme," 34, 64 (cf. pp. 68, 71). This is all the more significant with the "abbreviated expression" in that the certain, yet in no way serious, difficulty that two (or more) dependent genitives may cause (on this see, e.g., F. Blass and A. Debrunner, *Grammatik des neutestamentlichen Griechisch* [fourteenth ed.; Göttingen: Vandenhoeck & Ruprecht, 1976], 168) is avoided (on this cf. n. 95 below). Cf. n. 86 above.

93. On this last point see (at) n. 8 above.

94. Cf. Lohmeyer, "Probleme," 61-63.

95. What the ὑμῶν standing before the expression "of the work of faith and of the labor of love and of the patience of hope" refers to is contested (on this cf., e.g., T. Holtz, *Der erste Brief an die Thessalonicher* (EKKNT 13; Neukirchen-Vluyn: Neukirchener, 1986], 43 together with nn. 56-57); but in any case the pronoun is related also to ἔργον (cf. p. 43, further 2 Thess 1:11-12). Cf. n. 92 above.

96. Lohmeyer, "Probleme," 59 together with n. 3, contrasts this passage (inadvertently

designated 2 Tim 1:10 by him) with "the so-called deutero-Pauline Letters" (p. 59) and Rom 9:12 and sets in opposition correspondingly Tit 3:5 ("not by/from any works of righteousness that we had done" [cf. n. 147 below]) with the linguistic usage especially of Romans and Galatians. Moreover, he could have done this also for Eph 2:(8-)9 (["not by/from your own" stands in parallel to] "not by/from works" [cf. also v. 10]) (cf. Gaston, "Works," 104). Cf. n. 8 above.

97. On this passage see the previous note.

98. The phrases "works of the Lord/of Christ" (on this see n. 80 above) and "each one's works" (1 Cor 3:13) are to some extent comparable.

99. Cf. Lohmeyer, "Probleme," 59, also Dunn: "Perspective," 194; *Jesus, Paul, and the Law*, 250-51.

100. Cf. the plural formulations "good works" (Eph 2:10; 1 Tim 2:10) and "beautiful works" (1 Tim 5:10, 25; 6:18; Tit 2:7, 14; 3:8, 14; singular in 1 Tim 3:1). The antonyms "bad work" (Rom 13:3), "evil work" (2 Tim 4:18), and "evil works" (Col 1:21) play a lesser role in the Corpus Paulinum. "Dead works" (Heb 6:1; 9:14) and "unlawful works" (2 Pet 2:8) do not occur at all in Paul. To some extent these expressions with an oppositional function are "substituted for" in Paul by "works of darkness" (Rom 13:12; cf. Eph 5:11) and "works of the flesh" (Gal 5:19). Cf. also 1 John 3:8 (and John 8:41[-44]): "works of the devil."

101. On what is comparable in the "deutero-Pauline Epistles" cf. above (at) n. 96 (and [at] n. 100 [and on this Heiligenthal, "ἔργον," 124, further Moo, "Law," 96 n. 76]). And concerning the linguistic usage of the Apocalypse of John cf., e.g., at nn. 72-73 above and n. 76.

102. On this cf. Lohmeyer, "Probleme," 59, 64, 68, 71.

103. The emphasis on the positive evaluation of the law arises here because of the provocative formulation in Rom 7:7b.

104. So, e.g., Lohmeyer, "Probleme," 64; and Westerholm, *Israel's Law*, 117-18, 120. Cf. Bachmann, *Sünder*, 64 (with n. 190), 91 (with nn. 337-38) (likewise 95 [with n. 358]); there further bibliographical information.

105. Rom 3:20b (and 3:19) may be compared to 3:20a, in any case 2:21bα — but indeed also 2:19aα (on this see Bachmann, *Sünder*, 64-66) — to Gal 2:16aα, by, c; and 3:11a presents a parallel to 3:10a, further 5:4aβ (cf. also especially 3:18a, 21cβ [and on this Moo, "Law," 86]). Finally Gal 3:2, 5, 10 are to be understood in connection (with 2:21 and 3:11a, 12a as well as above all) with 3:13-14. (With reference to the "abbreviated expressions" "without works" [Rom 4:6] and "by/from works" [Rom 4:2; 9:12, 32; 11:6] cf. what is said in [and at] n. 9 above, further the references to νόμος in Rom 3:20; 4:13, 14, 16; and 10:5 [as well as Moo, "Law," 86]). Cf. n. 123 below, further (at) n. 141.

106. Whereas especially Moo, "Law," 94-96 (esp. 95), as already noted (in n. 9) above, misinterprets the parallelism by the emphatic inclusion of references to ἔργον from other contexts, in view of the parallelism Lohmeyer, "Probleme," 64, correctly accentuates: it "is evidently possible only if out of the more complete and more precise expression the word 'law' rather than the other word 'work' stands out, that is, if this work is viewed not as something achieved but as something to achieve, something demanded by the law." Cf. n. 69 above.

107. The, as it appears to me, serious fact can be added as confirmation that then and only then do the works of the law in Gal 3:10a correspond exactly to the plural expression πᾶσιν τοῖς γεγραμμένοις ἐν τῷ βιβλίῳ τοῦ νόμου of 3:10b (cf. Deut 27:26) and also to the pro-

nouns of (3:10b and) 3:12b (and Lev 18:5 LXX) (as similarly the "works" of Rom 9:32 correspond to the αὐτά in Rom 10:5 [and Lev 18:15 LXX]). On this see Bachmann, *Sünder*, 93, 95 (together with n. 359 [with bibliographic information also]).

108. On this cf. n. 123 below, and further on what applies to such use of the term νόμος without addition, Westerholm, *Israel's Law*, 107-8 (cf. 106, 110-11).

109. On this cf. (at) n. 8 above. Not only the singular distinguishes the passage from the examples of "works of the law" but in addition the absence of the oppositions of content (especially the opposition to πίστις Χριστοῦ; on this see at nn. 134-35 below, also n. 123 below) under consideration in them without exception — or almost without exception (Rom 3:20 is perhaps an exception). Further, in Rom 2:15 — the only place where the article is inserted — one has to do not with one of the prepositional expressions that dominate the field in the plural (cf. again at n. 8 above, further, e.g., Schreiner, "Works," 217 n. 1). Nevertheless, the contact between the singular and plural expression is not to be neglected because, for instance, both are found in biblical literature only in Paul.

110. On this and the following cf. Bachmann, *Sünder*, 96-97 (together with nn. 365-71 [with bibliographical information also]).

111. On this problem cf. E. Käsemann, *An die Römer* (HNT 8a, third ed.; Tübingen: Mohr, 1974), (59-)60 (cf. ET of the fourth ed., *Commentary on Romans* [Grand Rapids: Eerdmans, 1980], 64), and Heiligenthal, *Werke als Zeichen*, 283-84 together with n. 329. Incidentally in the Septuagint in Jer 38(31):33 the plural νόμοι is used (on this cf. H. Hübner, "νόμος," *Exegetisches Wörterbuch zum Neuen Testament* 2 [1981], 1158-72, here 1163 [cf. ET *EDNT* 2, 473], and [at] n. 117 below).

112. Cf. Cranfield, "Works," 94: The word designates here (in distinction from Rom 3:20 and from the other references to "works of the law," in which "obedience to the law" is meant [pp. 92, 100; cf. (at) nn. 12-14, 60 above]) "the work *as prescribed*" (cf. Westerholm, *Israel's Law*, 107-8). Differently, e.g., W. Bauer, *Griechisch-deutsches Wörterbuch zu den Schriften des Neuen Testaments und der frühchristlichen Literatur* (sixth ed.; Berlin/New York: de Gruyter, 1988), 623: "*action according to the law ('d. dem Gesetz entsprechende Handeln')*."

113. On this see, e.g., Heiligenthal, *Werke als Zeichen*, 282-83, and Cranfield, "Works," 94 (the latter refers for the singular to John 6:29 and Rom 8:4).

114. Käsemann, *Römer*, 57 (cf. p[p]. 58 [and 60]).

115. Differently from Paul, who thereby understands "the law as a single entity" (Moo, "Law," 75), especially Philo and Josephus (on this see, e.g., W. Gutbrod, "νόμος B.C.D," *TWNT* 4 [1942], 1029-77, here pp. 1043-46 [cf. ET *TDNT* 4, 1050-54]).

116. Cf. Moo, "Law," 80, also E. W. Stegemann, "Die umgekehrte Tora. Zum Gesetzesverständnis bei Paulus," *Jud* 43 (1987), 4-20, here p. 8.

117. Hübner, "νόμος," 1163 (cf. n. 111 above).

118. From the context of the references to "works (of the law)" compare, e.g., Rom 3:1, 30; 4:9-12; Gal 2:3, 7-9, 12 (cf. 5:2-3, 6, 11; 6:12-13, 15).

119. Lohmeyer, "Probleme," 36.

120. Gaston, "Works," esp. 100-106. For critical opinions on this thesis (on which cf. already n. 48 above): (e.g.) Westerholm, *Israel's Law*, 116-17; W. Stegemann, "Christliche Judenfeindschaft," 160; Bachmann, *Sünder*, 96 together with n. 362; Schreiner, "Works," (220-21 and) 231.

121. On this see Bachmann, *Sünder*, 100 n. 394 (where among others reference is made

to the genitive of content corresponding to the genitive of domain; the former occurs in relation to the νόμος in Eph 2:15 ["law of commandments"] and in a certain way also in Rom 3:27 ["(Gesetz) der Werke"]). Cf. also (at) n. 83 above.

122. These were presented before at n. 8 above.

123. It is not without relevance for the passages with the formulation "works of the law" that also for the abbreviation "works" (on this see [at] nn. 8-9 above) an interpretation with "regulations" comes through well, if not better. On this it should simply be noted: The passage in Rom 4:6, in which in view of 4:7-8 disregarding the fulfillments of the law (in which for David at least circumcision must be taken into account [cf. 4:12, 16]) would make no sense, can then be understood (and therefore also the passage 4:2 [on this cf. in addition once more (see n. 105 above) 4:13, 14, 16]) like Rom 3:28 in accordance with 3:21 (on this see at n. 105 above, further Bachmann, *Sünder*, 96) — and 7:8-9 — , just as the contrasts in 9:12 (where the fulfillments of commands could not be connected with the evil behavior of 9:11 [on this see also Bachmann, *Sünder*, 96]); Rom 9:32 and Rom 11:6 correspond to those oppositions, which, e.g., Rom 3:28 and Gal 3:2, 5 define (on this see n. 109 above and at nn. 134-35 below). If in Rom 9:31-32 — according to our thesis — νόμος and ἔργα are indeed closely connected (cf. section [ii] above), though not identified but rather distinguished, thus here νόμος alludes to another side of the law than the nomistic one (on this cf., e.g., Bachmann, *Sünder*, 150 n. 269); and this of course fits best, because Rom 9:31–10:4 has to do with teleology.

124. It is indeed — also completely aside from statements like Rom 2:13; 10:5; and Gal 3:12b — difficult to understand why the fact that "through the law comes knowledge of sin" (3:20b) may prove just that "on the basis of the *fulfillments* of the law (and not on the basis of *transgressions* of the law) no flesh will be justified before him [i.e., God]" (3:20a). And yet the γάρ at the beginning of 3:20b signals cause or reason. On this cf. Bachmann, *Sünder*, 96 together with n. 363 (bibliography), further at n. 167 below.

125. *WA* 57 [II], 5-108, here 79.4 — with reference to *PL* 26, 357(-58). Cf. *WA* 40 I, 397.5, 19-20.

126. *WA* 40 I, (1-)39–II, 184, here I, 396.34-35: "Sunt ergo omnino duae pugnantes sententiae Pauli et Mosi."

127. *WA* 2, 513.23-27; cited according to (line 26 and according to the translation mentioned in n. 30 above:) Mann, 131. Cf. *WA* 57 [II], 79.4; 40 I, 396, (esp.) 12, 31.

128. *WA* 2, 513.29-30 (Mann, 131). Of course Luther does not stop with these kinds of defeatist remarks. Rather he arrives particularly at the following interpretation of Gal 3:10a(-b), which promises to heal the logical damage: "*quicunque extra fidem sunt, operantur quidem opera legis, sed legem non implent. Opera enim legis simulata opera sunt*" (p. 513, lines 32-34; in lines 34-36 the Reformer refers for this to Gal 6:13 and 5:3). Cf. (at) nn. 28, 32-33, 45 above.

129. C. D. Stanley, "'Under a Curse': A Fresh Reading of Gal 3:10-14," *NTS* 36 (1990), 481-511, here p. 481.

130. For something more detailed on this: Bachmann, *Sünder*, 93-95.

131. Stanley, "Curse," 482-86 (cf. 509-10), who gives an overview of older and more recent attempts to resolve the conundrum (and rejects them all), understands Gal 3:10a as if it were a conditional sentence that applies to *Gentile* Christians (cf. esp. p. 498 n. 51) and "v. 10 as expressing the continuing 'potentiality' of the 'curse' threatened by the law" (p. 511). For

critical reflection on this see already Bachmann, *Sünder,* 94 n. 356 (with reference among others to Rom 2:12b).

132. On this see Bachmann, *Sünder,* 141-43, also p. 95 n. 357.

133. On this cf. (at) n. 168 below.

134. To the phrase "not by/from works (of the law)" there correspond the expressions "without works of the law" (Rom 3:28), "without works" (Rom 4:6), and, additionally, "without law" (Rom 3:21; 7:8, 9). On Rom 4:2 (and 4:6); 9:12, 32; 11:6 cf. (at) n. 9 above.

135. Cf. (at) nn. 105, 109, 123 above.

136. Here lies the correct claim in, e.g., Lohmeyer's interpretation that ἔργα are about "duty *(Dienst)* of the law" (on this see [at] nn. 14, 69 above); for prescriptions of the law are naturally aimed toward their execution, and this is true also for the Pauline ἔργα (νόμου) (on this see esp. Rom 4:4-5; 9:11-12; Gal 3:10-12; cf. Rom 2:14 [and Tit 3:5], further Cranfield, "Works," 94). Cf. (at) nn. 159-60 below.

137. On this see at nn. 70-78 above.

138. Billerbeck, *Kommentar,* 3.160. Cf n. 156 below. S. Ben-Chorin, *Paulus. Der Völkerapostel in jüdischer Sicht* (dtv/List Sachbuch 1550; Munich: Deutscher Taschenbuch Verlag, 1980), 56, holds: "it [i.e., "the word *Nomos*" in Paul] can stand for *Mizwoth ma'assioth,* for the ritual law."

139. In Billerbeck, *Kommentar,* 3.160 n. 1, and in Lohmeyer, "Probleme," 41, reference is made only to "a late midrash" (Gaston, "Works," 101) that bears the expression as a title.

140. Billerbeck, *Kommentar,* 3.160; Lohmeyer, "Probleme," (36 and) 40. Cf., e.g., Käsemann, *Römer,* 83.

141. Seen by Lohmeyer, "Probleme," 40, who however does not designate the equivalent to the same state of affairs in the Pauline writings (see p. 64, and section [ii] above).

142. Therefore, as Lohmeyer, "Probleme," 40, correctly emphasizes, "also here . . . the expression 'work' is only a variant of the concept command that tends toward the requirement 'to accomplish' [it], not toward the fact of 'having been accomplished.'"

143. Lohmeyer, "Probleme," 39-40, refers to texts such as Exod 36:1, 3 and Num 3:7, 8 (cf. further, for instance, Num 8:11 and 1[3] Esdr 7:9, also Jer 31[48]:10 and Bar 2:9 [where it ought to be concluded according to v. 10 — and v. 12 — that τὰ ἔργα αὐτοῦ must mean nothing other than τὰ προστάγματα κυρίου], which Westerholm, *Israel's Law,* 116, incorrectly claims for his view of "works of the law" ["deeds demanded by the law"]). From writings beyond the Septuagint Lohmeyer mentions ("Probleme," 39-40) *T. Levi* 19:1 and *T. Benj.* 5:3. Moreover, reference can be made here to Josephus, *Ant.* 20, 42, 43, 46 (see Bachmann, *Sünder,* 98) and of course to the New Testament passages already adduced in (and at) nn. 75-82 above.

144. On this see, e.g., (at) nn. 70-71 above.

145. On this see, e.g., H. Menge, *Langenscheidts Grosswörterbuch Griechisch Deutsch, unter Berücksichtigung der Etymologie* (27th ed. = second ed. of 1913; Berlin: Langenscheidt, 1991), 283-84, where with reference to the meaning of ἔργον (after "individual work, deed . . .") in the second position "incumbent work, duty, task, job, business . . ." (in Menge partly in emphatic print) are named (cf., e.g., Homer, *Iliad* 6.490 [and 6.492], also Mark 13:34). Cf. Heiligenthal, "ἔργον," 124: "ἔργον in the NT as in secular Greek means . . . *work, task*" (on this cf. n. 80 above). Cf. n. 156 below.

146. First edition 1959 (on this see, e.g., *Die Texte aus Qumran. Hebräisch und Deutsch.*

Mit masoretischer Punktation, Übersetzung, Einführung und Anmerkungen [ed. E. Lohse; Darmstadt: Wissenschaftliche Buchgesellschaft, 1971], 255[-59]).

147. If only because according to Moo, "Law," 91, there is "an equivalent Hebrew verbal parallel only in 4QFlor 1:7" (cf. Schreiner, "Works," 230[-31], further bibliography in Bachmann, *Sünder,* 98 n. 384 [see moreover W. Stegemann, "Christliche Judenfeindschaft," 160 n. 186]); the additional references to Qumran passages for "his works in the Torah" (1QS 5:21; 6:18 [cf. Dunn, *Jesus, Paul, and the Law,* 244, where reference is made in addition to 1QS 5:23 and to "an unpublished 4Q text," as which (see Dunn, "Response," 103-4) the letter 4QMMT to be presented forthwith is to be understood]; cf. Tit 3:5 [on this see n. 96 above]) and for "works of righteousness" (1QH 1:26; 4:31; cf. *Pss. Sol.* 18:8) serve only for the illumination of the broader background. Yet it appears, with respect to the latter expression, that it is not to be excluded that (also) here works are to be understood as commandments, for they are (in 1QH 1:26; 4:31) classed in God's domain and (in 1QH 1:26-27) contrasted with "works of deceit" (cf. *Pss. Sol.* 18:8 with v. 4). Cf. also (at) n. 83 above. With respect to Paul and 4QMMT, cf. P. J. Tomson, *Paul and the Jewish Law: Halakha in the Letters of the Apostle to the Gentiles* (CRINT 3.1; Assen/Maastricht: Van Gorcum, 1990), 66; M. Hengel, "Der vorchristliche Paulus," in *Paulus und das antike Judentum. Tübingen-Durham Symposium im Gedenken an den 50. Todestag Adolf Schlatters* (WUNT 58, ed. M. Hengel and U. Heckel; Tübingen: Mohr, 1991), 177-291/3, here 253-54 and 273 n. 306 (cf. ET *The Pre-Christian Paul* [Philadelphia: Trinity, 1991], 50-51, 141 n. 306); J. D. G. Dunn, "The Justice of God: A Renewed Perspective on Justification by Faith," *JTS* 43 (1992), 1-22, here pp. 13-14.

148. On this see (the bibliography at) Bachmann, *Sünder,* 98-99. Cautious doubts that the manuscript of 4QFlor 1:7 reads *twrh* were expressed first by J. Strugnell, "Notes en marge du volume V des 'Discoveries in the Judean Desert of Jordan,'" *RevQ* 7 (1969-71), 163-276, here p. 221. More vehemently now, G. J. Brooke, *Exegesis at Qumran: 4QFlorilegium in Its Jewish Context* (JSOTSup 29; Sheffield: JSOT, 1985), 108 (cf. pp. 87, 92, 192): "The reading *twdh . . .* is . . . confirmed from the original manuscript and earliest photographs."

149. "An Anonymously Received Pre-Publication of the 4QMMT," in *The Qumran Chronicle: Appendix "A," no. 2* (Krakow: Enigma, 1990), here 2-9, the text with an English translation. (Prof. Dr. H. Lichtenberger, Münster, who deserves gratitude, with the friendly mediation of E. W. Stegemann, Basle, allowed a copy to reach me.) The enumeration of the lines in this "pirated edition" is picked up in what follows, although it — and also the stock of letters — does not agree precisely with what E. Qimron and J. Strugnell, to whom the task of the critical edition has been entrusted (or indeed was entrusted) have so far published in relation to and from the document reconstructed from six fragmentary manuscripts (namely, primarily two essays with the same title: "An Unpublished Halakhic Letter from Qumran," one in *Biblical Archaeology Today: Proceedings of the International Congress on Biblical Archaeology,* Jerusalem, April 1984, Jerusalem, 1985, 400-407, the other in *The Israel Museum Journal* 4 [1985], 9-12); so Qimron and Strugnell, "Letter," (402 or respectively) 10, cite a passage as "C14-15," which in the Krakow edition begins in line C7 (cf. further n. 152 below). In spite of the scandal of decades of delay in the edition of the text, which Qimron and Strugnell call "one of the most important documents from Qumran" ("Letter," 400), much has already been written about it (see the bibliography compiled by Z. J. Kapera on pp. 10-11 of the fascicle of *The Qumran Chronicle* that has been mentioned).

150. Qimron and Strugnell, "Letter," 400: The writer is "possibly the Teacher of Righteousness himself."

151. H. Lichtenberger, "Literatur zum Antiken Judentum," *VF* 33 (1988), 2-19, here p. 13. Cf. L. H. Schiffman, "*Miqṣat Ma'aśeh Ha-Torah* and the Temple Scroll," *RevQ* 14 (1990), 435-57.

152. Whereas this corresponds to the stock of consonants noted by Qimron and Strugnell, "Letter," 400 (or 9 respectively; see p. 10, a copy of one of the fragments of the passage under consideration), which in the secondary literature, as far as I can tell, are unanimously accepted, the Krakow edition offers not *m'śy* but *m'śh* (by which, however, as, e.g., a comparison of Exod 18:20 LXX [ἔργα] with the Hebrew original shows [cf. at n. 154 below], a plural meaning must not be excluded [cf. E. Qimron, *The Hebrew of the Dead Sea Scrolls* (HSS 29; Atlanta: Scholars, 1986), 101, and the following note], and this all the less so since such an alternation can be almost typical for the Qumran texts [on this see M. H. Gottstein, "Studies in the Language of the Dead Sea Scrolls: 1. The Interchange of Final *Yod* and *He*," *JJS* 4 (1953), 104-5]). Cf. the reference from Qimron and Strugnell, "Letter," 406 (n. 7 on p. 401): "The variant readings of the several manuscripts are very interesting" (and cf. n. 149 above).

153. Qimron and Strugnell, "Letter," 401 (or 9 respectively); just so, remarkably (cf. the preceding note), the translation given in the Krakow edition. Cf. Lichtenberger, "Literatur," 13 ("part of the prescriptions of the Torah"), and C. K. Barrett, *Texte zur Umwelt des Neuen Testaments*, (UTB 1591, ed. C.-J. Thornton; second ed.; Tübingen: Mohr, 1991), 261-62 (no. 233), here 261 (line 7: "(something) from the entirety of the prescriptions of the Torah"), further, Qimron, *Hebrew*, 101.

154. Cf. n. 152 above.

155. So also Qimron and Strugnell, "Letter," 406 (n. 5 on p. 401).

156. On this see, e.g., Billerbeck, *Kommentar*, 1.345-46; 3.501-2; 4/1.560-61; A. Finkel, "Gerechtigkeit II. Judentum," *TRE* 12 (1984), 411-14, here p. 412; Qimron and Strugnell, "Letter," 406 (n. 5 on p. 401) who refer to, among others, *b. B. Qam.* 99b(-100a); *b. B. Meṣ.* 30b; *Mek.* Exod 18:20 (here, however, *also* interpretation by *m'śh ḥṭwb*); *Tg. Ps.-J.* Exod 18:20 (cf. also *CN* [*Tg. Neof.*] Exod 18:20). Qimron and Strugnell, "Letter," 406 (n. 5 on p. 401 [bibliography]), incidentally point out that there are "many further examples of *m'śjm* . . . with the meaning 'precepts'" in postbiblical literature (cf. M. Elon, "Ma'aseh," *EncJud* 11 [1971], 641-49, esp. 641). The word has then a spectrum of meaning that includes the two poles "deeds" and "precepts" analogous to the term *mṣwt* (on this see, e.g., Billerbeck, *Kommentar*, 3.161-62; cf. [at] nn. 67, 83 above) — and similarly like (ἔργον or) ἔργα (on this see, e.g., [at] nn. 144-45 above). Cf. (at) n. 136 above.

157. Billerbeck, *Kommentar*, 3.502 (cf. 1.345; 4/1.561).

158. On this cf. Tomson, *Paul*, 66, and Hengel, "Der vorchristliche Paulus," (253 and) 273 together with n. 306. Further conspicuous points of contact in content are: As in Gal 3:10-14(ff.) the theme of blessing and curse (from Deuteronomy 27–28 [cf. particularly Deut 30:1; Josh 8:34; Mal 2:2]) in connection with the question of observing the law plays an important role, so also in 4QMMT (C15ff.), and when (the justification of David the sinner and) David's reliance on forgiveness is expressed in Rom 4:6-8, so in a similar way in this Qumran document (C27-28; cf. C19ff., also C10-11).

159. On this see Qimron and Strugnell, "Letter," 401 together with n. 5.

160. On this cf. (at) n. 136 above. Cf. further Hengel, "Der vorchristliche Paulus," 253-54.

161. Cf. Schreiner, "Works," 226-29 (and 232-38), and Westerholm, *Israel's Law*, 170-71.

162. On this cf. (at) n. 132 above.

163. On this cf. at nn. 134-36 above.

164. Cf. n. 58 above, further Bachmann, *Sünder,* 63 (together with n. 184) and 88-89.

165. On this see (at) nn. 48, 58 above.

166. However, so far as for Paul soteriology and anthropology come into view from christology (cf. again Gal 2:21b [and on this (at) nn. 58, 164 above]; cf. Rom 3:27), the thesis that the notion that one is not justified by/from works of the law arises in Paul from "the fleshly condition of humanity" (W. Stegemann, "Christliche Judenfeindschaft," 165) can be repeated only conditionally, not as an absolute statement. Particularly the observation that πᾶς ζῶν is not used in Rom 3:20 and Gal 2:16, as in Ps 142:2 LXX, but πᾶσα σάρξ (W. Stegemann, "Christliche Judenfeindschaft," 164; similarly, e.g., already A. Schlatter, *Gottes Gerechtigkeit. Ein Kommentar zum Römerbrief* [Stuttgart: Calwer, 1935], 133; cf. ET *Romans: The Righteousness of God* [tr. Siegfried S. Schatzmann; Peabody: Hendrickson, 1995], 89-90) should not be given too much weight, because the Apostle does not pick up the σάρξ terminology of the thus formulated saying of the psalm in the (near) context (see rather Gal 2:16aα: ἄνθρωπος; but see also Gal 2:20c) and because the concept of the flesh is found also in *1 En.* 81:5, which is obviously likewise dependent on Ps 143(142):2 (cf. Wilckens, "Was heisst bei Paulus?" 90-91 together with n. 28, and Cosgrove, "Justification," 655 n. 9).

167. On this passage cf. (the previous note and) above (at) n. 124.

168. So indeed runs the Pauline verdict *post Christum crucifixum* (on this see [at] nn. 164, 166 above).

Notes to Chapter 2

1. J. D. G. Dunn, "4QMMT and Galatians," *NTS* 43 (1997), 147-53. Dunn refers in every case to the (in its unity not quite undisputed) document 4QMMT, which exists in six fragmentary manuscripts (4Q394-99 [= 4QMMT^{a-f}]), according to the "Composite Text" and the corresponding numbering of lines, that is, following E. Qimron and J. Strugnell, *Qumran Cave 4 5: Miqṣat Maʿaśe Ha-Torah* (Discoveries in the Judaean Desert 10; Oxford: Oxford University Press, 1994), 43-63. Such a way of proceeding should be also basically satisfactory for the limited aims of this contribution to the discussion (cf. however below [at] n. 58). Cf. n. 35 below.

2. These parallels are: separation (C7; Gal 1:15; 2:12); curse and blessing (C14ff.; Gal 3:8ff.); "works of the law" (C27; Gal 2:16ff.); Gen 15:6 (or Ps 106:31; 1 Macc 2:52; *Jub.* 30:17) (C31; Gal 3:6); calendar (A1ff.; Gal 4:10). It is unfortunate, as far as scholarly communication is concerned, how impervious the borders between, e.g., English and German literature have become in the meantime. Thus Dunn does not mention H.-W. Kuhn, "Die Bedeutung der Qumrantexte für das Verständnis des Galaterbriefs. Aus dem Münchener Projekt: Qumran und das Neue Testament," in *New Qumran Texts and Studies: Proceedings of the First Meeting of the International Organisations for Qumran Studies, Paris, 1992* (Studies on the Texts of the Desert of Judah 15, ed. G. Brooke; Leiden: Brill, 1994), 169-221 (cf. H.-W. Kuhn, "Die drei wichtigsten Qumranparallelen zum Galaterbrief. Unbekannte Wege der Tradition," in *Konsequente Traditionsgeschichte. Festschrift für Klaus Baltzer zum 65. Geburtstag* [OBO 126, ed. R. Bartelmus; Freiburg (Schweiz): Universitätsverlag, 1993], 227-54); M. Bachmann,

Notes to Page 19

"Rechtfertigung und Gesetzeswerke bei Paulus," *TZ* 49 (1993), 1-33, esp. 27-31 (cf. M. Bachmann, *Sünder oder Übertreter. Studien zur Argumentation in Gal 2,15ff.* [WUNT 59; Tübingen: Mohr, 1992], esp. 98-99); P. Grelot, "Les oeuvres de la Loi (A propos de 4Q394-398)," *RevQ* 16.63 (1994), 441-48.

3. See Dunn, "4QMMT," 152-53.

4. Probably C12 thinks of the path "of the Torah," as Qimron and Strugnell, *Miqṣat*, 59, add (cf. p. 139 [referring to Exodus 18 (meaning 18:20?)] and cf. [at] n. 63 below) — correspondingly perhaps also in Gal 3:19 (on this see for instance Bachmann, *Sünder*, 74 n. 244); in any case the deviation from the right way (according to Deuteronomy 27–30 [esp. 30:16-17]) is negatively evaluated — no differently from Gal 2:14, 18; 3:19. On this imagery within the framework of Galatians cf. Bachmann, *Sünder*, esp. 79-80.

5. On this cf. Dunn, "4QMMT," 148-50. (Here in n. 13: Discussion of how the lacuna at the end of C21 is to be filled in: whether a return to Israel or to the Torah [cf. Gal 2:18a] should be read.)

6. See esp. E. Qimron and J. Strugnell, "An Unpublished Halakhic Letter from Qumran," in *Biblical Archaeology Today: Proceedings of the International Congress on Biblical Archaeology, Jerusalem, April 1984* (ed. J. Amitai; Jerusalem: International Congress on Biblical Archaeology, 1985), 400-407, esp. 401-2. In the meantime the authors backed away from the assessment of the document as a letter or indeed as a private letter and now call it an "epistle" or "treatise" (see Qimron/Strugnell, *Miqṣat*, 113-14, 121); indeed Strugnell now thinks that parts B and C (of the "Composite Text" which also contains a part A) are "a legal code," comparable to Deuteronomy (*Miqṣat*, 203-6 [citation: 205]). On the other hand, other scholars continue to characterize 4QMMT as a letter (e.g., L. H. Schiffman, "The New Halakhic Letter [4QMMT] and the Origins of the Dead Sea Sect," *BA* 53 [1990], 64-73, esp. 67; H. Stegemann, *Die Essener, Qumran, Johannes der Täufer und Jesus* (Herder Spektrum 4249; Freiburg: Herder, 1993], 148-49; H. Lichtenberger, "Das Tora-Verständnis im Judentum zur Zeit des Paulus. Eine Skizze," in *Paul and the Mosaic Law: The Third Durham-Tübingen Research Symposium on Earliest Christianity and Judaism [Durham, September, 1994]* [WUNT 89, ed. J. D. G. Dunn; Tübingen: Mohr, 1996], 7-23, here p. 15).

7. Qimron and Strugnell make a quite similar judgment ("Letter," 401 together with n. 6; *Miqṣat*, 114 together with n[n]. [10-]14). The fact that 4QMMT must have been regarded as a document of "substantial authority" (*Miqṣat*, 112) on account of the considerable number of copies preserved at Qumran also finds its parallel in Paul's letters (cf., e.g., 1 Cor 5:9; 2 Cor 10:9-10; 1 Thess 5:27; 2 Pet 3:15-16).

8. On this cf. Qimron/Strugnell, *Miqṣat*, 109, 113. Among other things, in view of the formulation "we have written to you" (כתבנו אליך [C26; cf. C10]) the possibility of a prescript is certainly not to be excluded; this would particularly be compatible with the absence of a postscript, which is assured by the arrangement of the text (C32 in 4Q398 and 4Q399 respectively [see Qimron/Strugnell, *Miqṣat*, Plate VIII] at the end of the column or without any text following), as particularly the Epistle of James shows and the Murabba'at Letters make apparent (on this see, e.g., D. Pardee, *Handbook of Ancient Hebrew Letters: A Study Edition* [SBLSBS 15; Chico: Scholars, 1982], esp. 151-52 [cf. n. 18 below]). If one considers the features of content and form of the text 4QMMT, it thus appears quite possible (also Qimron/Strugnell, *Miqṣat*, 119-20; and Stegemann, *Essener*, 149-50, is evidently certain) that the interpretation of Ps 37:32-33 found in Qumran (4Q171 [= 4QPs^a] 4:8-9) refers precisely to

this document: "Its interpretation concerns the Wicked Priest who spied on the Teacher of Righteousness and tried to put him to death because of the precepts and the law [והתורה] which the latter had sent [שלח] to the former" (Qimron/Strugnell, *Miqṣat*, 120; however, the formulation referring to "precepts" [החוק] is textually uncertain). Cf. 1QpHab 5:9-12.

9. Thus the concluding remarks of 1 Corinthians, 1 Cor 16:5ff. (travel plans, exhortations, greetings, etc.), are preceded by passages that deal with individual topoi (cf., e.g., also Rom 12:1ff. in connection with 1:16/18ff.). And the fact that such passages are on various occasions introduced with περὶ δέ (1 Cor 7:1; 8:1; 12:1; 16:1; cf. 16:12) constitutes an additional parallel to 4QMMT (as is also mentioned by Qimron/Strugnell, *Miqṣat*, 113-14), namely, to the "incipit of each halakha in section B, ואף על," (p. 113; see, e.g., B13, 21, whereas for instance it is expressed more succinctly in B8, 72 by ועל) — and permits one (cf. p. 114) to take note of halakhic material in Paul and in this letter of his (e.g., 1 Cor 7:1ff.; 8:1ff. with 4QMMT B39ff. [cf. B75-76]; B36ff.: legitimate marriage relations; permissible eating of sacrifices?). Cf. n. 11 below.

10. On this see Qimron/Strugnell, *Miqṣat*, 114-15 and 117 ("a three-party situation"), further pp. 175-76 (Qimron).

11. The polemical orientation of the document becomes clear from the (to a certain degree stereotypical) way in which their own view of the individual halakhot can be introduced by "and concerning x: we are of the opinion" (e.g., B36, 55), whereas on various occasions "a divergent praxis of others, who are described in the third person plural" (e.g., B24, 75), functions to profile what is considered correct (citations: Qimron/Strugnell, *Miqṣat*, 110; cf. pp. 135, 137 [Qimron], and Lichtenberger, "Tora-Verständnis," 15). Cf. n. 9 above, further CD 2:14.

12. Qimron/Strugnell, *Miqṣat*, 59. Cf. pp. 99, 111, further Y. Sussmann, "The History of the Halakha and the Dead Sea Scrolls," in Qimron/Strugnell, *Miqṣat*, 179-200, here p. 192 (cf. [at] n. 32 below) — as well as C. K. Barrett, *Texte zur Umwelt des Neuen Testaments* (UTB 1591, second ed., ed. C.-J. Thornton; Tübingen: Mohr, 1991), 262, and Dunn, "4QMMT," 147-48. M. Abegg, "Paul, 'Works of the Law' and MMT," *BAR* 20 (1994), 52-55, 82, fills in C7 differently and points to a separation not from the people ([...מ]העם) but from the community ([...ה]עדה); in this case the letter would be about "an intra-communal dispute that precipitated a schism among sectarians," which, however, in my opinion fits less satisfactorily with the constellation of three groups.

13. Alongside Galatians, 2 Corinthians above all should be mentioned (e.g., 2 Cor 3:1; 10:2; 11:1-15).

14. One must distinguish a threefold use of "we" in Galatians: sometimes it very probably means Paul and his co-senders (so perhaps 1:8-9; similarly 2:4-5, 9-10); then without question Paul and (the) Jewish-Christians (so 2:15-17 and probably also 3:1–4:7 [with the exception of 3:14b; 4:6b]); finally it includes (as already in 1:3-4; 3:14b; 4:6b) Gentile Christians (as in 4:8ff., here 4:26 is the first instance). On this cf. T. L. Donaldson, "The 'Curse of the Law' and the Inclusion of the Gentiles," *NTS* 32 (1986), 94-112, esp. 95-99; Bachmann, *Sünder*, 137-39; J. Lambrecht, "The Universalistic Will of God: The True Gospel in Galatians," *Pauline Studies: Collected Essays* (BETL 115; Leuven: Leuven University Press, 1994), 299-306, here pp. 304-5.

15. See 4:17; 6:12-13 (cf. esp. 1:7, 9; 3:1; 5:7, 10, 12).

16. "Brothers," 1:11 and *passim;* "you" (plural), from 1:6 on until 6:18.

17. See esp. 4:17-21; 5:1, 2-10; 6:11-17.

18. Qimron/Strugnell, *Miqṣat,* 113, name as a certain parallel to C31-32 "אהוה שלום וכל בית ישראל, the closing greeting formula of one of the Bar Kokhba letters (Mur 42:7)" — after which only signatures follow (on this see P. Benoit, J. T. Milik, and R. de Vaux, *Les Grottes de Murabbaʿât* [Discoveries in the Judaean Desert 2; Oxford: Oxford University Press, 1961], 155-59, esp. 156-57; Pardee, *Handbook,* esp. 123-24, 151-52 [cf. above, n. 8]).

19. Dunn, "4QMMT," 153.

20. This, however, is the tendency of Dunn, "4QMMT," 152-53.

21. Cf. Sussmann, "History of the Halakha," 185: the author of the "personal epistle," which "is a polemical document about halakhic matters," directs an appeal to the addressees (designated by Sussmann, however, as "opponents") "and attempts to persuade them to accept his views regarding specific halakhot."

22. Thus however, e.g., H. D. Betz, *Galatians: A Commentary on Paul's Letter to the Churches in Galatia* (Hermeneia; Philadelphia: Fortress, 1979), 24-25 (and *passim*) — and under his influence also other scholars (on this see, e.g., Bachmann, *Sünder,* 11-18 [together with nn. 122, 124-25, 127]).

23. Cf. Bachmann, *Sünder,* 16-18 (together with nn. 114, 121, 125), and pp. 156-60, as well as R. D. Anderson, *Ancient Rhetorical Theory and Paul* (Contributions to Biblical Exegesis and Theology 18; Kampen: Kok Pharos, 1996), 111-23, esp. 112-17 (cf. [however] also pp. 166-67), on the point that Galatians tends now more often to be categorized as belonging to the *genus deliberativum* or as close to it.

24. Two copies of the letter (4Q395 and 4Q398) come from the late Hasmonean or early Herodian period (cf. Qimron/Strugnell, *Miqṣat,* esp. 14, 28 [A. Yardeni]), and reasons based on the content allow one to assume (on this see, e.g., Qimron/Strugnell, *Miqṣat,* 116-21, further p. 205 [Strugnell]) that it originated rather toward the beginning of the Hasmonean epoch (cf. already n. 8 above).

25. Nevertheless Judaism plays an important role here: Paul is a Jewish Christian (on this see, e.g., n. 14 above) and consequently a Jew, and as a Jew he has persecuted the Christian community (see 1:13-14), just as he is now exposed to such persecutions (see 5:11); according to 4:28-29 this holds also for the group identified by *"you"* (plural) or indeed for the larger community of Christians encompassing them, and according to 6:12 the *"they"* group appears to want to avoid being persecuted. In addition, the Gentile Christian addressees (see, e.g., 4:8) — and Gentile Christians generally — are included in the salvation that goes out from Israel (see esp. 4:4-7 [and on this cf. what is explained in detail in the immediately following text, as well as once again n. 14 above]).

26. Namely, in 3:1-14; 3:15-29; and 4:1-7. On this see Donaldson, "Curse of the Law," esp. 95, 98; Bachmann, *Sünder,* esp. 138; Lambrecht, "Universalistic Will," 304-5.

27. On Gal 4:17 cf. C. Burchard, "Nicht aus Werken des Gesetzes gerecht, sondern aus Glauben an Jesus Christus — seit wann?" in *Geschichte — Tradition — Reflexion. Festschrift für Martin Hengel zum 70. Geburtstag* (ed. H. Cancik, H. Lichtenberger, and P. Schäfer, 3 vols.; Tübingen: Mohr, 1996), 3.405-15, here p. 406 n. 6 (where he mentions a series of comparable passages): "ἐκκλείειν probably as also in Rom 3:27 is not 'to exclude' (*"[hin]ausschließen"*) but 'to keep excluded' *("außen vor halten")."*

28. On this see (at) nn. 1-2, 12 above. Cf., e.g., 1QS 5:14-18; CD 6:14-19 (cf. [at] n. 71 below).

29. On the limits of this pericope cf. Bachmann, *Sünder,* esp. 111-14, 123-30.

30. If Paul uses this way of expressing himself (on this cf., e.g., 1QS 4:17-18; Mark 7:5, 8), then this fact is just as remarkable as the use of the verb διώκειν concerning each of the three groups (on this see n. 25 above) for the triangle determining Galatians — and for its analogy to the triangle of the document 4QMMT —, particularly since in a somewhat parallel way he employs the term Ἰουδαϊσμός, which evidently finds a certain parallel in (being compelled to) ἰουδαΐζειν in 2:14. For its part this verb appears to lead up to the catchword ἔργα νόμου (first in 2:16) (which supposedly covers not least of all being compelled to be circumcised, περιτέμνεσθαι [esp. 6:12-13; on the question of being compelled to be circumcised cf. also 2:3 and cf. moreover 5:2]).

31. Cf. Burchard, "Nicht aus Werken," 410-14.

32. The rigid halakhic view evident in 4QMMT agrees in at least two points (B13-16 [red heifer], B55-58 [streams of liquid]) with what in the Talmudic literature is characterized as the attitude of "Sadducees" (on this see, e.g., Qimron/Strugnell, *Miqṣat,* 132 [Qimron]) and which is distanced from the less stringent judgment on the part of "Pharisees" (on this see esp. Sussmann, "History of the Halakha," 187-91), so that in this respect one can say that the "we" group has a "Sadducean" orientation and the "they" group a "Pharisaic" orientation (see Qimron/Strugnell, *Miqṣat,* 115-16, further 175-76 [Qimron], and Sussmann, "History of the Halakha, esp. 187). In this connection it is worth considering that for the "Pharisees" themselves in the case of halakhic differences, maintaining fellowship with one another was of fundamental importance (on this see, e.g., Sussmann, "History of the Halakha," 191 [cf. 198-99]). Thus Paul the Christian represents, so to say, "Pharisaic" concerns (see esp. Gal 2:9-10, 11-14; 3:28; 5:6; 6:15-16), whereas before his call he acted "Sadducean" — the term "Pharisee" in Phil 3:5 notwithstanding. The use of the verb פרש in 4QMMT C7(-8), which probably lies behind the noun "Pharisee," makes it possible to realize, however, that the rabbinic wording cannot simply be inserted back into the earlier time (on this see, e.g., Qimron/Strugnell, *Miqṣat,* 111; Sussmann, "History of Halakha," 192-99; cf. [at] n. 12 above). Taking into account this פרש reference, Phil 3:5-6 (cf. Acts 26:5) completely makes sense: it has to do with Paul as he also did not shrink back from seceding for halakhic reasons.

33. On this see, e.g., Bachmann, *Sünder,* esp. 110-11. Cf., e.g., Burchard, "Nicht aus Werken," esp. 406.

34. On these passages and on the thematic recourse to 2:18, 21 that occurs here cf. Bachmann, *Sünder,* esp. 111-18.

35. On this cf. Bachmann, "Rechtfertigung," 30-31 together with n. 158 (and cf. moreover CD 5:5-6 and on this [at] n. 57 below). In this essay, which appeared in 1993, I followed the designation of the lines in the "pirated edition" of 4QMMT published in 1990 (see Bachmann, "Rechtfertigung," 29 n. 149). Unfortunately this results in a slight deviation from the more recently accepted convention of the "Composite Text" (see n. 1 above) — which I now adapt.

36. On this see, e.g., Bachmann, "Rechtfertigung," 6-10 (together with n. 19: Luther, *WA* 30 II, 633.29-30; cf. Jas 2:24). In the September Testament of 1522 it says similarly: "on zu thun der werck des gesetzs, alleyn durch den glawben" (*WA.DB* [Deutsche Bibel] 7, 38). Cf. (at) n. 105 and section 3 below.

37. Grelot, "Oeuvres," 448 : "Notre text est le premier qui fournisse une équivalence

directe à l'expression paulinienne: [*ta*] *érga* [*tou*] *nómou*." Cf., e.g., Bachmann, "Rechtfertigung," 3, 27, 29-30, and Abegg, "Paul," 53, further also Burchard, "Nicht aus Werken," 411 ("only 4QMMT C27 has close contact with ἔργα νόμου"). M. Wolter, "Ethos und Identität in paulinischen Gemeinden," *NTS* 43 (1997), 430-44, here p. 433 n. 16, is unable to produce a single close parallel from Greek literature. The closest seems to be ἔργα ἀρετῆς (e.g., Diogenes Laertius 6.70). The two examples of νόμου (δὲ) ἔργα in a work under the name of Philostratus (Διάλεξις 2; see C. L. Kayser, ed., *Flavii Philostrati Opera* II [Leipzig: Teubner, 1871], 259, 260) offer, measured by Paul's expression, an inverted word order; furthermore, since the context is about what is created or effected (by the φύσις and) by the νόμος, this is a *genitivus subiectivus*, and this is hard to maintain for Paul (on this see Bachmann, "Rechtfertigung," esp. 23-24). Cf. (at) n. 80 below.

38. Dunn, "4QMMT," 150. For the first rendering, besides Qimron/Strugnell, *Miqṣat*, 63, reference is also made here to the (English) edition, for which (in the end) F. García Martínez is responsible (see, however, the following note); for the second, the edition prepared by G. Vermes. For a similar understanding of the expression, see, e.g., Schiffman, "New Halakhic Letter," 67: ". . . legal rulings of (that is, pertaining to) the Torah"; Barrett, *Texte zur Umwelt*, 262; B. W. W. Dombrowski, *An Annotated Translation of Miqṣat Maʿaśeh ha-Tôrâ (4QMMT)* (second ed.; Krakau-Weenzen: privately printed, 1993), 2 ("matters laid down in the law"; cf. pp. 21-22 [n. 7 on p. 2] and 26 [n. 54 on p. 6], further Burchard, "Nicht aus Werken," 411 n. 36: "Conceivably also 'something in matters of Torah?'"); H. Stegemann, "Die Bedeutung der Qumranfunde für das Verständnis Jesu und des frühen Christentums," *BK* 48 (1993), 10-19, here p. 15 ("Commandments of the Torah"); and F. Avemarie, "ἔργον κτλ II," *Theologisches Begriffslexikon zum Neuen Testament*, new ed., vol. 1 (1997), 57-59, here p. 59. Although Abegg, "Paul," 52 — like Dunn — regrets that the translation by Qimron and Strugnell "unfortunately obscures MMT's relationship to Paul's letters" and therefore for 4QMMT C27 is able to speak in favor of "works of the law" (cf. p. 54: "pertinent works of the law"), this serves him exclusively to emphasize the relation to the Pauline expression which is conventionally rendered by "works of the law." Actually Abegg, "Paul," 53, agrees with Qimron and Strugnell as well as with Schiffman: "These translations are accurate enough"; "The works of the law that the Qumran text refers to are obviously typified by the 20 or so religious precepts *(halakhot)* detailed in the body of the text."

39. Dunn, "4QMMT, 150 — with reference among others to the edition of the text by R. Eisenman and M. Wise, to an oral comment from F. García Martínez (see the previous note), and also to M. Abegg (whose rendering, as we also saw in the previous note, it would be better not to take up for this end). Cf. further, e.g., J. Maier, *Die Qumran-Essener. Die Texte vom Toten Meer* (3 vols., UTB 1862-63/1916; Munich/Basel: Reinhardt, 1995-96), 2.375 ("Torah practices [*"Torah-Praktiken"*]").

40. Dunn, "4QMMT," 150. This is of course already a quite weak argument inasmuch as it is necessary to shed light primarily on the *conjunction* of מעשים and תורה.

41. Bachmann, *Sünder*, esp. 93-98; "Rechtfertigung," esp. 15-28.

42. Dunn, "4QMMT," 150 (cf. p. 151 n. 21). Correspondingly also D. Flusser, "Die Gesetzeswerke in Qumran und bei Paulus," in *Geschichte — Tradition — Reflexion. Festschrift für Martin Hengel*, 1.395-403, here pp. 397-99.

43. Paleographic reasons and contextual arguments concur. On this see esp. Grelot, "Oeuvres," 443-45, and Kuhn, "Bedeutung," 202-9 (together with plates 8 and 9). Cf., e.g.,

J. Kampen, "4QMMT and New Testament Studies," in *Reading 4QMMT: New Perspectives on Qumran Law and History* (SBL Symposium Series 2, ed. J. Kampen and M. Bernstein; Atlanta: Scholars, 1996), 122-44, here pp. 138-39 together with n. 40.

44. So among others Dunn, "4QMMT," 150 (with reference also to 1QH 14:9 [formerly 6:9]) — and Burchard, "Nicht aus Werken," 411 (together with) n. 37 (with reference also to CD 20:6-7), who takes note besides of a text form for 1QS 5:23-24 in which it speaks of "his" or "their 'works' *in the Tora*" (see Maier, *Qumran-Essener*, 2.207: 4Q258 [= 4QS^d]). Cf. (at) nn. 70-71, 80 below.

45. When Burchard, "Nicht aus Werken," 411 n. 37, hereby explains, "that *twrh* . . . [is] constructed with a preposition," he may be right (cf. at nn. 55-56 below); this is however doubtful concerning his subsequent remark: "The passages speak no other language than that of 4QMMT." At least in B2 and C27 things are different (on this see what is immediately worked out in detail in the text).

46. On this see Qimron/Strugnell, *Miqṣat*, vii (Strugnell).

47. On this see Qimron/Strugnell, *Miqṣat*, 46, 139. This fact is not noted by Flusser, "Gesetzeswerke," 399-400 (cf. n. 91 below).

48. Dunn, "4QMMT," 150. According to the list in Qimron/Strugnell, *Miqṣat*, 147 (Qimron) showing what the discovered manuscripts provide, this has to do with "seventeen halakhic subjects," for which, partly, "several halakhot are given"; originally, to conclude from the status of preservation of the manuscripts, "a number of further halakhot" must have been mentioned in the document.

49. In C30 according to 4Q399 (= 4QMMT^f) it is expressed, however, more briefly מדברינו (see Qimron/Strugnell, *Miqṣat*, 46, 62-63, 93). Also the בכל אלה of C28 (cf. B1) is probably to be understood as summing up (see p. 62: "may well refer to the laws mentioned in section B").

50. On this see Qimron/Strugnell, *Miqṣat*, 46, 139. P. 139 n. 44: "דבר in the sense 'commandment' is found in the Bible . . . , as in . . . 'the ten commandments'. It is more widespread in the later books of the Bible than in the earlier ones" (cf. Schiffman, "New Halakhic Letter," 65). Cf. further, e.g., Deut 1:1 (cf. n. 6 above).

51. Dunn, "4QMMT," 150; cf. p. 151: "the rulings and [!] practices (works)" and (for C 30) "our works/practices." Moreover, Dunn (p. 150 n. 19) speaks of "ambiguity" in relation to מעשה; the word "can signify 'deed' as prescribed deed (hence 'precept') as well as a deed carried out." Cf. (at) n(n). (57-)59 below.

52. See (at) n. 11 above.

53. Cf. the interpretation of Num 21:16-18 in CD 6:3ff., esp. lines 8-9: "they are those who come in order to dig the well with *mechoqeqot* (statutes), which the *Mechoqeq* (law giver) had established" (Maier, *Qumran-Essener*, 1.16; the *Mechoqeq* is according to line 7 דורש התורה, "an authoritative Torah-giver ["*Torah-Erteiler*"] or ["*bzw.*"] 'a prophet like Moses' (Deut 18:18)" [p. 16 n. 54]).

54. On this see for instance Stegemann, *Essener*, 275-77. Cf., e.g., 1QS 8:15–9:2; CD 19:31–20:17; further, e.g., Gal (3:10 and) 6:13.

55. On this see n. 45 above. Cf. (at) nn. 69, 71 below; cf. further 1 Cor 4:17 (and, e.g., Rom 2:16) with 1 Cor 4:15.

56. Cf. (again) n. 45 above.

57. C25 (e.g.) also leads to this (cf. also C10-11) as well as the pertinent parallel in CD 5:5-6 already mentioned (n. 35 above).

58. For this reason — and because it is uncertain whether the passage in C18-24 actually occurs shortly before C27 (on this see Qimron/Strugnell, Miqṣat, 2, 36-37, 201-2, 205-6: J. Strugnell and H. Stegemann think the fragments in question do *not* belong here) — it is by no means convincing when Dunn, "4QMMT," 150, asserts in support of his understanding of the expression מעשי התורה in C27 in the sense of "deeds of the law": "Indeed, it is noticeable that Qimron and Martinez both translate the same term four lines earlier in MMT . . . as 'their deeds.'"

59. The fact that the word מעשים — here — can have these two distinct meanings, finds a parallel in some respects with the term מצו(ו)ת as it is used in rabbinic Judaism (on this see [H. Strack and] P. Billerbeck, *Kommentar zum Neuen Testament aus Talmud und Midrasch* [4 vols.; Munich: Beck, 1922-28], 3.161-62). Cf. Bachmann, "Rechtfertigung," 30 n. 156, further (at) n. 51 above.

60. Cf. Qimron/Strugnell, Miqṣat, 139: "The Dead Sea sectarians did not employ the term halakhot, which was used by their opponents." But cf. Flusser, "Gesetzeswerke," 400.

61. Qimron/Strugnell, Miqṣat, 139.

62. Qimron/Strugnell, Miqṣat, 139.

63. On this see (at) n. 4 above.

64. Cf. Qimron/Strugnell, "Letter," 406 (n. 5 to p. 401): "One could add many further examples of מעשים and עשה with the meaning 'precepts' and 'perform the precepts.'" Cf. D. Flusser, "Paul's Jewish-Christian Opponents in the Didache," in *Gilgul: Essays on Transformation, Revolution and Permanence in the History of Religion, dedicated to R. J. Zwi Werblowsky* (SHR 50, ed. S. Shaked, D. Shulman, and G. G. Stroumsa; Leiden: Brill, 1987), 71-90, here p. 82 together with nn. 19-20.

65. E. Qimron, *The Hebrew of the Dead Sea Scrolls* (HSS 29; Atlanta: Scholars, 1986), 101 (where in addition the meaning "precepts" is noted for מעשים). It is valid also beyond Exod 18:20 (e.g., Exod 5:4; 23:16): "in the Greek Bible the Hebrew מעשה is often translated in the plural" (Flusser, "Gesetzeswerke," 396). Cf. (at) nn. 75, 104 below.

66. On this see e.g. Qimron/Strugnell, Miqṣat, 133 (together with) n. 24.

67. Billerbeck, *Kommentar*, 1.345. On this see Bachmann, "Rechtfertigung," 30 together with n. 156; Qimron/Strugnell, Miqṣat, 133 n. 24 (references, bibliography). Cf. Flusser, "Gesetzeswerke," 396.

68. Qimron/Strugnell, Miqṣat, 139 (together with n. 42: bibliography). Cf. Qimron/Strugnell, "Letter," 401 together with n. 5, and Bachmann, "Rechtfertigung," 30 n. 156, further, e.g., D. Flusser, "Die jüdische und griechische Bildung des Paulus," in *Paulus: Zeuge Jesu und Völkerapostel* (ed. E. Schillebeeckx, D. Flusser, and E. Lessing; Freiburg: Herder, 1982), 151-81, here p. 166 (cf. [however at] n. 91 below); Schiffman, "New Halakhic Letter," 65; Kuhn, "Bedeutung," 210.

69. Without question this is the case in CD 2:14-15, as not least of all the parallel expression מצות אל from line 18 makes evident (cf. Bachmann, "Rechtfertigung," 18 n. 83). Also CD 1:1 belongs here, further possibly 1QS 4:4 as well as CD 13:7-8 (on this see [at] n. 73 below). Cf. also 1QH 13:36 (formerly 5:36). Similarly, e.g., 1QS 10:17 ("his 'works'"); 1QM 13:1 ("'works' of his truth").

70. So, e.g., מצות אל (see the previous note) and רצון אל (see, e.g., 1QS 9:13; cf.

Qimron/Strugnell, *Miqṣat*, 133 together with n. 24). Cf. further the expression מעשי הצדקה, already mentioned at n. 44 above (on this syntagma, which could quite perfectly mean the divine commands, see Bachmann, "Rechtfertigung," 28 n. 147).

71. So, e.g., מדרש התורה (e.g., CD 20:6; cf. n. 44 above), פרוש התורה (CD 4:6, 8; 6:14 [cf. (at) n. 28 above]; 13:6; cf. 14:18 [see n. 104 below]) and עצת התורה (e.g., 1QS 9:9; cf. with it, e.g., 1QS 8:1 ["council of fellowship"] and on this juxtaposition [at] nn. 53-55 above). Cf. also the textual variant to 1QS 5:1 in 4Q258, namely, "men of the Torah" (Maier, *Qumran-Essener*, 2.206).

72. On this see, e.g., nn. 69-71 above.

73. Because here with פרוש התורה (on this expression cf. the references adduced in n. 71 above) without question the content of Torah is in view, as it is mediated through a "guard" (מבקר) by means of instruction (lines 5-6), and because lines 7ff. also have to do with the "guard" who gives instruction, this suggests that particular halakhot are to be understood by such "'works' of God," which are to be studied (but cf., e.g., [1QH 13:36 and] 1QM 10:8). Cf. (at) n. 69 above.

74. In view of Rom 2:15 one perhaps ought not to say that "the phrase in Paul is always anarthrous" (Dunn, "4QMMT," 151 n. 21). Cf. Kampen, "4QMMT," 138-39 together with nn. 38, 43.

75. Similarly in Paul δικαιοσύνη θεοῦ (e.g., Rom 1:17) and ἡ δικαιοσύνη τοῦ θεοῦ (Rom 10:3) stand together.

76. On this see (at) n. 65 above.

77. Abegg, "Paul," 53 n. *, says with regard to the Septuagint (concordance): "The most common Greek word for *ma'ase* is *ergon*. The Greek word *nomos* most commonly translates *torah*." For this reason there could exist only "little doubt, that the Greek equivalent of *ma'ase ha-torah* is likely *ergon nomou*" (p. 53). With respect to 4QMMT C27, Burchard, "Nicht aus Werken," 411 n. 36, places the emphasis differently: "what in Greek, with an expression that might include (τὰ) ἔργα (τοῦ) νόμου, would hardly be translated correctly" (cf. [at] n. 80 below).

78. Billerbeck, *Kommentar*, 3.160 (cf. Bachmann, "Rechtfertigung," 27 together with n. 138, further, the following note).

79. So again in the 1976 British Bible Society translation, and indeed, according to Abegg, "Paul," 53, "consistently." Correspondingly it is also the case in a reprint of the translation of F. Delitzsch (first edition, 1877) published in London (n.d.) by the Trinitarian Bible Society, where, however, the article, which also Billerbeck did not use (see the previous note), is not present only in Rom 3:28.

80. So, however, the argument of Wolter, "Ethos," 432-33 together with n. 16 (who refers here to Philo, *Praem.* 82-83; Josephus, *Ag. Ap.* 2:291-92): "Thus in the end the understanding . . . presented again by M. Bachmann proves to be . . . not appropriate." Cf. (n. 37 above and) Burchard, "Nicht aus Werken," 410 n. 32 (cf. n. 77 above), who, however, still holds that in Rom 2:15 ἔργον could mean "task, function," and who moreover asks (p. 411 [together with] n. 39) whether references to "work" in the "Qumran writings," namely such references from 1QS (cf. [at] n. 44 above), "have not after all contributed to establish works of the law as a fixed expression."

81. On this cf. Bachmann, "Rechtfertigung," 16-18, 27-28 (and the criticism related to it by Burchard, "Nicht aus Werken," 410 n. 32).

82. On this see for instance H. Hübner, "νόμος," in *Exegetisches Wörterbuch zum Neuen Testament* 2 (1981), 1158-72 (cf. ET *EDNT* 2:471-77), here 1162-63.

83. On this see (at) n(n). (62-)68 above.

84. E. Lohmeyer, "Gesetzeswerke," in *Probleme paulinischer Theologie* (Stuttgart: Kohlhammer, 1955), 31-74 (orig. 1929), here pp. 39-40. Cf. now P. W. Ensor, *Jesus and His "Works": The Johannine Sayings in Historical Perspective* (WUNT 2.85; Tübingen: Mohr, 1996), 279-81.

85. See esp. Exod 18:20; 36:1, 3; Num 3:7, 8; 8:11; 1(3) Esdr 7:9; Tob 3:2 (cf. vv. 4-5); Pss 105(106):35, 39 (cf. v. 13); 110(111):7; Prov 16:9; Wis 9:9; Sir 42:15 (cf. vv. 21-22); Mic 6:16; Jer 31(48):10; Bar 2:9 (cf. vv. 10, 12); Dan 3:27; 1 Macc 2:51 (cf. vv. 53, 55, 58, 65, 67, 68 [and with these also v. 52: Gal 1:14; 3:5-6; Rom 4:2-3, 9]). Cf. Bachmann, "Rechtfertigung," 27-28 together with n. 143.

86. In *4 Ezra* 7:24 the formulation *opera eius* (i.e., God's) constitutes a parallel to *lex eius* (and to *sponsiones eius, legitima eius*), and in *1 En.* 5:1-4 the ἐντολαί of God (v. 4) stand in a relationship to God's ἔργα (v. 1). The conflict of νόμος κυρίου and ἔργα Βελιάρ in *T. Levi* 19:1 (cf. the ἔργα references in *T. Naph.* 2:10; *T. Benj.* 5:3) leads to a similar equation of νόμος and ἔργα (cf. *T. Iss.* 5:1, 3 and the following note). As the "works of Beliar" here and in *T. Benj.* 6:7 (cf. 7:1) confront the human being as something objective (and capable of being chosen) (cf. Lohmeyer, "Gesetzeswerke," [39-]40), it is the case evidently also in *4 Bar.* 8:2 (cf. v. 3) with "Babylon's works" and in *1 En.* 10:8 with the works taught by Azael (cf. 9:6; 13:2). As far as the passage in *2 Bar.* 57:2 is concerned, which is frequently invoked for comparison, one may say: "also here the expression 'work' is merely a variant of the concept commandment" (Lohmeyer, "Gesetzeswerke," 40; cf. Bachmann, "Rechtfertigung," 27 together with n. 142; Burchard, "Nicht aus Werken," 410-11 together with n. 34) — and besides reference should be made among other passages to CD 14:18 (on this see [at] n. 104 below). Cf. moreover *T. Dan* 6:9; *Pss. Sol.* 18:8 (cf. vv. 4, 10); *Aristeas* 18:4; 272:3, further Josephus, *Ant.* 20:42, 43, 46 (on this see Bachmann, *Sünder*, 98, and cf. Josephus, *J.W.* 5:401).

87. In John 6:28 τὰ ἔργα τοῦ θεοῦ (on this cf. [at] nn. 69-70) are (as similarly also in 9:4) characterized as something that has to be done (ἐργάζεσθαι) (on this see [at] nn. 64-66 above and at n. 97 below), and therefore also the same idea should be thought of with the singular, which appears immediately in 6:29 (cf. 12:[49-]50), especially because then in the following context the thought is about God's will (see 6:40; cf. 6:38-39), about instruction from God (see 6:45) (cf. the references to ἔργον in 4:34; 5:36; 9:4; 17:4). In Rev 2:26 the "one who conquers" is described also as ὁ τηρῶν ἄχρι τέλους τὰ ἔργα μου. Concerning this expression one must conclude already on the basis of the further uses of τηρεῖν in Revelation (see esp. 1:3; 3:8, 10; 12:17; 14:12; 22:7, 9) that what is meant is observing precepts (cf. Avemarie, "ἔργον," 59) — hardly giving attention to the activity of the earthly Jesus or to his salvific works for the community (against M. Karrer, *Die Johannesoffenbarung als Brief. Studien zu ihrem literarischen, historischen und theologischen Ort* [FRLANT 140; Göttingen: Vandenhoeck & Ruprecht, 1986], 106 [together with] n. 77 [who however claims here correctly that in the (seeming) parallels from 2:2 to 22:12 we have always to do with "works" not of a single person] and pp. 199-200). Because the writing to the community in Thyatira attacks the false teaching and prophecy of "Jezebel" (2:20, 24), the connection with the (prophetically mediated) instructions of Jesus (cf. again 1:3; 3:8; 22:7, 9, further 22:14 variant reading) makes especially good sense (and it is not improbable that the expression τὰ ἔργα

αὐτῆς [i.e., Jezebel's] of 2:22 is to be understood as a concept that is the opposite of Jesus' [prophetic] instructions [cf. the previous note] and refers to "the false immorality that the prophetess teaches" [so T. Zahn, *Die Offenbarung des Johannes* (2 vols., KNT 18; Leipzig/Erlangen: Deichertsche Verlagsbuchhandlung Dr. Werner Scholl, 1924-26), 1.294]). Cf. Bachmann, "Rechtfertigung," 16-17 (together with n. 80 [and n. 82]: "Works of the Lord [or Christ]" [1 Cor 15:58; 16:10 (ἐργάζεσθαι); Phil 2:30]; εἰς τὸ ἔργον [Acts 13:2; 14:26; 15:38] with reference to the "task of the mission" [R. Heiligenthal, "ἔργον," *Exegetisches Wörterbuch zum Neuen Testament* 2 (1981), 123-27 (cf. ET *EDNT* 2:49-51), here 124]; Jas 1:25).

88. Lohmeyer, "Gesetzeswerke," esp. 38-41, 46, 64, 66-68, 70-71 (cf., however, p. 67 [and *passim*]: "duty [*Dienst*] of the law"). Cf. E. Lohmeyer, *Grundlagen paulinischer Theologie* (BHT 1; Tübingen: Mohr, 1929), esp. 8-12.

89. First in Flusser, "Paul's Jewish-Christian Opponents," 82 n. 20 (cf. [at] n. 91 below). Cf. n. 35 above.

90. The "original *(originelle)* interpretation of ἔργα νόμου as commandments of the law" (Burchard, "Nicht aus Werken," 410 n. 32) is in part more or less cautiously rejected (see n. 80 above; cf. further S. Meiner, *Die Heimholung des Ketzers. Studien zur jüdischen Auseinandersetzung mit Paulus* [WUNT 2.87; Tübingen: Mohr, 1996], 225-26 together with n. 77 [cf., however, also n. 104 below]), in part reported as "of interest" (so [e.g.] by R. Heiligenthal in a review of Bachmann, *Sünder, TLZ* 118 [1993], 132-34, here p. 134), in part noted favorably (so in G. Strecker, *Theologie des Neuen Testaments*, revised, enlarged, and ed. by F. W. Horn [Berlin/New York: de Gruyter, 1996], 152 n. 50).

91. Flusser, "Jüdische und griechische Bildung," 166 (see nn. 64, 68, 89 above). To be sure, in the recent publication of this outstanding scholar (Flusser, "Gesetzeswerke") that touches this subject, he says: "in Judaism the works and the commandments are closely related" (p. 401) and "for Paul . . . the difference between these two terms cannot be demonstrated" (p. 400); but Flusser, who more recently of course also takes 4QMMT C27 into consideration (see pp. 399-400), in the meantime equates "works of the law" with "practice of the law" (pp. 399-400; cf. the immediately following [at] n. 92), and he assumes that Paul could have assessed these "works" — in distinction from the "commandments" — negatively (see pp. 402-3), not least for the reason that, according to Jewish use of language, "the commandments come from God and the works from human beings" (p. 401). However, 4QMMT is referred to in these considerations only quite superficially (thus without mentioning the relevant parallels in B1, B2, and C30), and as far as Paul is concerned, things are not much better (see pp. 402-3: Rom 2:15 as an exception; contexts such as Rom 3:20-22; Gal 2:15-21; 3:5-14 are ignored).

92. On this see Bachmann, "Rechtfertigung," 5-15 (esp. p. 5 [together with n. 14], and pp. 14-15 [in theological and exegetical literature "works of the law," where they are understood as action, strangely are equated, among other possibilities, with: our works, good works, evil works, action according to the Torah, transgression of the Torah!]). Cf. Burchard, "Nicht aus Werken," 410 (together with n. 32), further the previous note as well as (at) n. 98 below.

93. On this see (at) nn. 44-45, 55-56 above.

94. With respect to the coexistence there can be no doubt in that in the passages that are named — and only in these — either of the two expressions "by works (of the law)" (Rom 3:20; 4:2; 9:12, 32; 11:6; Gal 2:16; 3:2, 5, 10) and "apart from works (of the law)" (Rom 3:28; 4:6) are used. Only the singular expression of Rom 2:15 is used without a preposition.

95. Lohmeyer, "Gesetzeswerke," 34, 64, 68, 71, already referred to this emphatically (see Bachmann, "Rechtfertigung," 19 together with n. 92). Where the genitive νόμου is missing, this is most especially striking (on this see p. 19 n. 92). Therefore and in view of the use of language in 4QMMT and the parallels to this mode of expression, which are found in Paul, the assumption of Burchard, "Nicht aus Werken," 411 n. 37, seems to me to be tricky: "an indication of the possessive very probably is missing for ἔργα νόμου on account of the brevity," even more so the continuing remark: "if always like that in Paul, then perhaps also in its subsequent influence." Cf. (n. 55 above and) n. 105 below.

96. On this see, as far as 4QMMT is concerned, (at) nn. 44-45, 56-59 and (at) nn. 64-66 above and, for Paul, Bachmann, "Rechtfertigung," 19-20 (with further comparative references). Cf. n. 105 below.

97. On this see on the one hand (at) nn. 64-66, 87 above, on the other, e.g., Bachmann, "Rechtfertigung," 27 n. 136 and p. 31 (with further comparative references). Cf., however, Flusser, "Gesetzeswerke," 397.

98. On this see on the one hand (at) n. 61 above, on the other, e.g., Bachmann, "Rechtfertigung," 22-23. In view of the parallels, the genitive should be called a genitive of domain (i.e., a *genitivus partitivus*) (see pp. 23-24 together with n. 121, further Bachmann, *Sünder*, 100 n. 394). In the case of an inverted order it is a genitive of content, as with (ὁ) νόμος (τῶν) ἔργων (see Rom 3:27; cf. Eph 2:15 [and on this see at n. 104 below]). Cf. (at) n. 92 above.

99. On this see esp. Schiffman, "New Halakhic Letter," 65-66; Qimron/Strugnell, *Miqṣat*, 145-47 (Qimron; cf. pp. 198-99 [Sussmann]); Grelot, "Oeuvres," 447-48 — and cf. (at) nn. 12, 32, 48 above.

100. Cf. (at) nn. 2, 27-32 above. Provided one takes into consideration that the expression ἔργα νόμου in Paul, as Gal 3:10 especially shows (on this see [at] n. 103 below, further Bachmann, *Sünder*, 91-94), is by no means related exclusively to such prominent halakhic questions and does not mean the performance of halakhot, then one can only agree with Dunn, "4QMMT," 151, when he (continuing his famous thesis, encountered, however, already decades earlier in similar form [on this see, e.g., Bachmann, *Sünder*, 11 together with n. 75]) names as "principal point of parallel . . . that מעשי התורה and ἔργα νόμου both seem to refer to 'works of the law' understood as defining a boundary" (cf. Burchard, "Nicht aus Werken," [410 together with n. 33 and] 413-14 together with n. 49, further [at] n. 104 below).

101. On the following points (ii.a-h) see Bachmann, "Rechtfertigung," 20 (a), 22-24 (b), 21 (c), 24-26 (together with n. 124) (d), 14-15 (together with n. 66: C. H. Cosgrove, "Justification in Paul: A Linguistic and Theological Reflection," *JBL* 106 [1987], 653-70, here pp. 657-60, esp. 659-60) (g), 26-27 (h); *Sünder*, 93-95 (together with nn. 357, 359), 141-43 (e), 119-22 (f).

102. R. Heiligenthal, *Werke als Zeichen. Untersuchungen zur Bedeutung der menschlichen Taten im Frühjudentum, Neuen Testament und Frühchristentum* (WUNT 2.9; Tübingen: Mohr, 1983), 282. Cf. Strecker, *Theologie*, 152 (also on Rom 2:26). Cf. (however) n. 91 above.

103. Cf. n. 2 above (the theme of curse in 4QMMT) and (at) n. 54 above, also n. 100.

104. Cf. (at) n. 98 above and on the expressions adduced on the one hand CD 14:18 (פרוש המשפטים [cf. n. 71 above]) and on the other 2 *Bar.* 57:2 (cf. n. 86 above). These parallels, the contacts with the rabbinic interpretation of Exod 18:20 (on this see again [at] nn. 62-66 above), the reference to a regulation such as the prescript for circumcision (on this see

151

[at] n. 100 above), and the *plural* ἔργα νόμου — to which the law as a unity can stand over against (on this cf. the expression ὁ . . . πᾶς νόμος in Gal 5:14 after the expression ὅλος ὁ νόμος in Gal 5:3, which puts the adjective predicatively before article and noun [and cf. on this e.g. Bachmann, *Sünder*, 120 nn. 101-2]) — speak in favor of the thesis that with ἔργα νόμου Paul had in view primarily individual ceremonial commandments. One could contrast this area of the Torah with τὰ βαρύτερα τοῦ νόμου as named in Matt 23:23 — and these again could be set in opposition to τὰ βραχέα τῶν κριμάτων (cf. Matt 5:19), mentioned in Exod 18:22 (!). Cf. (at) n. 100 above.

105. Of course the opposition between "Christ" and "law" marked in Gal 2:21b can, in view of the other formulations and with decreasing familiarity with the Hebrew vocabulary behind ἔργα (νόμου), easily and quickly fade in importance and give space for the (mis)understanding that Paul wanted to contrast the attitude of believing with that of human performent(s) (cf. J. A. Fitzmyer, *Paul and His Theology: A Brief Sketch* [second ed.; Englewood Cliffs: Prentice Hall, 1989], 81). This happens to some extent already in Eph 2:8-9 — and it has often happened in the history of the church (cf. [at] n. 36 above) — and obviously Jas 2:14-26 takes its starting point from and goes against such a post-Pauline doctrine of grace (on this cf. Bachmann, "Rechtfertigung," 18-19). Incidentally in both passages ἔργα lacks the genitive νόμου, and whereas Eph 2:10 speaks right away about "*good* works," James 2:18 has "*my* works," indeed quite in contrast to Paul (on this see, e.g., [at] nn. 95-96 above).

106. On this see Gal 2:16 as well as, recently, Burchard, "Nicht aus Werken," esp. 408-10.

107. Cf., e.g., Rom 2:13, further, for instance, Flusser, "Jüdische und griechische Bildung," 166, and Bachmann, "Rechtfertigung," 31-32.

108. Cf. (at) nn. 36, 105 above, further Bachmann, "Rechtfertigung," esp. 1-10, 32-33.

109. Abegg, "Paul," 55 (cf. p. 53: "For the first time we can really understand what Paul is writing about"). Cf. Dunn, "4QMMT," 147.

Notes to Chapter 3

1. On what precedes and follows see, e.g., J. Lambrecht, 94-104; S. Westerholm, 143-44; and M. Bachmann 1992, 2-11 (cf. 91-101); 1993, esp. 1-5, 11-15.

2. On what precedes and follows see M. Bachmann 1992, 3-7 (with the objection of J. Neusner, 49-50: Sanders "brings to the Rabbinic sources the issues of Pauline scholarship and Paul" and "does not bring to the fore what Rabbinic sources themselves wish to take as their principal theme"), and for the first question that is to be asked immediately also Westerholm, esp. 143-50. Concerning the letter 4QMMT (now easily available in R. Eisenman and M. Wise, 1993, 193-201, 203-5) cf. M. Bachmann, 1993, 29-31 (together with n. 158).

3. This interpretation of the mosaic, defended especially by H.-P. Stähli (1985 and 1988), is, however, not undisputed (on this see the surveys of the history of interpretation by G. Stemberger, 182-87 [where he uses the following categories: 1. decoration, 2. depiction of the calendar, 3. the idea of the Messiah, 4. heterodox Judaism], 208-20, and by P. Prigent, [112-22 and] 165-73). There is no getting around, however, connotations that it has to do with the order of the world that stands under the universal God of the Jews (on this see, e.g., G. Stemberger, 209, 212; P. Prigent, 172). The special prominence of the theme of the Torah in

early Judaism speaks for the solution advocated here. At the same time the history of both the individual motifs and the combination of motifs that are to be outlined in what follows (literarily and iconographically) and the specific overall concept of the floor of Beth-Alpha, which likewise will be succinctly characterized, speak for the solution advocated here.

4. On Susiya see L. I. Levine, 123-28 (S. Gutman, Z. Yeivin, and E. Netzer), and G. Stemberger, 179: cf. pp. 178-80 concerning Japhia (zodiac or the twelve tribes), Kafr Bar'am (stone frieze [third century] with the zodiac [?]) and 'En-Gedi (zodiac inscription).

5. This can be observed especially in H.-P. Stähli (1985, 85-93; 1988, 61-68) — and in P. Prigent, (112-22, 167-71).

6. According to T. Veijola, (esp.) 152-54, the account in Gen 22:1-19, by the expression, among others, "the place which God showed him" (vv. 2, 3, 9) and by the term burnt offering (vv. 2, 3, 6, 7, 8, 13), is brought into line "consequently . . . with Jerusalem," in fact, "from the beginning on it was conceived of as a cult aetiology for Jerusalem" (p. 154).

7. To be sure, however, within the frame of Jewish interpretive traditions (on this see H. D. Betz, 157 together with n. 38 [and n. 40], and H.-G. von Mutius [with the references to literature there]). The rendering that follows in the text is according to W. Bauer, 1789-80.

8. So especially G. Klein, 209-10 (citation: p. 210), and H. Hübner, 28-29.

9. I will shortly seek to expound in more detail against the background of the history of research the solution that is advocated here (see chapter 4 of this volume), for which I have recently given succinct evidence against other interpretations (M. Bachmann, 1992, 148-49 together with n. 265), with reference to E. Bammel, 317-18 (together with nn. 3, 5).

10. It is (in view of this) hardly by chance that what is thematic in the three scenes in the history of art can be related to Christ not only covertly but clearly: The sacrifice of Isaac, the "only" son (Gen 22:2; cf. Rom 8:32), becomes a figure for the death of Jesus (on this see H.-P. Stähli, 1988, 65 together with n. 86); also early on Christ bears characteristics of the sun, the "sun of righteousness" (Mal 3:20 [or 4:2]; cf., e.g., 2 Cor 3:18; Rev 1:16; 21:23; 22:16), and this corresponds to the fact that already in the third century he is portrayed after the model of the Sol Invictus or of the Roman ruler as the Cosmocrator (cf. also the Pantocrator motif) quite similar to Ḥammath (and Beth-Alpha) (on this see, e.g., L. I. Levine, 66 [M. Dothan], further P. Prigent, 172); finally, as is well known, the cross quite quickly finds its place in the apse or on the altar.

11. Concerning the fruit-bearing tree in the Torah shrine scene depicted at Beth-Alpha, the focus on Aaron in the Sepphoris mosaic raises some doubt as to whether my reference to Sir 24:14, 19 (cf. *Pss. Sol.* 14:1-4) was really helpful. It seems more likely that this is a way of symbolizing "Aaron's rod" (Num 17:8; cf. Heb 9:4).

Notes to Chapter 4

1. Cf., e.g., A. Klöpper, "Zwei merkwürdige Aeusserungen des Apostels Paulus über die Genesis des Messaischen *(sic)* Gesetzes," *ZWT* 13 (1870), 78-115, here p. 97 (cf. p. 80, where it says on 3:19-20: "locus vexatissimus" [so also O. Zöckler, *Die Briefe an die Thessalonicher und der Galaterbrief* (Kurzgefaßter Kommentar zu den heiligen Schriften Alten und Neuen Testaments B,3, 1-126; second ed.; Munich: Beck, 1894), 104]), W. Bousset, *Der Brief an die Galater* (Schriften des Neuen Testaments 2, 31-74; third ed.; Göttingen: Vandenhoeck &

Ruprecht, 1917), 56, A. Stegmann, "Ὁ δὲ μεσίτης ἑνὸς οὐκ ἔστιν," *BZ* 22 (1934), 30-42, here p. 30, [K.] Bornhäuser, "Der 'Mittler'. Versuch einer Erklärung von Gal. 3,19.20," *NKZ* 39 (1928), 21-24, here p. 21, and A. Vanhoye, "Un médiateur des anges en Ga 3,19-20," *Bib* 59 (1978), 403-11, here p. 403, further (at) n. 4 below.

2. Cf., e.g., H. Schlier, *Der Brief an die Galater* (KEK 7; twelfth ed.; Göttingen: Vandenhoeck & Ruprecht, 1962), 161, and H. D. Betz, *Der Galaterbrief. Ein Kommentar zum Brief des Apostels Paulus an die Gemeinden in Galatien* (Hermeneia; Munich: Kaiser, 1988 [orig. (English): 1979]), 305. R. Kübel, *Bibelkunde. Erklärung der wichtigsten Abschnitte der h. Schrift und Einleitung in die biblischen Bücher 2: Das Neue Testament* (sixth ed.; Stuttgart: J. F. Steinkopf, 1896), 308, even speaks about it thus: "V. 20 . . . is considered the most difficult verse in the New Testament" (cf. O. Fritsch, "Galater 3,20," *Wissenschaftliche Beilage zum Jahresbericht der Margarethenschule zu Berlin* [Berlin: R. Gaertners Verlagsbuchhandlung H. Heyfelder, 1895], 5, and W. Siebert, "Exegetisch-theologische Studie über Gal 3,20 und 4,4," *NKZ* 15 [1904], 699-733, here p. 711).

3. T. D. Callan, "The Law and the Mediator: Ga 3:19b-20" (Ph.D. diss.; Yale University, 1976, under N. A. Dahl).

4. T. [D.] Callan, "Pauline Midrash: The Exegetical Background of Gal 3:19b," *JBL* 99 (1980), 549-67, here p. 549. Cf. (at) n. 1 above.

5. [G. C. F.] Lücke, "Noch ein Versuch über Galat. 3,20., mit besonderer Rücksicht auf die Auslegungen dieser Stelle von Dr. *Winer*, Dr. *Schleiermacher* und Prof. *Schmieder*," *TSK* 1 (1828), 83-109, here p. 83.

6. *Martin Luther: Werke: Kritische Gesamtausgabe* ("Weimarer Ausgabe," hereinafter *WA*) 2, (436-)451-618. Cf. the translation: J. Mann, *Martin Luther, Kommentar zum Galaterbrief 1519* (Calwer Luther-Ausgabe, ed. W. Metzger, 10; Munich/Hamburg: Siebenstern Taschenbuch Verlag, 1968).

7. Cf. concerning Gal 3:(19-)20 in the Short Commentary, in later editions of this work and in the exposition of 1531/35 (see *WA* 40 I II) (*WA* 2, [522-24,] 524; 40 I, [473-501,] 501-6), K. Wieseler, *Commentar über den Brief Pauli an die Galater. Mit besonderer Rücksicht auf die Lehre und Geschichte des Apostels* (Göttingen: Dieterich, 1859), 292-93 (together with 292 n. 1), Mann, *Kommentar*, 149-50 (together with n. 72), and J. Rohde, *Der Brief des Paulus an die Galater* (THK 9; Berlin: de Gruyter, 1989), 157 n. 21.

8. *WA* 2, 524. [*Luther's Works*, vol. 27, *Lectures on Galatians 1519* (St. Louis: Concordia, 1964), 272: "If anything still lies hidden more deeply, let others look for it; I reef my sails."] Cf. at n. 30 below.

9. Wieseler, *Commentar*, 288. Cf. Callan, "The Law," v: "this infamously enigmatic passage."

10. On this see F. Sieffert, *Der Brief an die Galater* (KEK 7; ninth ed., from the sixth edition newly revised; Göttingen: Vandenhoeck & Ruprecht, 1899), 210 n. *, Schlier, *Galater*, twelfth ed., 161 n. 2, and Betz, *Galaterbrief,* 305 n. 70.

11. Schlier, *Galater*, twelfth ed., 161 n. 2.

12. Lücke, "Noch ein Versuch," 83.

13. So Sieffert, *Galater*, ninth ed., 210 n. * (cf., e.g., Fritsch, "Galater 3,20," 5 [together with nn. 9-10]).

14. *Der Brief des Paulus an die Galater* (THK 9; reprint of the second ed.; Berlin: de Gruyter, 1964), 82.

15. Sieffert, *Galater,* ninth ed., 210 (cf. Zöckler, *Briefe,* 104: a "deluge of explanations," which incidentally according to Zöckler "results primarily from the diverging opinions with respect to the μεσίτης"). Cf. C. A. T. Keilius (i.e., Keil), "Proponitur exemplum iudicii de diversis singulorum scripturae sacrae locorum interpretationibus ferendi, examinandis variis interpretum de loco Gal. III,20. sententiis," *Opuscula academica ad N.T. interpretationem grammatico-historicam et theologiae christianae origines pertinentia,* ed. I. D. Goldhorn (Leipzig: I. A. Barth, 1821), 211-317 (orig.: 1809-12 [see p. 211 note of the editor; cf., however, Wieseler, *Commentar,* 288: 1800-1813]), 213: *non videbatur nobis vllus alius locus in medium proferri posse, qui maiori interpretationis diversitati obnoxius fuisset, quam nobilissimus ille epist. ad Gal. III,20. locus.*

16. Concerning this position cf. for example M. Frank, "Wörter, Wörter, Wörter. Eine Abrechnung mit dem Poststrukturalismus," *Die Zeit,* no. 38, September 11, 1992, 74-75.

17. To be mentioned above all: C. F. Bonitz, *Plurimorum de loco Pauli Gal. III.20. sententiae examinatae, novaque eius interpretatio tentata: Commentatio historico-exegetica* (Leipzig: Rabenhorst, 1800); idem, *Spicilegium observationum ad locum Pauli nobilissimum Gal III,20* (Leipzig: Rabenhorst, 1802); C. T. Anton, "explicatio loci Gal. III,20. critica, historica et exegetica" (second ed.; diss., University of Wittenberg, 1800), in *Sylloge Commentationvm Theologicarvm* 5 (ed. D. I. Pott; Helmstedt: Fleckeisen, 1804), 141-274; Keil, *"exemplum"*; G. H. F. Weigand, (*'ΕΝΟΣ: In nobilissimo Pauli ad Gal. III.20 effato, Haud Genitivo sed Nominativo casu esse positum, Examinatis aliorum CCXXXXIII Interpretum explicationibus* (Erfurt: J. C. Müller, 1821); H. E. Schmieder, "Nova interpretatio loci Paulini Galat. III.19-20," in *Memoriam anniversariam inauguratae ante hos CCLXXXIII. annos Scholae Provincialis Portensis* (Naumburg: C. A. Klappenbach, 1826), esp. 1-3; G. B. Winer, *Pauli ad Galatas epistola* (third ed.; Leipzig: A. P. Reclam, 1829), 163-76 (= Excursus III. In locum cap. 3 v. 20); Wieseler, *Commentar,* esp. 292-304; G. A. Fricke, *Das exegetische Problem im Briefe Pauli an die Galater C. 3,20 auf Grund von 3,15-25 geprüft* (Leipzig: A. Edelmann, 1880), esp. 3-8; Zöckler, *Briefe,* 102-5; Sieffert, *Galater,* ninth ed., 210-18 (more clearly: idem, *Kritisch exegetisches Handbuch über den Brief an die Galater* [KEK 7; seventh ed.; Göttingen: Vandenhoeck & Ruprecht, 1886], esp. 210-23); Fritsch, "Galater 3,20," esp. 5-8, 24-28; Siebert, "Exegetisch-theologische Studie," esp. 700-711; Callan, "The Law," esp. 1-30 (on the latter survey of the literature cf. below [at] n. 52). Strongly related to the history of interpretation are also J. Schulthess, *Engelwelt, Engelgesetz und Engeldienst, philologisch und litterarisch erörtert und auf die evangelische Gnade und Wahrheit zurückgeführt* (Zurich: Schulthess'sche Buchhandlung [F. Schulthess, S. Höhr], 1833), and F. W. Culmann, *Noch ein Wort zum Verständnis der Worte Gal. 3:20* (Strassburg: C. F. Schmidt, 1864); this is less explicitly the case in I. A. Noesseltus (i.e., Noesselt), "Prolusio in locum Paulli Apost. Gal. III,20," *Exercitationes ad sacrarum scripturarum interpretationem* (Halle: Curtian, 1803), 143-68 (see, however, p. 146 n. a [bibliography]).

18. "Der Mittler und das Gesetz: Das Gesetz und der eine Gott. Eine Untersuchung von Gal 3,19f.," *Christus und das Gesetz. Die Bedeutung des Gesetzes des Alten Testaments nach Paulus und sein Glauben an Christus* (Leiden: Brill, 1969), 73-111 (orig. [more shortly]: 1966) (cf. idem, *Der Brief des Paulus an die Galater* [Berlin/Hamburg: Lutherisches Verlagshaus, 1968], 147-55; in the Swedish and likewise in the English version of the commentary [1958 and 1961] Bring still advocated another view than the one from 1966 [on this see Bring, "Mittler," 73 n. 2]).

19. Bring, "Mittler," 87. Cf. p. 86: "The fact that Moses was not the mediator of one can

mean that he was a mediator — not of one but — *of many*, thus not only Israel's mediator but the mediator also of the Gentiles."

20. "Galater iii.20: Die Universalität des Heils," *NTS* 13 (1966-67), 258-70.

21. Mauser, "Galater iii.20," 270. (On ἑνός in 3:16 see p. 269 n. 1 [on this cf. (at) nn. 158 and 168 below].)

22. On this see Bring, "Mittler," 91-93 (see idem, *Galater*, 149), and Mauser, "Galater iii.20," 268-69. Cf. (at) nn. 92-94, 195-96 below.

23. On this see Bring, "Mittler," 91-94 (cf. idem, *Galater*, 150-53).

24. On this see Mauser, "Galater iii.20," 268-69 (cf. p. 265).

25. "Exegetisch-theologische Studie," 711-33, esp. 720-29.

26. Siebert, "Exegetisch-theologische Studie," 724 and *passim*.

27. Siebert, "Exegetisch-theologische Studie," 729. It should be added here that one "partially saw both natures of Christ, the divine and the human, indicated in the passage" (Zöckler, *Briefe*, 104 [bibliographical references]).

28. On the textual tradition see Lücke, "Noch ein Versuch," 105-9, and Sieffert, *Galater*, ninth ed., 209(-210) n. ** ("The witnesses speak unanimously for authenticity").

29. On this see Lücke, "Noch ein Versuch," 101-9. According to him 3:20a would be inserted, taking 3:19 and 3:20b into consideration, in view of 3:21 (see pp. 103-4). On predecessors and successors of Lücke in accepting such an interpolation see Fritsch, "Galater 3,20," 7, Sieffert, *Galater*, ninth ed., 209(-210) n. **, and Siebert, "Exegetisch-theologische Studie," 699 (cf. Callan, "The Law," 23-24 together with n. 42). E. de Witt Burton (*A Critical and Exegetical Commentary on the Epistle to the Galatians* [ICC; Edinburgh: T&T Clark, 1921], 192) also considers the possibility of the introduction of a gloss.

30. On this see (at) n. 8 above.

31. Cf., e.g., K. H. Sack, "Versuch einer Erklärung von Gal. 3,20," *Tübinger Zeitschrift für Theologie* 1831/issue 1, 106-11, and Bornhäuser, "Mittler" (see n. 1 above), further Lücke, "Noch ein Versuch" — who moreover says expressly (p. 84): "hardly any [interpretation] surfaces still with any special confidence, indeed even the most scholarly and most thorough is very content to be only supposition and at best to have discovered what is most probable." Cf. n. 168 below (Steudel), further the following note.

32. Callan, "The Law," 214 (who calls his work only "a new attempt" [p. v]); cf. idem, "Pauline Midrash," 565, 567.

33. "Noch ein Versuch," 84.

34. Lücke, "Noch ein Versuch," 85 (cf. p. 102).

35. Lücke, "Noch ein Versuch," 106: "absolute insolubility of the exegetical difficulties."

36. For the context has nothing to do with this (so, e.g., Burton, *Critical and Exegetical Commentary*, 191, and Rohde, *Brief des Paulus*, 157).

37. On this see just Sieffert, *Galater*, ninth ed., 210 n. * and p. 211 (cf. pp. 205-6, further on the effect of this line of thought in Luther the literature mentioned in n. 7 above).

38. Sieffert, *Galater*, ninth ed., 210 n. *. Cf. Fritsch, "Galater 3,20," 5.

39. Sieffert, *Galater*, ninth ed., 210 n. *.

40. E.g., J. A. Bengel is interested in determining such a relationship (*Gnomon Novi Testamenti* . . . [reprint of the third ed. of 1772; Tübingen: Schramm, 1855], 727): *Non est alius Deus ante legem, alius deinceps: sed unus idemque Deus. Ante legem egit sine mediatore; ergo mediator Sinaiticus non est Dei, sed legis; Dei autem promissio.*

41. On the question of the hermeneutical relevance of this crime, which I refer to here with the metonym "Auschwitz," simply cf. M. Bachmann, *Sünder oder Übertreter. Studien zur Argumentation in Gal 2,15ff.* (WUNT 59; Tübingen: Mohr, 1992), 3 n. 11 (bibliography).

42. Indeed in this respect comparably important are only Matt 27:25; John 8:44; 1 Thess 2:14-16; Rev 2:9; 3:9 (cf. also 2 Corinthians 3–4) — and John 4:22; Romans 9–11.

43. On this question cf. n. 128 below.

44. On this list cf., e.g., J. B. Lightfoot, *St. Paul's Epistle to the Galatians* (London: Macmillan, 1865), 144, and Rohde, *Brief des Paulus*, 153.

45. On this see, e.g., S. Westerholm, *Israel's Law and the Church's Faith: Paul and His Recent Interpreters* (Grand Rapids: Eerdmans, 1988), (176-)177.

46. So, e.g., J. Gründler, "Noch einmal: Der 'Mittler,'" *NKZ* 39 (1928), 549-52, here p. 550-51, and Bring, *Galater*, 148 (cf. idem, "Mittler," 84, also p. 81 n. 1).

47. A large number of interpreters in support. At least some representatives of this group stand close to the concept now to be characterized (cf., e.g., G. Ebeling, *Die Wahrheit des Evangeliums. Eine Lesehilfe zum Galaterbrief* [Tübingen: Mohr, 1981], 259-60, and D. Lührmann, *Der Brief an die Galater* [ZBK, Neues Testament 7; second ed.; Zurich: Theologischer Verlag, 1988], 63-64). H. Schlier, *Galater*, twelfth ed., 161-62, however, has distanced himself from this concept rather clearly, after he had assumed a background of an "early Gnostic" type in the previous addition of his commentary (eleventh ed., 1951) and here found expressed "that the law is not given by God, . . . because the unity of God excludes that person in whose hand the law indeed was found" (p. 116; cf. on this the statements which Schlier made in a letter on August 19, 1939, to R. Bultmann, and which he [in the opening] summarized while he was working on the second installment of his Galatians commentary as follows: "I have . . . thought about the passages 3:19-20; 4:3, 5, 8ff., and I am more and more convinced that Paul took up Gnostic ideas" [R. von Bendemann, *Heinrich Schlier. Eine kritische Analyse seiner Interpretation paulinischer Theologie* (BEvT 115; Gütersloh: Kaiser, 1995), 91 n. 338]).

48. *Das Gesetz bei Paulus. Ein Beitrag zum Werden der paulinischen Theologie* (FRLANT 119; third ed.; Göttingen: Vandenhoeck & Ruprecht, 1982), 28 (printed with emphasis by Hübner). Cf. idem, "Intertextualität — die hermeneutische Strategie des Paulus. Zu einem neuen Versuch der theologischen Rezeption des Alten Testaments im Neuen," *TLZ* 116 (1991), 881-98, here p. 889 (cf. col. 894): "Paul may speak in a defamatory way about the law of Moses" ("he does not speak in a defamatory way about the Scripture itself").

49. Hübner — and not only Hübner (but, e.g., also G. Klein, "Individualgeschichte und Weltgeschichte bei Paulus. Eine Interpretation ihres Verhältnisses im Galaterbrief," *Rekonstruktion und Interpretation. Gesammelte Aufsätze zum Neuen Testament* [BEvT 50; Munich: Kaiser, 1969], 180-224 [orig., apart from the postscript (221-24): 1964], 209-10] — joins the concept of the role of the μεσίτης with an evaluation of the angels of v. 19, according to which they "are to be understood" not only as the "originators of the law," but indeed "as demonic beings, who in opposition to God did not desire the salvation of humankind" (Hübner, *Gesetz*, 28-29; somewhat more cautious idem, *Biblische Theologie des Neuen Testaments* [2 vols.; Göttingen: Vandenhoeck & Ruprecht, 1990-93), 1.92 ["The religion of the angelic law stands on the side of the flesh, the religion of the gospel on the side of the Spirit; in this regard the law actually stands . . . against the promise"] and 2.82-83 together with n. 137). In similar conceptions the angels of v. 19 are in various cases brought into connection with

the elements (of the world) in 4:3, 9 (τὰ [...] στοιχεῖα [τοῦ κόσμου]) or even identified with them (cf., e.g., A. Ritschl, *Die christliche Lehre von der Rechtfertigung und Versöhnung 2: Der biblische Stoff der Lehre* [third ed.; Bonn: Adolph Marcus, 1889], 249-53, esp. 253, A. Schweitzer, *Die Mystik des Apostels Paulus* [Tübingen: Mohr, 1930], 71-72, Schlier, *Galater*, eleventh ed., 136 ["The στοιχεῖα τοῦ κόσμου are the ἄγγελοι from 3:19"; different, however, idem, *Galater*, twelfth ed., 194], B. Reicke, "The Law and This World According to Paul. Some Thoughts concerning Gal 4$_{1-11}$," *JBL* 70 [1951], 259-76 [orig. (Swedish): 1943], esp. 262-63, M. F. Lacan, "Le Dieu unique et son médiateur. Galates 3:20," in *L'homme devant Dieu. Mélanges offerts au Père Henri de Lubac. Exégèse et patristique* [Théologie 56; Paris: Aubier, 1963], 113-25, here pp. 123-24, Klein, "Individualgeschichte," 209 n. 105, D. Lührmann, *Das Offenbarungsverständnis bei Paulus und in den paulinischen Gemeinden* [WMANT 16; Neukirchen-Vluyn: Neukirchener, 1965], 67-69 [cf., however, idem, "Tage, Monate, Jahreszeiten (Gal 4,10)," in *Werden und Wirken des Alten Testaments. Festschrift für Claus Westermann* (ed. R. Albertz et al.; Göttingen/Neukirchen-Vluyn: Vandenhoeck & Ruprecht/Neukirchener, 1980), 428-45, here pp. 430-31, 442-43], and M. Mach, "Tora-Verleihung durch Engel," in *Das Alte Testament als geistige Heimat. Festgabe für Hans Walter Wolff*, ed. M. Augustin/J. Kegler [EHS 23.177; second ed.; Frankfurt am Main/Bern: Lang, 1984], 51-70, here p. 62 [cf. M. Mach, *Entwicklungsstadien des jüdischen Engelglaubens in vorrabbinischer Zeit* (Texte und Studien zum Antiken Judentum 34; Tübingen: Mohr, 1992), 294, 297]). On this see H. Räisänen, *Paul and the Law* (WUNT 29; Tübingen: Mohr, 1983), 131-32, Betz, *Galaterbrief*, 301-3 together with n. 58, Rohde, *Brief des Paulus*, 156 (together with nn. 16, 18-19), Westerholm, *Law*, 176-79, D. B. Wallace, "Galatians 3:19-20: A *crux interpretum* for Paul's View of the Law," *WTJ* 52 (1990), 225-45, (235,) 241-43, and Bachmann, *Sünder*, 146 together with n. 254. The expression (τὰ) στοιχεῖα (τοῦ κόσμου), as it is used in Gal 4:3, 9, (however) speaks precisely against a somewhat narrow connection with the angels from 3:19 (cf. P. Vielhauer, "Gesetzesdienst und Stoicheiadienst im Galaterbrief," *Oikodome. Aufsätze zum Neuen Testament 2* (TB 65, ed. G. Klein; Munich: Kaiser, 1979], 183-95 [orig.: 1976], esp. 189-90). This is so first of all because one does not find in Galatians 3–4 an explicitly established connection (see Räisänen, *Law*, 131). Second, especially the term στοιχεῖα in one of the "perhaps closest 'parallels' to Gal 4:10" (Lührmann, "Tage," 442 n. 76), namely, Wis 7:17-19, serves to characterize the structure and the order of the cosmos. And third, over against the state of the discussion up until then, some years ago D. Rusam, "Neue Belege zu den στοιχεῖα τοῦ κόσμου (Gal 4,3.9; Kol 2,8.20)," *ZNW* 83 (1992), 119-25, by means of the Thesaurus Linguae Graecae has been able not only to increase the number of ancient comparative passages for the expression with the genitive attribute considerably but also to make probable: "The supposition..., the στοιχεῖα τοῦ κόσμου have to do with 'living spirits,' lacks any lexical basis, since not a single instance for this word association can be found. The material that has been furnished [by the author, that is, Rusam] strengthens the concept represented by J. Blinzler, G. Delling, E. Schweizer, and P. Vielhauer, that the στοιχεῖα τοῦ κόσμου have to do with the four or five physical elements" (p. 125, here nn. 28-33 bibliography; cf. further Bachmann, *Sünder*, 123-24 [together with] n. 122 [and nn. 126-27]).

50. The question about a possible development leading toward toning down the Pauline view, specifically concerning the assessment of the law, between Galatians and Romans (on this see, e.g., Bachmann, *Sünder*, 8 together with n. 41 [bibliography]) cannot be pursued further here (cf. nevertheless [at] n. 194 below). Indeed this question belongs to those

problems that shift Gal 3:19-20 and Gal 3:20 to the center of contemporary discussions about the Pauline understanding of the law, as Wallace, "Galatians 3:19-20," (225-)227-29, correctly emphasizes.

51. Klein, "Individualgeschichte," 210. Cf. idem, "Gesetz III: Neues Testament," *TRE* 13 (1984), 58-75, here p. 67.

52. Not very satisfactory, as an example, is the proceeding of Callan, "The Law," 1-30 (cf. [at] n. 17 above). For when close to the beginning of his report on the history of research he puts forth (pp. 4-5) three "common arguments" (p. 4) (μεσίτης = Moses; μεσίτης in v. 19b and in v. 20 ultimately with an identical reference; ἑνός and εἷς are used with the same meaning [cf. below (at) nn. 68, 98-99, 106]), which serve him to eliminate such interpretations, "which, it seems . . . , can rather readily be dismissed" (p. 4), so those arguments which speak for such proposals that have fallen through that sieve can of course hardly be recognized. (Similarly circular in my opinion also: Callan, "Pauline Midrash" [cf. here 549 with 564-67].)

53. Cf. Lücke, "Noch ein Versuch," 101: "I really know no better interpretation than those [three: namely, those of G. B. Winer, of F. D. E. Schleiermacher, and of C. A. T./K. A. G. Keil] I have criticized. If there were a better one, it would have been found long ago." Perhaps a better one has been found!

54. F. Mußner, *Der Galaterbrief* (HTK 9; Freiburg: Herder, 1974), 248-50 (sketch: 249). On this see n. 63 below.

55. *Brief des Paulus,* 157, where as evidence he refers particularly to "the grammatical structure of this verse" (evidently he means v. 20), but without characterizing this structure more precisely (see, however, p. 158: "ὁ μεσίτης [has] generic meaning . . . because ὁ is not equivalent to οὗτος" [on this see at n. 100 below]). Oepke, *Brief des Paulus,* 83, expresses himself more clearly: "The first δέ introduces this ['general sentence,' i.e., 3:20a] as a major premise for v. 19, especially for its last words, the second δέ by contrast introduces v. 20b as the second, contrasting minor premise to v. 20a" (cf. idem, "μεσίτης κτλ.," *TWNT* 4 [1942], 602-29 [cf. ET *TDNT* 4, 598-624], here p. 622, further n. 63 below). Cf. also Sieffert, *Galater,* ninth ed., 216 ("the two clauses in 3:20 just have the form of major and minor premises of a syllogism"), further (at) nn. 66, 68, 69, 84, 86 below.

56. *Brief des Paulus,* 84. Cf. (at) nn. 70, 82 below.

57. Schlier, *Galater,* twelfth ed., 161; still differently: eleventh ed., 114-15. Cf. further, e.g., Hübner, *Gesetz,* 28.

58. D. Sänger, "μεσίτης κτλ.," *EWNT* 2 (1981), 1010-12 (cf ET *EDNT* 2, 410-11), here 1011.

59. On this cf., for example, J. Dopp, *Formale Logik* (Philosophia Lovaniensis [Deutsche Ausgabe] 3; Einsiedeln: Benziger, 1969), 108-9, 111-16, 141(-142) (together with n. 38).

60. On this cf., e.g., Dopp, *Formale Logik,* 141-42.

61. On this cf. again Dopp, *Formale Logik,* 109, 111-16.

62. Oepke, *Brief des Paulus,* 83; cf. idem, "μεσίτης," 622.

63. On this see Callan, "The Law," esp. (4 and) 24 (cf. p. 26): "20th century interpretation of the passage . . . has been . . . almost unanimous in seeing v 20a as a universal statement about mediation in general." When on p. 26 (correspondingly: Callan, "Pauline Midrash," 566 n. 36) he counts Mußner's interpretation (*Galaterbrief,* 248-50 [on this cf. at n. 54 above]) among the exceptions, this is hardly correct. It is true, Mußner actually (hardly different from Oepke [on this see n. 55 above]) emphasizes an "adversative connection with

v. 19" (*Galaterbrief*, 248); but he does also say that Paul "then notices, *in a generally valid formulation*, that the mediator is not mediator of a singularity" (p. 248[-249] n. 25; emphasis added), and he argues also with respect to the mediator in 1 Tim 2:5-6 and *T. Dan* 6:2: "the singularity here always is contrasted to a plurality." Cf. (at) n. 89 below.

64. Cf., e.g., Sieffert, *Galater*, seventh ed., 211-23, esp. 211, 217 (cf. ninth ed., 212-14), Ritschl, *Rechtfertigung und Versöhnung*, 2.250, Oepke, *Brief des Paulus*, 83 (cf. idem, "μεσίτης," 622), and Betz, *Galaterbrief*, 305. Beyond this alternative the attempt has to be positioned, according to which the ἑνός in 3:20a (in spite of the ἑνός in 3:16) should be understood not as masculine but as neuter (so particularly C. Holsten [*Deutung und Bedeutung der Worte des Galater-Briefes cap. 3,21 in ihrem Zusammenhange* (Rostock: Stiller'sche Buchhandlung, 1853), esp. 29-31; *Das Evangelium des Paulus I: Die äußere entwicklungsgeschichte des paulinischen evangeliums 1: Der brief an die gemeinden Galatiens und der erste brief an die gemeinde in Korinth* (Berlin: G. Reimer, 1880), esp. 105-6]; on this see, e.g., Sieffert, *Galater*, seventh ed., 221 together with n. *).

65. On this see Callan, "The Law," esp. (4 and) 24-25 (cf. p. 26). Cf. V. Stolle, "Die Eins in Gal 3:15-29," in *Theokratia II: 1970-72. Festgabe für Karl Heinrich Rengstorf zum 70. Geburtstag*, ed. W. Dietrich, P. Freimark, and H. Schreckenberg (Leiden: Brill, 1973), 204-13, here p. 208 together with n. 4: The concept of "brokering between two parties" (p. 208) "in recent times . . . has strongly receded" (n. 4) — but it occurs, nevertheless, in F. Siegert, *Argumentation bei Paulus, gezeigt an Röm 9–11* (WUNT 34; Tübingen; Mohr, 1985), 193. Cf. (at) nn. 93, 117 below.

66. On this see Callan, "The Law," esp. 25, where he says of the twentieth century in view of this alternative: "most have understood it to mean that Moses acted as mediator of the angels, rather than God." Cf. H. Merklein, *Studien zu Jesus und Paulus* (WUNT 43; Tübingen: Mohr, 1987), 71 n. 177: "Normally the 'one' is understood as referring to God and as the contrast to the multiplicity of the angels." It is not completely clear how one should understand Rohde, *Brief des Paulus*, 153-59; for on the one hand he says that "Moses received the law through angels" (p. 156), and he positively refers (p. 156 n. 36) to Oepke (see [at] n. 56 above), on the other hand he says: "The appearance of a mediator presupposes the presence of two parties" (p. 158).

67. On this see Callan, "The Law," esp. (4 and) 26; cf. pp. 27-30, where Callan himself — over against the prevailing view — comes near to a preference of the concept expressed especially by Stolle, "Eins," esp. 207-8, 210, who thinks of a *genitivus qualitatis* (cf. [however] Callan, "Pauline Midrash, 566-67 [p. 567: "The advantage of this interpretation is that it allows for v 20b to be taken at full weight, but the use of a cardinal number as a qualitative genitive is unparalleled and somewhat unlikely"]).

68. One customarily "starts" with both (cf. with respect to ἑνός/εἷς already n. 52 above, further, e.g., Wieseler, *Commentar*, 289 [where he says that "the εἷς obviously takes up the ἑνός"], and on the syllogism hypothesis cf. [at] n. 55 above). Characteristically: Callan, "The Law," 5 ("it seems most likely to me that v 20a and 20b are in some sense antithetical and that the antithesis lies in the contrast between ἑνὸς οὐκ ἔστιν and εἷς ἐστιν; consequently I reject interpretations which give ἑνός and εἷς different meanings"), and F. F. Bruce, *The Epistle of Paul to the Galatians: A Commentary on the Greek Text* (NIGTC; Eerdmans: Grand Rapids, 1982), 179 ("We can scarcely hope to grasp Paul's meaning unless we posit a logical relation between ἑνός in the former clause and εἷς in the latter" [critical against this already

Bachmann, *Sünder*, 148 n. 265]). Rather to the point indeed is what Lücke, "Noch ein Versuch," 86, says on the comparison of 3:20b with 3:20a: "The form of the sentence is entirely the same"; but it is not entirely right (see F. Reithmayr, *Commentar zum Briefe an die Galater* (Munich: J. J. Lentner [E. Stahl], 1865), 283: "parallel except for the word order"), and it can, as Lücke's thesis of a double interpolation (on this see [at] n. 29 above) shows, be explained quite differently. Cf. (at) nn. 98-99, 106, 116 below.

69. Thus not only (Oepke, who takes 3:20a as the major premise in view of [the end of] 3:19 and also with respect to 3:20b, and) Rohde (on this see [at] n. 55 above), but also an abundance of authors (cf., e.g., Wieseler, *Commentar*, 297, Sieffert, *Galater*, ninth ed., 216, and Mußner, *Galaterbrief*, 249).

70. Cf. with respect to the (traditional) logical terminology in question Dopp, *Formale Logik*, 110-11, 141-42.

71. H. Lietzmann, *An die Galater* (HNT 10; third ed.; Tübingen: Mohr, 1932), 23, who (according to his first premise [p. 22]: "the μεσίτης is οὐκ ἑνός, ἀλλὰ πολλῶν") continues: ἀλλὰ πολλῶν (cf. [at] nn. 116-17 below).

72. More disturbing for those who make out in 3:20a and 3:20b premises of a syllogism is perhaps that no real agreement with respect to the content of this syllogism exists among them. It shall only be mentioned that on the assumption that two parties should stand over against the ἑνός, 3:20b must refer to one of the two parties and the *conclusio* perhaps can mean that "there was, besides God, a second party" (Burton, *Critical and Exegetical Commentary*, 191; similarly, e.g., Winer, *Pauli ad Galatas epistola*, 88-89, somewhat different Kern, "Noch eine Erörterung von Gal 3,19.20," *Tübinger Zeitschrift für Theologie* 1830/issue 3, 157-69, esp. 167-68), and that if in accordance with the thesis that ἑνός finds its opposite in the people of Israel, it can be concluded: "Moses was not μεσίτης of the one God but of the multiplicity of Israelites" (T. Zahn, *Der Brief des Paulus an die Galater* [KNT 9; second ed.; Leipzig: A. Deichert'sche Verlagsbuchhandlung Nachf., 1907], 177). Also where Moses is thought of as the representative of the angels, 3:20b can be, however, not only the occasion to conclude, as outlined, that the mediator is not of God, at any rate not directly, but it can be related also (at the same time) to the direct action of the one God as it appears especially in the events connected with the promise (cf., e.g., A. Hilgenfeld, "Paulus und die Urapostel, der Galaterbrief und die Apostelgeschichte und die neuesten Bearbeitungen," *ZWT* 3 [1860], 101-68, 205-39, 236-39, Klöpper, "Zwei merkwürdige Aeusserungen," 107-9, Ritschl, *Rechtfertigung und Versöhnung*, 2.250-51, further, Schlier, *Galater*, twelfth ed., 161, Sänger, "μεσίτης," 1011, also [at] n. 82 below [Mußner; Rohde]). (Again differently Betz, *Galaterbrief*, 304-8, esp. 307-8: in the "proof" one has to supply "as the presupposition the old rule . . . 'like to like'" [cf. Merklein, *Studien*, 71 (see n. 97 below)].) Cf. (at) nn. 81-82, 93 below.

73. See (at) n. 54 above.

74. Cf. (at) nn. 63, 66 above.

75. *Galaterbrief*, 248-49.

76. Cf., e.g., Zahn, *Brief des Paulus*, 177, Stegmann, "μεσίτης," 30, and Callan, "The Law," 2.

77. Cf. (at) n. 55 above.

78. See on this tradition, which particularly could be attached to Deut 33:2 (LXX) and Ps 68:18 (cf. on this S. M. Olyan, *A Thousand Thousands Served Him: Exegesis and the Naming of Angels in Ancient Judaism* [Texte und Studien zum Antiken Judentum 36; Tübingen: Mohr, 1993], esp. 15-16), e.g., (H. L. Strack and) P. Billerbeck, *Kommentar zum*

Neuen Testament aus Talmud und Midrasch (4 vols.; Munich: Beck, 1922-28), 3.554-56, Schlier, *Galater*, twelfth ed., 156-57, and Callan, "Pauline Midrash," 550-54. Mach's attempt ("Tora-Verleihung," 54-62; cf. idem, *Entwicklungsstadien,* 285-86 together with n. 16 and p. 307 n. 80), in spite of what he too concedes to be a widespread concept in Judaism that "God is accompanied by angels" ("Tora-Verleihung," 55), to deny nevertheless the traditional character of the more special view of angels mediating the law is not able to convince. It is already doubtful whether one really has to understand the passage usually quoted as evidence from Josephus, *Ant.* 15:136 (see, e.g., Billerbeck, *Kommentar,* 3.556) as concerning human messengers (as Mach ["Tora-Verleihung," 57-58; *Entwicklungstadien,* 307 n. 80] thinks, and indeed in connection with R. Marcus's note in the LCL edition and with W. D. Davies, "A Note on Josephus, Antiquities 15:136," *HTR* 47 [1952], 135-40, as well as F. R. Walton, "The Messenger of God in Hecateus of Abdera," *HTR* 48 [1955], 255-57; differently, however,, e.g., Betz, *Galaterbrief,* 301-11 [together with] n. 55, A. J. Bandstra, "The Law and the Angels: *Antiquities* 15.136 and Galatians 3:19," *CTJ* 24 [1989], 223-40, and R. N. Longenecker, *Galatians* [WBC 41; Dallas: Word, 1990], 140) rather than angels; for with δι' ἀγγέλων in *Ant.* 15:136 it is not beyond all doubt that this has the prophets of *Ag. Ap.* 1:37 in mind, because there (see, however, at any rate *Ag. Ap.* 1:39) it is (rather) about knowledge of something narrated, of "events" (Mach, *Entwicklungsstadien,* 307 n. 80), but here it is about τὰ κάλλιστα τῶν δογμάτων καὶ τὰ ὁσιώτατα τῶν ἐν τοῖς νόμοις, and besides this the term ἄγγελος in *Ant.* 15:136 makes sense just in that it on the one hand allows the killed envoys of the Arabians to be subsumed, on the other hand, however, it is able to suggest by its more narrow meaning to what extent God becomes present in the messenger. (If, however, the prophets were meant in *Ant.* 15:136, then the topos of the violent death of such characters [see, e.g., *Ant.* 9:265] would be at cross purposes with the intention of the speaker, that is, to emphasize what is outrageous in the hostile deeds.) But even if one should not take this passage into account, there still remain (cf. further 4Q 521 (2) 2:2 ["the precepts of the holy ones" (cf., e.g., Jude 14-15, and on this n. 188 below); according to H. Stegemann, *Die Essener, Qumran, Johannes der Täufer und Jesus. Ein Sachbuch* (Herder/Spektrum 4249; Freiburg: Herder, 1993), 50, this has to do with "nothing other than the commandments . . . of the Torah, which God had revealed to Moses 'through (his holy) angels'"], and also *Apocalypse of Moses* 1 and n. 138 below: angels generally as mediators) *Jubilees* (see esp. 1:27-29; 6:22; 30:12, 31; 50:1ff.; cf., e.g., 2:9; 3:10-14), rabbinic comments (on this see again Billerbeck, *Kommentar,* 3.556, and Betz, *Galaterbrief,* 302 n. 55: reference esp. to *Pesiq. Rab.* 21 [103b]; Betz names further '*Abot R. Nat.* [recension B] 2, where, it is true, angelic mediation of the Law is rejected, but where of course a corresponding tradition is presupposed [Davies, "Note," 140 n. 2, tries, on the basis of such a tradition, in which a hostile stance of some rabbinic statements becomes recognizable with the possibility that not until "after the close of the New Testament period efforts were made in some quarters to belittle the role of the angels on Mt. Sinai," "to make it clear that the angels did not receive the Law from Yahweh"; Longenecker, *Galatians,* 140, follows this thesis of a Jewish correction directed at certain Christian interpretations of the presence of angels in the giving of the law (see below: *Barn.* 9:4, further n. 80)]), and above all the New Testament parallels in Acts 7:53 (cf. 7:38) and Heb 2:2 (on this see [at] nn. 137, 186-89 below; cf. also the notice from Papias cited by F. Siegert, "Unbeachtete Papiaszitate bei armenischen Schriftstellern," *NTS* 27 [1981], 605-14, here p. 606, according to which to "Michael and his hosts, who are the guardians of the world," applies: "they gave laws and made the prophets wise"). With respect to such a tradition, it is therefore (as one is able especially to learn from Davies, "Note," 139-40 together with n. 11) a fallacy to evaluate a vote against an interpretation of the δι' ἀγγέλων in Josephus, *Ant.* 15:136 as concerning the participation of angels in the giving of the law as "decisive" (Mach, *Entwicklungsstadien,* 307 n. 80) according to the question of such a tradition. And to maintain that Acts 7:53 (and Heb 2:2 [?]) depend(s) (only) on Gal 3:19 (Mach, "Tora-Verleihung," 61) is a *petitio principii.* At any rate, in view of Gal 1:8 and 4:14, the (uncorrected) thesis does not hold that in Galatians Paul "understood the angels negatively" (Mach, ibid., 62-63 [citation: 63]; idem, *Entwicklungsstadien,* 285-86; on this see Bachmann, *Sünder,* 146 together with n. 151); for this reason one will also not be able to agree with the view that the heavenly beings in 3:19 should be understood as an "inversion of the tradition of the wisdom of the angels" (Mach, *Entwicklungsstadien,* 285 n. 16) — and this in analogy to the *later* statement in *Barn.* 9:4 (cf. Mach, "Tora-Verleihung," 284[-286]; idem, *Entwicklungsstadien,* 63 together with n. 64), according to which an ἄγγελος πονηρός influenced the Israelites (with respect to circumcision) (cf. Bachmann, *Sünder,* 147 n. 259: critique on a similar argument in H.-J. Schoeps, *Paulus. Die Theologie des Apostels im Lichte der jüdischen Religionsgeschichte* [Tübingen: Mohr, 1959], 191). When Mach (*Entwicklungsstadien,* 285 n. 16) assesses *Jubilees* as the "closest parallel" to the concept of the mediation of the law as it is found in Gal 3:19, and when according to him in both the "halakhic interpretation of the Torah" is thematic, then this should at least be capable of consensus, especially since such an accent occurs in the majority of the comparable passages touched upon (cf. once again [at] nn. 187-89 below).

79. The expression that Paul uses corresponds precisely to the formulation of Heb 2:2 (cf. Acts 7:53) and Josephus, *Ant.* 15:136 (on this see the previous note), but he does not use either the high number (see already Deut 33:2 [LXX]; Ps 68:18 [cf. Ezek 43:2 LXX and on this see Olyan, *Thousand,* 50-51 together with n. 74]; cf. Heb 12:22, also Dan 7:10) set by the tradition (see on this again the previous note) nor does it say δι' πολλῶν ἀγγέλων (so correctly Sieffert, *Galater,* ninth ed., 213). Cf. Merklein, *Studien,* 71 n. 177, and also A. Suhl, "Die Galater und der Geist. Kritische Erwägungen zur Situation in Galatien," in *Jesu Rede von Gott und ihre Nachgeschichte im frühen Christentum. Beiträge zur Verkündigung Jesu und zum Kerygma der Kirche. Festschrift für Willi Marxsen zum 70. Geburtstag,* ed. D.-A. Koch, G. Sellin, and A. Lindemann (Gütersloh: Mohn, 1989), 267-96, here pp. 290-91, who names further difficulties of the conventional interpretation, which, not least in view of the context (on it see section 5 of this study below), does not hold. Finally: To express the origin of the law from angels, the formulation δι' ἀγγέλων fits decisively worse than ὑπ' ἀγγέλων (on this see, e.g., Bachmann, *Sünder,* 146 together with nn. 252-53 [bibliography]; cf. on the other hand Hübner, *Gesetz,* 28, further n. 165 below).

80. As far as I can tell (similarly: Stegmann, "μεσίτης," 40-41; cf. Longenecker, *Galatians,* 142), in the span of time that interests us there is no direct evidence for this view (cf., however, Schlier, *Galater,* twelfth ed., 157, 159-62: references among others to Acts 7:38; *Jub.* 1:27ff., and *Apocalypse of Moses* 1 as well as to Gnostic sources), and the tradition connected with Isa 63:9 LXX (on this see recently Mach, *Entwicklungsstadien,* 92-94 together with n. 72), according to which it is not an "angel" but none other than God who deals with Israel, is only occasionally applied to the Mosaic law (on this see, e.g., Callan, "Pauline Midrash," 556-57 [bibliography]; cf. C. H. Giblin, "Three Monotheistic Texts in Paul," *CBQ* 37 [1975], 527-47, here p. 541 n. 63, and n. 78 above), and therefore hardly allows for the conclu-

sion that here such a view of Moses as an agent is taken up with a polemic intent. Cf. Suhl, "Die Galater und der Geist," 290.

81. On this see (at) nn. 56, 71-72 above.

82. Mußner, *Galaterbrief*, 249 (who however does not, as does not even Oepke [see at n. 56 above], present the bare formulation of the *conclusio* drawn directly from the premises that are asserted). Similarly, e.g., Rohde, *Brief des Paulus*, 158-59. Klöpper, "Zwei merkwürdige Aeusserungen," 105-9, clearly distinguishes the true "Conclusio" (p. 105) or "the suppressed conclusion" (p. 107) from the still necessary "conclusion concerning the inferiority of the law" (p. 108). Similarly C. Burchard, "Noch ein Versuch zu Galater 3:19 und 20," *Spuren eines Weges. Freundesgabe für Bernd Janowski*, ed. T. Podella/P. Riede (Heidelberg, 1993), 63-81, here p. 73. Cf. nn. 66, 72 above.

83. On this see, e.g., Siegert, *Argumentation bei Paulus*, 191-95, 237-40, 261, and Bachmann, *Sünder*, 20 (together with) n. 137 and p. 48 n. 132 (cf. p. 35 n. 64).

84. See (at) n. 55 (and n. 68) above.

85. On this see already Bachmann, *Sünder*, 148 n. 265. Years ago E. Bammel, "Gottes ΔΙΑΘΗΚΗ (Gal. III.15-17) und das jüdische Rechtsdenken," *NTS* 6 (1959-60), 313-19, here p. 317 n. 5, had pointed out over against the usual interpretations that "in v. 20a δέ and not μέν" occurs, and he suggested accordingly "to place a full stop" after v. 20a. Cf. (at) nn. 91, 97, 182 below.

86. An (only seeming) exception is 1 Cor 15:13 (cf. Rom 3:5a; 11:17), if one should understand this verse (or v. 16 [here however already: εἰ γάρ]) and the clearly later following sentence in 3:20a (νυνὶ δέ) in the sense of premises for a conclusion (on this see, e.g., Bachmann, *Sünder*, 49 n. 132; idem, "Zum 'argumentum resurrectionis' von 1 Kor 15:12ff nach Christoph Zimmer, Augustin und Paulus," *LB* 67 [August 1992], 29-39, esp. 29-33, 35 [bibliography]). But this passage shows quite well that here the δέ is oriented not (also) forward — toward the second premise — but (exclusively) toward the preceding context. With respect to content, in 1 Cor 15:13a reference is made to 15:12b, and even this reference back is signaled by εἰ δέ, just as the εἰ δέ functions in 15:12a (see 15:[1-]11b); 15:14a (see 15:13b); 15:17a (see 15:16b) also analogously (cf. Rom 8:9-11, 13, 17; 11:12, 16-18). Cf. (at) n. 122 below.

87. On this and on the following examples (to which one can possibly add Gal 3:10, 11a [and, as far as the δέ in the second premise is concerned, 3:11b, 12a]) see Bachmann, *Sünder*, 35 (together with) n. 64, p. 53 n. 142, p. 95 n. 357, and p. 142 n. 229 (further again p. 148 n. 265).

88. Incidentally in this way premises are often marked also outside the Corpus Paulinum (see H. Lausberg, *Elemente der literarischen Rhetorik. Eine Einführung für Studierende der klassischen, romanischen, englischen und deutschen Philologie* [third ed.; Munich: Max Hueber, 1967], 370).

89. Also Vanhoye, "médiateur," esp. 408, puts another model beside Mußner's sketch (p. 405) (on this cf. L. Salvadori, "'Mediatore d'angeli' (Gal 3,19-20)," *Ricerche bibliche e religiose* 17 [1982], 143-45, here pp. 144-45). But inasmuch as the model takes account of an agent of the angels it shares essential difficulties of the suggestion under consideration, and it adds further problems, when it allows this mediator to be mentioned in Gal 3:20a and to be distinguished from Moses (as he should be in view in 3:19), especially the difficulty of an ambiguous use of language, of an ambiguity that is hardly transparent.

90. Thus in recent times above all Stolle, "Eins," 208, Lacan, "Dieu unique," 121-22, Giblin, "Three Monotheistic Texts," 540-41, and Callan, "The Law," 212 (cf. idem, "Pauline

Midrash," 556-57, where in n. 36 Mußner is assessed as a predecessor [on this see n. 63 above]). Cf. n. 97 below.

91. On this see Bammel, "Gottes ΔΙΑΘΗΚΗ," 317 n. 2: "Moses is . . . mediator of/for many" (cf. [at] nn. 97, 168 below).

92. Cf. U. Borse, *Der Brief an die Galater* (RNT; Regensburg: F. Pustet, 1984), 135 ("The Old Testament confession of the one God serves him [Paul] as the basis"), and Stolle, "Eins," 212 ("Reference to the shema Israel"; Giblin, "Three Monotheistic Texts," 542, follows Stolle [cf. further Wallace, "Galatians 3:19-20," 244]; similarly already Bornhäuser, "Mittler," 22-23). Of course the term κύριος that occurs before εἷς in Deut 6:4 (on this see Callan, "The Law," 195-96) is missing in Paul here, but not only here (cf. [also on this at] nn. 195-96 below). On the wider background of the "formula" see, e.g., Callan, "The Law," 195-201, and Betz, *Galaterbrief,* 307 n. 79 (bibliography). Cf. Bachmann, *Sünder,* 146 n. 249.

93. This premise is difficult to understand on the one hand on account of the amplifications, which are not trivial and which are made the burden of the recipient (on this see [at] nn. 76-80 above). On the other hand, the alleged general sentence constitutes in itself a certain imposition, because the concept of the μεσίτης in no way expresses in itself the notion that such a mediator would necessarily have to represent a group (as for example Zahn, *Brief des Paulus,* 176, Schlier, *Galater,* eleventh ed., 115, Giblin, "Three Monotheistic Texts," 540 n. 60, and Callan, "The Law," 25, mention correctly and to be precise against formulations such as the one from Klöpper, "Zwei merkwürdige Aeusserungen," 106, that the Apostle wanted "to be conceded . . . as an empirical fact, that only a plurality of individuals makes use of a mediator," which of course, as Klöpper admits, would hold "only at large"), as the prevailing convention wants (and also the assumption that a duality of parties has to be imagined is not without difficulties [on this see, e.g., again Schlier, *Galater,* eleventh ed., 115, and Callan, "The Law," 25]). That also the second premise and the *conclusio* are also not without problems was already the issue in n. 72 above. Little plausible furthermore is, precisely with the clearest versions of the syllogism thesis, that given only the evidence in Rom 3:30 and 1 Cor 8:4, 6 (on this see [at] nn. 195-96 below), for Paul the undoubtedly significant formulation of monotheism in Gal 3:20b should simply express a numerical fact (cf. the corresponding criticism in Callan, "The Law," 216 [and Wallace, "Galatians 3:19-20," 244]).

94. PL 82:481: Ὁ καὶ τὴν ἐπαγγελίαν τῷ Ἀβραὰμ δεδωκώς, καὶ τὸν νόμον τεθεικώς, καὶ νῦν τῆς ἐπαγγελίας ἡμῖν ἐπιδείξας τὸ πέρας. Οὐ γὰρ ἄλλος μὲν ἐκεῖνα θεὸς ᾠκονόμησεν, ἄλλος δὲ ταῦτα. Critical with respect to this are for example Wieseler, *Commentar,* 290, and Sieffert, *Galater,* seventh ed., 209 n. *, whereas Reithmayr, *Commentar,* 283, refers to this positively — nevertheless taking 3:20a and 3:20b as premises of a syllogism (pp. 282-86).

95. At any rate it is remarkable that at the beginning of Theodoret's brief commentary on 3:20a a reference to the people occurs: Ἐμεσίτευσε γὰρ τῷ λαῷ καὶ τῷ θεῷ (PL 82:481).

96. With respect to 3:20a Keil, "*exemplum,*" 234 together with n. 9, and — in dependence on him — Callan, "The Law," 12 together with (n. 18 [ἑνός to be sure related to the seed in 3:16, 19, but thereby σπέρμα in accordance with 3:29 understood collectively] and) n. 19, provide an overview (cf. Sieffert, *Galater,* seventh ed., [221-]222 together with n. *, and Siebert, "Exegetisch-theologische Studie," 704), and as far as 3:20b is concerned Sieffert, *Galater,* ninth ed., 215 with n. *** (reference esp. to C. F. Schmid, *Biblische Theologie des Neuen Testaments* [third ed., ed. C. Weizsäcker; Stuttgart: S. G. Liesching, 1864], 521-22, and Fritsch, "Galater 3,20," 15), facilitates a certain orientation (see further Bonitz, *interpretatio,*

57-71, and Fritsch, "Galater 3,20," 24[-28]). For an early interpretation of the entire verse in the sense characterised I. G. Rosenmüllerus (i.e., Rosenmüller), *Scholia in Novum Testamentum.* Vol. 4: *Continens Pauli epistolas ad Corinthios, Galatas, Ephesios, Philippenses, Colossenses et Thessalonicences* (third ed.; Nürnberg: Felsecker, 1790), 388-90 (analogously already in first ed., 1780, there pp. 367-68), should be mentioned. On 3:20a (among other things) he says: *Dicit igitur Apostolus, munus illud Mosis, internuncii et mediatoris in legislatione, ad prolem illam unicam Abrahamicam,* ᾧ ἐπήγγελται *sine adiecta legis durae conditione, haud pertinuisse* (p. 389), and he comments on 3:(20a-)20b (among other things) as follows: *Quamquam Deus misit Mosen ad Israelitas, ad promulgandam legem, noluit tamen, ut pacto cum Abrahamo aliquid statueretur contrarium* (pp. 389-90).

97. Bammel, "Gottes ΔΙΑΘΗΚΗ," 317 together with n. 2 (and nn. 3, 5), who confines himself to few notes (cf. nn. 85, 91 above as well as [at] nn. 168, 182 below). His proposals were taken up by me (Bachmann, *Sünder,* 148 together with n. 265; the present essay presents something like an explanation of this note) and earlier by Suhl, "Die Galater und der Geist," 291-93 (esp. 293). Suhl refers more intensively to Merklein, *Studien,* 70-71, whose interpretation of 3:20a (p. 71: "With the first half of the verse it is disputed whether the law mediated by Moses . . . is the fulfillment of the promise, which is aimed toward the 'one' seed of Abraham (Gal 3:16), i.e., Christ (Gal 3:19)"; cf. Stolle, "Eins," 207-10) he picks up (Suhl, "Die Galater und der Geist," 292), whereas he rejects (p. 293 together with n. 86) Merklein's interpretation of 3:20b (Merklein, *Studien,* 71: "The second half of the verse certainly derives from an analogical line of thought and emphasizes likewise the 'One' in v. 20a as a direct manifestation of the likewise 'one' God" [cf. n. 72 above]) with reference to Bammel, "Gottes ΔΙΑΘΗΚΗ," 317 n. 5. Regarding 3:20b Suhl (p. 292), however, remains trapped in the usual explanation, in that he thinks that Paul uses "the principle that an individual does not need a mediator" (cf. [at] n. 93 above).

98. Cf. Bring, "Mittler," 86 (cf. idem, *Galater,* 148): "One appears to start from it as a matter of self-evidence, that 'one' is related to the same referent." On the judgments alluded to by Bring see already (at) nn. 52, 68 above (and further, e.g., Sieffert, *Galater,* seventh ed., 222 n. *).

99. Klein, "Individualgeschichte," 210 n. 110, who here among other things challenges Bring's concept ("Mittler," 86; *Galater,* 148-49) (cf. [at] nn. 18-19, 22-23 above), according to which ἑνός and εἷς cannot be associated (directly) — as in a reduced way then also according to Stolle, "Eins," 207-8 (together with p. 208 n. 1) (cf. nn. 67, 97 above).

100. So, e.g., Lightfoot, *St. Paul's Epistle,* 147, Sieffert, *Galater,* ninth ed., 212, Oepke, *Brief des Paulus,* 83, and Rohde, *Brief des Paulus,* 158 (see n. 55 above).

101. Sieffert, *Galater,* ninth ed., 217.

102. So especially clear J. C. K. von Hofmann, *Der Schriftbeweis. Ein theologischer Versuch* II.2 (second ed.; Nördlingen: Beck, 1860), 55. On the problem cf. also Lücke, "Noch ein Versuch," 86, and Winer, *Pauli ad Galatas epistola,* 89 together with n. 27.

103. So, e.g., Sieffert, *Galater,* seventh ed., 222 n. *, also Giblin, "Three Monotheistic Texts," 538 n. 51, and Suhl, "Die Galater und der Geist," 292.

104. So, e.g., Keil, "*exemplum*," 222-23, Winer, *Pauli ad Galatas epistola,* 164-65, and Sieffert, *Galater,* ninth ed., 210-11.

105. Suhl, "Die Galater und der Geist," 292. Under the category of "reading habit(s)" it possibly would be to classify, when, e.g., Sieffert, *Galater,* ninth ed., 215(-216) n. *** (cf. pp.

212, 218-19), conceives of the following v. 21, "that the law stands in conflict with the promise," on account of which v. 20 could not have to do with the "identity of the God, who has given the promise and the law" (on this see [at] nn. 176-83 below).

106. Cf. (once again at) nn. 52, 68, 98 above.

107. Cf. C. L. Bavervs (i.e., Bauer), *Logica Pavllina, vel notatio rationis, qva vtatvr Pavllvs apostolvs in verbis adhibendis, interpretando, definiendo, envntiando, argvmentando, et methodo vniversa: in vsvm exegeseos et doctrinae sacrae* (Halle: Waisenhaus, 1774), 2-8, i.e., the passage, where he deals with words that are used with a double meaning in one and the same context; here, 3, also the example just to mention first. Concerning this rhetorical characteristic outside the Pauline writings, cf. for example Siegert, *Argumentation bei Paulus*, 44, 46 (together with nn. 70, 77), also p. 239 — and the following note.

108. On homonymy see esp. Lausberg, *Elemente*, 142-52 — further the previous note.

109. On this hotly debated subject cf., e.g., on the one hand H. Räisänen, "Sprachliches zum Spiel des Paulus mit ΝΟΜΟΣ," *The Torah and Christ. Essays in German and English on the Problem of the Law in Early Christianity* (Publications of the Finnish Exegetical Society; Helsinki: The Finnish Exegetical Society, 1986), 119-47, on the other hand, Hübner, *Gesetz*, 118-29 (bibliography).

110. Also Hübner, *Gesetz*, 125, 129, does not assert such an identity.

111. So C. L. Bauer, *Logica Pavllina*, 2-3.

112. That the ἄνθρωπος οὐκ ἔστιν from Eccl 7:20 has been altered to οὐδὲ εἷς in Rom 3:10b may be influenced by the fact that in the passage from Ps 13(14):1-3, which is clearly taken up in Rom 3:11-13, ἕως ἑνός is used twice (Ps 13:1, 3).

113. In the ἑνός in Rom 5:17-18 (employed differently [?]) Rosenmüller, *Scholia* 4, third ed., 389, saw a parallel to Gal 3:20a(-20b [?]).

114. More precisely the correspondence can be noted as follows:
Adam: δι' ἑνὸς ἀνθρώπου (5:12)
τοῦ ἑνός (5:15, 17)/δι' ἑνὸς ἁμαρτήσαντος (5:16)/ἐξ ἑνός (5:16)
διὰ τοῦ ἑνός (5:17)
δι' ἑνὸς παραπτώματος (5:18)
διὰ τῆς παρακοῆς τοῦ ἑνὸς ἀνθρώπου (5:19)
Christ: τοῦ ἑνὸς ἀνθρώπου Ἰησοῦ Χριστοῦ (5:15)
διὰ τοῦ ἑνὸς Ἰησοῦ Χριστοῦ (5:17)
δι' ἑνὸς δικαιώματος (5:18)
διὰ τῆς ὑπακοῆς τοῦ ἑνός (*v.l.*: τ. ἑ. ἀνθρώπου) (5:19)

115. Less closely than the comparative formulations under consideration, the passages Rom 12:4-5; 1 Cor 6:16-17; 10:17; 12:9ff. are related to Gal 3:20 (and even less 1 Cor 4:6), where in each case the relationship of affinity and difference is (further) clarified by substantives that come up. Cf. (at) nn. 195-96 below.

116. The argument in Zahn, *Brief des Paulus*, 176 together with n. 40, is convincing. Since μεσίτης has the article, in terms of the content the negation does not (as, e.g., in Ps 13[14]:1; cf. Gal 3:28) belong together with the following word, ἐστίν (as also not in Rom 8:9; 1 Cor 14:33), to which rather "an anarthrous μεσίτης as predicative noun has to be supplemented" (Zahn, *Brief des Paulus*, 176 n. 40, where he refers to Rom 2:28-29; 3:29; 1 Cor 15:39; cf. again 1 Cor 14:33). Then the negation is related to ἑνός, and if the wording deviates from the usual sequence, thus, to "give the ἑνός stronger emphasis and thereby to make dispens-

able the formal pronouncement of the opposite" (Zahn, *Brief des Paulus*, 176 n. 40, who among other things compares the placement of "all" in Num 23:13 and in 1 Cor 15:51, further the position of the "one" in Matt 5:18; 10:29). Cf. (however [at] n. 68 above and cf.) E. Schwyzer, *Griechische Grammatik, auf der Grundlage von Karl Brugmanns Grammatik 2: Syntax und syntaktische Stilistik* (Handbuch der Altertumswissenschaft II,I,2, supplemented and ed. A. Debrunner; second ed.; Munich: Beck, 1959), 596; F. Blass and A. Debrunner, *Grammatik des neutestamentlichen Griechisch* (fourteenth ed.; Göttingen: Vandenhoeck & Ruprecht, 1976), 433,2 together with n. 3, and W. Bauer, *Griechisch-deutsches Wörterbuch zu den Schriften des Neuen Testaments und der frühchristlichen Literatur* (sixth ed.; Berlin/New York: de Gruyter, 1988), 1194.

117. Thus, as mentioned ([at] n. 71 above), (e.g.) Lietzmann, *An die Galater*, 22, but of course also Zahn, *Brief des Paulus*, 176-77: "A self-evident *contrast* is, however, always only the direct *opposite;* the negation of unity, that is, of the singular, includes in itself the assertion of multiplicity, that is, of the plural" ("and," the author continues in view of an frequently advocated thesis [on this see, e.g., (at) nn. 65, 93 above], "in no way that of the duality, that is, of the dual"). Zahn, *Brief des Paulus*, 40, illustrates word order and additions among other things with the German sentence: "'*Einer* bringt das nicht fertig,' sondern nur mehrere."

118. The fact that in Paul on various occasions the "many" appear as facing the "one" (see Rom 5:15, 16, 17, 19 [cf. 5:12, 18, further Rom 12:4; 1 Cor 12:12, 13, 19, and Gal 3:28, also 1 Cor 9:24: "all"]; 12:4-5; 1 Cor 10:17; 12:12, 14, 20; Gal 3:16) also speaks for this.

119. Blass/Debrunner, *Grammatik*, 252.

120. *Gnomon*, 727.

121. Bengel, *Gnomon*, 727: "*Mediator ille*, Moses." See for example Rosenmüller, *Scholia* 4, third ed., 389: "Ὁ δὲ *ille autem*, ὁ pro οὗτος, ut Matth. XII,3.11.39. ὁ δὲ εἶπεν" (see n. 123 below), further, e.g., H. Riesenfeld, "The Misinterpreted Mediator in Gal 3:19-20," in *The New Testament Age. Essays in Honor of Bo Reicke*, vol. 2, ed. W. C. Weinrich (Macon: Mercer University Press, 1984), 405-11, here p. 407, and Burchard, "Noch ein Versuch," 73.

122. Cf. on this see already n. 86 above, further Giblin, "Three Monotheistic Texts," 541 (together with) n. 61; among other things, Giblin refers to the serial occurrences of δέ in Rom 5:4-5; 1 Cor 11:3 and 12:9-10, where the particle, according to him, is "clearly explicative." On the older discussion on the δέ in Gal 3:20a cf., e.g., Sieffert, *Galater*, ninth ed., 210. Sieffert himself likewise supports an understanding as "explanation."

123. Giblin, "Three Monotheistic Texts," 540-41 (together with n. 61), who cites alongside Rom 10:17 also 1 Cor 10:4 and 2 Cor 3:16-17 (and compares Rom 9:30 [on this cf. Blass/Debrunner, *Grammatik*, 447 together with n. 5], further the passages mentioned in the previous note and — without δέ — Rom 3:21; Gal 4:21; 5:13). Cf. (Wallace, "Galatians 3:19-20," 244, and above all) Callan, "The Law," 212, who draws attention also to Gal 4:24-25 (as well as to Eph 4:8-9; Heb 2:7-9). If one does not insist on maintaining that with its first occurrence the substantive must not have the article (on this cf. 1 Cor 8:1 [variant reading]), it is possible to cite 1 Cor 15:55-56 as a further parallel (cf. also 1 Cor 3:7-8, further 1 Cor 5:12-13; Gal 5:17). Our passage has less much in common with the "but he" (see n. 121 above); that it is used "for continuing the narrative," however, in the New Testament is encountered "only in the historical writings" (Blass/Debrunner, *Grammatik*, 251 n. 1; cf. 447,1e together with n. 7).

124. On this see, e.g., B. M. Metzger, *A Textual Commentary on the Greek New Testament*

(London/New York: United Bible Society, 1971), 596: δέ has better witnesses than γάρ, and the (secondary) "juxtaposition of γὰρ Ἀγάρ led to the accidental omission sometimes of γάρ and sometimes of Ἀγάρ." This latter omission led moreover to a *lectio facilior*.

125. As 1 Cor 10:4 (... ἡ πέτρα δὲ ἦν ὁ Χριστός) shows, Paul was quite able to make such a formulation.

126. On this see, e.g., Bachmann, *Sünder*, 131-32.

127. Cf. also in 1 Cor 10:1ff. on the one hand 10:1-5, on the other the passage 10:6ff. (which, however, constantly refers back to the Old Testament event). Also reference can be made to Romans 9–11 (cf. esp. 9:4, 8; 10:5; 11:1).

128. On this see (at) nn. 166-67 below. Also the condition contrary to fact in 3:21 (on this cf. n. 181 below) must indicate an analogous temporal gap. Whereas in the protasis the aorist "ἐδόθη ... ties us to the historical moment of the giving of the law" (Zahn, *Brief des Paulus*, 179), the apodosis has the imperfect ἦν, and the Pauline parallels (1 Cor 11:31 and esp. Gal 1:10 [cf. 1 Cor 12:19]) confirm the rule that "for what is not real in the present often the imperfect" is used (E. Bornemann, *Griechische Grammatik*, with collaboration by E. Risch [Frankfurt am Main: Diesterweg, 1973], 223 n. *). This should not be canceled by the fact that the "imperfect of εἶναι, which of course has no aorist" (Blass/Debrunner, *Grammatik*, 360,3 n. 5), may be understood as "ambiguous" (360,3; here in note 5 explanatory examples are discussed [Matt 23:30; John 18:36; Heb 11:15] or cited [additional: Heb 8:7], presenting "ambiguity" in so far as in any case also the present aspect still plays a role) (differently: Zahn, *Brief des Paulus*, 179, and, somewhat more cautious, Mußner, *Galaterbrief*, 251 [together with n. 36], who lay emphasis only on the past). In addition, one has to take into account that Paul could have expressed himself otherwise, e.g., by means of the aorist of δικαιοῦσθαι (cf. Rom 4:2; 8:30; 1 Cor 6:11). Moreover, the protasis and the apodosis of 3:21c are clearly taken up again by 3:22a on the one hand and 3:22b on the other hand (on this see Bachmann, *Sünder*, 51-52 together with n. 136); since now 3:22b does not remain fixed on the "historical moment of the giving of the law," this will also not be the case in 3:21cβ (against Zahn, *Brief des Paulus*, 179, who brings up just 3:22 for his interpretation). Incidentally, from these observations, but also in view of the Pauline use of τί οὖν (see esp. 1 Cor 3:5; 14:15 [cf. 14:26]; cf. Rom 3:1, 9; 6:1, 15; 11:15, also Rom 7:7; 1 Cor 10:19), it seems reasonable (so correctly for instance Sieffert, *Galater*, ninth ed., 201) (the τί not to take adverbial [against Bauer, *Wörterbuch*, 1633, Longenecker, *Galatians*, 137, and Wallace, "Galatians 3:19-20," 231-32] and) to fill in the elliptical formulation of Gal 3:19a (in any case not with ἦν, but) with ἐστίν (cf. the question of "Socrates" cited by Betz, *Galaterbrief*, 290 n. 2, from the beginning of *Minos* [313a]: ὁ νόμος ἡμῖν [Betz: ἡμῶν] τί ἐστιν;) and to understand the question precisely according to the present meaning of the law: "how does it therefore (...) stand with regard to the law?" (so Sieffert, *Galater*, ninth ed., 201), "What then is the law for?" (so Betz, *Galaterbrief*, 289-90 [cf. Blass/Debrunner, *Grammatik*, 480,3 n. 9]; on the other hand Rohde, *Brief des Paulus*, 152 [cf. p. 154, but also p. 153], offers the past tense). Cf. at n. 43 above.

129. On this see (at) nn. 116-18 above.

130. As in Exodus 19ff. the people (עַם/λαός; so, e.g., Exod 19:9, 25; 24:3, 8) and (the sons of) Israel (בְּנֵי יִשְׂרָאֵל/[υἱοὶ] Ἰσραήλ; so, e.g., Exod 20:22; 24:5) are named, so it says, e.g., in Heb 7:11 (cf. 1 Cor 10:7 [Exod 32:6]) λαός and in Acts 7:37(ff.) (cf. 2 Cor 3:7, 13, also Rom 9:31, further 9:4 [Ἰσραηλῖται]) (υἱοὶ) Ἰσραήλ.

131. So correctly von Hofmann, *Schriftbeweis* II.2, 56.

132. Paul could spare himself the trouble of expressly establishing the reference, because in 3:16 he had already appropriately specified the ἑνός there — and the τῷ σπέρματι — namely, by ὅς ἐστιν Χριστός (on this see [at] nn. 157-63 below). Cf. (at) nn. 168, 183 below.

133. On this see (at) nn. 55, 59-63 above.

134. On this see, e.g., Oepke, "μεσίτης," 605.

135. Cf. Philo, *Her.* 205-6. To a certain degree in Job 9:33 ἀνὰ μέσον ἀμφοτέρων stands in parallel to ὁ μεσίτης ἡμῶν.

136. Reference is made to Lev 26:46 in *'Abot R. Nat.* (recension A) 1, and thereby the verse gives occasion for the following consideration: "Moses merited becoming God's messenger to the children of Israel" (tr. J. Goldin, *The Fathers According to Rabbi Nathan* [Yale Judaica Series 10; New Haven: Yale University Press, 1955], 4; Goldin refers to a reading that offers not "messenger," but "middleman" [p. 175 (n. 8 on p. 4); cf. (at) n. 142 below]). The passage in Exod 25:21-22 (v. 22: ἀνὰ μέσον τῶν δύο χερουβιμ), which Merklein mentions (*Studien*, 70[-71]), is (as it seems) less closely related to Gal 3:19-20 (cf. Suhl, "Die Galater und der Geist," 292).

137. Betz, *Galaterbrief*, 303. In n. 64, he adduces (as parallels to Lev 26:46): Num 4:37, 41, 45, 49; 9:23; 10:13; 15:23; 17:5; 33:1; 36:13; Josh 21:2; 22:9; Judg 3:4; 1 Chr 16:40; 2 Chr 33:8; Ps 76(77):21; Bar 2:28. Also Wis 11:1 (ἐν χειρὶ προφήτου ἁγίου) refers to Moses, whereas the "formula" (which in Num 33:1 and Ps 76[77]:21 is also extended to Aaron) in Josh 14:2 is transferred, so to say, to Joshua (cf. Hilgenfeld, "Paulus," 237 n. 1). The ἐν χειρί in the "formula" (cf. Acts 7:35: σὺν χειρί) is without question a Hebraism (on this see, e.g., Longenecker, *Galatians*, 140). To think of the tradition which finds expression in this way is also suggested in view of the fact that it is taken up also in 1QS 8:15. Indeed it seems necessary inasmuch as the verb צוה applied in this passage is used in the Pentateuch often in the context with the giving of the law by Moses and is translated in the Septuagint by συντάσσειν (so, e.g., Exod 35:29, but also in Num 15:23 just referred to), therefore by a word which closely corresponds to the διατάσσειν in Gal 3:19bβ — not least of all according to the evidence in Acts 7:44 (cf. on this, e.g., Exod 35:29) and Acts 7:53 (cf. on this [at] n. 78 above and [at] nn. 186-89 below). Cf. (at) n. 78 above and (at) nn. 143, 186-89 below.

138. *Mos.* 2:166. Cf. *Somn.* 1:142-43 (here as in *T. Dan* 6:2 the term refers to angels; however, at the same time, reference is made to Exod 20:19!) — further *Spec. Laws* 1:116.

139. *As. Mos.* 1:14; 3:12. For 1:14 a Greek version is preserved (in Gelasius of Cyzicus, *Historia Ecclesiastica* 2.17.7; cf. Oepke, "μεσίτης," 621 n. 73), according to which God has destined Moses as τῆς διαθήκης αὐτοῦ [θεοῦ] μεσίτην *(arbiter testamenti illius)*.

140. Heb 8:6 (cf. 8:5: Moses); 12:24 (cf. 12:18-21: Sinai events; Moses). Cf. 9:15.

141. Cf. for instance Callan, "Pauline Midrash," 555 (and Sänger, "μεσίτης," 1012).

142. Examples in Billerbeck, *Kommentar*, 3.512, 514-16, 556 (cf. Oepke, "μεσίτης," 619-20; Callan, "Pauline Midrash," 555), and S. Lieberman, *Hellenism in Jewish Palestine: Studies in the Literary Transmission, Beliefs and Manners of Palestine in the I Century B.C.E.–IV Century C.E.* (Texts and Studies of the Jewish Theological Seminary of America 18; New York: Jewish Theological Seminary of America, 1950), 81 n. 271. It deserves to be noticed that this terminology "in the main (is) employed exclusively for Moses as the one commissioned by God" (Oepke, "μεσίτης," 619). Moreover: "Moses was also called ביניי, middleman" (Lieberman, *Hellenism*, 81 n. 271), further שליח (see ibid.; cf. K. H. Rengstorf, "ἀποστέλλω κτλ.," *TWNT* 1

[1933], 397-448 [cf. ET *TDNT* 1, 398-447], here pp. 419-20, and further the passage in *As. Mos.* 11:17, in which Moses is designated as *magnus nuntius*, finally n. 136 above).

143. Billerbeck, *Kommentar*, 3.556, presents a translation of the passage in question, *y. Meg.* 4.74d.9. Cf. (at) n. 137 above.

144. On this see esp. Oepke, "μεσίτης," 603-4.

145. Citations: Oepke, "μεσίτης," 622.

146. Oepke, "μεσίτης," 622.

147. Lieberman, *Hellenism*, 81-82: "The Samaritan Marqah [Memar Marqah VI §2], in enumerating the titles of Moses, calls him מיסטה, μεσίτης . . . , and נומיקה, νομικός" (on this cf. H. Baneth, "Des Samaritaners Marqah an die 22 Buchstaben, den Grundstock der hebräischen Sprache anknüpfende Abhandlung," [Ph.D. diss., University of Halle-Wittenberg, 1888], 48[-49] [here lines 5-6] together with n. 89, and J. MacDonald, *Memar Marqah: The Teaching of Marqah* [2 vols., BZAW 84; Berlin: de Gruyter, 1963] 1.135 [here line 7] as well as 2.219 [together with n. 24, where MacDonald supposes that מיסטה — in the present translation understood as "teacher" — would be "possibly a denominative from Latin *just-*, or connected with μήστωρ"; especially in view of the almost direct juxtaposition with נומיקה the thesis of Lieberman will, however, be preferred, which MacDonald does not discuss]). Whereas "the rabbis admittedly know the loan word מֵסוֹן = μέσον" (Oepke, "μεσίτης," 619), things stand differently in their field with the word μεσίτης — differently also from Marqah's work, which probably originated at the latest in the fourth century (on this see MacDonald, *Memar*, 1.XX). Callan, "Pauline Midrash," 555, and Longenecker, *Galatians*, 141, take up Lieberman's notion.

148. Callan, "Pauline Midrash," 555. Cf. Lührmann, *Brief an die Galater*, 63 ("'Mediator' may be a common title for Moses"), further Sänger, "μεσίτης," 1011.

149. See, e.g., Rosenmüller, *Scholia* 4, third ed., 388-89, Wieseler, *Commentar*, 287, 291, Kern, "Noch eine Erörterung," 157-58, Bousset, *Brief an die Galater*, 56, Gründler, "Noch einmal," 550-51, and Giblin, "Three Monotheistic Texts," 538, also Schlier, *Galater*, twelfth ed., 161, and Betz, *Galaterbrief*, 305.

150. The thesis often advocated, that 3:20 explains as (an) interpolation or gloss, has already been mentioned (at) n. 29 above. More cautiously Wieseler, *Commentar*, 303, speaks of "the parenthetical thought of v. 20," and Callan ("The Law," ii, 211-12, 214, 219; "Pauline Midrash," 565) assesses both 3:19b-20 and 3:20a in this sense (as similarly already A. Keller, "Ueber Gal. 3,20," *Tübinger Zeitschrift für Theologie* 1830/issue 3, 119-47, here p. 147).

151. Thus among the authors named or alluded to in the previous note, e.g., Wieseler, *Commentar*, 288-89, and Burton, *Critical and Exegetical Commentary*, 191. Differently, however, Callan ("The Law," ii, 212; "Pauline Midrash," 566). Cf. (at) nn. 62-63, 121-23 above.

152. On this cf. for the moment only Betz, *Galaterbrief*, 283-86 together with nn. 31, 48-53 (bibliography).

153. On this see, e.g., G. Quell and J. Behm, "διαθήκη," *TWNT* 2 (1935), 106-37 (cf. ET *TDNT* 2, 106-34), here pp. 109, 127.

154. Bammel, "Gottes ΔΙΑΘΗΚΗ," esp. 314-15, has suggested thinking about the "enactment on the part of a healthy person" (מתנת בריא), as it is documented in numerous Jewish texts. This has been taken up especially by Mußner, *Galaterbrief*, 237-38, and Betz, *Galaterbrief*, 280-81 (cf. Bachmann, *Sünder*, 145). What can be said in favor of this thesis alongside its considerable power of explanation with respect to the details of the text (on

this see, e.g., Bammel, "Gottes ΔIAΘHKH," esp. 316-18), is among other things that analogies to this legal institution are not missing either in the oriental realm beyond Palestine (on this see Bammel, "Gottes ΔIAΘHKH," 315, and Betz, *Galaterbrief*, 280 together with n. 19) or (otherwise) in the Greco-Roman sphere (on this see Longenecker, *Galatians*, 129-30). The difficulty noted by Longenecker, *Galatians*, 130, that (especially) with διαθήκη as a legal term concerning inheritance the addressees had become accustomed to associate an enactment that could be withdrawn, in addition, can be relativized. The readers and hearers are prevented from focusing on an understanding of the word in the sense of not taking effect until the death of the testator (that is, on an understanding, according to which a transfer of property could still be amended at an earlier time) by the association of the concept with the story of Abraham, that is, with the biblical form of speaking about the "covenant" (see Gal 3:16-17; cf. 4:24). Cf. (however) Burchard, "Noch ein Versuch," 65.

155. In this Paul is without question closer to the Greek version of Exod 12:40-41 than to the Hebrew, because the information about the number is different in the Hebrew, where only the sojourn in Egypt is in view, than in the Septuagint, where reference is made to the time in Egypt *and* in Canaan. Moreover, if the Apostle lets this period begin with Abraham, then he thus belongs to a wide stream of tradition as the calculation in this respect in Demetrius (Eusebius, *Praeparatio Evangelica* 9.21.16, 18-19) and a passage in Josephus (*Ant.* 2:318; cf. however: *J.W.* 5:382; *Ant.* 2:204) show. D. Lührmann, "Die 430 Jahre zwischen den Verheißungen und dem Gesetz (Gal 3,17)," *ZAW* 100 (1988), 420-23 (esp. 421), has undertaken to make it plausible that such a numbering is prepared for already in the Pentateuch (beginning with the chronological notices in Gen 12:4 and 16:3).

156. On this distinction, concerning the promise of the land and concerning the promise of posterity, see, e.g., Betz, *Galaterbrief*, 283 n. 30. Cf., however, Sir 44:21.

157. Ebeling, *Wahrheit*, 255, even says that today this interpretation seems like "sleight of hand." He correctly adds to this that the Apostle moves here nevertheless within what was for him "a familiar rabbinic hermeneutic." H.-G. von Mutius, "Ein judaistischer Beitrag zu Galater 3,16," *Biblische Notizen* 11 (1980), 35-37, with *Bereshit Rabba* 6:9 (on Gen 1:18) gives an example, evaluated as amoraic, that the term זרע, originally understood in the collective sense, now is referred to a singular person; here actually the "seed" from Gen 48:19 points to Joshua (cf. further Mußner, *Galaterbrief*, 238-40, also Longenecker, *Galatians*, 131-32).

158. Bauer, *Wörterbuch*, 1789-90. On the attempt to provide a collective interpretation, among other things, of the ἑνός see (at) n. 21 above and n. 168 below.

159. That is, (at) n. 132 above.

160. Thus one gets the impression with Sieffert (*Galater*, ninth ed., 192-96) and with W. Radl (*Galaterbrief* [Stuttgarter Kleiner Kommentar, Neues Testament 9; Stuttgart: Katholisches Bibelwerk, 1985], 54) that what is at stake is simply a grammatical verification of the singular (form and) meaning of the expression τῷ σπέρματι, which hence could be used to make a claim for Christ (cf. [at] n. 163 below). Even Mußner (*Galaterbrief*, 237-40) considers only in a parenthesis (p. 238) whether Paul "possibly challenges the objection that with the 'descendants' of Abraham all Israel could be meant" (similarly Longenecker, *Galatians*, 130-32, here 131).

161. Cf. Rohde, *Brief des Paulus*, 150: "That the promise does not hold for the people of Israel . . . is . . . an important presupposition for the following remarks of the Apostle."

162. *Galaterbrief*, 283.

163. "Eins," 205. Cf. (at) n. 160 above.

164. On this see, e.g., Bachmann, *Sünder,* 50-51 (together with nn. 134-35) and p. 145 (together with n. 246). Cf. (at) nn. 178-79 below.

165. Whereas Hübner was once (*Gesetz,* [28-]30) certain of this, that in the "main clause 'It was added on account of the transgressions' the intention of the angels [should be] articulated," he does now (*Biblische Theologie,* 2.83 n. 138) no longer exclude the possibility that προσετέθη could be a divine passive. However, he finds it necessary to add: "One can, however, not *postulate* a divine passive and then from this postulate deduce that God is the true giver." But whether one ought to speak here of a *"petitio principii"* (ibid.) seems in view of the passive forms of 3:21f(f.) (and indeed in view of the ἐπήγγελται in 3:19, which probably has to be understood analogously [on this see esp. Zahn, *Brief des Paulus,* 173 n. 32; cf. Mußner, *Galaterbrief,* 246 n. 6, and Betz, *Galaterbrief,* 300 n. 43, the latter of whom refers to Blass/Debrunner, *Grammatik,* 311,1 n. 1]) very questionable (especially because the δι' ἀγγέλων in 3:19 "first appears to speak for the mediation of the law given by God through angels" [Hübner, *Gesetz,* 28; on this cf. already n. 79 above]). Cf. Mußner, *Galaterbrief,* 247 n. 17, Räisänen, *Law,* 123, Suhl, "Die Galater und der Geist," 290(-291), Wallace, "Galatians 3:19-20," 234-36, 241-43, Bachmann, *Sünder,* 145 (together with) n. 248, and Burchard, "Noch ein Versuch," 67 (together with n. 29).

166. The fact (already mentioned [at] n. 128 above) is especially strongly accented by Merklein, *Studien,* 70 (cf. Suhl, "Die Galater und der Geist," 291).

167. Concerning the various interpretive attempts with respect to this difficult formulation, cf., e.g., Sieffert, *Galater,* ninth ed., 201-3, M. Lehninger, "Exegetische Studie über Gal. 3,19," *TQ* 33 (1936), 41-56, here pp. 50-55, Rohde, *Brief des Paulus,* 154-55, Wallace, "Galatians 3:19-20," 236-38, and Bachmann, *Sünder,* 74 n. 244. I oppose (*Sünder,* 74 n. 244 [and pp. 146-49]) the customary interpretation (in more recent times rejected, e.g., also by Mußner, *Galaterbrief,* 246 together with n. 5, Giblin, "Three Monotheistic Texts," 539-40, U. Wilckens, *Der Brief an die Römer,* vol. 1 [EKK 6, 1; Neukirchen-Vluyn: Neukirchener, 1978], 177, D. J. Lull, "'The Law Was Our Pedagogue': A Study in Galatians 3:19-25," *JBL* 105 [1986], 481-98, here pp. 484-85, J. D. G. Dunn, *Jesus, Paul, and the Law: Studies in Mark and Galatians* [London: SPCK, 1990], 262 [n. 4 to p. 250], and Burchard, "Noch ein Versuch," 68-69, as well as in a cautious way by Longenecker, *Galatians,* 138[-139]), according to which the law was given "in order to bring about transgressions" (Hübner, *Gesetz,* 27), thus, therefore, because a causative understanding of the χάριν is by no means linguistically necessary (see, e.g., 1 Macc 6:13; 2 Macc 4:16) and because that interpretation seems to be governed by statements from Romans (see Rom 7:5ff.; cf. 5:20), not, however, from the context of our passage (see Gal 3:10-13, 21-25; cf. 2:15-17, also 4:1-11), which is — in harmony with the Torah's decreeing characteristic brought to expression by διαταγείς in 3:19 — concerned with the point, that the law shows aberrant behavior to be punishable (and seeks to prevent it [cf. (at) n. 191 below, further Schlier, *Galater,* twelfth ed., 153 (together with) n. 1]). To understand the words τῶν παραβάσεων χάριν in this sense, it is, alongside the context, of course possible also to consider diachronically parallels like *Jub.* 1:5ff. (esp. v. 22) and Justin, *Dial.* 21:1 (Sabbath command and other decrees enacted by God διὰ τὰς ἀδικίας ὑμῶν καὶ τῶν πατέρων ὑμῶν [cf. 19:6; 20:1]); 67:4, 8, 10 and like Rom 3:20. Cf. (at) nn. 186-91 below.

168. On this see (at) n. 132 above and (at) n. 183 below. Similarly (but even then a bit differently) Bammel, "Gottes ΔΙΑΘΗΚΗ," 317 n. 2: In 3:20a "it is a matter of the comple-

mentary statement to v. 16b: the νόμος is not related to Christ" (cf. [at] nn. 91, 97 above). Differently F. Steudel ("Auch ein Versuch, die Stelle Gal. III,16 zu erklären, nebst einer Anfrage ueber die Deutung von Gal. III,19.20," *Archiv für die Theologie und ihre neueste Literatur* 1 [1816], 124-43, esp. 124-30, 137-41; "Wiederholte Anfrage wegen einer Auffassung der Stelle Gal. 3,20," *Tübinger Zeitschrift für Theologie* 1830/issue 3, 148-56, esp. 148, 151), who to be precise relates the ἑνός in 3:16 as well as in 3:20a to the collective ("seed") of the saved (see 3:28-29), but then of course is unable to link the concluding expression in 3:16 (which he unconvincingly paraphrases: "and this great promised thing is Christ" ["Auch ein Versuch," 131]) and therefore Christ directly with the ἑνός (on Steudel's approach see Sieffert, *Galater*, seventh ed., [221-]222 [together with] n. *). Cf. (at) nn. 21, 158 above.

169. On these two points see (at) nn. 160-63 and (at) nn. 52, 68, 98-99, 106-18 above.

170. Bachmann, *Sünder*, 136-38 (bibliography; cf. Burchard, "Noch ein Versuch," 79 n. 92, further W. J. Dalton, "The Meaning of 'We' in Galatians," *ABR* 38 [1990], 33-44).

171. "The Curse of the Law and the Inclusion of the Gentiles: Galatians 3.13-14," *NTS* 32 (1986), 94-112, here esp. 95-99.

172. Gal 3:13a, 14b, 23-25; 4:3, 5b, 6b. Cf. the "I" in 3:15, 17; 4:1.

173. Gal 3:1-5, 26-29; 4:6a. Cf. (3:7, 15 and) the "you" (singular) in 4:7.

174. Cf. Bachmann, *Sünder*, 148(-149) n. 265.

175. Bachmann, *Sünder*, 30-54, esp. 31, 33-40.

176. So, e.g., Holsten, *Deutung*, 33-34 (cf. Holsten, *Evangelium* I,1, 107-8), Sieffert, *Galater*, ninth ed., 215(-216) n. *** (cf. pp. 212, 218-19), J. Lambrecht, "The Line of Thought in Gal 2.14b-21," *NTS* 24 (1978), 484-95, here p. 492, and Hübner, *Gesetz*, 30-31. Cf. n. 105 above.

177. On this see, e.g., Longenecker, *Galatians*, lxxxviii-c.

178. So probably the majority of commentators,, e.g., Oepke, *Brief des Paulus*, 84-85, Schlier, *Galater*, twelfth ed., 163, Mußner, *Galaterbrief*, 250-51, and Ebeling, *Wahrheit*, 261-62. Cf. further for instance Fritsch, "Galater 3,20," 18, and Bachmann, *Sünder*, 50-51 together with n. 135 and pp. 145-46 together with n. 250 (bibliography).

179. On this see (at) n. 164 above.

180. This is in the instances where Paul uses μὴ γένοιτο not without parallels; on this see, e.g., Bachmann, *Sünder*, 48-54 (where I deal especially with the μὴ γένοιτο in Rom 3:6; 6:2a, 15d; 1 Cor 6:15c, and Gal 2:17c).

181. On this see already n. 128 above (bibliography).

182. On this see Bachmann, *Sünder*, 145-46 (together with n. 250; here the reference to Bammel, "Gottes ΔΙΑΘΗΚΗ," 317-18, where it says: "as a result of the fact that it is a matter of *two* works of the *one* God, the problem of ἐπαγγελία-νόμος becomes such a pointed one and establishing the relationship of the two quantities becomes so urgent" [317; p. 317 n. 5: reference to 3:20b]). Cf. (at) n. 97 above.

183. On this see (at) nn. 132, 168 above.

184. At and in nn. 170-73 above.

185. Both components run through 3:15-17 (on this see [at] nn. 153-63 above) by way of 3:19-20a (on this see [at] nn. 166-68 above) at least up until this point.

186. See, however, n. 167 above (on the transgressions) as well as (at) nn. 49, 78-80 (and n. 137) (on the angels).

187. On this cf., e.g., Mußner, *Galaterbrief*, 255, and Betz, *Galaterbrief*, 312.

188. Cf. further for instance *1 En.* 1:9/Jude 14-15 (cf. v. 9), also Exod 23:20-21 (on the "an-

gel of the Lord" cf., e.g., E. E. Urbach, *The Sages. Their Concepts and Beliefs* [Jerusalem: Publications of the Perry Foundation in the Hebrew University of Jerusalem, 1975] [orig. (Hebrew): 1969], 137-38, and Olyan, *Thousand*, 17-18) as well as CD 2:5-6; 4Q400 (1) [ShirShabb] [1:5, 14 and] 1:16f(f.) (see C. Newsom, *Songs of the Sabbath Sacrifice: A Critical Edition* [Harvard Semitic Studies 27; Atlanta: Scholars, 1985], 89 [and on this pp. 30, 105]; cf. 4Q 521 (2) 2:2-3); *Jub.* 1:24-25 (and v. 29); 15:26-27 (cf. also 4:21-24; 30:21-22); *T. Levi* 3:2-3; *T. Naph.* 8:4, 6; *Herm. Sim.* 8:3:3 (= *Herm.* 69:3). Cf. n. 78 above.

189. O. Hofius, "Das Gesetz des Mose und das Gesetz Christi," *Paulusstudien* (WUNT 51; Tübingen: Mohr, 1989), 50-74 (orig.: 1983), regards the angels in Gal 3:19 as "advocates of the divine holiness and of the *middat had-dîn*, of the strict judicial justice of God" (cf. Bachmann, *Sünder*, 147 together with n. 259 [bibliography]). On this cf. Urbach, *Sages*, 135-58 (esp. 137-39, 149), Billerbeck, *Kommentar*, 3.555-56, P. Schäfer, *Rivalität zwischen Engeln und Menschen. Untersuchungen zur rabbinischen Engelvorstellung* (SJ 8; Berlin/New York: de Gruyter, 1975), 30-32, 64, 65-67, Bandstra, "Law," esp. 239-40, and Mach, *Entwicklungsstadien*, 255-57 (cf. pp. 61-62 [here points 6, 10, 11, and 14], also pp. 105-12), further Olyan, *Thousand*, 2, 15, 99 and *passim*, as well as (again) nn. 78, 167 above.

190. On this metaphor see, e.g., Bachmann, *Sünder*, 147-48 together with nn. 260-64 (bibliography).

191. Cf. Bachmann, *Sünder*, (147-48 together with n. 264 and p.) 150 (together with) n. 272: as Phil 4:7 and 1 Peter 1:5 show (cf., however, 2 Cor 11:32), the φρουρεῖν in 3:23 could point in this direction. Cf. Burchard, "Noch ein Versuch," 76-78, further n. 167 above.

192. Cf. (at) nn. 156-63 above.

193. Cf. Bammel, "Gottes ΔΙΑΘΗΚΗ," 317 n. 3: "Both quantities are separate according to the subject matter as well as according to their intention."

194. Bammel, "Gottes ΔΙΑΘΗΚΗ," 317 (who by "in this direction" has in view an angel-God dualism, as it occasionally is claimed on the basis of Gal 3:15ff.); similarly, e.g., Westerholm, *Law*, 176(-179). On the thesis of an especially negative view of the law in Galatians cf. (at) n. 50 above (bibliography), further for instance J. Becker, *Paulus. Der Apostel der Völker* (second ed.; Tübingen: Mohr, 1992; cf. ET of first edition, *Paul: Apostle to the Gentiles* [Louisville: Westminster/John Knox, 1993]), 367, and Hübner, *Biblische Theologie*, 2.35-37.

195. At notes 114-15 above.

196. On this and on the passage to name immediately in the text cf. again Rom 10:12 (as well as Eph 4:5-6; Col 3:11 and 1 Tim 2:5-6). As in Paul, who at the same time articulates his (well-known) christological emphasis, "the oneness of God . . . finds its focus in the realization of an undivided, inner-related community of persons" (Giblin, "Three Monotheistic Texts," 547; cf. Mauser, "Galater iii. 20," 266-68, further, e.g., G. W. Hansen, *Abraham in Galatians: Epistolary and Rhetorical Contexts* [JSNTS 29; Sheffield: JSOT, 1989], 133, and Wallace, "Galatians 3:19-20," 244), so there exists also in the broader Greek and (Jewish) Hellenistic sphere a close "connection between the oneness of God and his universality" (Callan, "The Law," 200; on this see pp. 196-201). Cf. (at) nn. 22-24, 92-94 above.

Notes to Chapter 5

1. F. J. Matera, *Galatians* (SP 9; Collegeville: Liturgical, 1992), 172: "This is, without doubt, one of the most puzzling and disturbing passages in the whole of Galatians"; "a great company of exegetes protests that this is one of the most confusing passages of the New Testament" (on this see the bibliographic references in M. Bachmann, *Sünder oder Übertreter. Studien zur Argumentation in Gal 2,15ff.* [WUNT 59; Tübingen: Mohr, 1992], 130 n. 161). Concerning the offensive element cf. (at) nn. 16-20 below.

2. The opposition seems to be more important to Paul than the way of speaking about δύο διαθῆκαι (cf., e.g., U. Luz, "Der alte und der neue Bund bei Paulus und im Hebräerbrief," *EvT* 67 [1967], 318-36, here pp. 319-20). For whereas he takes up the attached formulation μία μέν in 4:24, differently than expected, not by (ἡ) ἑτέρα δέ or a synonymous phrase (on this see esp. F. Mußner, *Der Galaterbrief* [HTKNT 9; Freiburg: Herder, 1974], 320-21; cf., for instance: D. Lührmann, *Der Brief an die Galater* [ZBK, Neues Testament 7; second ed.; Zurich: Theologischer Verlag, 1988], 79; E. Gräßer, *Der Alte Bund im Neuen. Exegetische Studien zur Israelfrage im Neuen Testament* [WUNT 35; Tübingen: Mohr, 1985], 77), with the δέ close to the beginning of 4:26 he nevertheless offers something similar to such a resumption after all. As a result another covenant is not now placed alongside the one that has been named, but rather the Jerusalem above is opposed to the present Jerusalem in 4:25 (on this see Mußner, *Galaterbrief*, 321, 325; G. Bouwman, "Die Hagar- und Sara-Perikope (Gal 4,21-31). Exemplarische Interpretation zum Schriftbeweis bei Paulus," *ANRW* 2.25.4 [1987], 3135-55, here p. 3144; G. Jankowski, *Friede über Gottes Israel. Paulus an die Galater* [Texte & Kontexte 13; Berlin: Lehrhaus, 1990], 93; Matera, *Galatians*, 176). Cf. (at) nn. 57-71 below, esp. n. 59.

3. At the window furthest to the west on the south aisle — its name is on account of some coats of arms of the cloth weavers and traders' guild situated nearby — the (three) medallions set into the tracery are (in the base) indeed old (on this and on the medallions see F. Geiges, *Der mittelalterliche Fensterschmuck des Freiburger Münsters. Seine Geschichte, die Ursachen seines Zerfalles und die Manahmen zu seiner Wiederherstellung; zugleich ein Beitrag zur Geschichte des Baues selbst* [Freiburg: Herder, 1931], 87-92 [together with nn. 3-4]; I. Krummer-Schroth, *Glasmalereien aus dem Freiburger Münster* [Freiburg: Herder, 1967], 178; E. Adam, *Das Freiburger Münster* [Große Bauten Europas 1; third ed.; Stuttgart: Müller und Schindler, 1981], 80; K. Kunze, *Himmel in Stein. Das Freiburger Münster. Vom Sinn mittelalterlicher Kirchenbauten* [ninth ed.; Freiburg/Basel/Wien: Herder, 1995], 52-53). The present condition of the medallions with the women is being shown by the colored fig. 41 and 42 in Kunze, *Himmel*, whereas our illustration, which lines up the medallions too closely (cf. H. Schreckenberg, *Die Juden in der Kunst Europas. Ein historischer Bildatlas* [Göttingen/Freiburg: Vandenhoeck & Ruprecht/Herder, 1996] 54 fig. 2), reproduces fig. 245 and 246 at Geiges, *Fensterschmuck*, i.e., blueprints which were drawn up (1898) before the restoration of the stained glass windows (cf. Geiges, *Fensterschmuck*, fig. 247-48: photographs of the old condition), in which a gap was necessary to be filled especially at the head of the left woman's mount (where a lion's head had to be supplied).

4. Of the relevant literature dealing particularly with iconography, the following publications are named: A. Oepke, *Das neue Gottesvolk in Schrifttum, Schauspiel, bildender Kunst und Weltgestaltung* (Gütersloh: Bertelsmann, 1950); P. Bloch, "Nachwirkungen des Alten

Bundes in der christlichen Kunst," in *Monumenta Judaica. 2000 Jahre Geschichte und Kultur der Juden am Rhein. Handbuch* (ed. K. Schilling; second ed.; Cologne: Joseph Melzer, 1964), 735-81; R. L. Füglister, *Das Lebende Kreuz. Ikonographisch-ikonologische Untersuchung der Herkunft und Entwicklung einer spätmittelalterlichen Bildidee und ihrer Verwurzelung im Wort* (Einsiedeln/Zurich/Cologne: Benziger, 1964); W. Seiferth, *Synagoge und Kirche im Mittelalter* (Munich: Kösel, 1964); B. Blumenkranz, *Juden und Judentum in der mittelalterlichen Kunst* (Franz Delitzsch-Vorlesungen 1963; Stuttgart: Kohlhammer, 1965); W. Greisenegger, "Ecclesia," *LCI* 1 (1968), 562-69; W. Greisenegger, "Ecclesia und Synagoge," *LCI* 1 (1968), 569-78; W. Greisenegger, "Synagoge," *LCI* 4 (1972), 231-32; G. Schiller, *Ikonographie der christlichen Kunst* (5 vols.; Gütersloh: Bertelsmann, 1966-91), 2.117-18, 121-24; 4.1.38-68; N. Bremer, *Das Bild der Juden in den Passionsspielen und in der bildenden Kunst des deutschen Mittelalters* (EHS 1.892; Frankfurt: Peter Lang, 1986); H. Schreckenberg, *Die christlichen Adversus-Judaeos-Texte und ihr literarisches und historisches Umfeld (1.-11.Jh.)* (EHS 23.172; Frankfurt: Peter Lang, 1982); H. Schreckenberg, *Die christlichen Adversus-Judaeos-Texte (11.-13.Jh.). Mit einer Ikonographie des Judenthemas bis zum 4. Laterankonzil* (EHS 23.335; Frankfurt: Peter Lang, 1998); H. Schreckenberg, "Die patristische Adversus-Judaeos-Thematik im Spiegel der karolingischen Kunst," *Bijdr* 49 (1988), 119-38; Schreckenberg, *Bildatlas;* H. Jochum (ed.), *Ecclesia und Synagoga. Das Judentum in der christlichen Kunst. Ausstellungskatalog* (Saarbrücken: Museum, 1993).

    5. Oepke, *Gottesvolk,* 205 n. 2 (cf. p. 302) in view of Gal 4:21-31 writes: "The later symbolic representation of the church and synagogue in the form of women in the plastic arts and in the religious drama of the Middle Ages perhaps goes back to the passage at hand. In any case it paves the way" (similarly K. Haacker, "Paulus und das Judentum im Galaterbrief," in *Gottes Augapfel. Beiträge zur Erneuerung des Verhältnisses von Christen und Juden* [ed. E. Brocke and J. Seim; Neukirchen-Vluyn: Neukirchener Verlag, 1986], 94-111, here p. 98). Of course one has to reckon with an abundance of further influential factors (among which are: the exegesis of the Song of Songs; the Roman *Judaea-capta* coins, on which *Judaea* is personified allegorically in the form of a woman set several times in contrast over against a victorious armed soldier [on this see Schreckenberg, *Ikonographie,* 450-53, and H. Schwier, *Tempel und Tempelzerstörung. Untersuchungen zu den theologischen und ideologischen Faktoren im ersten jüdisch-römischen Krieg (66-74 n. Chr.)* (NTOA 11; Freiburg Schweiz/Göttingen: Universitätsverlag/Vandenhoeck & Ruprecht, 1989), 287-90; cf. nn. 75, 90, below]) (on this see only the remarks which follow in the text above and section 5 of this essay, further from the literature cited in the preceding note, e.g., Oepke, *Gottesvolk,* 301-32[-338]). Oepke's judgment, however, seems to be rather cautious, when one thinks about the opposition expressed particularly concisely, as it is, in Gal 4:21–5:1 taking into account the διαθήκη concept, about (partly to be emphasized immediately in the text above) the striking correspondences between this pericope and presentations of the *ecclesia-synagoga* motif (with reference to "Jerusalem" in the early period on various occasions [e.g., Jochum, *Ecclesia,* fig. 2, 8; on this see Schreckenberg, *Bijdr* 49, 125]) and about the possible after-effect of the exegesis in the ancient church of this Pauline passage (cf. Schreckenberg, *Bijdr* 49, 137 [p. 127 n. 35], further n. 15 below) and not the least about the allusions to just this passage found in the remarks of Innocent III on the relationship of Christianity and Judaism (on this see Schreckenberg, *Ikonographie,* 408, 410, 414; cf. pp. 99, 279, 283). Cf. n. 13 below.

    6. With respect to our theme, the (former) mark of the color yellow really carries

through (see, e.g., Jochum, *Ecclesia*, fig. 26b, 30, or Schreckenberg, *Bildatlas*, 66 fig. 17 and p. 58 table 2; see, however, the earlier documents Jochum, *Ecclesia*, fig. 17, 18) not until after the fourth Lateran Council (with its clothing regulations for Jews and "Saracens," naming, by the way, no characteristic color [see, e.g., Bremer, *Juden*, 34-36; Schreckenberg, *Ikonographie*, 423-25]). Not least of all as a result this woman so assessed becomes the "representative of contemporary Judaism" (Greisenegger, *LCI* 1, 572; cf., for instance, Oepke, *Gottesvolk*, 332, further: Geiges, *Fensterschmuck*, 87; Bremer, *Juden*, 188-89).

7. The fact that the tetramorph as a mount of the *ecclesia* is at least also reminiscent of the writers of the Gospels (see Schiller, *Ikonographie*, 2.172 together with n. 128) — and in addition possibly reminiscent of Christ — is made certain by formulations from the Middle Ages (on this see: Geiges, *Fensterschmuck*, 87 together with n. 3; Kunze, *Himmel*, 53), especially by one of the inscriptions concerning the scene, which connects the church/tetramorph and synagogue/ass under the cross, in the Hortus Deliciarum of Herrad of Landsberg; the Hortus was lost in 1870, but to a large extent can be reconstructed from, among other things, tracings (on this work see, e.g., Schreckenberg, *Ikonographie*, 601, and on that scene: pp. 314, 601-3; reproductions in R. Green [and others] [ed.], *Herrad of Hohenbourg: Hortus Deliciarum* [2 vols., SWI 36; London/Leiden: E. J. Brill, 1979], 1. folio 150r/plate 93 [in color, without inscriptions; cf. Jochum, *Ecclesia*, fig. 40] and 2. fig. 234 [black and white, with inscriptions; cf. Schiller, *Ikonographie*, 4.1. fig. 111, or Schreckenberg, *Bildatlas*, 43 fig. 14]). It says there: *Ecclesia. Quatuor evangeliste animal ecclesie* (Schreckenberg, *Ikonographie*, 603). As is well known, Irenaeus (*Adversus haereses* 3.11.8) related the "beings" of the biblical texts that have been mentioned not only to Christ as the Word of God but also to the fourfold shape of the gospel (and to four covenants of the history of redemption). On the replacement of the symbolism referring to the Gospels as well as to the Evangelists by a symbolism of only the four writers see H. H. Hofstätter, "Evangelistenbild und Evangeliensymbole"/"Evangelisten und Evangelistensymbole," *Das Münster* 37 (1984), 231-34/321-24, esp. 322-23.

8. Again the interpretation can be made certain by a glance at the Hortus Deliciarum, in that there the woman on the right holds a complete baby goat (similarly Jochum, *Ecclesia*, fig. 11, or Schreckenberg, *Bildatlas*, 39 fig. 4 [a miniature, likewise from the twelfth century]: the woman who has been cast out "has as an attribute ... the baby-goat of the Old Testament cult of sacrifices in her arm" [Schreckenberg, *Ikonographie*, 547]; cf. also Schreckenberg, *Bildatlas*, 54 fig. 1; p. 58 table 3; p. 60 table 6) — and also (among other things) a "knife for sacrifice or for circumcision" (Schreckenberg, *Ikonographie*, 602). If then the ram's head at the end of the twelfth century becomes almost a stereotype (see, e.g.: H. Sachs, *Mittelalterliches Chorgestühl* [Leipzig: Koehler & Amelang, 1964], fig. 53; Jochum, *Ecclesia*, fig. 16, 27, 28b, 41, 42, 43, further 44, or Schreckenberg, *Bildatlas*, 52 fig. 31; p. 53 fig. 34, further p. 69 fig. 2), it should be permissible for this to be connected with the fact that in addition it is an attribute (like the ram in general — which one also comes across as an animal on which the synagogue rides [see Schiller, *Ikonographie*, 2.172 together with fig. 527] — and no differently from the swine [on this see n. 14 below as well as Sachs, *Chorgestühl*, 42 together with fig. 60-61; cf., however, also Schiller, *Ikonographie*, 4.1, 52]), which indicates unchastity (on this see: Greisenegger, *LCI* 1, 571, 574, 577; Greisenegger, *LCI* 4, 232; L. Wehrhahn-Stauch, "Bock," *LCI* 1 [1968], 314-16, here pp. 315-16). For a portrayal like that of the *Tucherfenster* such a nuance is all the less likely to be excluded, just as according to the Hortus Deliciarum

it is likewise not missing with the ass as a mount: *Animal Synagoge asinus stultus et laxus* (Schreckenberg, *Ikonographie*, 602; cf. H. Schmidt and M. Schmidt, *Die vergessene Bildersprache christlicher Kunst. Ein Führer zum Verständnis der Tier-, Engel- und Mariensymbolik* [Munich: Beck, 1982], 88-90). Without question the ram's head with the naked synagogue in the "altar canopy of the Church in Aal from the second half of the thirteenth century" (Blumenkranz, *Juden*, 58; see fig. 70 [or Schreckenberg, *Bildatlas*, 53 fig. 35]) is to be understood in this way, inasmuch as this woman, apart from the crown that is falling off and the veil over the eyes, is shaped quite similarly like, for example, the famous seductress in the foyer of the Freiburg Cathedral (see Kunze, *Himmel*, fig. 93; cf. Wehrhahn-Stauch, *LCI* 1, 315) — which probably is to be connected with the figures of the foolish virgins and of the synagogue which are placed diagonally opposite (see Kunze, *Himmel*, fig. 39, 91; cf. Schreckenberg, *Bildatlas*, 55 fig. 2), as not only the arrangement of the sculptures in this foyer suggests (on this see G. Münzel, *Der Skulpturenzyklus in der Vorhalle des Freiburger Münsters* [Freiburg: Herder, 1959], 68-70), but also certain iconographic parallels lead one to suppose (see on this Sachs, *Chorgestühl*, fig. 53 [foolish virgin and synagogue with ram's head, around 1360], and further H. Appuhn [ed.], *Heilsspiegel. Die Bilder des mittelalterlichen Erbauungsbuches* [Speculum humanae salvationis, Die bibliophilen Taschenbücher 267; Dortmund: Harenberg, 1981], fig. referring to chapter 34c [and on this see pp. 113-14: Here, likewise ca. 1360, "the first of the five wise . . . virgins is depicted by the flag of victory and chalice as *Ecclesia*, . . . the first of the foolish virgins [is depicted] by the blindfold over the eyes, the crown that is falling off, and the ram's head as *Synagoga*"; cf. on this and on similar groupings in addition R. Körkel-Hinkfoth, *Die Parabel von den klugen und törichten Jungfrauen (Mt. 25, 1-13) in der bildenden Kunst und im geistlichen Schauspiel* (EHS 28.190; Frankfurt: Peter Lang, 1994), 85-88]). Both here and there, however, the ram's head is connected with a fur hide thrown over the shoulder. Cf. (at) n. 12 below.

9. Cf. (at) nn. 59-63 below.

10. Geiges, *Fensterschmuck*, fig. 242-43 (cf. fig. 244).

11. A certain development is reflected in this; for in older portrayals of the *ecclesia-synagoga* motif — so, e.g., in the Hortus Deliciarum (on this see n. 7 above) — as a rule the two women belong directly under the cross, and indeed in just this arrangement (on this see, e.g., Greisenegger, *LCI* 1, 572-73, 575). In any case the left side as the heraldic right side, compared with the other side, is the positive one (cf. on this, e.g., Schreckenberg, *Bijdr* 49, 125, with reference to Matt 25:33, 41).

12. On this see, e.g.: Oepke, *Gottesvolk*, 332-33; Bloch, *Monumenta*, 752-53; Greisenegger, *LCI* 1, 571-72; Schiller, *Ikonographie*, 2.123-24. Cf. (at) n. 8 above (and Schreckenberg, *Ikonographie*, 602-3).

13. A crown *(corona)* and a spear-flag *(hasta signifera, flammula, vexillum)* point in any case to political-military elements in the prior history of the *ecclesia-synagoga* portrayal (on this see, e.g.: Schreckenberg, *Ikonographie*, 452 [cf. on this n. 5 above]; Schreckenberg, *Bijdr* 49, 125-26) — including Gal 4:30. But not until relatively late did the contraposition develop "into an authentic struggle . . . , as pictures of tournaments depict it" (Greisenegger, *LCI* 1, 576), especially the depiction in the Freiburg Cathedral. Not the least the pseudo-Augustinian writing "Altercatio Ecclesiae et Synagogae" (*PL* 42:1131-40) will have exerted influence on the still less aggressive contraposition of church and synagogue in the Carolinian portrayals (on this see, e.g.: Seiferth, *Synagoge*, 56-65; Schreckenberg, *Ikonographie*, 479-80;

Schreckenberg, *Bijdr* 49, 125 together with n. 24); in the "Altercatio" incidentally the debate of these communities, portrayed here as women, concerning freedom or slavery (*PL* 42, 1131-32) that befits them our passage Gal 4:21–5:1 will reverberate, inasmuch as the verse Gen 25:23 (or Rom 9:12), which is quoted in this context (*PL* 42, 1131) asserts only the factor of slavery, indeed not that of freedom and especially not the motif of the contraposition of two mothers. When in a sermon of Martin Luther of March 16, 1539, on this passage (WA 47, 678-85) it says (p. 679, lines 31-32): *Haec pugna et altercatio inter hos 2 populos semper fuit* (cf. p. 638, line 6: *Sic Deus pinxit hanc pugnam, quae ab initio mundi duravit* [and to be sure the struggle between the true church, characterized by promise among other things, and the false church, characterized by works among other things]), the concept of combat indicates the intensification that has occurred in the meantime. Moreover, one will at least be able to ask whether now here artistic portrayals of the motif may exercise influence on the exegesis of Gal 4:21-31. Cf. n. 5 above and nn. 15, 55 below.

14. Sachs, *Chorgestühl*, 32-33 together with fig. 43 (cf. Schreckenberg, *Bildatlas*, 65 fig. 14). (Whereas Sachs, *Chorgestühl*, 31 [cf. p. 17], speaks of "the first half of the fourteenth century," it is dated at the beginning of the fifteenth century in Schiller, *Ikonographie*, 4.1, 59 together with fig. 140, and in Jochum, *Ecclesia*, 92 [together with fig. 38].) As in Freiburg, the head of the figure that symbolizes Judaism is falling over backward; but differently from there this figure and the one opposite now in each case is — according to the genre — a man and the animals that are being ridden, namely a horse *(ecclesia)* and a swine *(synagoga* [cf. n. 8 above]). Above all: The church, which here carries a shield (with the symbol of a fish; cf., e.g., Jochum, *Ecclesia*, fig. 37), now contacts with its lance the opponent, the synagogue.

15. In any case from the second century on this passage has been understood in this way: According to Tertullian (*Adversus Marcionem* 5.4.8) who himself also interprets it as having to do with Judaism and Christianity, Marcion had already pointed to the synagogue and the church (on this see J. L. Martyn, "The Covenants of Hagar and Sarah," in *Faith and History. Essays in Honor of Paul W. Meyer*, ed. J. T. Caroll and others [Atlanta: Scholars, 1990], 160-93, here pp. 164-67; cf. [however] A. v. Harnack, *Marcion. Das Evangelium vom fremden Gott. Eine Monographie zur Geschichte der Grundlegung der katholischen Kirche* [TU 45, second ed.; Leipzig: Hinrichs, 1924], 75*[-76*] n. 21). For the subsequent centuries Schreckenberg, *Umfeld*, 306, 332, 496, names as representatives of such an interpretation Ambrose of Milan, Maximus of Turin, and Abogard of Lyon (cf. n. 21 below); from the field of Greek exegesis one could also name John Chrysostom (*PG* 61:662-63). Cf. also Augustine, *De trinitate* 15.9.15, further for a later time: n. 5 above; Martyn, "Covenants," 167-68; (at) n. 46 below. (It should be especially mentioned that the interpretation with respect to synagogue and church is also documented by the *Glossa ordinaria* [see *PL* 114, 581-82] and that Luther [on him see already n. 13 above] in his continuous comments on Galatians, given that with the verb ἀλληγορεῖν and the concept "Jerusalem," which "in the Middle Ages was time and again mentioned as a model example" [F. Ohly, *Schriften zur mittelalterlichen Bedeutungsforschung* (Darmstadt: Wissenschaftliche Buchgesellschaft, 1977), 14] for the fourfold meaning of the biblical text, constantly comes to speak of this interpretive technique [e.g., WA 57.2, 95-96] and thereby relates *allegorice* to *Sinagoga et Ecclesia* [e.g., 1516/17: WA 57.2, 96, line 2], without, however, placing emphasis on it.) Cf. (at) nn. 19-21, 103 below.

16. Thus, but without the hypothetical "if," G. Ebeling, *Die Wahrheit des Evangeliums. Eine Lesehilfe zum Galaterbrief* (Tübingen: Mohr, 1981), 381 (cf., e.g.: D.-A. Koch, *Die Schrift*

als Zeuge des Evangeliums. Untersuchungen zur Verwendung und zum Verständnis der Schrift bei Paulus [BHT 69; Tübingen: Mohr, 1986], 204 n. 12, also p. 209; F. S. Malan, "The Strategy of Opposing Covenants. Galatians 4:21–5:1," Neot 26 [1992], 425-40, here pp. 433, 436). See S. Ben-Chorin, Paulus. Der Völkerapostel in jüdischer Sicht (Munich: P. List, 1980 [orig. 1970]), 132: In Gal 4:21-31 Paul offers "a complete turnaround of the patriarchal legend." (Under that assumption such judgments would not thereby become invalid, that Paul at any rate fits basically into the intensification of the Old Testament contraposition of Hagar/Ishmael and Sarah/Isaac in Jewish interpretive traditions [see, e.g., Philo: Cher. 9; Sobr. 7–9 (cf. Bar 3:23); see further n. 32 below]; on this see M. C. Callaway, "The Mistress and the Maid: Midrashic Traditions Behind Galatians 4:21-31," RadRel 2 [1975], 94-101, esp. 99; on the exegesis and history of interpretation of Genesis 16–21 cf. the Habilitationsschrift of T. Naumann [Bern, 1996; typescript]: "Ismael. Studien zu einem biblischen Konzept der Selbstwahrnehmung Israels im Kreis der Völker aus der Nachkommenschaft Abrahams," further, concerning Gal 4:27 and Isaiah 54, F. F. Bruce, "'Abraham Had Two Sons': A Study in Pauline Hermeneutics," in New Testament Studies: Essays in Honor of Ray Summers in His Sixty-Fifth Year, ed. H. L. Drumwright and C. Vaughan [Waco: Word, 1975], 71-84, here p. 82 [cf. n. 103 below]).

17. So H. D. Betz, Der Galaterbrief. Ein Kommentar zum Brief des Apostels Paulus an die Gemeinden in Galatien (Hermeneia; Munich: Kaiser, 1988 [orig., English, 1979]), 420, who (in n. 55 refers to H.-J. Schoeps, Paulus. Die Theologie des Apostels im Lichte der jüdischen Religionsgeschichte [Tübingen: Mohr, 1959], 248, and) proceeds accordingly. Incidentally, Schoeps, Paulus, 252 n. 1, points out that in Pesiq. Rab Kah. 22:1 "there is" (probably) something like "an . . . ironical take on this [Pauline] allegory" (on this see, e.g., Bouwman, "Hagar- und Sara-Perikope," 3149; cf. Schreckenberg, Umfeld, 166): "R. Berechiah, citing R. Levi, said: You find that when our mother Sarah gave birth, the nations of the world declared — and may be forgiven for repeating what they said — that Sarah did not give birth to Isaac. It was Hagar, Sarah's handmaid — she gave birth to him, they said. [To prove that Sarah had indeed given birth to Isaac], what did the Holy one do? He withered up the nipples of the noblewomen of the world's nations, so that they came and kissed the dust of Sarah's feet, pleading with her: Do a good deed and give suck to our children. Thereupon our father Abraham said to Sarah: 'Sarah, this is no time for modesty. Hallow the Holy One's name. Sit down in the marketplace and give suck to their children.' Hence it is said Sarah gave children suck (Gen 21:7)" (Pesikta dĕ-Raḇ Kahăna. R. Kahăna's Compilation of Discourses for Sabbaths and Festal Days, translated from Hebrew and Aramaic by W. G. (G. Z.) Braude and I. J. Kapstein [The Littman Library of Civilization; London: Routledge & Paul, 1975], 345).

18. F. Nietzsche, Werke in drei Bänden (ed. K. Schlechta; fifth ed.; Munich: Carl Hanser, 1966), 1.1010-1279, here p. 1068. This does not have to do especially with Gal 4:21–5:1, but in general with the early "attempt" — later supplied with arbitrary philological assistance — "to pull the Old Testament out from under the body of the Jews, with the claim that it contains nothing other than Christian doctrines and belongs to Christians as the true people of Israel: whereas the Jews had only arrogated it for themselves" (1068).

19. Examples (in F. Mußner, "Theologische 'Wiedergutmachung'. Am Beispiel der Auslegung des Galaterbriefes," FrRu 26 [1974], 7-11, here p. 10, and) in the two following notes as well as in n. 46 below. Cf. n. 15 above.

20. J. Becker, *Paulus. Der Apostel der Völker* (second ed.; Tübingen: Mohr, 1992; cf. ET of the first edition, *Paul: Apostle to the Gentiles* [Louisville: Westminster/John Knox, 1993]), 116, 492. Cf. J. Becker, *Der Brief an die Galater* (NTD 8, 1-85; third ed.; Göttingen: Vandenhoeck & Ruprecht, 1985), (55-)58. Similarly, e.g., also R. R. Ruether, *Faith and Fratricide: The Theological Roots of Anti-Semitism* (New York: Seabury, 1974), (102-)103: "Those who believe in Christ are the offspring of the free woman, while those still under the Mosaic covenant are the offspring of the slave woman. . . . The slave woman and her children are cast out, so they may not inherit together with the children of the free woman." From there the author arrives at the assessment: "Paul's position was unquestionably that of anti-Judaism" (p. 104). When U. Luz, *Das Geschichtsverständnis des Paulus* (BEvT 49; Munich: Kaiser, 1968), 285, says with Gal 4:30 in view: "Here the rejection of the Jews is explicitly expressed" (cf. U. Wilckens, *Der Brief an die Römer* [3 vols., EKKNT 6; Neukirchen-Vluyn: Neukirchener Verlag, 1978-82], 2.185; H. Frankemölle, "Juden und Christen nach Paulus. Israel als Volk Gottes und das Selbstverständnis der christlichen Kirche," *TGl* 74 [1984], 59-80, here p. 75; P. Fiedler, "'Das Israel Gottes' im Neuen Testament — die Kirche oder das jüdische Volk?" in *Christlicher Antijudaismus und jüdischer Antipaganismus. Ihre Motive und Hintergründe in den ersten drei Jahrhunderten* [ed. H. Frohnhofen, Hamburger Theologische Studien 3; Hamburg: Steinmann u. Steinmann, 1990], 64-87, here p. 70), so this fits in as well as the comment on Gal 4:25 in Betz (*Galaterbrief*, 423): "This is one of the sharpest attacks of Paul on the Jews." Indeed G. Klein, "Individualgeschichte und Weltgeschichte bei Paulus. Eine Interpretation ihres Verhältnisses im Galaterbrief," in *Rekonstruktion und Interpretation. Gesammelte Aufsätze zum Neuen Testament* (BEvT 50; Munich: Kaiser, 1969), 180-224 (orig., apart from the "Nachtrag" [221-24], 1964), is even a bit more blatant when he says that "Paul . . . with the passage vv. 21-31 destroys Israel's dignity" (216). Cf. (at) n. 103 below.

21. "Der Galaterbrief — Situation und Argumentation," *ANRW* 2.25.4 (1987), 3067-3134, here p. 3121: "the . . . line of argument with the appeal in v. 30, which is aimed directly at the community, leads to this: that . . . the Apostle . . . proves that the separation from the heretics is a necessity . . . demanded by the law" (cf. pp. 3128-29, 3132). Similarly, e.g.: T. Zahn, *Der Brief des Paulus an die Galater* (KNT 9; second ed.; Leipzig: Deichert, 1907), 242-43; G. Dehn, *Gesetz oder Evangelium? Eine Einführung in den Galaterbrief* (UCB 9; third ed.; Berlin: Furche-Verlag, 1938), 161-62; Mußner, *Galaterbrief*, 331-32; Callaway, "Mistress and the Maid," 99; Betz, *Galaterbrief*, 66, 430-31; G. W. Hansen, *Abraham in Galatians. Epistolary and Rhetorical Contexts* (JSNTSup 29; Sheffield: JSOT, 1989), 48, 144-46 (and *passim*); R. B. Hays, *Echoes of Scripture in the Letters of Paul* (New Haven: Yale University Press, 1989), 116; R. N. Longenecker, *Galatians*, WBC 41; Dallas, TX: Word, 1990), 217; Malan, "Strategy of Opposing Covenants," 436-37; Matera, *Galatians*, 173, 178; J. D. G. Dunn, *The Theology of Paul's Letter to the Galatians* (New Testament Theology; Cambridge: Cambridge University Press, 1993), 97; A. C. Perriman, "The Rhetorical Strategy of Galatians 4:21–5:1," *EvQ* 65 (1993), 27-42, esp. 40-41 (in which Perriman however thinks less about the driving out of the Judaizers or Jews than about a rejection concerning "the Sinaitic covenant and its implications"). Cf. J. Rohde, *Der Brief des Paulus an die Galater* (THKNT 9; Berlin: Evangelische Verlagsanstalt, 1989), 204-5, where from such exposition another line of interpretation is distinguished, according to which the driving out is not a matter for the addressees but for God (so, e.g.: A. Oepke, *Der Brief des Paulus an die Galater* [THKNT 9; second ed.; Berlin: Evangelische

Verlagsanstalt, 1957 (=1964)], 115; Luz, *Geschichtsverständnis*, 285; cf. Koch, *Schrift*, 211). At any rate in either case from the time of the early church onward that testimony of Gal 4:30 "was customarily assessed as proof for the loss of being chosen, and the disinheritance and rejection of the Jewish people in redemptive history" (Schreckenberg, *Umfeld*, 63; cf. pp. 100, 122, also 496 [Agobard of Lyon (cf. n. 15 above) phrases with reference to Gal 4:30: *Expulsus ergo est de paterna domo Judaicus populus, atque ab haereditate filiorum Ecclesiae, quae per Christum libera effecta est, segregatus*; according to him the Jews are *filii ancillae* and *exhaeredati* (*PL* 104, 96)]). Cf. (at) n. 103 below.

22. That it is better to give the thesis such a nuance (cf. H. Schlier, *Der Brief an die Galater* [KEK; fourth ed.; Göttingen: Vandenhoeck & Ruprecht, 1965], 227) is emphasized among the authors in the previous note especially by: Mußner, *Galaterbrief*, 332 (cf. pp. 325, 327, further, Mußner, "Theologische 'Wiedergutmachung,'" 10); Matera, *Galatians*, 178. Differently, e.g., Betz, *Galaterbrief*, 430. Cf. (at) n. 46 below.

23. It is to some extent comparable when Paul in Rom 11:2(-3) in the reference to 1 Kgs 19:10, 14 does not actually allow Elijah to speak but rather "the Scripture," of course "in Elijah . . . how he pleads with God against Israel" (cf. further Rom 9:25 with Hos 2:23-25). The parallel becomes even more striking when one takes into account that according to Gen 21:(11-)12 God takes up and affirms Sarah's word (cf. 1 Kgs 19:[15-]18 with vv. 10, 14) — and that according to *Tg. Ps.-J.* Gen 21:12 she is held to be a prophet (cf. J. B. Lightfoot, *The Epistle of St. Paul to the Galatians* [London: Macmillan, 1865], 184).

24. This detail and, connected with it, the orientation of the formulation toward Abraham would make an appeal to Paul's addressees more difficult (cf. on this n. 36 below), and indeed not only in that case, that it had to do with driving out opponents.

25. Cf., for instance, U. Borse, *Der Brief an die Galater* (RNT; Regensburg: Pustet, 1984), 176.

26. The Septuagint in contrast to the Hebrew wording does not repeat the preposition ("with") before the name Isaac.

27. So above all: Schlier, *Galater*, 228; W. Radl, *Galaterbrief* (Stuttgarter Kleiner Kommentar, Neues Testament 9; Stuttgart: Katholisches Bibelwerk, 1985), 76.

28. Cf. Borse, *Galater*, 176-77 (who incidentally advocates reading ἄρα at the beginning of the verse with the majority text [cf. on this Rom 8:12], not διό [so Nestle-Aland[27], in agreement with Sinaiticus and Vaticanus among others [p. 177], and [in spite of the undisputed first person plural] also not ἡμεῖς δέ [thus, probably under the influence of the ὑμεῖς (variant reading ἡμεῖς) δέ (see on this the immediately following note) from 4:28, among others Alexandrinus and Ephraemi rescriptus]); Gräßer, *Bund*, 74, 76; I. Broer, "'Vertreibe die Magd und ihren Sohn!' Gal 4:21-31 im Horizont der Debatte über den Antijudaismus im Neuen Testament," in *Der bezwingende Vorsprung des Guten. Exegetische und theologische Werkstattberichte*, ed. K. Schoenborn and S. Pfürtner (Münster/Hamburg: Lit, 1994), 167-98, here p. 190.

29. The formulation of 4:28 accords precisely with the naming of the ἀδελφοί in 4:31, but hardly with the personal pronoun. For in 4:28 ὑμεῖς . . . ἐστέ "is strongly supported by early and diverse witnesses" (B. M. Metzger, *A Textual Commentary on the Greek New Testament* [London/New York: United Bible Societies, 1971], 597), and in view of the first person plural in 4:26, 31 (cf. the previous note) and in 5:1 the reading offered in the majority of manuscripts, ἡμεῖς . . . ἐσμέν, must be assessed as the *lectio facilior* (see Metzger, *Textual*

Commentary, 597; cf. Becker, *Galater,* 55), particularly as reference to "you" (plural) is to be found only at a somewhat greater distance (4:21; 5:1b).

30. Suhl, "Der Galaterbrief — Situation und Argumentation," 3120, according to whom 4:31 and 5:1 pick up much more, namely, primarily Galatians 3. (That chapter 3 also stands in the background can and ought not to be disputed [on this see, e.g., (at) n. 35 below]; but in my opinion 4:31[–5:1] has to do above all with the conclusion of the section that begins with 4:21.) Inasmuch as Suhl finds "the break before 4:31" (p. 3132), he stands after all close to the not insignificant number of authors who take 4:31 with what follows (on this and against it see: Schlier, *Galater,* 228 [together with n. 3]; Bachmann, *Sünder,* 105-7 [together with n. 23], 111-15, 130 n. 162). Cf. n. 40 below.

31. Correspondingly also Rom 10:8 (see v[v]. 8[-10]) — although here (according to the majority of textual witnesses) righteousness by faith speaks and not the Scripture (see v. 6).

32. See the references in: (H. L. Strack and) P. Billerbeck, *Kommentar zum Neuen Testament aus Talmud und Midrasch* (4 vols.; Munich: Beck, 1922-28), 3.410, 575-76; R. Le Déaut, "Traditions targumiques dans le Corpus Paulinien? (Hebr 11,4 et 12,24; Gal 4,29-30; II Cor 3,16)," *Bib* (1961), 28-48, here pp. 39-41; Mußner, *Galaterbrief,* 329-30 together with n. 69; Callaway, "Mistress and the Maid," 98-99; C. K. Barrett, "The Allegory of Abraham, Sarah, and Hagar in the Argument of Galatians," in *Essays on Paul* (London: SPCK, 1982), 154-70 (orig. 1976), 164-65 together with n. 31; W. A. Meeks, "'And Rose Up to Play': Midrash and Paraenesis in 1 Corinthians 10:1-22," *JSNT* 16 (1982), 64-78, here pp. 69-70; Longenecker, *Galatians,* 201-3, 205, 217. Since there are also other striking points of contact between Gal 4:21–5:1 and the Targumim (on this see: Déaut, "Traditions targumiques," 42, 37-43; M. McNamara, *Palestinian Judaism and the New Testament* [GNS 4; Wilmington: Glazier, 1983], 247-52; M. G. Steinhauser, "Gal 4,25a: Evidence of Targumic Tradition in Gal 4,21-31?" *Bib* 70 [1989], 234-40 [esp. striking: the themes "children" and "slavery" can be accentuated in the Targumim and the place name "Shur" in Gen 16:7 can here become "Hagra" (cf. Gal 4:24-25!)]; on this cf. nn. 16, 23 above and n. 82 below), it is especially relevant (cf.: Mußner, *Galaterbrief,* 330; Steinhauser, "Gal 4,25a," 239 n. 35) that precisely also here the expression מצחק from Gen 21:9 is understood negatively, indeed partially in the sense of aggression (see the helpful synoptic compilation by P. Naumann, *Targum. Brücke zwischen den Testamenten* 1 [Konstanz: Christliche Verlagsanstalt, 1991], 114-15, 127: idolatry [*CN (Tg. Neof.)* Gen 21:9; *Tg. Ps.-J.* Gen 21:9, 11; *Tg. J. II (Frg. Tg.)* Gen 21:9]; improper deeds [*CN (Tg. Neof)* Gen 21:9]; doing improper things [*Tg. J. II (Frg. Tg.)* Gen 21:9]; quarrel [*Tg. Ps.-J.* Gen 21:10; 22:1; cf. Ms. EE of the Cairo genizah Gen 21:10]; attempt to kill [Ms. LL of the Cairo genizah Gen 21:9]).

33. Similarly in particular: Schlier, *Galater,* 226-27; Barrett, "Allegory," 165; Radl, *Galaterbrief,* 75-76; Broer, "Vertreibe die Magd," 188-89. To connect the διώκειν in Gal 4:29 not with the other references for this verb, but with the ὠδίνειν in 4:19, as occurs in Martyn, "Covenants," 179-80 together with n. 40, seems, however, too bold (cf. nn. 41, 46 below). Cf. (at) nn. 66-68 below.

34. With the repeated use of the adversative particle a correspondence to the pitch of Gal 4:28 arises (cf. Rom 5:13-15, further Gal 4:7-8). This would not be the case, however, if the aggression named in Gal 4:29 had been taken up by a demand for an opposing aggression in 4:30.

35. So, e.g.: Mußner, *Galaterbrief,* 333; Haacker, "Paulus und das Judentum," 100-101 (cf. n. 30 above). This connection is also emphasized by Becker, *Galaterbrief,* 55(-56), who, how-

ever, sees in it one of the signs for "explaining . . . vv. 28-30 as a Pauline insertion in an older exegesis" (cf. n. 52 below). That, as he thinks, Gal 4:31 cannot be understood as the conclusion of 4:29-30 will not be maintained, precisely because of the consideration of this connection.

36. Cf. K. Berger, "Abraham in den paulischen Hauptbriefen," *MTZ* 17 (1966), 47-89, here p. 62, further (at) nn. 27-28, 33, 35 above, also (at) n. 43 below. (Since the "brothers" are addressed in 4:31, indeed addressed concerning their status, the reversed facts of the matter in 4:30 are all the more significant, as Schlier, *Galater*, 227, aptly describes them: "No address to the community takes place, which after all is typically molded in advance not through Abraham but through Sarah and Isaac" [on this cf. n. 24 above].)

37. Cf. further, for instance: G. Delling, "στοιχέω," *TWNT* 7 (1964; cf. ET *TDNT* 7), 669; Lührmann, *Galater*, 79; Betz, *Galaterbrief*, 422; Longenecker, *Galatians*, 213.

38. Indeed in the essay referred to in n. 2 above, esp. 3144-45. I have more recently taken up the structural diagram (p. 3145) with the addition of 5:1 (on this cf. n. 40 below) and slightly modified it (Bachmann, *Sünder*, 131 [together with] n. 165) — in the course of which some errors in versification slipped in, which I have corrected in the diagram that follows.

39. On this see the previous note. The contraposition is simplistic among other things inasmuch as in it on the one hand certain elements of the text (e.g., Gal 4:24a) are at least not translated as catchwords and inasmuch as on the other hand in this process of transformation the finite verb form in Gal 4:25c now becomes a noun.

40. That the pericope does not end until Gal 5:1 and (not with 4:30 [on this cf. n. 30 above] or) not with 4:31 (cf. n. 38 above) is a minority opinion, which nevertheless is advocated by the following authors among others: Zahn, *Galater*, 244-45; R. Bring, *Der Brief des Paulus an die Galater* (Berlin/Hamburg: Lutherisches Verlagshaus, 1968), 203-4; F. F. Bruce, *The Epistle to the Galatians* (NIGTC; Grand Rapids: Eerdmans, 1982), 226; Haacker, "Paulus und das Judentum," 98; P. Stuhlmacher, "Die Stellung Jesu und des Paulus zu Jerusalem. Versuch einer Erinnerung," *ZTK* 86 (1989), 140-56, here pp. 152-53; Jankowski, *Galater*, esp. 96; Malan, "Strategy of Opposing Covenants," 425-26, 438-39; Perriman, "Rhetorical Strategy," 29-32 (cf. Borse, *Galater*, 178; G. A. Kennedy, *New Testament Interpretation through Rhetorical Criticism* [SR; Chapel Hill: University of North Carolina Press, 1984], 150; Martyn, "Covenants," 164 n. 11). This view of things is substantiated not only by the ring composition already mentioned, but, as will be made clear immediately, also by the all-embracing coherence of the letter (on this cf. Bachmann, *Sünder*, esp. 105-7, 111-12).

41. There can be no doubt that a correspondence exists between Gal 4:21 and 5:1 in terms of content (insofar as with ὑπὸ νόμον in 4:1-7 [vv. 4-5; cf. vv. 2, 3] reference is made to the status of a δοῦλος [vv. 1, 7; cf. v. 3] and insofar as the term "yoke" [as in Acts 15:10] is reminiscent of the Jewish expression "yoke of the law" [on this see, e.g.: Ben-Chorin, *Paulus*, 132-33; Longenecker, *Galatians*, 224-25]); moreover, both verses happen to pick up 4:9: 4:21 with θέλειν, 5:1 with πάλιν as well as with the vocabulary of slavery (on this cf. [at] n. 49 below). This reference back to 4:9 is decisively clearer than such a reference to 4:12-20, to which Martyn, "Covenants," esp. 170-71, and under his influence also Matera, *Galatians*, esp. 173, appeal. In spite of certain contacts between 4:21–5:1 and 4:12-20 (esp. 4:19: τέκνα or τεκνία, πάλιν, labor pains or motherhood) the differences, however, strike one's eye immediately. In 4:26, 31 (cf. 5:1a) the Apostle, although he is, according to 4:19, in labor pains, counts himself among the children of a mother (on this cf. Martyn, "Covenants," 183-84), and according to

4:27 she suffers no birth pangs in contrast to the Apostle, as conversely no γεννᾶν (4:23, 24, 29) is expressed with respect to him. (Besides, on the question whether in 4:19 τέκνα actually is the correct reading as in 4:25, 27, 28 cf. Longenecker, *Galatians*, 188 n. g, 195, on ὠδίνειν [and its alleged closeness to διώκειν in 4:29] n. 33 above, and on πάλιν [which understood as repetitive corresponds only indirectly to the restitutive πάλιν in 5:1] n. 45 below as well as Bachmann, *Sünder*, 129-30.) Cf. n. 46 below.

42. Borse, *Galater*, 179, says correctly: "others are not thought about here . . . , who could force them [the Galatians] under the yoke of the law, but they themselves are in danger of submitting to a compulsion." The fact that the imperative ἐνέχεσθε follows the active στήκητε weighs in favor of taking it in the middle voice. Cf. Bachmann, *Sünder*, 123-24.

43. Cf. Bachmann, *Sünder*, 130, further (at) nn. 27-28, 33, 35-36 above as well as (at) n. 71 below. J. Lambrecht, "The Universalistic Will of God. The True Gospel in Galatians," in *Pauline Studies. Collected Essays* (BETL 115; Leuven: University of Leuven Press, 1994), 299-306, here p. 300, says in view of the entire writing that the writer "re-evangelizes the Galatians," and that he does this with the goal: "they should not turn back again to slavery."

44. Bachmann, *Sünder*, esp. 123-35. In my opinion the third section (5:2–6:17) has to do with the Christian life, which, correctly understood, makes a direct orientation toward the Torah unnecessary (see, e.g., Bachmann, *Sünder*, 110-11, 158).

45. Hardly any different from the use at the beginning, in Gal 4:9b (cf. n. 41 above, further [at] n. 49 below).

46. Matera, *Galatians*, 176, correctly summarizes (as similarly already Martyn, "Covenants," 168-69): "The majority of commentators identify the children of the slave woman with Judaism." With this option (represented, e.g., by: H. Lietzmann, *An die Galater* [HNT 10; third ed.; Tübingen: Mohr, 1932], 30; Betz, *Galaterbrief*, 422-23, 430-31; Ebeling, *Wahrheit*, 318; Rohde, *Galater*, 194; cf. further the examples and references in [and at] nn. 15, 19-20 above) at least Jewish Christianity is sometimes not counted within the negative corporate entity (so Koch, *Schrift*, 204, speaks of a "contraposition of Israel . . . and the community made up of Jews and Gentiles" [differently expressly Rohde, *Galater*, 194, insofar as he determines just "the Gentile Christian believers" as *oppositum*]). Above all Mußner, *Galaterbrief*, 325 (cf. Mußner, "Theologische 'Wiedergutmachung,'" 10), points exactly to this sub-group here excluded (on this cf. [at] nn. 21-22 above); he evidently thinks more precisely — thereby circumventing the difficulty that results otherwise from the "we" in 4:26, 31 (cf. 5:1a) (on this cf. n. 41 above) — about the "Judaists who hold on to the law" (Mußner, *Galaterbrief*, 327) (following him also Schreckenberg, *Umfeld*, 89, 99, 100, 122 [cf. further, for instance, B. Corsani, "L'interpretazione tipologica della storia di Agar e Sara," *Parola spirito e vita* 24 (1991), 213-24, esp. 220-23]; against such an approach, e.g.: Koch, *Schrift*, 211 n. 47 [who maintains: "Sinai is the identifying marker of Israel altogether and not only of Jewish Christianity"]; Fiedler, "Israel Gottes," 70; Broer, "Vertreibe die Magd," 185-86). Similarly, e.g., Mußner, *Galaterbrief*, 26, 325 (a Judaistic "slogan . . . 'Jerusalem is our mother'"), Bouwman, "Hagar- und Sara-Perikope," 3144 ("Opponents, which interpret the two women as types of the church of the circumcised and the church made up of Gentiles"); differently J. G. Gager, *The Origins of Anti-Semitism: Attitudes toward Judaism in Pagan and Christian Antiquity* [Oxford: Oxford University Press, 1983], 242 [together with n. 19], according to whom Paul himself intends to distinguish here "between Israel (Isaac) and the nations (Ishmael)" [see, however, (at) n. 53 below]), and Martyn, "Covenants," esp. 174 n. 34, assume a Pauline

revision of statements of the Jewish opponents ("the Teachers"). When Martyn ("Covenants," esp. 179-83), however, thinks (cf. Matera, *Galatians*, 173, 176-79 [who in the end, nevertheless, stands closer to Mußner's view, in spite of his taking up Martyn's proposal]) that the Apostle wants — with reference to what is said in 4:12-20 about his labor pains — to drive at two different Christian groups, more precisely: "two different ways in which churches are being born" (Martyn, "Covenants," 179, here in italics), "the law-observant mission to Gentiles" (p. 183), defined by Jerusalem, on the one hand, and "the Law-free mission pursued by himself and his co-workers" (p. 183) on the other hand, this stands in conflict not least (cf. n. 41 above, where still other difficulties of this approach are addressed) with the "we" in 4:26, 31 (cf. 5:1a). Even with respect to his position, all the more with respect to the opinions of those who understand the Hagar corporate entity directly of Judaists, particularly Mußner, Schreckenberg, and Matera, that objection has to be added which will be raised immediately in the text (above) over against the conventional conception, if one pointedly applies this objection to those suggested solutions. But Martyn and these authors have nevertheless rendered considerable service to be able to draw attention to the weaknesses of the traditional consensus (see esp. Mußner, "Theologische 'Wiedergutmachung,'" 10; Matera, *Galatians*, 176-77 [Paul's opponents not Jews but Judaists; the contraposition between Judaism and Christianity anachronistic]). On the view which breaks loose from the consensus in another, in a very interesting way, which particularly Bouwman, "Hagar- und Sara-Perikope," esp. 3151, has developed, see (at) nn. 54-55 below.

47. When Longenecker, *Galatians*, 225, after interpreting 4:22-31, at least close to the conventional view of the Hagar corporate entity (see esp. pp. 211, 219), says in relation to 5:1: "The use of the word πάλιν . . . does not mean that before becoming believers in Christ the Galatians had been under the 'yoke' of the Jewish law," this is an urgently necessary protection against this background — and in view of 4:8 — for the reader instructed by Longenecker otherwise would have to understand Paul exactly in the meaning thus rejected.

48. On this see, e.g., D. Rusam, "Neue Belege zu den στοιχεῖα τοῦ κόσμου (Gal 4,3.9; Kol 2,8.20)," *ZNW* 83 (1992), 119-25.

49. On this cf. (at) nn. 41, 45 above.

50. On this see, e.g., Bachmann, *Sünder,* 124 together with n. 127 (with reference to Zahn, *Galater,* esp. 207). Over against those who "in Christ Jesus" have achieved "freedom," among whom there is the non-Jew Titus, according to Gal 2:1-5 the attempt of enslaving, of καταδουλοῦν (2:4) — only in the case of those of Jewish origin: of enslaving again — is, of course, possible.

51. The former as one put "under the law" brings about not least the redemption of those "under the law," the latter, who advanced especially in Ἰουδαισμός (Gal 1:13-14), is determined by his vocation to proclaim ἐν τοῖς ἔθνεσιν (Gal 1:16), and this means: among the non-Jewish nations. Both reflect a priority of Judaism in redemption history.

52. That the first person plural in Gal 2:15-17 refers exclusively to Jewish Christians is clear in view of the context and in view of the contraposition carried out in 2:15. From this an analogous answer stands to reason for the controversial problem with reference to the meaning of the "we" in the part of the letter that follows 2:15-21, namely 3:1–4:7 (on this see, e.g., Bachmann, *Sünder,* 136 together with n. 193 [bibliography]; cf. esp. pp. 27-29, 123-24, 134-35 with respect to the divisions of the text). T. L. Donaldson, "The 'Curse of the Law' and the Inclusion of the Gentiles: Galatians 3,13-4," *NTS* 32 (1986), 94-112, has provided further

important reasons for such a solution. According to him, here Paul gives three times (see 3:13-14; 3:23-29; 4:3-7) — and not least of all by means of the first person plural — a christologically thought out interpretation of the traditional eschatological schema, according to which "salvation is extended to the Gentiles, who share on equal terms with the Jews" (p. 98). The "we" would therefore be used inclusively only at the conclusion of the adaptations of that traditional idea, now including the Gentile Christians, that is, in 3:14b and 4:5b, 6b. Besides me (Bachmann, *Sünder,* esp. 137-39; I, however, understand the first person plural in 4:5b, which indeed is followed by a second person plural in 4:6a, in an exclusive sense) Lambrecht, "The Universalistic Will," 304-5, has adapted this approach as a solution (who in so doing gives up his earlier inclusive interpretation of "we" [especially in 3:13; on this see p. 304 n. 6]), not however D. Sänger, *Die Verkündigung des Gekreuzigten und Israel. Studien zum Verhältnis von Kirche und Israel bei Paulus und im frühen Christentum* (WUNT 75; Tübingen: Mohr, 1994), 273 (together with) n. 466. Inasmuch as in 3:14 Paul speaks of the blessing of Abraham extending to the ἔθνη and in 3:26-29 and 4:6a uses the second person plural (as in 4:7 the second person singular) with a corresponding intention, it stands of course beyond doubt that salvation and the need for salvation also have to be expressed for Gentile Christians — and this is just what happens with the "we" in 3:14b and 4:6b (cf. 1:4; 5:5, 25). But the Apostle very carefully nuances in this part of the letter with respect to salvation history (and Justin incidentally does this, by the way, in a slightly different manner, *Dialogue with Trypho* 95.1[-3] [as needs to be said in view of Sänger's reference to this passage]). And although outside of 2:15–4:7 "we" is not found used exclusively for Jewish Christians (on this see Bachmann, *Sünder,* 136-37 together with n. 198), the juxtaposition of the second person plural and the inclusive "we," which, of course, is reminiscent particularly of 3:14 and 4:6(-7) and which determines 4:21–5:1, reveals that the differentiation is here not possibly given up. (That this juxtaposition is prepared for in the letter also speaks against evaluating it, as Becker, *Galater,* 55, suggests, in terms of source criticism [cf. n. 35 above].)

53. Cf. nn. 41, 46, 52 above (and Broer, "Vertreibe die Magd," 187), further with respect to the questions of text criticism nn. 28-29 above.

54. Bouwman, "Hagar- und Sara-Perikope," 3151.

55. Cf. Bouwman, "Hagar- und Sara-Perikope," 3149 ("way[s] of living," according to "the pair of concepts flesh-spirit") and 3152 ("The two women are symbols of two ways of living, which are not typical for Judaism on the one hand or Christianity on the other, but which are found in both religions") — and cf. Luther's statements, cited in n. 13 above. Similarly, yet without maintaining any factual juxtaposition also with respect to the past, already: Schlier, *Galater,* (223-)224 ("The present Jerusalem . . . is the representation of the world, which is subjugated to the order of the law, of sin, and of death," and it "is the Jerusalem above which lives in the church, the kingdom that reigns in freedom on the basis of the divine promise"); Berger, "Abraham in den paulischen Hauptbriefen," 63 ("one more 'dogmatic' problem"; "not 'Jews' and 'Christians,' but only 'those under the law' and 'those who are free from the law'") and 87 (further cf. G. Wagner, "Les enfants d'Abraham ou les chemins de la promesse et de la liberté. Exégèse de Galates 4,21 à 31," *RHPR* 71 [1991], 285-95, esp. 287). Comparable statements, *among others,* in Luz, "Der alte und der neue Bund," 321-22; Luz, *Geschichtsverständnis,* 283-84; Betz, *Galaterbrief,* 325; Broer, "Vertreibe die Magd," 192 (cf. p. 195 n. 110). Cf. (at) n. 46 above and n. 69 below.

56. On this see n. 2 above as well as the diagram of the structure at p. 92.

57. Cf., for instance, Klein, "Individualgeschichte," 216-17, Koch, *Schrift*, 210, and now P. Söllner, *Jerusalem, die hochgebaute Stadt. Eschatologisches und Himmliches Jerusalem im Frühjudentum und im frühen Christentum* (TANZ 25; Tübingen/Basel: A. Francke, 1998), 143-69, esp. 151, 156.

58. And in agreement with him: Bouwman, "Hagar- und Sara-Perikope," 3149, 3151.

59. Thus recently H. Lichtenberger, "Alter Bund und Neuer Bund," *NTS* 41 (1995), 400-414, here p. 414 (cf., for instance, Lührmann, *Galater*, 79; Gräßer, *Bund*, 73 n. 304, also p. 77). Although the terminological facts are plain — and although they are in view of the history of the Jerusalem motif extremely striking (on this see, e.g., [at] nn. 60-62, 85 below) — this is often applied to the old and new covenants: in the course of, or at least in a certain proximity to, the common interpretation of our passage toward *synagoga* and *ecclesia* (on this see [at] nn. 15, 46 above; cf. at n. 9 above) and on the basic way of speaking about the δύο διαθῆκαι (esp. emphatically, e.g.: Luz, "Der alte und der neue Bund," 320; Luz, *Geschichtsverständnis*, 57, 130, 283-85; Becker, *Galater*, 56-57; similarly even: Gräßer, *Bund*, 73, 75, 77; E. W. Stegemann, "Zwischen Juden und Heiden, aber 'mehr' als Juden und Heiden? Neutestamentliche Anmerkungen zur Identitätsproblematik des frühen Christentums," *Kirche und Israel* 9 [1994], 53-69, here p. 62; cf. further, for instance, Stuhlmacher, "Stellung Jesu," 152-53). This is problematic not only on account of the absence of the adjectives or ordinal numbers in question. Two further arguments are to be mentioned. First (on this see n. 2 above), the term διαθήκη is left out after Gal 4:24 — and the μία μέν, which refers to it, should in itself not indicate a chronological sequence or a contraposition, as likewise the ἕνα in 4:22bα should not, which is taken up anew by the ἕνα in 4:22bβ, now aimed at Isaac (on this see W. Bauer, *Griechisch-deutsches Wörterbuch zu den Schriften des Neuen Testaments und der frühchristlichen Literatur* [sixth ed.; Berlin/New York: de Gruyter, 1988], 467, *s.v.* εἷς 5a, also 5d; in p. 1019, *s.v.* μέν 1c, incidentally also the ὁ μέν . . . ὁ δέ in 4:23 is judged as employed "not for emphasizing differences"; cf. F. Blass and A. Debrunner, *Grammatik des neutestamentlichen Griechisch* [fourteenth ed.; Göttingen: Vandenhoeck & Ruprecht, 1976], 249, 3 together with nn. 7-9). Second, if one wants to arrange the Hagar or Sinai covenant as the "old covenant" prior to a "new covenant," marked by the woman giving birth to the second child, one would come into considerable conflict with the sequence of the Abrahamic διαθήκη and the giving of the law in chapter 3 (see esp. 3:17) (cf., for instance, Bouwman, "Hagar- und Sara-Perikope," 3151; Martyn, "Covenants," 186), which at best one can escape with the bold thesis of a profound dialectic (as especially is attempted in Gräßer, *Bund*, 68-69, 75 [cf.: Klein, "Individualgeschichte," 216-17; Luz, "Der alte und der neue Bund," 321-22]).

60. In view of this city (or less probably its temple [cf. *1 En.* 89:50; 91:9]) already *1 En.* 90:29 speaks about a new house that takes the place of the first, older one. On later rabbinic linguistic usage that distinguishes between a Jerusalem in the world to come (של עולם הבא) and a Jerusalem in this world (של עולם הזה) see, e.g., Billerbeck, *Kommentar*, 3.22, 87, 573 (cf. also Billerbeck, *Kommentar*, 4.2, 815 and *passim*, with respect to the related way of speaking about the two aeons or worlds). Cf (at) nn. 69, 88 below.

61. "The earliest reference for the idea of the heavenly Jerusalem is found in Gal 4:26," says B. Ego, *Im Himmel wie auf Erden. Studien zum Verhältnis von himmlischer und irdischer Welt im rabbinischen Judentum* (WUNT 2.34; Tübingen: Mohr, 1989), 15. Of course also in comparison with *1 En.* 90:29 (see the previous note), for instance, the parallels are of a later date. Two parallels, which probably refer to the "interim place of rest of the devout souls"

(O. Hofius, *Katapausis. Die Vorstellung vom endzeitlichen Ruheort im Hebräerbrief* [WUNT 11; Tübingen: Mohr, 1970], 188 [p. 73 n. 439]; cf. pp. 181-82 [p. 57 n. 359]), are to be named above all (cf. Heb 11:6 and 2 Tim 4:18, also: Eph 2:6; Phil 3:20; Col 3:1), i.e., Heb 12:22 ('Ιερουσαλὴμ ἐπουράνιος) and *4 Bar.* 5:34 (cf. 5:32) (ἡ ἄνω πόλις 'Ιερουσαλήμ). On the rabbinic juxtaposition of Jerusalem below (של מטה) and Jerusalem above (של מעלה) see again Billerbeck, *Kommentar*, 3.573 (cf. the detailed presentation in Ego, *Himmel*, esp. 172-76).

62. All the less likely because the two comparable passages in Heb 12:22 and *4 Bar.* 5:34, as expressed in the previous note, should not simply be taken to mean the consummation of the end.

63. On this see (at) nn. 8-9 above.

64. This would have been especially obvious. For instance, the rabbinic terminology (on this see n. 61 above) points in this direction, just as also the New Testament (John 8:23; Acts 2:19 [Joel 3:1, variant reading]) juxtaposition (not the first to do so) of ἄνω and κάτω (on this see, e.g., Bauer, *Wörterbuch*, sixth ed., 152, *s.v.* ἄνω) and the comparison especially with Heb 12:25 (cf. 12:22); Phil 3:19-20 (cf. 3:14); Col 3:1-2.

65. This dissonance is extremely strident and, as far as I can see, it has no close parallel — certainly not in the rabbinic terminology mentioned in nn. 60-61 above — although it stands to reason, of course, that, with the somewhat eschatological views associated with Jerusalem as a place, spatial and temporal qualifications could blend, as is the case, e.g., in Heb 12:22-24 ("heavenly Jerusalem" and "heaven" next to the "mediator of the new covenant") and *2 Bar.* 4:1-7 (cf. also Rev 3:12; 21:2, 10). In the latter context, Jerusalem is given over for destruction (by the Babylonians) and for a limited phase abandoned, and it is contrasted as this and as present Jerusalem with the future Jerusalem which God from the beginning made ready. Whereas there "this city" is clearly characterized locally — "this building, which now is built up in your midst" (*JSHRZ* 5.2, 124 [A. F. J. Klijn]) — this is simply not the case for the Jerusalem in Gal 4:25b (in spite of 4:25a). Already for this reason it is awkward here to point directly to Jerusalem as a place as it is named with some emphasis in Galatians 1–2 (so indeed especially: H. W. Bartsch, "Geographische Bezeichnungen für Israel im Neuen Testament," in *Jüdisches Volk-gelobtes Land. Die biblischen Landverheißungen als Problem des jüdischen Selbstverständnisses und der christlichen Theologie* [ed. W. P. Eckert et al., ACJD 3; Munich: Kaiser, 1970], 290-304, here pp. 295-96; Lührmann, *Galater*, 77; Schreckenberg, *Umfeld*, 63; Haacker, "Paulus und das Judentum," 99; Martyn, "Covenants," 181-83; Matera, *Galatians*, 177) — furthermore since the γάρ in 4:25c should not be understood as causal and the sentence need not be understood as expressing political dependence (on the Roman Empire) (so, however, Bartsch and Haacker, similarly also Schreckenberg; differently Lührmann, who understands the γάρ in the consecutive sense [for this possibility see Bauer, *Wörterbuch*, sixth ed., 305, *s.v.* γάρ 3, also 4]). Moreover, the simple connection of 4:25 with chapters 1–2 is problematic for two other reasons: The term Ἀραβία (4:25) occurs in 1:17 without any negative connotation, and the feminine form of Jerusalem, used in 4:25(-26) — and standing closer to the Hebrew name and for this reason dominating the field in the Septuagint — is not employed in 1:17, 18 and 2:1, where rather the neuter Ἱεροσόλυμα is used (compare on this, e.g., M. Bachmann, *Jerusalem und der Tempel. Die geographisch-theologischen Elemente in der lukanischen Sicht des jüdischen Kultzentrums* [BWANT 109; Stuttgart: Kohlhammer, 1980], 13-66 [bibliography], esp. 22-26, further [at] n. 73 below).

Notes to Pages 96-97

What is said in no way rules out a less direct, a more sophisticated and undecided relationship with the place of Jerusalem in chapters 1–2 (as the starting point of the efforts to Judaize in Galatia) (on this see at n. 72 below).

66. On this see at nn. 31-33 above. Cf., for instance, Stegemann, "Zwischen Juden und Heiden," 62-63.

67. With the one exception of Gal 4:29a — of course also with the exception of the quotations (4:27, 30). Cf. Koch, *Schrift*, 210.

68. On this cf. esp. Gal 3:20; 2 Cor 3:12-18 (see, however, 3:13, 14a).

69. Likewise such positions, in my opinion, cannot be maintained in full measure on the basis of Paul's vocabulary and especially the double νῦν (Gal 4:25b, 29b), according to which "that νῦν (in v. 25b) is not to be defined historically, but includes 'the entire length of this aeon'" (Klein, "Individualgeschichte," 217 n. 128, with reference to G. Stählin, "νῦν [ἄρτι]," *TWNT* 4, 1099-1177 [cf. ET *TDNT* 4, 1106-23], here p. 1107; similarly: Luz, "Der alte und der neue Bund," 322; Perriman, "Rhetorical Strategy," 34, 41 [cf. besides n. 55 above]). Here, however, the terminology relating to this (on this see, e.g., [at] n. 60 above) is (differently, e.g., from 1 Tim 6:17[-19]) notably not used (cf., however, nevertheless Gal 1:14 [and along with it: Tit 2:12-14; *Barn.* 4:1]).

70. Cf. (at) nn. 44, 52 above.

71. Cf. Koch, *Schrift*, 211, further (at) nn. 27-28, 33, 35-36, 43 above.

72. Cf. n. 65 above. In another context he chooses a clearly different vocabulary, e.g., in Phil 3:17-21.

73. The feminine is emphasized — as belonging to a chain of feminine terms (broken only by "Mount Sinai") — especially by: Borse, *Galater*, 171; Jankowski, *Galater*, 89. This seems more sensible than to insist here on the "sacred connotations" of the linguistic usage (already mentioned in n. 65 above) in the Septuagint (Longenecker, *Galatians*, 213; cf., e.g., Rohde, *Galater*, 200 n. 61) (which indeed also otherwise are too strongly emphasized in the explanations of the analysis of Ἰερουσαλήμ/Ἱεροσόλυμα in the New Testament [on this see, e.g.: Bachmann, *Jerusalem*, 24-25, 42-43; J. T. Sanders, *The Jews in Luke-Acts* [London: SCM, 1987], 35-36). The νῦν Ἰερουσαλήμ unquestionably belongs on the negative side. Rather, the feminine fits in much better with the double finding that in the New Testament the idea of Jerusalem above or new Jerusalem is consistently connected with the expression Ἰερουσαλήμ (Gal 4:26; Heb 12:22; Rev 3:12; 21:2, 10) — never with Ἱεροσόλυμα — and that in this (as in Matt 23:27 parallel to Luke 12:34) the city is understood throughout as a female person (see esp. Gal 4:[25-]26; Rev 21:2) and/or as a corporate entity. In any case the latter applies also to the νῦν Ἰερουσαλήμ in Gal 4:25; moreover it is indeed notable as well that on account of the ἄνω Ἰερουσαλήμ in 4:26, in which both findings are valid, an antonym νῦν Ἱεροσόλυμα would hardly be possible. On this in more detail: Bachmann, *Jerusalem*, 22-23 (esp. n. 41) and p. 25.

74. *ZTK* 56 (1989), 261-81 (p. 263 n. 5: further important bibliographical references).

75. See Steck, "Zion," 271-72 (here n. 57: reference to the formulation "a city and mother in Israel" in 2 Sam 20:19), also pp. 274-75: on differences in the field of the eastern Semitic and on similiarities in the western Semitic sphere, where "early the concept of the city-goddess" (p. 275) has been developed (cf. n. 90 below). Cf. already K. Albrecht, "Das Geschlecht der hebräischen Hauptwörter," *ZAW* 15 (1895), 313-25; 16 (1896), 41-121, here pp. 56-60 (esp. 59) and pp. 120-21.

76. See Steck, "Zion," 278-79 (together with n. 107). Concerning the aftereffects see for the moment only pp. 262, 281: Gal 4:26; Revelation 21; *4 Ezra* 9:26–10:59; Philipp Nicolai's hymn "Wachet auf, ruft uns die Stimme" (*Evangelisches Gesangbuch*, no. 147).

77. Cf. *4 Ezra* 10:6-7 ("Zion, mother of us all" [so JSHRZ 5.4, 377 (J. Schreiner)]); *2 Bar.* 3:1, 3. Further parallels in Billerbeck, *Kommentar*, 3.574.

78. For this and the previous concepts: (further) references in Steck, "Zion," 270-71.

79. On this see Steck, "Zion," 276-79 (cf. J. Jeremias, *Kultprophetie und Gerichtsverkündigung in der späten Königszeit Israels* [WMANT 35; Neukirchen-Vluyn: Neukirchener Verlag, 1970], 33-37, according to whom in Nah 3:4 originally Jerusalem was thought of as a whore [see pp. 36-37, on the related image of denudation also used in Isa 47:3a]). Cf. A. Y. Collins, "Feminine Symbolism in the Book of Revelation," *BibInt* 1 (1993), 20-33, here p. 26, further M. Bachmann, "Offb 17,5: Hurenmutter?" in *Religionspädagogische Grenzgänge. Für Erich Bochinger und Martin Widmann von der Landesfachschaft Evangelische Theologie/Religionspädagogik in Baden-Württemberg* (ed. G. Büttner and J. Thierfelder; Arbeiten zur Pädagogik 26; Stuttgart: Calwer, 1988), 95-98, here p. 96 together with n. 11.

80. Citations: Steck, "Zion," 279, 278, 280.

81. Steck, "Zion," 280. Since also "these texts . . . , as Lam 4:21-22 and above all Isaiah *51ff., with its orientation on Isaiah 47, show, are [designed] as counter images to the corresponding portrayal of enemies" (p. 280), this has to do with, so to speak, counterstatements of counterstatements.

82. Cf. Bruce, "Abraham Had Two Sons," 81. Isa 54:1, quite clearly associated with Jerusalem already by means of the context (see, e.g., 54:3 [on this cf. n. 84 below] and 54:12-13), will have suggested for Paul being taken up in the argument. The verse is also understood as relating to Jerusalem in the Targumim (see, e.g.: Koch, *Schrift*, 209 [together with] n. 34; Longenecker, *Galatians*, 215) and (on account of the same theme of "childlessness") associated with Sarah in *Pesiq. Rab.* 32:2 (see Longenecker, *Galatians*, 215; cf. Bouwman, "Hagar- und Sara-Perikope," 3150 [together with n. 78: reference to Callaway, "Mistress and the Maid," 97, which in turn refers to the material relating to this from the Cairo Genizah researched by J. Mann, *The Bible as Read and Preached in the Old Synagogue. A Study in the Cycles of the Readings from Torah and Prophets, as well as from Psalms, and in the Structure of the Midrashic Homilies* (Cincinnati, OH: Jewish Publication Society, 1940), esp. LII-LIII, 122]: "In the ancient Palestinian Cycle, Isaiah 54 was the haftara . . . for Genesis 16" [cf. Jankowski, *Galater*, 87, 93]), as then already in Isa 51:1-3 Abraham and Sarah are connected with Zion (see Hays, *Echoes*, 119). Cf. (at) n. 32 above.

83. Cf. Isa 23:8, 16-17; Nah 3:4-5.

84. Steck, "Zion," 280; p. 280 (together with n. 114) references, among which is Isa 54:3. From such statements it is understandable that "very early in the apocalyptic tradition about Jerusalem a universalistic character" is encountered (W. W. Reader, *Die Stadt Gottes in der Johannesapokalypse* [diss. thesis theol.; University of Göttingen, 1971], 28; p. 29 see among other references *1 En.* 90:30-35; Gal 4:26-28; Heb 12:22 [cf. *Pss. Sol.* 14:29-36, esp. v. 31]). Cf. (at) nn. (85 and) 89, 90 below.

85. Cf. Isa 54:10; 55:3; 56:4(-5), 6(-7); 61:8. Cf. (at) nn. 59-60 above.

86. On this see above all C. Deutsch, "Transformation of Symbols: The New Jerusalem in Rv 21_1-22_5," *ZNW* 78 (1987), 106-26, esp. (110 n. 29, pp. 111-13 and) 122-24, further: Bachmann, "Offb 17,5," esp. 96 (together with n. 9); Collins, "Feminine Symbolism," esp. 25-

26 (see R. H. Gundry, "The New Jerusalem: People as Place, Not Place for People," *NovT* 29 [1987], 254-64, here pp. 257-58).

87. Cf. 2 Cor 11:2, also Josephus, *J.W.* 6:301.

88. Cf. (at) nn. 60(-65) above.

89. On this see Bachmann, "Offb 17,5," 96. Cf. Deutsch, "Transformation of Symbols," 120-21, 126, and (at) nn. 84-85 above.

90. So, for instance, also Collins, "Feminine Symbolism," 26-27. She thinks (as most commentators [on this see O. Böcher, *Die Johannesapokalypse* (EdF 41; third ed.; Darmstadt, 1988), 87-96; E. Lohmeyer and J. Sickenberger, among others, are exceptions; cf. now M. Rissi, *Die Hure Babylon und die Verführung der Heiligen. Eine Studie zur Apokalypse des Johannes* (BWANT 136; Stuttgart/Berlin/Cologne: Kohlhammer, 1995), 49-73, who originally thought of "the godlessness of the syncretistic religions ('Religionswesen') of the world" (p. 55), whereas those who, according to him, have given new interpretations to Revelation 17 by vv. 9-14 and again by vv. 15-17, at any rate, however, agree in that "both see Rome as the whore" (p. 72)]]) of the "woman on the scarlet beast" (Rev 17:3) more precisely as the goddess Roma (Collins, "Feminine Symbolism," 27: "It is a parody of the honor given Roma: her supporters worship a prostitute, not a goddess!"). This thought actually suggests itself (not only from the perspectives of the history of tradition [cf. nn. 5, 75 above]) (cf. Rev 13:14-15), especially if one is permitted to assume familiarity among the addressees (cf. Rev 13:17) with the "depiction of female city divinities ["Stadttychen"] on Phoenician-Hellenistic and Roman coins" (Steck, "Zion," 275 together with n. 89, with reference to: O. Keel, *Deine Blicke sind Tauben. Zur Metaphorik des Hohen Liedes* [SBS 114/115; Stuttgart: Katholisches Bibelwerk, 1984], fig. 5 [city goddess from Gaza at the time of Hadrian]; O. Keel, *Das Hohelied* [ZBK, Altes Testament 18; Zurich: Theologischer Verlag, 1986], fig. 112 ["Magna Mater Cybele," "here probably as the guardian goddess of Rom"; 67 BCE; in addition, a lion is added to the female head (cf. also fig. 45 and *passim*)]).

91. Bibliographical evidence in Deutsch, "Transformation of Symbols," 122(-123) n. 98 (P. Carrington; J. Sweet), who just like Collins, "Feminine Symbolism," 26, rejects this view.

92. That here one needs to reckon with the reception of a pagan myth already taken over earlier into the Jewish sphere, see R. Bergmeier, "Altes and Neues zur 'Sonnenfrau am Himmel (Apk 12)'. Religionsgeschichtliche und quellenkritische Beobachtungen zu Apk 12_{1-17}," *ZNW* 73 (1982), 97-109 (here p. 103 on the uncertain origin of the number 12 in v. 1). Cf. E. Lohse, "Synagogue of Satan and Church of God. Jesus and Christians in the Book of Revelation," *SEÅ* 58 (1993), 105-23, here pp. 117-18.

93. On this cf., e.g.: Lohse, "Synagogue of Satan," 116-19; F. W. Horn, *Zwischen der Synagoge des Satans und dem neuen Jerusalem. Die christlich-jüdische Standortbestimmung in der Apokalyse des Johannes* (Gerhard-Mercator-Universität, Veröffentlichungen des Fachbereichs 1: H. 6; Duisburg: Gerhard-Mercator-Universität, 1994), 17-19.

94. On this see, e.g.: Lohse, "Synagogue of Satan," 117; Horn, *Synagoge des Satans*, 19 — where reference is made to Judges 17-18; *T. Dan* 5:6-7 and Irenaeus, *Adversus haereses* 5.30.2.

95. Perhaps directed (not to Christians, but) to Jews in Asia Minor (so Lohse, "Synagogue of Satan," 106-7, and Horn, *Synagoge des Satans*, 8 together with n. 1) — whether these are negatively assessed on account of blasphemy against Christ (so Lohse, "Synagogue of Satan," 119-20) or, as the immediate context of Rev 2:9 could suggest (cf., for instance, also Acts

13:45, 50), on account of cooperation with the political authorities that led to acts of persecution against Christians (so Horn, *Synagoge des Satans*, esp. 8-9).

96. Inasmuch as in Rev 3:9 with the future falling down of the "Jews," who are addressed here, an allusion is made to the passage Isaiah 60 (i.e., 60:14), which is so important for Revelation 21–22 (see esp. 21:24-26), the synagogue of Satan thus in a way stands over against Zion/Jerusalem.

97. Further parallels for this — and correspondences to the other "geographical" terms in Rev 11:8 — in A. J. Beagley, *The 'Sitz im Leben' of the Apocalypse with Particular Reference to the Role of the Church's Enemies* (BZNW 50; Berlin: de Gruyter, 1987), 67 (cf. Horn, *Synagoge des Satans*, 15 n. 28).

98. The beast that comes out of the ἄβυσσος (Rev 11:7; 17:8) represents a further obvious point of contact between Revelation 11 and 17(–18). Cf. M. Bachmann, "Himmlisch: Der 'Tempel Gottes' von Apk 11,1," *NTS* 40 (1994), 474-80, here p. 479 (together with) n. 34.

99. On this cf. (at) nn. 84-85, 89.

100. The correspondence between Jerusalem and Rome — among other things thus pronounced — is strongly emphasized by Horn, *Synagoge des Satans*, 14-17, according to whom in the Apocalypse Jews (on the one hand "a Judaism . . . , which in its character has become so similar to the satanic power of Rome that the distinguishing features disappear" [p. 14] and on the other hand 'Israel within Israel' [p. 14]) and Christians must allow themselves to be assessed "according to the yardstick of their relationship to the cult of the emperor" (p. 25 [cf. p. 7]) (cf. n. 102 below).

101. So (following, among others, C. H. Giblin, "Revelation 11.1-13: Its Form, Function and Contextual Integration," *NTS* 30 [1984], 433-59, here p. 438, and), in contrast with the usual interpretation referring to the earthly temple destroyed by the Romans in the year 70, recently Bachmann, "Himmlisch" (esp. p. 477).

102. Cf.: Deutsch, "Transformation of Symbols," 124 ("the New Jerusalem of 21_1–22_{25} serves not only as a polemic against Rome, but also against the non-messianic Jewish community, i.e., those Jews who have not accepted Jesus as the Christ"); Horn, *Synagoge des Satans*, 19 ("the dividing line runs through the Christian communities and through the Jewish synagogues equally" [cf. n. 100 above]).

103. Since one would have to agree with Mußner ("Theologische 'Wiedergutmachung,'" 10) (on this see, e.g., [at] nn. 15, 19-21 above) when he says with reference to Gal 4:21-31: "Especially in the interpretation of this text anti-Judaism in Christian exegesis has celebrated its particular triumph," it is of some relevance that there are exegetical particulars which lead us to move away from the conventional line of interpretation (as is the case, though from [something of] another point of view, in certain features [on this see (at) nn. 46, 54-55], particularly in Mußner [see Mußner, "Theologische 'Wiedergutmachung,'" 10], Bouwman [see Bouwman, "Hagar- und Sara-Perikope," 3152: "On the basis of this passage one . . . cannot accuse Paul of anti-Judaism"], and Martyn [see Martyn, "Covenants," 188-89; see further, once again, Gager, *Origins of Anti-Semitism*, 242]). If the observations summarized here are somewhat correct, one incidentally gets the impression that Paul, who in Galatians can speak not only about the "church of God" (1:13), but in conclusion also about "the Israel of God" (6:16), finds himself in this letter, which unquestionably demonstrates polemical elements, in closer proximity to Romans (4 and) 9–11 (esp. 9:4, 6-13, 22-24, 33; 10:17, 19-21; 11:1, 11-16, 17-32) (cf., for instance: Schlier, *Galater*, 227; Longenecker, *Galatians*,

217; also Broer, "Vertreibe die Magd," [172-74, 191, and] 193-94) than is often assumed (cf. esp.: Luz, *Geschichtsverständnis*, 285-86; Wilckens, *Römer*, 2.184-85; Betz, *Galaterbrief*, 430-31; U. Schnelle, *Wandlungen im paulinischen Denken* [SBS 137; Stuttgart: Katholisches Bibelwerk, 1989], 80, 85; Fiedler, "Israel Gottes," esp. 85) — and so also methodologically, in his dealings with the Old Testament. (It is therefore no longer [and it was never] valid, what Bruce, "Abraham Had Two Sons," [83-]84, feels obliged to express: Whereas in Paul's other actualizations of Old Testament statements "the Old Testament narrative is left intact, in the Galatians passage the analogy finds itself up against the historical facts that Isaac was the ancestor of the Jews, while Ishmael's descendants were Gentiles" [cf. (at) n. 16 above, further Gager, *Origins of Anti-Semitism*, 242].)

Notes to Chapter 6

1. On this see (at) nn. 12, 30 below.
2. F. Mußner, "'Volk Gottes' im Neuen Testament," in *Praesentia Salutis. Gesammelte Studien zu Fragen und Themen des Neuen Testaments* (KBANT; Düsseldorf: Patmos, 1967), 244-52 (orig. [in a somewhat other form] 1963), 248-49 — with reference to H. Schlier, *Der Brief an die Galater* (KEK 7; third ed.; Göttingen: Vandenhoeck & Ruprecht, 1962), 283.
3. Mußner, "Volk Gottes," 248. Cf. (at) nn. 25, 111-12 below.
4. F. Mußner, "Gesetz, Abraham, Israel nach dem Galater- und Römerbrief," in *Die Kraft der Wurzel. Judentum-Jesus-Kirche* (Freiburg: Herder, 1987), 27-38 (orig. 1983), 34. Cf. F. Mußner, *Der Galaterbrief* (HTKNT 9; Freiburg: Herder, 1974), 417 together with n. 61. Cf. (at) nn. 16-17 below.
5. Mußner, "Gesetz," 34. Cf., e.g., F. F. Bruce, *The Epistle of Paul to the Galatians: A Commentary on the Greek Text* (NIGTC; Grand Rapids: Eerdmans, 1982), 275.
6. Mußner, "Gesetz," 34-35. Similarly undecided the statements in D. Lührmann, *Der Brief an die Galater* (ZBK, Neues Testament 7; second ed.; Zurich: Theologischer Verlag, 1988), 102, and in W. Schrage, "'Israel nach dem Fleisch' (1 Kor 10:18)," in *"Wenn nicht jetzt, wann dann?" Aufsätze für Hans-Joachim Kraus zum 65. Geburtstag*, ed. H.-G. Geyer et al. (Neukirchen-Vluyn: Neukirchener Verlag, 1983), 143-51, here p. 145.
7. Mußner, "Gesetz," 35. Cf., for instance, J. D. G. Dunn, *A Commentary on the Epistle to the Galatians* (BNTC; London: Black, 1993), 344: "The precise referent has been a source of unresolved debate" (cf. further p. 346).
8. Cf. H. D. Betz, *Der Galaterbrief. Ein Kommentar zum Brief des Apostels Paulus an die Gemeinden in Galatien* (Hermeneia; Munich: Kaiser, 1988; orig. [English] 1979), 546: "an extremely difficult problem in New Testament research."
9. If one with respect to the Christians still makes a distinction between "judaizing" people and people who are "free of the law" and distinguishes that Judaism which was found at the time of Galatians from "eschatological" Judaism, the crucial variants of the spectrum are complete (on this cf., e.g., F. J. Matera, *Galatians* [SP 9; Collegeville: Liturgical, 1992], 232, where six possibilities of exegesis are given; similarly W. Kraus, *Das Volk Gottes. Zur Grundlegung der Ekklesiologie bei Paulus* [WUNT 85; Tübingen: Mohr, 1996], 251 [together with nn. 331-34: bibliography]). R. N. Longenecker, *Galatians* [WBC 41; Dallas: Word, 1990], 298-99, proposes a quite independent solution, which in my opinion, however, cannot be

verified for methodological reasons and which does *not* go particularly well with the singularity of the expression "the Israel *of God*" (on this cf. [at] n. 103 below). According to this proposition, Paul probably uses here "a self-designation of his Jewish-Christian opponents in Galatia" (p. 298), and he does this to oppose them and the Galatians, who are addressed by this group with the Israel-formula, in a final point: "what the Judaizers were claiming to offer his converts they already have 'in Christ' by faith: that they . . . can be called 'the Israel of God' together with all Jews who believe" (p. 299). Similarly to Longenecker for instance already Betz, *Galaterbrief,* 547-48; cf. also Kraus, *Volk Gottes,* 252 n. 338: "'The Israel of God' is . . . a polemical concept in Galatians that is directed against the Galatian opponents" (cf., however, [at] nn. 58-59 below).

10. J. Roloff, *Die Kirche im Neuen Testament* (GNT 10; Göttingen: Vandenhoeck & Ruprecht, 1993), (125-)126. Cf. (at) n. 118 below.

11. Citations (of which the first is partly italicized in the original): Roloff, *Kirche,* 125, 125, 126, 126.

12. H. D. Betz, *Galaterbrief,* 546 (cf., e.g., P. Richardson, *Israel in the Apostolic Church* [SNTSMS 10; Cambridge: Cambridge University Press, 1969], 74: "the common position"). G. Schrenk, "Was bedeutet 'Israel Gottes'?" *Jud* 5 (1949), 81-94, here p. 87 (together with) n. 12 (cf. p. 85 [together with] nn. 7-8), Schlier, *Galater,* 283 (together with) n. 2, and Richardson, *Israel,* 83 n. 2, name as representatives of the older exegesis: Eusebius of Emesa, Chrysostom, Theodoret of Cyrrhus, Luther, and Calvin. The fact that "most new exegetes" follow the customary interpretation (Schrenk, "Israel Gottes," 87 n. 12, with reference to J. B. Lightfoot, C. Holsten, M. Kähler, R. A. Lipsius, H. Lietzmann, W. Bauer, A. Oepke, and N. A. Dahl, to whom Schlier, *Galater,* 283 n. 2, adds: F. Sieffert, A. Bisping, M. J. Lagrange, O. Kuß, and S. Lyonnet) is also valid for the time after 1949 or correspondingly 1962 (on this see [at] n. 1 above; cf. [at] n. 30 below). Besides H. Schlier, (the early) F. Mußner and J. Roloff (on this see [at] nn. 2, 10-11 above) the following people shall be named especially: C. Müller, *Gottes Gerechtigkeit und Gottes Volk. Eine Untersuchung zu Römer 9–11* (FRLANT 86; Göttingen: Vandenhoeck & Ruprecht, 1964), 97 (cf. p. 99); U. Luz, *Das Geschichtsverständnis des Paulus* (BEvT 49; Munich: Chr. Kaiser, 1968), 270, 285; W. Klaiber, *Rechtfertigung und Gemeinde. Eine Untersuchung zum paulinischen Kirchenverständnis* (FRLANT 127; Göttingen: Vandenhoeck & Ruprecht, 1982), 28; J. Becker, *Der Brief an die Galater* (NTD 8; third ed.; Göttingen: Vandenhoeck & Ruprecht, 1985), 84; E. Gräßer, *Der Alte Bund im Neuen. Exegetische Studien zur Israelfrage im Neuen Testament* (WUNT 35; Tübingen: Mohr, 1985), 222-23 (cf. p. 19 n. 53); H. Merklein, *Studien zu Jesus und Paulus* (WUNT 43; Tübingen: Mohr, 1987), 75; Matera, *Galatians,* 232; Kraus, *Volk Gottes,* 116, 251-52, 355, 359 (cf. [at] nn. [115-]118 below).

13. G. Schrenk, "Der Segenswunsch nach der Kampfepistel," *Jud* 6 (1950), 170-90, here pp. 180-83 (citations: 182 [twice], 183). Cf. also p. 185: "Also in Galatians Paul remains faithful to his people." Cf. (at) n. 33 below.

14. Citations: Schrenk, "Israel Gottes," 81, 81, 88.

15. Schrenk, "Israel Gottes," (89-)90. Cf. (at) n. 72 below and Kraus, *Volk Gottes,* 188(-189).

16. Schrenk, "Segenswunsch," 178(-179).

17. Schrenk, "Israel Gottes," 81 (on this cf. [at] nn. 27, 29, 51 below). On p. 94 n. 29, Schrenk lists as forerunners of this view: Ephraem Syrus, Ambrosiaster, Gaius Marius Victorinus, T. Beza, H. Grotius, W. Estius, J. A. Bengel, L. J. Rückert, C. Schöttgen, M. L. de

Wette, G. H. A. Ewald, C. J. Ellicott, B. Weiß, J. C. K. von Hofmann, T. Zahn, A. Schlatter, W. Bousset, E. de Witt Burton, and E. Kühl; cf. Schlier, *Galater*, 283 n. 3, who also names E. Wörner and A. Schäfer (cf. from more recent times: P. von der Osten-Sacken, "Römer 9-11 als Schibbolet christlicher Theologie," in *Evangelium und Tora. Aufsätze zu Paulus* [TB 77; Munich: Kaiser, 1987], 294-314, here p. 305 together with n. 12). At least for E. de Witt Burton, *A Critical and Exegetical Commentary on the Epistle to the Galatians* (ICC; Edinburgh: Clark, 1921), 357-58 ("the mercy of God through which they may obtain enlightenment and enter into peace, upon those within Israel who even though as yet unenlightened are the true Israel of God" [p. 358]) the limitation to Jewish *Christians*, however, must be a delicate matter (on this see Richardson, *Israel*, 83 n. 1), and in more recent times (cf. Schrenk, "Israel Gottes," 86 [together with] n. 11, who mentions only T. Morus and K. F. Zimmer as older representatives of this view) a wider circle of Jews is assumed — more or less defined — among others, by the following authors: W. D. Davies, "Paul and the People of Israel," *NTS* 24 (1978), 4-39, here p. 10 (together with n. 2); P. Richardson (on this see [at] nn. 26, 29 below); F. Mußner (on this see [at] nn. 4-5 above); D. Lührmann (on this cf. n. 6 above); H. Kremers, *Judenmission heute? Von der Judenmission zur brüderlichen Solidarität und zum ökumenischen Dialog* (Neukirchen-Vluyn: Neukirchener Verlag, 1979) 38; H. Kuhli, "'Ἰσραήλ," *EWNT* 2 (1981), 495-501 (cf. ET *EDNT* 2, 202-4), here 501; J. G. Gager, *The Origins of Anti-Semitism. Attitudes toward Judaism in Pagan and Christian Antiquity* (New York/Oxford: Oxford University Press, 1983), 228-29; K. H. Schelkle, *Israel im Neuen Testament* (Darmstadt: Wissenschaftliche Buchgesellschaft, 1985), 50 (together with) n. 7; E. W. Stegemann, "Zwischen Juden und Heiden, aber 'mehr' als Juden und Heiden? Neutestamentliche Anmerkungen zur Identitätsproblematik des frühen Christentums," *KuI* 9 (1994), 53-69, here p. 62 ("either . . . Israel in general or — more probably. . . the early Jerusalem Christian community").

18. So the evaluation of N. A. Dahl, "Zur Auslegung von Gal. 6,16," *Jud* 6 (1950), 161-70, here p. 162.

19. Dahl, "Auslegung," 162: "This is correct." Cf. N. A. Dahl, *Das Volk Gottes. Eine Untersuchung zum Kirchenbewußtsein des Urchristentums* (second ed.; Darmstadt: Wissenschaftliche Buchgesellschaft, 1963; orig. 1941), 210 (cf. p. 1, 213): "The transfer to the church of Christ is present only in Gal 6:16."

20. Dahl, "Auslegung," 163. Cf. (on the other hand at nn. 73, 76 below and) the following note.

21. Dahl, "Auslegung," 163. Cf. (W. Gutbrod, "'Ἰουδαῖος κτλ. Im Neuen Testament," *TWNT* 3 [1938] 376-94 [cf. ET *TDNT* 3, 375-91], here p. 390, and) H. D. Betz, *Galaterbrief*, 547 n. 105, who at least agrees with Schrenk (see at n. 15 above) on the view that with respect to the expression (ὁ) Ἰσραὴλ κατὰ πνεῦμα Paul "never . . . uses" it, but who nevertheless says: "But Gal 4:21-31, esp. 4:29 and Rom 2:17-29; 9–11 show that he could have used it if he had wanted to." (However, obviously he did not want to.)

22. Dahl, "Auslegung," 163.

23. Richardson, *Israel*, 83 n. 2 (cf. p. 74).

24. On this see Richardson, *Israel*, 9-14.

25. Richardson, *Israel*, 80.

26. Richardson, *Israel*, 82. On this cf. (at) nn. 16-17 above.

27. On this see (at) n. 17 above (and [at] n. 29 below).

28. On this see Schrenk: "Israel Gottes," 92-93; "Segenswunsch," 177-79.

29. Schrenk, "Segenswunsch," (173-)174 (cf. p. 178: The Apostle wants to denote "only the remnant of Israel"). Cf. (at) nn. 17, 27 above and (at) n. 103 below. Also Richardson, *Israel*, 82, however, understands the genitive in the sense of a restriction: Paul blesses "an Israel (of God) within (all) Israel."

30. Schrenk, "Segenswunsch," 190 (cf. Schrenk, "Israel Gottes," 91-92). Dahl, "Auslegung," 161, regards this interpretation more cautiously as belonging to the "customary exegetical opinions" — and therefore a reviewing would be recommendable. Cf. (at) nn. 1, 12 above.

31. Schrenk, "Israel Gottes," 86.

32. Citations: Kraus, *Volk Gottes*, 251. Cf. p. 252: "There no longer remains a space for an independent quality of Israel post Christum natum" in Galatians. On this cf. at n. 82 below.

33. Citations (among which the second is highlighted in the original): Schrenk, "Segenswunsch," 183, 182. Cf. (at) n. 13 above.

34. Schrenk, "Segenswunsch," 181, exactly also refers to this (namely, to T. Zahn, *Der Brief an die Galater* [Kommentar zum Neuen Testament 9; second ed.; Leipzig: Deichert'sche Verlagsbuchhandlung Nachf., 1907], 119[-135]).

35. M. Bachmann, *Sünder oder Übertreter. Studien zur Argumentation in Gal 2,15ff.* (WUNT 59; Tübingen: Mohr, 1992); that recourse can be found on p. 108 (together with nn. 39-43).

36. Cf. esp. Bachmann, *Sünder*, 101-2, 110-11, 153.

37. On this see, e.g., Bachmann, *Sünder*, 134-39, where I particularly take up proposals from T. L. Donaldson, "The Curse of the Law and the Inclusion of the Gentiles: Galatians 3.13-14," *NTS* 32 (1986), 94-112, esp. 95-99. Cf. J. Lambrecht, "The Universalistic Will of God. The True Gospel in Galatians," in *Pauline Studies. Collected Essays* (BETL 115; Leuven: Leuven University Press, 1994), 299-306, here pp. 304-5. Cf. J. D. G. Dunn, *Galatians*, 345-46, who (against Dahl, "Auslegung") refers to Paul's "earlier description of his fellow Jews as heirs still in their minority (see . . . iii.23–iv.3)."

38. On this see, e.g., Bachmann, *Sünder*, 119-22. Cf. J. D. G. Dunn, "Paul: Apostate or Apostle of Israel?" *ZNW* 89 (1998), 256-71, here pp. 270-71.

39. On this see (Bachmann, *Sünder*, 130-32 [together with n. 173], further) my essay: "The Other Woman: Synchronic and Diachronic Observations on Gal 4:21–5:1," which is printed in this present volume (and appeared in a somewhat different version in *Jud* 54 [1998], 144-64).

40. On this see esp. Zahn, *Galater*, 103-5 (with reference among other things to 1 Macc 6:58; 11:62). Cf. (however) for instance H. D. Betz, *Galaterbrief*, 187-91.

41. On this see, e.g., Bachmann, *Sünder*, 112-18 (esp. 113 together with n. 67). Cf. at n. 58 below.

42. Cf., e.g., Bachmann, *Sünder*, 113 n. 66.

43. Zahn, *Galater*, 284-85, adds to the introductory τοῦ λοιποῦ in 6:17 the term Ἰσραήλ from the previous sentence and understands it "in contrast to the people for whom peace and mercy had just been wished personally." He translates accordingly: "Of the remaining (Israel) let no one cause me trouble and annoyance . . ." (p. 285). But where Paul otherwise uses λοιπός personally, he puts it in the plural (e.g., Gal 2:13) — which is also possible here ("Of the remaining Israelites") — whereas he always uses the singular adverbially (cf. esp.

2 Cor 13:11; Phil 3:1; 4:8; 1 Thess 4:1; cf. further 2 Thess 3:1; Eph 6:10). Cf. A. Oepke, *Der Brief des Paulus an die Galater* (THKNT 9; reprint of the second ed.; Berlin: Evangelische Verlagsanstalt, 1964), 163.

44. But cf. at least 2 Cor 13:11; 1 Thess 5:27-28; Phlm 20 (and further Eph 6:23).

45. Cf. H. D. Betz, *Galaterbrief*, 551: "What is strange is the form of address, 'brothers,' which is so important in this letter, but which occurs in no other Pauline benediction." If one attempts to interpret this curiosity with Lührmann, *Galater*, 103 (cf., e.g., Matera, *Galatians*, 233) as follows: "In spite of all the harshness of the dispute, the Galatians remain brothers," one wonders whether a further reference of this kind after the fairly analogous examples of "brothers" in the letter (1:11; 3:15; 4:12, 28, 31; 5:13; 6:1) and above all after the blessing in 6:16, if understood in the usual sense, would really still be needed.

46. Schrenk, "Israel Gottes," 84 (together with) n. 7 (who names representatives of the view in question). Cf. Oepke, *Galater*, 163: "so the majority."

47. Kraus, *Volk Gottes*, 251, who in n. 337 refers to F. Blass and A. Debrunner, *Grammatik des neutestamentlichen Griechisch* (fourteenth ed.; Göttingen: Vandenhoeck & Ruprecht, 1976), 442, 6, and to J. Rohde, *Der Brief des Paulus an die Galater* (THKNT 9; first ed. of the rev. ed.; Berlin: Evangelische Verlagsanstalt, 1989), 278.

48. On this cf. for example Zahn, *Galater*, 282-83, and Oepke, *Galater*, 163.

49. In addition to the — Pauline — passages listed in W. Bauer, *Griechisch-deutsches Wörterbuch zu den Schriften des Neuen Testaments und der frühchristlichen Literatur* (sixth ed.; Berlin/New York: de Gruyter, 1988), 787, see on the one hand Zahn, *Galater*, 283 n. 45, on the other hand the separate categorization of examples of καί connected with the demonstrative pronoun (as in 1 Cor 2:2) in Schrenk, "Israel Gottes," 85 n. 9. That Rom 1:5, which is not discussed by Zahn and Schrenk, with δι' οὗ ἐλάβομεν χάριν καὶ ἀποστολήν provides an example of an epexegetical (or explanatory) καί, may already be doubted on account of the first person plural (cf. in contrast 1:1, 8).

50. Zahn, *Galater*, 283 (cf., particularly as far as τουτέστιν is concerned, the examples appealed to in the previous note, e.g., for καὶ τοῦτο) — who in n. 44 for the omission of καί mentions the manuscript D. Cf., e.g., Schrenk, "Israel Gottes," 86.

51. When, e.g., according to Schrenk, "Israel Gottes," 85 n. 9, Paul adds "the particular to the general" (that is: "the Jews who believe in Christ" [on this see, e.g., (at) n. 17 above]; cf., e.g., 1 Cor 9:5), and when, for instance, according to Oepke, *Galater*, 163 (cf. F. Sieffert, *Der Brief an die Galater* [KEK 7; ninth (fourth) ed.; Göttingen: Vandenhoeck & Ruprecht, 1899], 362), to the contrary "the καί places the whole beside the part" (that is: beside "all Christians in Galatia, who in faith will become obedient to God," as a more comprehensive corporate entity "the New Testament people of God in general" [p. 362]), then with respect to both, Zahn's older, perhaps somewhat too firmly expressed doubts are still of importance (*Galater*, 283 [on this cf., e.g., Acts 5:29; Rom 1:13; Gal 2:13]): "In the last case πᾶς (πάντες) or ὅλος after καί could not be absent if a plural expression with οἱ λοιποί was not preferred. The first case, however, could only be accepted with the reading στοιχοῦσιν," whereas with the future tense Paul will have in mind "a second circle which goes beyond such Galatians who follow the guiding principle which is described (in 6:14-15). Cf. Kuhli, "'Ισραήλ," 500-501, and Schrage, "Israel nach dem Fleisch," 145.

52. Schrenk, "Israel Gottes," 86 n. 10.

53. Schrenk, "Israel Gottes," 86 n. 10 (cf. Schrenk, "Segenswunsch," 177 together with

n. 8, and Dahl, "Auslegung," 167) — where among other things Matt 5:45; Heb 10:16; Rev 19:16 are referred to. Richardson's objection (*Israel*, [80-]81 [together with] n. 1) against this overview and its evaluation have not convinced me; for the fact that in the examples nothing corresponding to the insertion of καὶ ἔλεος is to be found, changes nothing in the cooperation of two prepositional expressions.

54. Cf., however, (at) nn. 48, 53 above.

55. On this cf., e.g., Zahn, *Galater*, 282, and Longenecker, *Galatians*, 298, further (at) nn. 90-110 below.

56. In F. Staudinger, "ἔλεος," *EWNT* 1 (1980), 1046-52 (cf. ET *EDNT* 1, 429-31), here 1049, it says rightly (cf. esp. Rom 11:31[-33]): "Paul explicates God's ἔλεος/ἐλεεῖν in Rom 9; 11; 15 as an eschatological act in redemptive history in Jesus Christ." In the rest of the New Testament primarily the examples in Matt 5:7; 2 Tim 1:18; James 2:13 and Jude 21 may be compared (cf. Zahn, *Galater*, 282 [together with] n. 43), which for their part are not found in isolation in tradition-history (on this see for this moment only the formulation of the Eighteen Benedictions mentioned at nn. 3, 25 above as well as Dunn, *Galatians*, 344). Cf. section 2.4 below.

57. In the undisputed Pauline Epistles, the substantive occurs three times in Romans (9:23 [on this see, e.g., 9:24!]; 11:31 [on this see, e.g., 11:28-29!]; 15:9 [on this see, e.g., 15:8, 10!]) — and "outside of Romans only in Gal 6:16, here also characteristically connected with the catchword Ἰσραήλ" (so D. Sänger, *Die Verkündigung des Gekreuzigten und Israel. Studien zum Verhältnis von Kirche und Israel bei Paulus und im frühen Christentum* [WUNT 75; Tübingen: Mohr, 1994], 132 n. 348). The main emphasis of the use of the verb can be indicated with the mention of Romans 9–11 (9:15, 16, 18; 11:30, 31, 32; further [and differently]: Rom 12:8; 1 Cor 7:25; 2 Cor 4:1; Phil 2:27). Again, in no way does Paul stand alone here, as for instance 1 Pet 2:10 and in Jewish literature the Eighteen Benedictions show (on this see again at nn. 3, 25 above, further, e.g., Dunn, *Galatians*, [343-]344). Primarily on account of the term "mercy" Dunn, *Galatians*, 344, says: "Paul has deliberately introduced a strongly Jewish benediction, whose very Jewish character would be unmistakable" (that is, "to all the Christian Jews in Galatia and to those most influenced by them"). Cf. section 2.4 below.

58. On this see (at) n. 41 above.

59. Cf. Dunn, *Galatians*, 345: "Paul holds out an olive branch to his opponents." Cf., however, n. 9 above.

60. Namely (at) nn. 4-6, 14-17(-24) above and at the conclusion of section 1.

61. On the correspondence of Rom 11:1-2 with Rom 9:4-5, cf. Kraus, *Volk Gottes*, 308: "The designation 'his people' corresponds . . . with regard to content to the privileges in 9:4-5." Cf. Rom 11:4, where in contrast to 3 Kgdms (1 Kgs) 19:18 Paul adds ἐμαυτῷ in order to accent God's attachment to the "remnant" of Israel and thereby to Israel (on this see Kraus, *Volk Gottes*, 309 together with n. 252).

62. H. Kuhli, "Ἰσραηλίτης," *EWNT* 2 (1981), 501-4 (cf. ET *EDNT* 2, 204-5), here 503-4.

63. Kuhli, "Ἰσραηλίτης," 503.

64. The belonging together is supported by the rhetorical connection of the three elements that can be found in 2 Cor 11:22 (see Kuhli, "Ἰσραηλίτης," 503) and by the parallels (see esp. Rom 11:1; Phil 3:5).

65. Kuhli, "Ἰσραηλίτης," 503.

66. With respect to the very close relationship of 2 Cor 3:16 to Romans 11 (esp. 11:23) cf. Sänger, *Verkündigung*, 178-79.

67. On this see, e.g., Richardson, *Israel,* 128 together with n. 6 (cf. p. 82). Today, it is hardly denied "that with 'all Israel' the Jews and not the Jewish and Gentile Christians are meant" (Kraus, *Volk Gottes,* 321 [together with n. 343], with reference among other things to Rom 11:25b). On this more precisely: R. Stuhlmann, *Das eschatologische Maß im Neuen Testament* (FRLANT 132; Göttingen: Vandenhoeck & Ruprecht, 1983), 179-81 (cf. p. 178: "Πᾶς is . . . not to be understood . . . as numerically complete, but as an emphatic counterconcept to λεῖμμα"). P. J. Tomson, "The Names Israel and Jew in Ancient Judaism and in the New Testament," *Bijdr* 47 (1986), 120-40, 268-89, 285 together with n. 159 (cf. p. 286 together with n. 161 as well as n. 73 below), refers rightly to CD 16:1 as an important parallel, where it says: "a covenant with you and with all Israel" (so E. Lohse, ed., *Die Texte aus Qumran. Hebräisch und Deutsch. Mit Übersetzung, Einführung und Anmerkungen* [second ed.; Darmstadt: Wissenschaftliche Buchgesellschaft, 1971], [98-]99). Further, compare for instance *m. Sanh.* 10:1 (according to which כל ישראל will have a place in the eon to come) and *T. Benj.* 10:11 (καὶ συναχθήσεται πᾶς Ἰσραὴλ πρὸς κύριον) (see Kraus, *Volk Gottes,* 321 together with n. 342); beyond this cf. Merklein, *Studien,* 308-9, and (at) nn. 98, 100, 101, 109, 131 as well as at n. 106 below.

68. Kuhli, "'Ἰσραήλ,'" 500.

69. With respect to the grammatical classification of ἀπὸ μέρους cf. Kraus, *Volk Gottes,* 320 n. 335. Besides, one will probably have to follow his argumentation (pp. 308-12), that already in Rom 11:1-2 with the "remnant" the entity πᾶς Ἰσραὴλ in 11:26 is in view (cf. p. 321 [together with n. 344]: "'Remnant' . . . as 'earnest' for the full number").

70. Schrage, "'Israel nach dem Fleisch,'" esp. 144-50 (together with nn. 2-8, 32-33 [with reference to other interpretations]). The criticism by Kraus, *Volk Gottes,* 189 n. 225, is not convincing because in view of the "unity of the context 1 Cor 10:1-22" (p. 188 n. 219) the present tense in v. 18b hardly allows, as he thinks, a "reference backward" to be "unlikely." Rather the forms of the present tense are "evidence for the fact that from v. 14 onward the current problem of the participation of Corinthians in pagan cult meals comes to the fore," namely against the background of the "typology of vv. 1ff." that works with "the unique historical episode of the golden calf" (citations: Schrage, "'Israel nach dem Fleisch,'" 149). Cf. the similar sequence of Gal 4:22-23 and Gal 4:24-31 as well as of 2 Cor 3:7-11 and 2 Cor 3:12-18 (and on this my contribution in this collection of essays [see n. 39 above]: "The Other Woman: Synchronic and Diachronic Observations on Gal 4:21–5:1," there esp. [at] n. 68).

71. Schrage, "'Israel nach dem Fleisch,'" 150. Differently, e.g., H. D. Betz, *Galaterbrief,* 547.

72. Schrage, "'Israel nach dem Fleisch,'" 150. Schrage himself avoids the addition ὁ Ἰσραὴλ κατὰ πνεῦμα (see pp. 144-45, 150-51), which from the Pauline use of language is not compulsory (on this see, e.g., Kuhli, "'Ἰσραήλ,'" 500, and at n. 15 above). Cf. Stegemann, "Zwischen Juden und Heiden," 62.

73. Cf., however, at n. 20 above. With the results gathered, especially with the result that in Paul (at least beyond Gal 6:16) "there is, in fact, no instance of his using Ἰσραήλ except of the Jewish nation or a part thereof" (E. de Witt Burton, *Galatians,* 358; cf. Davies, "Paul and the People," 10, and Gager, *Origins,* 228-29), even the cautious comments of Dunn (*Galatians,* 345) seem not to be compatible (cf. n. 114 below) when he says that "the Israel of God" means "the Jewish people precisely in their covenant identity," but adds, "*not* as excluding Jews as a whole, but as *including* Gentile believers (cf. Rom ix.6; xi.17-26; 1 Cor x.18)."

In my opinion Tomson, "The Names Israel and Jew," 288 (cf. [at] n. 117 below), expresses it somewhat more correctly when he says: "The most prominent misunderstanding is that for Paul the name Israel would represent a spiritual reality only. The reserve *(sic)* is true. Israel for Paul is . . . real Israel, his own people." According to Tomson (p. 285 [cf. n. 67 above]) this means for Gal 6:16: "There are two communities Paul belongs to: the new Christian community and the people of Israel. And his non-Jewish readers are begged not to stand off but to respect this." Cf. (at) nn. 117, 137 below.

74. On this cf. on the one hand (at) nn. 55, 56 above, on the other hand (at) nn. 61, 66 above.

75. On this see (at) nn. 23, 24 above.

76. On these see (at) nn. 20-22 above.

77. It should therefore be stated that in Paul "the use of λαὸς θεοῦ concerning the Ekklesia . . . occurs only in . . . quotations" (Kraus, *Volk Gottes,* 119; cf. pp. 115, 302), as the Apostle uses in general "λαός in a striking way exclusively in biblical quotations" (H. Frankemölle, "λαός," *EWNT* 2 [1981], 837-48 [cf. ET *EDNT* 2, 339-44], here 841) (see furthermore Rom 10:21; 11:1-2; 15:10-11; 1 Cor 10:7; 14:21; cf. [however] Tit 2:14).

78. On these comments on tradition-history cf., e.g., Kraus, *Volk Gottes,* 223-25, 275, 280, 302.

79. Kuhli, "'Ἰσραήλ," 499 (cf. Kuhli, "'Ἰουδαῖος," 475-76, on the background of such linguistic use, especially on the rather compelling distinction between Ἰουδαῖος and Ἰσραήλ in 1 Maccabees [on this see more particularly K. G. Kuhn, "'Ἰουδαῖος κτλ. In der nach-at.lichen jüdischen Literatur," *TWNT* 3 (1938), 360-70 (cf. ET *TDNT* 3, 359-69), here pp. 361-62]). Cf. Tomson, "The Names Israel and Jew," 284-85.

80. O. Betz, "Ἰουδαΐζω κτλ.," *EWNT* 2 (1981), 470-72 (cf. ET *EDNT* 2, 192-93), here 472.

81. On the meaning of 2:14b in connection with 2:15-21 see Bachmann, *Sünder,* 153-56, esp. 155.

82. See at n. 32 above.

83. On this cf., e.g., H. D. Betz, *Galaterbrief,* 283.

84. Differently, e.g., Davies, "Paul and the People," 9(-10).

85. On this see my contribution (printed in this collection of essays): "Investigations on the Mediator: Galatians 3:20 and the Character of the Mosaic Law," there esp. (at) nn. 92-118, 157-64, 196.

86. On this cf., e.g., n. 70 above (together with the bibliographical reference given there at the end).

87. On this see also my essay on Gal 4:21ff. mentioned in n. 39 (and n. 70) above, there esp. sections 2-5. Cf. at n. 133 below.

88. On this see, e.g., Kraus, *Volk Gottes,* 296-99.

89. On 3:1–4:7 as a passage that retrospectively looks back on the conversion see, e.g., (at) n. 36 above.

90. Richardson, *Israel,* 76. According to him, elsewhere it holds for Paul (with the exception of Eph 6:23-24): "the order is based on the logic of God's activity among men: source then benefits" (p. 77 [together with n. 5]).

91. Cf. Longenecker, *Galatians,* 298, who stresses the sequence of 5:1-11 ("peace," "reconciliation") and 5:12-21 ("grace," "the gift of grace") (and cf. [at] nn. 55-57 above).

92. On the question to what extent Gal 6:16 is to be considered part of the conclusion, see, e.g., Bachmann, *Sünder*, 158 together with n. 307 (and p. 114 together with n. 74).

93. Citations: Dahl, "Auslegung," 164.

94. On this cf. Dahl, "Auslegung," 164-65, and Longenecker, *Galatians*, 298.

95. On this see (at) n. 57 above.

96. On this and on the complete paragraph see, e.g., M. Bachmann, "4QMMT and Galatians, מעשי התורה and ΕΡΓΑ ΝΟΜΟΥ," *ZNW* 89 (1998), 91-113, here pp. 91-94 (together with nn. 1, 6, 8, 18), reprinted in this collection of essays. In the following comments I refer to the "Composite Text" and the translation (merely expanded by some of my notes in brackets) by E. Qimron and J. Strugnell, *Qumran Cave 4*, vol. 5, *Miqṣat Ma'aśe Ha-Torah* (Discoveries in the Judaean Desert 10; Oxford: Oxford University Press, 1994), 43-63, there 62-63.

97. On this cf. J. D. G. Dunn, "4QMMT and Galatians," *NTS* 43 (1997), 147-53, here pp. 151-52.

98. Text (expanded again with my note in brackets) and translation by D. Pardee, *Handbook of Ancient Hebrew Letters: A Study Edition* (SBLSBS 15; Chico: Scholars, 1982), 123-24 (cf. pp. 120, 127, 151-52). In lines 7-13 six signatures are added to the writing itself.

99. In pap Mur 42:7 it may have played a quite concrete role that in the case of a theft of a cow one had to defend oneself against a similar reproach as it can be found in a letter by Bar Kochba himself (5/6 Ḥev 12:3-4): "you are — eating and d[r]inking from the goods of Beth-Israel and not giving a thought to your brothers" (Pardee, *Handbook*, [142-]143; cf. p. 125).

100. The formulation שלום על ישראל is documented in inscriptions in the ancient synagogues in 'En-Gedi, Gerasa, Ḥusifa and Jericho; the inscription in Gerasa speaks more exactly of "all Israel" (cf. [at] n. 67 above) and adds "amen, amen" (cf. [at] nn. 112, 120 below), as in Ḥusifa perhaps also an "amen" follows (see F. Hüttenmeister and G. Reeg, *Die antiken Synagogen in Israel* [Beihefte zum Tübinger Atlas des Vorderen Orients 12; Wiesbaden: Reichert, 1977], 111, 129, 183, 190 [Hüttenmeister]).

101. Dunn, *Galatians*, (343-)344, furthermore names a more or less extracanonical parallel, namely 11QPs^a 23:(10-)11, where not only the eternal blessing of God following Ps 133:3 is mentioned (lines 10-11), but where it also says: שלום על ישראל (line 11).

102. Cf. (at) nn. 107, 113 below.

103. On this see, e.g., Richardson, *Israel*, 76 ("a unique phrase"), and Longenecker, *Galatians*, 299 ("The phrase . . . is not found in the extant writings of Second Temple Judaism or later rabbinic Judaism"); cf. (at) nn. 9, 29 above. With respect to a suggestion of J. C. K. von Hofmann, Zahn himself, *Galater*, 284 n. 48, think that "Paul has Ps 73:1 in mind and . . . has connected ישראל as status constructus with אלהים, remains questionable," and that suggestion is totally rejected by Sieffert, *Galater*, 361 n. *.

104. In the Septuagint text of Ps 84(85):11 as well as of Isa 54:10 both terms occur quite close together, and in the Sinaiticus version of Tob 7:12 (cf. *1 En.* 5:5-6) it says: ἐφ' ὑμᾶς ἔλεος καὶ εἰρήνην (cf. Richardson, *Israel*, 77 together with n. 6, and Dunn, *Galatians*, 344).

105. On this cf. Richardson, *Israel*, 78 n. 3.

106. In view of Gal 6:16 (not least of all with respect to its more precise identification of "Israel"), this formulation appears especially noteworthy: ἐλέησον λαόν, κύριε, κεκλημένον ἐπ' ὀνόματί σου καὶ Ἰσραήλ, ὃν πρωτογόνῳ ὡμοίωσας.

107. Cf. Dunn, *Galatians*, 344, further Richardson, *Israel*, 78, 218-19, who accentuates strongly that in this corpus of texts "as a refrain . . . is the idea that God's mercy is only for the select group" (p. 78; cf. at n. 102 above and at n. 113 below).

108. Cf. M. Black, *The Book of Enoch* or *1 Enoch. A New English Edition. With Commentary and Textual Notes* (SVTP 7; Leiden: Brill, 1985), 12-13, 108, further p. 327, as far as the text is concerned (which is quoted in the following according to M. Black, ed., *Apocalypsis Henochi Graece* [PVTG 3; Leiden: Brill, 1970], 19).

109. De Witt Burton, *Galatians*, 357-58.

110. Sieffert, *Galater*, 361.

111. See esp. Schrenk, "Israel Gottes," 93 (cf., e.g., Zahn, *Galater*, 284 n. 48, further at nn. 3, 25 above). Cf. (H. L. Strack and) P. Billerbeck, *Kommentar zum Neuen Testament aus Talmud und Midrasch*, 4 vols. (Munich: Beck, 1922-28), 3.578-79 (and 4.211-14).

112. Texts in W. Staerk, ed., *Altjüdische liturgische Gebete* (KlT 58, second ed.; Berlin: de Gruyter, 1930), 14-19, 31-32 (and in G. Dalman, *Die Worte Jesu. Mit Berücksichtigung des nachkanonischen jüdischen Schrifttums und der aramäischen Sprache*, vol. 1 [Leipzig: J. C. Hinrichs'sche Buchhandlung, 1898], 301-4, 305-6). Other versions of the Kaddish in Staerk, *Gebete*, 30-31, and Dalman, *Worte*, 305.

113. On this see, e.g., (at) nn. 96-97, 102, 107 above.

114. Cf. Dunn, *Galatians*, 344-45: If "the Israel of God" means "believers in Christ, particularly Gentile believers" (344), "we would have to say that Paul modified his position . . . in Rom ix-xi" (345). However, if Gal 6:16 deals with "the Jewish people as a whole" (p. 345), the result is: "the corollary that the development of thought between Galatians and Romans is not so great as is often claimed" (p. 345). Dunn argues, as it was already mentioned (in n. 73 above), for the second interpretation and says (*Galatians*, 345): "Paul deliberately refrains from driving a . . . wedge between ethnic Israel and the new movement among Gentiles." Cf. Dunn, "Apostate," 269: "Romans gives us just the same picture as Galatians. The gospel was a fulfillment of Israel's own hopes" (cf. p. 264 together with n. 25).

115. Citations: Kraus, *Volk Gottes*, 358.

116. Kraus, *Volk Gottes*, 358. — Kraus's position is also not so easy to understand, because with respect to the topic of the people of God he on the one hand thinks that he can claim "a new step in reflection" (*Volk Gottes*, 354) for Galatians, but on the other hand he has to state that the Apostle could here "in his course of argumentation fall back on earlier statements and pre-Pauline traditions on baptism . . . (cf. 1 Cor 1:30; 6:11)."

117. Citations: Tomson, "The Names Israel and Jew," 285, 288. Cf. nn. 67, 73 above and (at) n. 137 below.

118. Citations: Kraus, *Volk Gottes*, 355 (cf. [at] nn. 10, 12 above).

119. Kraus, *Volk Gottes*, 355.

120. Cf., e.g., Dunn, *Galatians*, 343, 347-48, further, with respect to "amen," (at) nn. 100, 112 above.

121. On this see esp. J. L. Martyn, "Apocalyptic Antinomies in Paul's Letter to the Galatians," *NTS* 31 (1985), 410-24. Cf. Bachmann, *Sünder*, 79 (together with n. 267) and pp. 115-17, 132-33, 160-61.

122. On this see section 2.1 ([at] nn. 34-40) above, further (at) nn. 82-89 above.

123. *Pss. Sol.* 17:45 (cf. 17:42): ἐπὶ Ἰσραὴλ τὸ ἔλεος . . . ; 17:43-44: ἐν συναγωγαῖς or ἐν συναγωγῇ φυλῶν. Cf. de Witt Burton, *Galatians*, 418, further (at) n. 107 above.

124. On this see J. Roloff, "ἐκκλησία," *EWNT* 1 (1980), 998-1011 (cf. ET *EDNT* 1, 410-15), here (1000-)1002(-1003) (cf. Roloff, *Kirche,* 83-84, 96-97), and Merklein, *Studien,* 301.

125. So Kraus, *Volk Gottes,* 125(-126) — in debate with other positions (esp. that of W. Schrage). Cf. Roloff, *Kirche,* esp. 96, further Merklein, *Studien,* esp. 307, 309, 312, also Dunn, "Apostate," 261 (together with n. 17).

126. See, e.g., Kraus, *Volk Gottes,* 124(-125). Cf., however, H. Frankemölle, "συναγωγή," *EWNT* 3 (1983), 702-10 (cf. ET *EDNT* 3, 293-96), here 704-5.

127. On this see esp. Merklein, *Studien,* 308-12. Cf. section 2.4 above (as well as [at] nn. 67, 123).

128. On this see the cross references given in n. 122 above.

129. So also Kraus, *Volk Gottes,* esp. 10-11, 351-52. But he thinks that in Galatians, as indicated (at) nn. 115-19 above, he is able to discern a minimization of the redemptive-historical component. However, it also does not convince me how he interprets Gal 3:23 and 4:1-7 (on this and against this see, e.g., Bachmann, *Sünder,* 124, 146-51 [together with nn. 127, 263-64, 272, 277]).

130. On this see esp. (at) nn. 34-40 above.

131. On this see, e.g., Kraus, *Volk Gottes,* 223-25, 228. Cf. (at) nn. 76-78 above, further from the comparative texts which we have referred to above particularly *Pss. Sol.* 17:27 (πάντες υἱοὶ θεοῦ εἰσιν αὐτῶν [cf. 17:31 and cf. on this Gal 4:26-28]) and *1 En.* 1:8d (καὶ ἔσονται πάντες τοῦ θεοῦ).

132. On this cf. (at) n. 85 above.

133. Namely at nn. 86-87 above.

134. On this and on the following cf. (at) n. 121 above, particularly Bachmann, *Sünder,* 79, 115-17, 132-33, further pp. VII, 65-78, 101-2.

135. In a certain respect the eschatological perspective is already important for the phrase ὁ Ἰσραὴλ τοῦ θεοῦ (on this see Kraus, *Volk Gottes,* 125-26; cf. Merklein, *Studien,* 303-4, 311).

136. One can illustrate the sequence of the ecclesiological statements of Galatians under consideration if one makes use of the "set theory" diagram, which I developed in the essay mentioned in n. 39 above (see there esp. at n. 53); here the diagram (since the iconographic comparison that was of interest there does not play a role here) is turned around the vertical axis and then the individual sectors are numbered as follows:

Jerusalem above	I Jews	II Gentiles	(SARAH) / Freedom
present Jerusalem	III	IV	HAGAR / Slavery

For then sector I belongs, if one is permitted to say so, to Gal 1:13ff., the combination of sectors I and II to 3:1ff., the contraposition of this combination and of the connection of sectors III and IV (better: IV and III) to 4:21ff., whereas in 6:16 on the one hand the combination of sectors I and II and on the other hand, so to speak vertical to it, the connection of sectors I and III has to be considered.

137. On this cf. Tomson's statements quoted above in n. 73 and at n. 117, further n. 114 above.

Bibliographical Appendix

(see Preface [at] n. 5)

M. Bachmann, Review of: F. Vouga, An die Galater, Handbuch zum Neuen Testament 10 (Tübingen: Mohr, 1998), *Theologische Literaturzeitung* 125 (2000), 521-23

———, Review of: K. Kuula, The Law, the Covenant and God's Plan. Vol. 1: Paul's Polemical Treatment of the Law in Galatians, Publications of the Finnish Exegetical Society 72 (Helsinki/Göttingen: The Finnish Exegetical Society/Vandenhoeck & Ruprecht, 1999), *Biblica* 82 (2001), 121-26

———, "Die Botschaft für alle und der Antijudaismus. Nachdenken über Paulus und die Folgen," *Ernstfall Frieden. Biblisch-theologische Perspektiven*, ed. M. Hofheinz/G. Plasger (Wuppertal: foedus-Verlag, 2002), 57-74

———, "*Verus Israel*: Ein Vorschlag zu einer 'mengentheoretischen' Neubeschreibung der betreffenden paulinischen Terminologie," *New Testament Studies* 48 (2002), 500-512

———, "Zur Entstehung (und zur Überwindung) des christlichen Antijudaismus," *Zeitschrift für Neues Testament* (Tübingen) 10 (5th year) (2002), 45-54

———, "Gal 1,9: 'Wie wir schon früher gesagt haben, so sage ich jetzt erneut,'" *Biblische Zeitschrift*, Neue Folge 47 (2003), 112-15

———, Review of: D. Kremendahl, Die Botschaft der Form. Zum Verhältnis von antiker Epistolographie und Rhetorik im Galaterbrief, Novum Testamentum et Orbis Antiquus 46 (Freiburg Schweiz/Göttingen: Universitätsverlag/Vandenhoeck & Ruprecht, 2000), *Biblica* 84 (2003), 139-45

———, Review of: Gemeinde ohne Tempel/Community without Temple. Zur Substituierung und Transformation des Jerusalemer Tempels und seines Kults im Alten Testament, antiken Judentum und frühen Christentum, ed.

B. Ego/A. Lange/P. Pilhofer, Wissenschaftliche Untersuchungen zum Neuen Testament 118 (Tübingen: Mohr, 1999), *Orientalistische Literaturzeitung* 98 (2003), 251-69

——— and G. Ballhorn, "Auseinandersetzungen um Verhaltensregeln im frühen Christentum als Indizien eines Ringens um Identität und Universalisierung der Religionsgemeinschaft," *Römische Reichsreligion und Provinzialreligion. Globalisierungs- und Regionalisierungsprozesse in der antiken Religionsgeschichte. Ein Forschungsprogramm stellt sich vor*, ed. H. Cancik/J. Rüpke (Erfurt: Universität, 2003), 85-93

M. Bachmann, "Nicht von außen kommende 'Gegner,' sondern galatischjüdische 'Beeinflusser'? Zu Mark D. Nanos' Dissertation und ihrer These vom synagogalen sozialen Kontext des Galaterbriefs," *Biblische Zeitschrift*, Neue Folge 48 (2004), 97-103

——— (and J. Woyke) ed., *Lutherische und Neue Paulusperspektive. Beiträge zu einem Schlüsselproblem der gegenwärtigen exegetischen Diskussion*, Wissenschaftliche Untersuchungen zum Neuen Testament 182 (Tübingen: Mohr, 2005)

M. Bachmann, "Vorwort," *Paulusperspektive*, VII-XIII

———, "Keil oder Mikroskop? Zur jüngeren Diskussion um den Ausdruck ἔργα νόμου," *Paulusperspektive*, 69-134

———, "Von den Schwierigkeiten des exegetischen Verstehens. Erwägungen am Beispiel der Interpretation des paulinischen Ausdrucks '<Werke> des Gesetzes,'" *Kontexte der Schrift. Vol. I: Text, Ethik, Judentum und Christentum, Gesellschaft. Ekkehard W. Stegemann zum 60. Geburtstag*, ed. G. Gelardini (Stuttgart: Kohlhammer, 2005), 49-59

———, "Ausmessung von Tempel und Stadt. Apk 11,1f und 21,15ff auf dem Hintergrund des Buches Ezechiel," *Das Ezechielbuch in der Johannesoffenbarung*, ed. D. Sänger, Biblisch-Theologische Studien 76 (Neukirchen-Vluyn: Neukirchener Verlag, 2006), 61-83

———, "Zur Rezeptions- und Traditionsgeschichte des paulinischen Ausdrucks ἔργα νόμου: Notizen im Blick auf Verhaltensregeln im frühen Christentum als einer 'Gruppenreligion,'" *Gruppenreligionen im römischen Reich. Sozialformen, Grenzziehungen und Leistungen*, ed. J. Rüpke, Studien und Texte zu Antike und Judentum 43 (Tübingen: Mohr, 2007), 69-86

———, "Auseinandersetzungen um Verhaltensregeln im frühen Christentum als Indizien eines Ringens um Identität und Universalisierung der Religionsgemeinschaft," *Antike Religionsgeschichte in räumlicher Perspektive.*

Bibliographical Appendix

Abschlussbericht zum Schwerpunktprogramm 1080 der Deutschen Forschungsgemeinschaft "Römische Reichsreligion und Provinzialreligion," ed. J. Rüpke, unter Mitarbeit von F. Fabricius (Tübingen: Mohr, 2007), 213-22

———, "J. D. G. Dunn und die Neue Paulusperspektive," *Theologische Zeitschrift* 63 (2007), 25-43

———, "Christus, 'das Ende des Gesetzes, des Dekalogs und des Liebesgebots'?" *Theologische Zeitschrift* 63 (2007), 171-74

———, "Zur Argumentation von Gal 3.10-12," *New Testament Studies* 53 (2007), 524-44

———, "Neutestamentliche Hinweise auf halakhische Regelungen," *Nuovo Testamento. Teologie in dialogo culturale. Scritti in onore di Romano Penna nel suo 70° compleanno,* ed. N. Ciola/G. Pulcinelli, Supplementi: alla Rivista Biblica 50 (Bologna: Edizioni Dehoniane, 2008), 449-62

———, "Was für Praktiken? Zur jüngsten Diskussion um die ἔργα νόμου", *New Testament Studies* 55 (2009), 35-54

———, Review of M. Tiwald, *Hebräer von Hebräern. Paulus auf dem Hintergrund frühjüdischer Argumentation und biblischer Interpretation,* Herders Biblische Studien 52 (Freiburg/Basel/Wien: Herder, 2007), *Biblische Zeitschrift. Neue Folge* 53 (2009)

———, "Biblische Didaktik ohne historische Rechenschaft? Einige Notizen und das Beispiel der (paulinischen) Rechtfertigungsbotschaft," *Erstaunlich lebendig und berstürzend verständlich? Studien und Impulse,* ed. M. Bachmann/J. Woyke (Neukirchen-Vluyn: Neukirchener, 2009)

———, "Bermerkungen zur Auslegung zweier Genitivverbindungen des Galaterbriefs: 'Werke des Gesetzes' (Gal 2,16 u.ö.) und 'Israel Gottes' (Gal 6,16)," *Umstrittener Galaterbrief. Studien zur Situierung und zur Theologie des Paulus-Schreibens,* ed. M. Bachmann/B. Kollmann, Biblisch-Theologische Studien (Neukirchen-Vluyn: Neukirchener, 2009)

Index of Scripture and Other Literature

OLD TESTAMENT		17:11	46, 74	24:7 LXX	75
		17:13	46, 74	25:23	180n.13
Genesis		17:14	46, 74	26:4-5	43
1	44, 59	17:19	46, 74	26:5	42-43
1:14	59	17:21	46, 74-75	48:19	172n.157
1:14-18	44	18:1-16	59		
1:18	172n.157	18:10-15	59	**Exodus**	
1:27	52	21	91	5:4	147n.65
2:2	132n.79	21:1-21	86	12:40-41	172n.155
12:4	172n.155	21:7	181n.17	12:40-41 LXX	47, 75
12:7	75	21:9	90	18	141n.4
13:15	75	21:9-10	91	18:20	16, 25-28, 125n.3
13:16	75	21:10	89		(Pref. '99),
15:5	75	21:11-12	183n.23		139n.152, 141n.4,
15:6	16, 116, 140n.2	21:12	75, 89, 183n.23		147n.65, 149n.85,
15:18	46, 74	22	37, 42-43		151n.104
16–21	181n.16	22:1	42	18:22	152n.104
16	192n.82	22:1-19	152n.6	19ff.	72, 169n.130
16:1-7	86	22:2	42, 152n.6, 153n.10	19:9	169n.130
16:3	172n.155	22:3	152n.6	19:25	169n.130
16:7	184n.32	22:7	152n.6	20:4	35
16:27	86	22:8	152n.6	20:19	170n.138
17	43	22:9	37, 152n.6	20:22	169n.130
17:2	46, 74	22:12	37	23:16	147n.65
17:4	46, 74	22:13	37, 152n.6	23:20-21	174n.188
17:7	74	22:15-18	43	24:3	169n.130
17:8	47, 75, 114	22:16ff.	75	24:5	169n.130
17:9	46, 74	22:18	42, 47, 75	24:8	169n.130
17:10	46, 74	24:7	75	25:21-22	170n.136

210

Index of Scripture and Other Literature

25:22	170n.136
27:20	36
32:6	90, 169n.130
34:34	87
34:35	111
35:29	170n.137
36:1	137n.143, 149n.85
36:3	137n.143, 149n.85

Leviticus
16:12	113
17–26	73
18:4-5 LXX	30
18:5	30, 45
18:5 LXX	135n.107
18:15 LXX	135n.107
26:46	73, 170nn.136-37

Numbers
3:7	137n.143, 149n.85
3:8	137n.143, 149n.85
4:37	170n.137
4:41	170n.137
4:45	170n.137
4:49	170n.137
8:11	137n.143, 149n.85
9:23	170n.137
10:13	170n.137
15:23	170n.137
17:5	170n.137
17:8	153n.11
21:16-18	146n.53
23:13	168n.116
33:1	170n.137
36:13	170n.137

Deuteronomy
1:1	146n.50
4:5-6	44
4:19	35
5:5	73
5:8	35
6:4	50, 69, 165n.92
18:18	146n.53
27–30	141n.4
27–28	34, 139n.158
27:26	13-14, 30, 134n.107
30:1	139n.158
30:16	141n.4
33:2 LXX	161n.78, 163n.79

Joshua
8:34	139n.158
14:2	170n.137
21:2	170n.137
22:9	170n.137

Judges
3:4	170n.137
17–18	193n.94

1 Samuel
12:22	110

2 Samuel
7:8	27
20:19	191n.75

1 Kings
19:10	183n.23
19:14	183n.23
19:15-18	183n.23
19:18	90, 183n.23, 200n.61

2 Kings
23:5	35
23:11	35

1 Kingdoms
12:22	110

3 Kingdoms
19:18	200n.61

1 Chronicles
16:40	170n.137

2 Chronicles
3:1	42
14:1	26
33:8	170n.137

Nehemiah
1:5	117
9:32	117

Job
9:33	73, 170n.135

Psalms
13(14):1	167n.112, 167n.116
13(14):1-3	167n.112
13(14):3	167n.112
19	45, 59
19:2-7	45
25:4-17	14
31(32):1-2	109
32(33):22	117
37:32-33	141n.8
68:18	161n.78, 163n.79
73:1	203n.103
76(77):12	132n.79
76(77):21	170n.137
84(85):11	203n.104
93(94):14	110
97(98):3	117
104	45
104:2-4	45
105:5-11	43, 76
105(106):13	149n.85
105(106):35	149n.85
105(106):39	149n.85
106:31	16, 140n.2
110(111):7	149n.85
119(118)	127n.9
119(118):32	127n.9
119(118):35	127n.9
124(125):1	117
124(125):1-2	117
124(125):2	117
124(125):3	117

INDEX OF SCRIPTURE AND OTHER LITERATURE

124(125):5	117	56:6-7	192n.85	Hosea	
127(128):1	117	60	193n.96	1:6	117
127(128):2	117	60:14	193n.96	1:7	117
127(128):5	117	61:8	98	1:9–2:1	113
127(128):6	117	61:18	192n.85	1:25	117
133:3	203n.101	62:4-5	97	2:1	111, 113
142:2 LXX	140n.166			2:1-4	98
143(142):2	3, 32, 140n.166	Jeremiah		2:23-25	183n.23
		4:4	113	2:25	113

Proverbs
8:22ff.   44
16:9   149n.85

Ecclesiastes
7:20   70, 167n.112

Isaiah
1:21-26   98
10:22   111
14:1   117
23:8   192n.83
23:16-17   192n.83
47   98, 192n.81
47:1-3   98
47:5-8   98
47:8-9   98
47:11   98
50:1   97
51ff.   192n.81
51:1-3   192n.82
52:2   97
54   181n.16, 192n.82
54:1   98, 192n.82
54:3   192n.82, 192n.84
54:4   98
54:4-5   98
54:6   98
54:6-7   97-98
54:10   192n.85, 203n.104
54:12-13   192n.82
55:3   192n.85
56:4   192n.85
56:4-5   192n.85
56:6   192n.85

Jeremiah
22:8   99
27(50):29   132n.79
31(48):10   137n.143, 149n.85
31(48):33   12
50:12   97

Lamentations
1:1   98
4:21-22   192n.81
5:16   88

Ezekiel
1   87
1:10   87
10   87
10:14   87
16   97-98
16:8   98
16:30-31   98
16:35-37   98
16:59-62   98
17–18   98
19   98
19:7-9   98
20:9   98
21–22   98
37:27   113
39:25   117
43:2 LXX   163n.79
44:7   113

Daniel
3:27   149n.85
4:27   99
7:10   163n.79

Joel
3:1 (var.)   190n.64

Amos
5:15   117

Micah
6:16   149n.85
7:20   117

Nahum
3:4   98, 192n.79
3:4-5   98, 192n.83

Zechariah
1:12   117
1:17   117

Malachi
2:2   139n.158
3:20(4:2)   153n.10

NEW TESTAMENT

Matthew
5:7   200n.56
5:18   168n.116
5:19   152n.104
5:45   200n.53
10:29   168n.116
23:23   152n.104
23:27   129n.33, 191n.73
23:30   169n.128

Index of Scripture and Other Literature

27:25	109, 157n.42	7:37ff.	169n.130	2:25-29	113
		7:38	52, 82, 162n.78, 163n.80	2:26	12-13, 28-29, 151n.102
Mark					
7:5	144n.30	7:44	170n.137	2:28-29	167n.116
7:8	144n.30	7:53	52, 82, 162-63nn.78-79, 170n.137	3:1	113, 135n.118, 169n.128
13:34	137n.145				
		11:15	109	3:5	2, 32
Luke		13:2	132n.80, 150n.87	3:5a	164n.86
12:34	191n.73	13:45	193-94n.95	3:6	174n.180
22:20	87, 96	13:50	193-94n.95	3:9	113, 169n.128
		14:26	132n.80, 150n.87	3:10b	167n.112
John		15:10	185n.41	3:10-13	70
3:20	132n.79	15:23-29	125n.5	3:11-13	167n.112
4:22	157n.42	15:38	132n.80, 150n.87	3:19	134n.105
4:34	10, 149n.87	26:5	144n.32	3:20	2-3, 13-14, 18, 23, 28-30, 33-34, 126n.9, 134n.105, 135n.109, 140n.166, 150.94, 173n.167
5:36	10, 149n.87	26:24	14		
6:28	10, 149n.87				
6:29	10, 135n.113, 149n.87	**Romans**			
6:38-39	149n.87	1–8	113	3:20b	134n.105
6:40	149n.87	1:4	112	3:20ff.	126n.9
6:45	149n.87	1:7	115	3:20-22	150n.91
8:23	190n.64	1:13	199n.51	3:21	12, 29, 136n.123, 137n.134, 168n.123
8:39	126n.9	1:16	113		
8:41	134n.100	1:16ff.	142n.9	3:21-22	29
8:41-44	134n.100	1:17	1-3, 125n.4 (Ch. 1), 148n.75	3:22	10, 14, 30
8:44	157n.42			3:23-26	17
9:4	10, 149n.87	1:18ff.	142n.9	3:24	10
12:49-50	149n.87	1:32	13, 29	3:25-26	2, 32
12:50	149n.87	2–3	17	3:26	14, 30
14:10	133n.82	2:6	11, 28, 132n.79	3:27	30, 107, 136n.121, 140n.166, 143n.27, 151n.98
14:10–15:10	133n.82	2:6-7	28		
14:12	133n.82	2:7	11, 28		
14:12–15:12	133n.82	2:10	16	3:28	2-4, 12, 14, 23, 25, 28-29, 126n.9, 136n.123, 137n.134, 148n.79, 150n.94
17:4	10, 149n.87	2:13	17, 136n.124, 152n.107		
18:36	169n.128				
		2:14	12, 28-29, 137n.136		
Acts		2:14-15	13, 28-29	3:29	84, 167n.116
2:19	190n.64	2:15	12, 26, 29, 126n.8, 135n.109, 148n.74, 150n.91, 150n.94	3:29-30	83-84, 113-14
5:11	109			3:30	84, 135n.118, 165n.93
5:29	199n.51				
7:2ff.	82	2:16	146n.55	3:31	30, 80
7:35	170n.137	2:17-29	197n.21	4ff.	126n.9
7:37	169n.130	2:23	107	4	114, 194n.103

213

INDEX OF SCRIPTURE AND OTHER LITERATURE

4:1	113	5:16	167n.114, 168n.118	9–11	111-12, 157n.42, 169n.127, 194n.103, 197n.21, 200n.57, 204n.114
4:2	2, 14, 28, 30, 90, 126n.9, 134n.105, 136n.123, 137n.134, 150n.94, 169n.128	5:17	167n.114, 168n.118
		5:17-18	167n.113
		5:18	80-81, 167n.114, 168n.118
				9	200n.56
4:2ff.	126n.9	5:19	167n.114, 168n.118	9:1	169n.130
4:2-3	149n.85	5:20	127n.10, 173n.167	9:1-2	110
4:2-4	28, 30	6:1	169n.128	9:1-5	110
4:2-5	126n.9	6:2a	174n.180	9:3	112-13
4:3	14, 16, 90	6:2-3	80	9:4	74, 80, 110, 169n.127, 194n.103
4:4	28	6:15	80, 169n.128
4:4-5	16, 137n.136	6:15d	174n.180	9:4-5	110, 115, 200n.61
4:5	14, 90	7	12	9:5	110, 112
4:5-9	23	7:5ff.	173n.167	9:6	23, 111, 201n.73
4:6	25, 28, 126n.9, 134n.105, 136n.123, 137n.134, 150n.94	7:7	11, 169n.128	9:6-7	115
		7:7b	134n.103	9:6-9	115
		7:7ff.	127n.10	9:6-13	75, 194n.103
4:6-8	139n.158	7:8	137n.134	9:7	113
4:7-8	109, 136n.123	7:8-9	136n.123	9:8	112-13, 169n.127
4:9	109, 149n.85	7:9	137n.134	9:10-13	126n.9
4:9ff.	75	7:12	11-12, 17	9:11	136n.123
4:9-12	135n.118	7:14	11	9:11-12	11, 137n.136
4:11-12	109, 113	7:16	11	9:12	2, 14, 28, 30, 126n.9, 134n.105, 134n.96, 136n.123, 137n.134, 150n.94, 180n.13
4:11-14	75	7:22	11, 29
4:12	114, 136n.123	7:25	11, 29
4:13	14, 23, 104, 134n.105, 136n.123	8:2	70
		8:3-8	114
4:14	14, 134n.105, 136n.123	8:4	13, 29, 135n.113	9:15	200n.57
		8:7	11, 29	9:16	126-27n.9, 200n.57
4:16	14, 23, 75, 114, 134n.105, 136n.123	8:9	167n.116	9:18	200n.57
		8:9-11	164n.86	9:23	200n.57
4:16-17	113	8:10	70	9:24	113, 200n.57
4:18	23, 75	8:11	70	9:25	103, 117, 183n.23
5	115	8:12	183n.28	9:25-26	113
5:4-5	168n.122	8:13	164n.86	9:26	113
5:9-10	115	8:14	113	9:27	111
5:12	167n.114, 168n.118	8:15	86, 113	9:27b	111
5:12ff.	70	8:17	164n.86	9:30	14, 168n.123
5:13	127n.10	8:19	113	9:31	110-11, 126n.9, 169n.130
5:13-15	184n.34	8:21	86
5:14	109	8:23	113	9:31-32	136n.123
5:14a	127n.10	8:30	169n.128	9:31–10:4	136n.123
5:14b	127n.10	8:32	153n.10	9:32	2, 14, 28, 30, 126n.9, 134n.105,
5:15	167n.114, 168n.118	9–16	113

214

Index of Scripture and Other Literature

		135n.107, 136n.123,	11:14	112	2:2	199n.49
		137n.134, 150n.94	11:15	169n.128	3:5	169n.128
9:32 (var.)	2, 23, 28		11:16-18	164n.86	3:7-8	168n.123
9:33	194n.103		11:17	111, 164n.86	3:7-11	201n.70
10:1 (var.)	111		11:17-26	201n.73	3:13	134n.98
10:2-4	131n.58		11:17-32	194n.103	3:14	11
10:3	148n.75		11:23	200n.66	3:15	11
10:4-5	90		11:25	111-12	4:6	167n.115
10:5	14, 30, 45, 126n.9,		11:25b	201n.67	4:15	146n.55
	134n.105, 135n.107,		11:26	23, 101, 111, 201n.69	4:17	146n.55
	136n.124, 169n.127		11:28-29	200n.57	5:9	141n.7
10:6	14, 184n.31		11:30	200n.57	5:12-13	168n.123
10:8	184n.31		11:31	200n.57	6:11	169n.128, 204n.116
10:8-10	184n.31		11:31-32	108	6:15c	174n.180
10:12	113, 175n.196		11:32	200n.57	6:16-17	167n.115
10:17	71, 194n.103		12:1ff.	142n.9	7:1	142n.9
10:18-21	110		12:4	168n.118	7:1ff.	142n.9
10:19	111		12:4-5	167n.115	7:19	12, 28-29
10:19-21	194n.103		12:8	200n.57	7:25	200n.57
10:19–11:10	112		13:3	11, 134n.100	8:1	142n.9
10:21	110-11, 202n.77		13:10	16	8:1 (var.)	168n.123
11	90, 101, 123,		13:12	134n.100	8:1ff.	142n.9
	200n.56, 200n.66		14:13	70	8:4	50, 165n.93
11:1	110, 113, 126n.9,		15	121, 200n.56	8:4-6	83
	169n.127, 194n.103,		15:7-12	121	8:5	83
	200n.64		15:8	200n.57	8:6	50, 70, 165n.93
11:1-2	110, 200n.61,		15:9	200n.57	8:6a	83
	201n.69, 202n.77		15:10	200n.57	8:6b	83
11:1-2a	90		15:10-11	202n.77	9:1	11
11:1-4	114		15:16-21	121	9:5	199n.51
11:2	183n.23		15:25-27	121	9:13	16
11:2b	90		15:31	121	9:20	105
11:2-3	183n.23		15:33	115	9:24	168n.118
11:3	110		16:7	110, 113	10	103, 111
11:4	90, 200n.61		16:11	110, 113	10:1ff.	169n.127, 201n.70
11:5	90, 111		16:20	115-16	10:1-5	169n.127
11:6	2, 14, 28, 30,		16:21	110, 113	10:1-11	111
	126n.9, 134n.105,		16:27	120	10:1-22	201n.70
	136n.123, 137n.134,				10:3-4	112
	150n.94		**1 Corinthians**		10:4	168n.123, 169n.125
11:7	111-12		1:1	199n.49	10:6	111
11:11-16	194n.103		1:3	115	10:6ff.	169n.127
11:11-32	111		1:8	199n.49	10:7	90, 112, 169n.130,
11:12	110-11, 164n.86		1:30	53, 204n.116		202n.77

215

INDEX OF SCRIPTURE AND OTHER LITERATURE

10:9	112	16:22	116	1:2	19-20, 104
10:11	111			1:3	115
10:11-13	111	**2 Corinthians**		1:3-4	142n.14
10:14	112, 201n.70	1:2	115	1:4	17, 19, 120, 188n.52
10:17	167n.115, 168n.118	3-4	157n.42	1:5	120
10:18	101, 103, 111, 112, 201n.73	3	87, 96	1:6-6:18	142n.16
		3:1	142n.13	1:7	142n.15
10:19	112, 169n.128	3:6	96	1:8	163n.78
10:22	112	3:7	87, 111, 169n.130	1:8-9	142n.14
11:3	168n.122	3:7ff.	71	1:9	93, 142n.15
11:25	87, 96	3:7-11	71	1:10	169n.128
11:31	169n.128	3:8	71	1:11	142n.16, 199n.45
12:1	142n.9	3:9b	71	1:11-2:14	106
12:4-5	168n.118	3:11b	71	1:13	91, 106, 113, 121, 194n.103
12:9ff.	167n.115	3:12ff.	71		
12:9-10	168n.122	3:12-18	191n.68, 201n.70	1:13ff.	206n.136
12:12	168n.118	3:13	71, 87, 111, 169n.130	1:13-14	22, 121, 143n.25, 187n.51
12:13	168n.118	3:13b-16	111		
12:14	168n.118	3:14	87, 96	1:14	113, 149n.85, 191n.69
12:19	168n.118, 169n.128	3:14a	71		
12:20	168n.118	3:16	200n.66	1:15	140n.2
13:9	17	3:16-17	168n.123	1:15-16	22
14:21	202n.77	3:18	153n.10	1:15-17	122
14:33	167n.116	4:1	200n.57	1:16	20, 122, 187n.51
15:1-11b	164n.86	6:16	103, 113	1:17	93, 97, 106, 190n.65
15:5ff.	142n.9	6:18	27	1:18	97, 190n.65
15:9	121	9:8	11	1:22-23	106, 121
15:11b	164n.86	10:2	142n.13	1:23	22, 91
15:12a	164n.86	10:9-10	141n.7	2	97
15:12b	164n.86	11:1-15	142n.13	2:1	93, 97, 102, 190n.65
15:13	164n.86	11:2	193n.87	2:1-5	187n.50
15:13b	164n.86	11:15	11	2:3	93, 113, 122, 135n.118, 144n.30
15:14a	164n.86	11:18ff.	111		
15:16	164n.86	11:22	110, 114, 200n.64	2:4	86
15:16b	164n.86	11:32	175n.191	2:4-5	142n.14
15:17a	164n.86	13:11	115, 199nn.43-44	2:7	93
15:39	167n.116	14:15	169n.128	2:7-9	20, 106, 113, 135n.118
15:51	168n.116	14:26	169n.128		
15:55-56	168n.123			2:8	106
15:58	132n.80, 150n.87	**Galatians**		2:8-9	102
16:1	142n.9	1-2	190-91n.65	2:9	106
16:10	16, 132n.80, 150n.87	1	95, 97	2:9-10	121-22, 142n.14, 144n.32
		1:1	106, 120		
16:12	142n.9	1:1-5	120	2:10	121

216

Index of Scripture and Other Literature

2:11-14	122, 144n.32	2:20-21	10, 17	3:10a	30, 134n.105, 134n.107, 136n.128, 136n.131
2:12	22, 113, 135n.118, 140n.2	2:21	105, 131nn.57-58, 134n.105, 144n.34		
2:12-14	29	2:21b	17, 30, 80, 105, 123, 140n.166, 152n.105	3:10a-b	136n.128
2:13	113, 198n.43, 199n.51	2:21bα	14	3:10b	29-30, 70, 134n.107, 135n.107
2:14	19, 113, 141n.4, 144n.30	2:26	152n.106	3:10-12	30, 137n.136
2:14b	202n.81	3–6	93	3:10-13	30, 173n.167
2:14-15	105	3–4	158n.49	3:10-14	139n.158
2:15	105, 113, 187n.52	3	91, 97, 184n.30, 189n.59	3:10-14ff.	139n.158
2:15ff.	27, 80	3:1	10, 142n.15	3:11	14, 62
2:15-17	22, 95, 142n.14, 173n.167, 187n.52	3:1ff.	22	3:11a	134n.105, 164n.87
2:15-17a	80, 105	3:1-5	174n.173	3:12	14, 45, 52, 62
2:15-21	22, 102, 105, 122, 150n.91, 187n.52, 202n.81	3:1-14	105, 143n.26	3:12a	134n.105
		3:1-29	114	3:12b	30, 70, 135n.107, 136n.124
		3:1–4:7	22, 78, 93, 105, 114-15, 122, 142n.14, 187n.52, 202n.89	3:13	62, 106, 188n.52, 191n.68
2:15–4:7	188n.52			3:13a	174n.172
2:16	2-3, 5-6, 19, 28, 30, 33-34, 140n.166, 144n.30, 150n.94	3:1–6:17	105, 122	3:13-14	10, 122, 134n.105, 188n.52
		3:2	2, 14, 17, 19, 28, 30, 62, 134n.105, 136n.123, 150n.94	3:13-14a	122
2:16aα	14, 134n.105, 140n.166			3:13–4:6	95
		3:2-3	122	3:14	14, 17, 62, 105, 188n.52
2:16a	14	3:2-5	122		
2:16ba	14	3:2-14	86	3:14a	191n.68
2:16b	14	3:3	86	3:14b	78, 81, 105, 142n.14, 174n.172, 188n.52
2:16bγ	14, 134n.105	3:5	2, 14, 17, 19, 28, 30, 62, 134n.105, 136n.123, 150n.94		
2:16c	14, 134n.105			3:14-19	86
2:16ff.	140n.2			3:15	74-75, 174nn.172-73, 199n.45
2:16-17	10, 105	3:5-6	149n.85		
2:16-17a	106	3:5-14	150n.91	3:15ff.	51, 175n.194
2:16-19	105	3:6	16, 106, 116, 140n.2	3:15-17	174n.185
2:17a	14, 30	3:6-7	122	3:15-18	46, 74, 76-77
2:17b-18	105	3:6–4:7	114	3:15-29	34, 46, 55, 59, 82, 91, 105, 143n.26
2:17c	174n.180	3:7	113, 122, 174n.173		
2:18	19, 30, 93, 123, 141n.4, 144n.34	3:8	14, 20, 82, 105	3:16	19, 47-50, 59, 62-63, 70, 72, 75, 77-79, 81, 83, 105, 114, 122, 156n.21, 160n.64, 165n.96, 166n.97, 168n.118, 170n.132, 174n.168
		3:8ff.	140n.2		
2:18a	141n.5	3:8-9	114		
2:19aα	14	3:9	14, 113		
2:19-20	105	3:10	2, 13, 17, 19, 28-30, 62, 134n.105, 146n.54, 150n.94, 151n.100, 164n.87		
2:20	17, 30, 93				
2:20c	140n.166				
2:20d	105			3:16b	174n.168

217

INDEX OF SCRIPTURE AND OTHER LITERATURE

3:16-17	49, 172n.154
3:16-18	75
3:16-29	114
3:17	59, 62, 74-75, 127n.10, 174n.172, 189n.59
3:17-18	75
3:17-19	106, 122
3:18	49, 51, 59, 62, 67-68, 76-77, 93, 122
3:18a	14, 134n.105
3:19	19, 49-52, 59, 62-63, 65-66, 68-69, 71-74, 76-78, 81, 105-6, 114, 127n.10, 141n.4, 156n.29, 157-58n.49, 160n.63, 161n.69, 163n.78, 165n.96, 166n.97, 173n.165, 173n.167, 175n.189
3:19a	169n.128
3:19bα	77
3:19b	68, 72, 77, 79, 81, 159n.52, 170n.137
3:19bγ	82
3:19ff.	77
3:19-20	49, 73-74, 78, 81, 122, 153n.1, 159n.50, 170n.136
3:19-20a	77-78, 81-82, 174n.185
3:19-25	49, 59
3:19b-20	60, 171n.150
3:20	20, 50, 60-84, 122, 159n.50, 159n.52, 159n.55, 167n.115, 171n.150, 191n.68
3:20a	49-51, 61-62, 65-74, 76, 78-83, 106, 136n.124, 156n.29, 160n.64, 160n.68, 161n.69, 161n.72, 164nn.85-86
3:20a-20b	166n.96, 167n.113
3:20b	50-51, 61-62, 65, 67-70, 74, 79, 81-83, 114, 136n.124, 156n.29, 160n.68, 161n.69, 161n.72, 165-66nn.93-97, 174n.182
3:21	49, 51, 59, 62, 77-78, 80, 82, 156n.29, 169n.128
3:21b	52, 80
3:21c	14, 80, 134n.105, 169n.128
3:21ff.	74, 173n.165
3:21-25	173n.167
3:21-29	78
3:22	51-52, 62, 77, 82-83, 105
3:22a	169n.128
3:22b	169n.128
3:23	62, 175n.191, 205n.129
3:23-24	105, 122
3:23-25	80, 82, 106, 122, 174n.172
3:23-29	188n.52
3:24	52, 62, 102
3:24-25	80
3:25	93
3:26	46, 82-83, 105, 113-14
3:26-29	20, 48, 83, 105, 114, 122, 174n.173, 188n.52
3:27	122
3:27-28	107
3:28	48, 51-52, 82-83, 113-14, 122, 144n.32, 167n.116, 168n.118
3:28d	67-68
3:28-29	59, 67-68, 83, 105, 174n.168
3:29	19, 62, 72, 77, 91, 104, 106, 113-14, 122, 165n.96
3:29a	67-68
3:29b	91
4	86-89, 94, 97-98
4:1	27, 106, 110, 174n.172, 185n.41
4:1ff.	80
4:1-5	110
4:1-7	91, 94, 105, 143n.26, 185n.41, 205n.129
4:1-11	173n.167
4:2	185n.41
4:3	94-96, 158n.49, 174n.172, 185n.41
4:3-6a	122
4:3-7	188n.52
4:4	19, 62, 72, 95, 102, 105-6, 122
4:4-5	122
4:4-7	143n.25
4:5	106
4:5b	174n.172, 188n.52
4:6	86, 105, 114, 122
4:6a	174n.173, 188n.52
4:6b	78, 105, 142n.14, 174n.172, 188n.52
4:6-7	105, 113, 114, 122
4:7	93, 106, 114, 174n.173, 185n.41, 188n.52
4:7-8	184n.34
4:8	94, 123, 143n.25, 187n.47
4:8ff.	142n.14
4:8-9	94-96, 105-6
4:8-11	94

Index of Scripture and Other Literature

4:8–5:1	22, 105	4:24d	92	4:31	85-86, 88, 90-91, 95-97, 183n.29, 184n.30, 185nn.35-36, 185nn.40-41, 186-87n.46, 199n.45
4:9	94, 158n.49, 185n.41	4:24-25	71, 85, 89, 106, 115, 168n.123, 184n.32		
4:9b	93, 186n.45	4:24-31	201n.70		
4:9c	93	4:25	85-86, 91, 94-97, 106, 114-15, 176n.2, 186n.41, 190n.65, 191n.73		
4:10	29, 44, 52, 59, 106, 140n.2			4:31–5:1	184n.30
4:12	109, 199n.45			5:1	86, 92-96, 106, 114-15, 123, 143n.17, 185nn.40-41, 186-87n.41, 187n.47
4:12-20	185n.41	4:25a	92, 190n.65		
4:13–6:13	86	4:25b	92, 190n.65, 191n.69		
4:14	163n.78				
4:17	22, 142n.15, 143n.27	4:25c	92, 185n.39	5:1a	88, 95-96, 185n.41, 186-87n.46
4:17-18	22	4:25-26	115, 190n.65, 191n.73		
4:17-21	143n.17			5:1b	95-96, 184n.29
4:19	93, 184n.33, 185n.41	4:26	85-86, 88, 90-91, 95-97, 106, 115, 142n.14, 185n.41, 186-87n.46, 189n.61, 191n.73, 192n.76	5:1-11	202n.91
4:21	52, 92-98, 106, 115, 123, 168n.123, 184nn.29-30, 185n.41			5:2	105, 107, 123, 144n.30
				5:2-3	93, 113, 135n.118
				5:2-4	52, 106
4:21ff.	71, 102, 202n.87, 206n.136			5:2-10	143n.17
		4:26a	92	5:2-12	22, 107, 109
4:21-23	71	4:26b	92	5:2–6:17	105, 106
4:21-31	177n.5, 180n.13, 181n.16, 194n.103, 197n.21	4:26-28	192n.84, 205n.131	5:2b-4	107
		4:27	85, 90, 92, 181n.16, 186n.41, 191n.67	5:3	29, 93, 136n.128, 152n.104
4:21–5:1	85-100, 106, 114-15, 123, 177n.5, 180n.13, 181n.18, 184n.32, 188n.52	4:28	85-86, 90, 92, 95-97, 106, 113, 115, 183nn.28-29, 184n.34, 186n.41, 199n.45	5:4	30, 80, 123
				5:4a	14, 134n.105
				5:5	19, 188n.52
				5:5–6:18	86
4:22	86, 92, 115			5:6	30, 106-7, 113, 135n.118, 144n.32
4:22bα	189n.59	4:28-29	115, 143n.25		
4:22b	189n.59	4:28-30	185n.35	5:7	142n.15
4:22ff.	90	4:28–5:1	106	5:7-10	107
4:22-23	85, 106, 201n.70	4:29	86, 90-92, 96, 103, 106, 112, 114, 184nn.33-34, 186n.41, 197n.21	5:10	110, 142n.15
4:22-29	104			5:10-12	110
4:22-31	187n.47			5:11	91, 93, 106, 113, 135n.118, 143n.25
4:23	86, 92, 115, 186n.41, 189n.59				
		4:29a	96, 191n.67	5:12	107, 142n.15
4:24	74, 85-86, 94, 96-97, 115, 172n.154, 186n.41, 189n.59	4:29b	96, 191n.69	5:12-21	202n.91
		4:29-30	185n.35	5:13	86, 106, 168n.123, 199n.45
		4:30	71, 86, 89-91, 106, 184n.34, 185n.36, 185n.40, 191n.67		
4:24a	92, 185n.39			5:14	30, 52, 106, 152n.104
4:24b	92				
4:24c	92	4:30-31	92-93, 106	5:16-18	106

219

INDEX OF SCRIPTURE AND OTHER LITERATURE

5:17	168n.123	6:17b	107	4:9	115
5:19	13, 134n.100	6:18	108, 120, 123	4:19	115
5:21–6:17	186n.44			4:20	120
5:22	106	**Ephesians**			
5:23	106	2:6	190n.61	**Colossians**	
5:25	106, 188n.52	2:8-9	134n.96, 152n.105	1:10	11
6:1	199n.45	2:9	126n.8, 134n.96	1:21	134n.100
6:2	52, 106	2:10	134n.100, 152n.105	3:1	190n.61
6:4	11	2:11ff.	103	3:1-2	190n.64
6:8	80-81, 106	2:12	111	3:11	175n.196
6:10	16	2:15	30, 136n.121, 151n.98		
6:11-13	117, 119			**1 Thessalonians**	
6:11-16	22	4:5-6	70, 175n.196	1:1	115
6:11-17	107, 109, 143n.17	4:8-9	168n.123	1:3	11
6:11-18	116-17	5:11	134n.100	2:14-16	157n.42
6:12	52, 91, 106, 107, 113, 143n.25	6:3	199n.44	4:1	199n.43
		6:10	199n.43	5:13	11
6:12-13	93, 106-7, 112-13, 135n.118, 142n.15, 144n.30	6:23	115	5:23	115
		6:23-24	202n.90	5:27	141n.7
				5:27-28	199n.44
6:12-15	123	**Philippians**			
6:12-17	107	1:2	115	**2 Thessalonians**	
6:13	107, 136n.128, 146n.54	1:6	11	1:11-12	133n.95
		2:13	14	2:17	11
6:13a	107	2:27	200n.57	3:1	199n.43
6:13b	107	2:30	132n.80, 150n.87	3:16	115-16
6:14	107	3:1	199n.43		
6:14-15	108, 116	3:2ff.	111	**1 Timothy**	
6:14-16	20	3:3	113	1:2	109, 115
6:15	52, 93, 107, 113, 117, 123, 135n.118	3:3-4	112	2:5	62, 70
		3:4-6	22	2:5-6	160n.63, 175n.196
6:15-16	19, 109, 144n.32	3:5	111, 144n.32, 200n.64	2:10	134n.100
6:16	101-4, 106-7, 109-13, 120, 123, 194n.103, 197n.19, 200n.57, 201-2n.73, 203n.92, 203n.106, 204n.114, 206n.136	3:5-6	144n.32	3:1	134n.100
		3:6	121	5:10	11, 134n.100
		3:7-8	111	5:25	134n.100
		3:9-11	111	6:17	191n.69
		3:14	190n.64	6:17-19	191n.69
		3:17-21	191n.72	6:18	134n.100
6:16a	108, 123	3:19-20	190n.64		
6:16b	108	3:20	190n.61	**2 Timothy**	
6:16-17	107	3:20-21	111	1:2	115
6:17	107-8, 117, 119, 123, 198n.43	4:7	115, 175n.191	1:9	11, 132n.79
		4:8	199n.43	1:10	134n.96
6:17a	107			1:18	200n.56
				2:21	11

220

Index of Scripture and Other Literature

3:17	11
4:14	11
4:18	134n.100, 190n.61

Titus

1:4	115
1:16	11
2:12-14	191n.69
2:14	134n.100, 202n.77
2:7	134n.100
3:1	11
3:5	11, 126n.8, 134n.96, 137n.136, 138n.147
3:14	11
3:18	134n.100

Philemon

3	115
20	199n.44

Hebrews

2:2	52, 82, 162-63nn.78-79
2:7-9	168n.123
6:1	134n.100
7:11	169n.130
8-9	96
8:5	170n.140
8:6	62, 170n.40
8:7	96, 169n.128
8:8	96, 109
8:9	96
8:13	96
9:4	153n.11
9:14	134n.100
9:15	62, 96
9:18	96
10:16	200n.53
10:16-17	96
11:6	190n.61
11:15	169n.128
12:18-21	82, 170n.140
12:22	163n.79, 190nn.61-62, 190n.64, 191n.73, 192n.84
12:22-24	190n.65
12:24	62, 96, 170n.140
12:25	190n.64
13:20	116

James

1:25	132n.80, 150n.87
2:10	29-30
2:13	200n.56
2:14	133n.90
2:14-20	133n.86
2:14-26	10, 152n.105
2:18	10-11, 133n.90
2:21	10, 43
2:22	10-11, 133n.90
2:24	10, 128n.19, 144n.36
2:25	10
2:26	10
3:13	11

1 Peter

1:2	115
1:5	175n.191
2:10	116-17, 200n.57
3:6	27
5:13	99
5:14	116

2 Peter

1:2	115
2:8	134n.100
3:15-16	141n.7
3:16	32

1 John

3:8	134n.100

2 John

3	115

3 John

15	116

Jude

2	115
14-15	162n.78, 174n.188
21	200n.56

Revelation

1:3	132n.76, 149n.87
1:4	115
1:16	153n.10
2:2	149n.87
2:9	9, 99, 157n.42, 193n.95
2:18-29	9
2:19	132n.75, 132n.79
2:20	149n.87
2:22	132n.76, 150n.87
2:23	9-10, 132n.79
2:24	149n.87
2:26	10, 149n.87
3:8	10, 132n.76, 149n.87
3:9	99, 157n.42, 193n.96
3:10	10, 149n.87
3:12	96, 190n.65, 191n.73
4:6-7	87
7:3-8	99
11	99-100, 194n.98
11:1	99
11:2	99
11:2-10	100
11:7	194n.98
11:8	99, 194n.97
11:9	99
11:9-10	99
12	99
12:1	99
12:17	10, 149n.87
13:14-15	193n.90
13:17	193n.90
14:1	99
14:12	10, 149n.87
14:13	132n.78

15:3	133n.82	22:12	149n.87	Prayer of Manasseh	
15:3-4	133n.82	22:14	132n.76	8	42
16:19	99	22:14 (var.)	149n.87	14–15	118
17–18	100, 194n.98	22:16	153n.10		
17	99, 193n.90, 194n.98			Sirach	
		APOCRYPHA		7:8-9	34
17:2	98-99			11:21-28	34
17:3	193n.90	Baruch		17:12	34
17:5	99	2:9	137n.143, 149n.85	17:24-26	34
17:6	98	2:10	137n.143, 149n.85	24	34, 44-45
17:7	98	2:12	137n.143, 149n.85	24:8	44
17:8	194n.98	2:28	170n.137	24:9	44
17:8-12	99	3:9–4:4	44	24:10-11	45
17:9-14	193n.90	3:23	181n.16	24:10-12	44
17:13-14	98	3:31–4:4	44	24:14	45, 153n.11
17:15	99	3:37	44	24:19	45, 153n.11
17:15-17	193n.90	4:1	44	24:22	45
17:18	99			24:23	44
18	99	1(3) Esdras		36:11	117
18:2	99	7:9	137n.143, 149n.85	40	45
18:3	99			42:15	149n.85
18:10	99	Judith		42:21-22	149n.85
18:16	99	6:19	117	44:18	46
18:18	99			44:19	113
18:19	99	1 Maccabees		44:19-21	43, 76, 113
18:21	99	2:49-52	43	44:19-23	43
18:24	98	2:51	149n.85	44:20	43, 46
19:2	99	2:52	16, 45, 140n.2, 149n.85	44:21	47, 172n.156
19:16	200n.53			44:22	46
20:4	109	2:53	149n.85	45	45
21–22	100, 193n.96	2:55	149n.85	50	45
21	192n.76	2:58	149n.85		
21:2	96, 190n.65, 191n.73	2:65	149n.85	Tobit	
		2:67	149n.85	3:2	149n.85
21:10	190n.65, 191n.73	2:68	149n.85	3:4-5	149n.85
21:12-13	99	6:13	173n.167	7:12	203n.104
21:23	153n.10	6:58	198n.40	8:4	117
21:24	99	11:62	198n.40	13:10	117
21:24-26	193n.96				
21:26	99	2 Maccabees		Wisdom	
22:2	99	4:16	173n.167	6:16-20	44
22:3	99			6:18b	34
22:7	132n.76, 149n.87	4 Maccabees		7–8	45
22:9	132n.76, 149n.87	18:1	43, 47, 76, 114	7	44, 59

Index of Scripture and Other Literature

7:17	44	8:3	149n.86	1:27-29	162n.78		
7:17-19	158n.49			1:29	175n.188		
7:18	44	1 Enoch		2:9	162n.78		
7:19	44	1	119	3:10-14	162n.78		
7:21	44	1:1	149n.86	4:21-24	175n.188		
7:22	44	1:4	118, 149n.86	6:22	162n.78		
7:25	45	1:4-7	118	15:26-27	175n.188		
7:25ff.	44	1:7	118	30:12	162n.78		
7:26	45	1:8	118	30:17	140n.2		
7:29	45	1:8a	118	30:21-22	175n.188		
8:1	45	1:8b	118	30:31	162n.78		
9:4ff.	45	1:8c	118	50:1ff.	162n.78		
9:9	149n.85	1:8d	118, 205n.131				
10:5	43	1:9	118, 174n.188	Psalms of Solomon			
11:1	170n.137	9:6	149n.86	2:35	118		
13	44	10:8	149n.86	2:35-37	118		
13:3	44	13:2	149n.86	4:25	118		
18:4	44	27:4	117	6:6	118		
		72–82	45	7:6	118		
		81:5	140n.166	7:10	118		
OLD TESTAMENT PSEUDEPIGRAPHA		89:50	189n.60	9:8	118		
		90:29	189nn.60-61	9:8-9	118		
		90:30-35	192n.84	9:11	118		
Apocalypse of Moses		91:9	189n.60	10	121		
1	162n.78, 163n.80			10:3	118		
		Epistle of Aristeas		10:6	118, 121		
Assumption of Moses		18:4	149n.86	10:6-7	118		
1:14	170n.139	272:3	149n.86	10:6-8	118		
2:166	170n.138			10:7	121		
3:12	170n.139	4 Ezra	34	10:8	121		
11:17	171n.142	7:24	149n.86	11:1	118		
		9:26–10:59	192n.76	11:9	118		
2 Baruch		10:6-7	192n.77	14:1-4	153n.11		
3:1	192n.77			14:29-36	192n.84		
3:3	192n.77	Joseph and Aseneth		14:31	192n.84		
4:1-7	190n.65	19:5-8	113	15:13	118		
57:2	15, 43, 149n.86, 151n.104	19:8	113	16:15	118		
				17	121		
67:7	99	Jubilees	45	17:21-22	121		
78:2	115	1:5ff.	173n.167	17:27	205n.131		
		1:22	173n.167	17:30-31	121		
4 Baruch		1:23	113	17:31	205n.131		
5:32	190n.61	1:24-25	175n.188	17:42	204n.123		
5:34	190nn.61-62	1:27ff.	163n.80	17:42-46	121		
8:2	149n.86						

INDEX OF SCRIPTURE AND OTHER LITERATURE

17:43-44	204n.123	4:6	148n.71	12:31 (4:31)	24
17:45	118-19, 204n.123	4:8	148n.71	13:36 (5:36)	147n.69, 148n.73
18:3	118	5:5-6	144n.35, 147n.57		
18:4	138n.147, 149n.86	6:3ff.	146n.53	14:9 (6:9)	146n.44
18:8	138n.147, 149n.86	6:7	146n.53		
18:10	149n.86	6:8-9	146n.53	**1QM**	
		6:14	148n.71	4:10	121
Testament of Benjamin		6:14-19	143n.28	10:8	148n.73
5:3	137n.143, 149n.86	13:5-6	148n.73	13:1	147n.69
6:7	149n.86	13:6	148n.71		
7:1	149n.86	13:6-8	26	**1QpHab**	
10:11	201n.67	13:7ff.	148n.73	5:9-12	142n.8
		13:7-8	147n.69		
Testament of Dan		14:18	148n.71, 149n.86, 151n.104	**1QS**	148n.80
5:6-7	193n.94			4:4	147n.69
6:2	160n.63, 170n.138	16	45	4:17-18	144n.30
6:9	149n.86	19:31–20:17	146n.54	5:1	148n.71
		20:6	148n.71	5:14-18	143n.28
Testament of Levi		20:6-7	146n.44	5:21	24, 138n.147
3:2-3	175n.188			5:23	24, 138n.147
10:1	137n.143	**Other Cairo Genizah Documents**		5:23-24	146n.44
19:1	149n.86	*Ms. EE*		5:24	24
		Gen 21:10	184n.32	6:18	24, 138n.147
Testament of Naphtali		*Ms. LL*		8:1	148n.71
2:10	149n.86	Gen 21:9	184n.32	8:15	170n.137
8:4	175n.188			8:15–9:2	146n.54
8:6	175n.188	**Naḥal Ḥever texts**		9:9	148n.71
		12:3-4	203n.99	9:13	147n.70
Testament of Zebulun				10:17	147n.69
8:1-2	117	**Temple Scroll**	45, 139n.151		
				1QSa	
		Wadi Murabbaʿat texts	141n.8	1:25	121
DEAD SEA SCROLLS AND RELATED TEXTS		42:2	117	**4Q171**	
		42:7	117, 143n.18, 203n.99	4:8-9	141n.8
Cairo *Damascus Document*		42:7-13	203n.98	**4Q174**	
1:1	147n.69			3:7	24
2:5-6	175n.188	**1QH**			
2:14	142n.11	1:26	138n.147	**4Q258**	148n.71
2:14-15	133n.83, 147n.69	1:26-27	138n.147		
2:18	133n.83, 147n.69	4:31	138n.147	**4Q259**	
3	45	9:26 (1:26)	24	5:10-11	59
3:2-3	43				

Index of Scripture and Other Literature

4Q381 (1)		B39ff.	142n.9
8	59	B55	142n.11
		B55-58	144n.32
4Q395	143n.24	B68	20
		B72	142n.9
4Q398	141n.8, 143n.24	B75	19, 142n.11
		B75-76	142n.9
4Q399	141n.8, 146n.49	B81	19
		C	19, 125n.5, 141n.6
4Q400 (1) (ShirShabb)		C7	20, 138n.149, 140n.2, 142n.12, 144n.32
1:5	175n.188		
1:14	175n.188		
1:16ff.	175n.188	C7-8	20, 22, 144n.32
		C10	141n.8
4Q521 (2)		C10-11	139n.158, 147n.57
2:2	162n.78	C12	19, 25, 141n.4
2:2-3	175n.188	C14ff.	140n.2
		C14-15	138n.149
4QFlor		C15ff.	139n.158
1:7	15, 24, 138n.147, 138n.148	C16	19
		C18-24	147n.58
		C19ff.	139n.158
4QMMT	34, 138n.147, 139n.158, 140n.1, 141nn.6-7, 142n.9, 144n.30, 144n.35	C21	19, 141n.5
		C23	25, 28, 147n.58
		C23-32	23
		C24	16
A	19, 141n.6	C25	19, 147n.57
A1ff.	140n.2	C25-26	23
B	19, 141n.6, 142n.9, 146n.49	C26	20, 141n.8
		C27	19-20, 23-28, 30, 116-17, 125n.3 (Pref. '99), 140n.2, 145nn.37-38, 146n.45, 147n.58
B1	20, 24, 25, 146n.49, 150n.91		
B1-2	16		
B2	16, 19, 25-26, 28, 146n.45, 150n.91		
		C27-28	139n.158
B6	20	C27-31	28
B8	142n.9	C28	20, 25, 146n.49
B10	20	C28-30	25, 116
B13	142n.9	C28-32	20
B13-16	144n.32	C29	16
B21	142n.9	C30	20, 24-25, 116, 146n.49, 146n.51, 150n.91
B24	142n.11		
B36	142n.11		
B36ff.	142n.9	C30-32	19, 117

C31	23, 25-26, 28, 140n.2
C31-32	20, 28, 116, 143n.18
C32	16, 141n.8
C33	16

4QPs^a
4:8-9	141n.8

11QPs^a
23:10-11	203n.101
23:11	203n.101

PHILO

De cherubim
9	181n.16

Quis rerum divinarum heres sit
205-6	170n.135

De vita Mosis
2:166	170n.138

De praemiis et poenis
82–83	148n.80

De sobrietate
7-9	181n.16

De somniis
1:142-43	170n.138

De specialibus legibus
1:116	170n.138

JOSEPHUS

Against Apion
1:37	162n.78
1:39	162n.78

2:291-92	148n.80	*Tg. J. II*		APOSTOLIC FATHERS	
		Gen 21:9	184n.32	AND EARLY CHRISTIAN	
Jewish Antiquities				WRITERS	
2:204	172n.155	*Tg. P.-J.*			
2:318	172n.155	Gen 21:9	184n.32	**Augustine**	
9:265	162n.78	Gen 21:10	184n.32	*De Trinitate*	
15:136	162-63nn.78-79	Gen 21:11	184n.32	15.9.15	180n.15
20	137n.143	Gen 21:12	183n.23		
20:42	149n.86	Gen 22:1	184n.32	**Barnabas**	
20:43	149n.86	Exod 18:20	139n.156	4:1	191n.69
20:46	149n.86			9:4	162-63n.78
42	137n.143				
43	137n.143	OTHER JEWISH		**Chrysostom**	
46	137n.143	WORKS		PG 61:662-63	180n.15
		'Abot R. Nat.		**Eusebius**	
Jewish War		1 (recension A)	170n.136	*Praeparatio Evangelica*	
5:382	172n.155	2 (recension B)	162n.78	9.21.16	172n.155
5:401	149n.86			9.21.18-19	172n.155
6:301	193n.87	**Bar Kochba Documents**			
		letter 5/6	203n.99	**Gelasius of Cyzicus**	
				Historia Ecclesiastica	
MISHNAH, TALMUD,		*Ber. Rab.*		2.17.7	170n.139
AND TARGUMIC		6:9	172n.157		
TEXTS				**Hermas**	
		Eighteen		*Similitude*	
b. B. Meṣ.		**Benedictions**	200nn.56-57	8:3:3	
30b	139n.156			(= *Herm.* 69:3)	175n.188
		Mek.			
b. B. Qam.		Exod 18:20	139n.156	**Irenaeus**	
99b(-100a)	139n.156			*Adversus haereses*	
		Memar Marqah		3.11.8	178n.7
m. Sanh.		VI §2)	171n.147	5.30.2	193n.94
10:1	201n.67				
		Pesiq. Rab.		**Justin**	
y. Meg.		21	162n.78	*Dialogue with Trypho*	
4.74d.9	171n.143	32:2	192n.82	11:5	103
				19:6	173n.167
		Pesiq. Rab Kah.		20:1	173n.167
CN (Tg. Neof.)		22:1	181n.17	21:1	173n.167
Gen 21:9	184n.32			67:4	173n.167
Exod 18:20	139n.156			67:8	173n.167
				67:10	173n.167
Frg. Tg.				95:1	188n.52
Gen 21:9	184n.32			95:1-3	188n.52

Index of Scripture and Other Literature

123:7-8	103	Theodoret of Cyrus		Homer	
		PL 82:481	165nn.94-95	*Iliad*	
Pseudo-Augustine				6.490	137n.145
Altercatio Ecclesiae et Synagogae		**CLASSICAL AND HELLENISTIC WRITERS**		6.492	137n.145
				Philostratus	
PL 42:1131-40	179-80n.13			Διάλεξις 2	145n.37
		Diogenes Laertius			
Tertullian		6.70	145n.37		
Adversus Marcionem					
5.4.8	180n.15				

Index of Authors

Abegg, M., 31, 142n.12, 145nn.37-38, 145n.39, 148n.77, 148n.79, 152n.109
Albrecht, K., 191n.75
Anderson, R. D., 143n.23
Anton, C. T., 155n.17
Appuhn, H., 179n.8
Asmussen, Hans, 5, 129nn.34-37
Avemarie, F., 145n.38, 149n.87

Bachmann, M., 52, 78, 80, 85, 93, 105, 124n.1 (Pref. '99), 126n.7, 127n.10, 129n.29, 130n.48, 131n.57, 133n.88, 134nn.104-5, 135n.107, 135n.110, 135n.120, 135-36n.121, 136nn.123-24, 136n.130, 137nn.131-32, 137n.143, 138nn.147-48, 140n.164, 140-41n.2, 141n.4, 142n.14, 143nn.22-23, 143n.26, 144n.29, 144nn.33-37, 145n.41, 147n.59, 147n.67, 148n.70, 148n.78, 148nn.80-81, 149n.85, 150n.87, 150n.90, 150n.92, 151nn.95-98, 151nn.100-101, 152nn.104-5, 152nn.107-8, 152n.1-2, 153n.9, 157n.41, 158n.50, 158n.49, 161n.68, 163nn.78-79, 164n.83, 164n.85-87, 165n.92, 166n.97, 169n.126, 169n.128, 173nn.164-65, 173n.167, 174n.170, 174nn.174-75, 174n.178, 174n.180, 174n.182, 175nn.189-91, 176n.1, 184n.30, 185n.40, 186nn.41-44, 187n.50, 187-88n.52, 190n.65, 191n.73, 192n.79, 192n.86, 193n.89, 194n.98, 194n.101, 198nn.35-39, 198nn.41-42, 202n.81, 203n.92, 203n.96, 204n.121, 205n.129, 205n.134
Bammel, Ernst, 47, 69, 153n.9, 164n.85, 165n.91, 166n.97, 171-72n.154, 173-74n.168, 174n.182, 175nn.193-94
Bandstra, A. J., 162n.78, 175n.189
Baneth, H., 171n.147
Barrett, C. K., 139n.153, 142n.12, 184nn.32-33
Bartsch, H. W., 190n.65
Bauer (Bavervs), C. L., 167n.107, 167n.111
Bauer, W., 135n.112, 153n.7, 196n.12
Baur, J., 125n.1
Beagley, A. J., 194n.97
Becker, Jürgen, 89, 175n.194, 182n.20, 184n.29, 184-85n.35, 188n.52, 189n.59, 196n.12
Behm, J., 171n.153
Ben-Chorin, S., 137n.138, 181n.16, 185n.41
Bendemann, R. von, 157n.47
Bengel, Johann Albrecht, 71, 156n.40, 168nn.120-21, 196n.16
Benoit, P., 143n.18
Berger, K., 185n.36, 188n.55
Bergmeier, R., 193n.92
Bertram, G., 132nn.70-71, 133n.81
Betz, H. D., 46-47, 50, 55, 75-76, 143n.22, 153n.7, 154n.10, 154n.2, 158n.49, 160n.64, 161n.72, 162n.78, 165n.92, 170n.137,

Index of Authors

171n.149, 171n.152, 171-72n.154, 172n.156, 172n.162, 174n.187, 181n.17, 182nn.20-22, 185n.37, 186n.46, 188n.55, 195n.103, 195n.8, 196n.9, 196n.12, 197n.21, 198n.40, 199n.45, 201n.71, 202n.83
Betz, O., 202n.80
Billerbeck, P., 3, 7-8, 15, 26, 126n.9, 128n.14, 137nn.138-40, 139n.156-56, 147n.59, 147n.67, 148nn.78-79, 161-62n.78, 170n.142, 171n.143, 175n.189, 184n.32, 189n.60, 192n.77, 204n.111
Bisping, A., 196n.12
Black, M., 204n.108
Blank, J., 127n.11
Blinzler, J., 158n.49
Bloch, P., 176-77n.4, 179n.12
Blumenkranz, B., 177n.4, 179n.8
Böcher, O., 193n.90
Bonitz, C. F., 155n.17, 165-66n.96
Bornemann, E., 169n.128
Bornhäuser, K., 154n.1, 156n.31, 165n.92
Borse, U., 165n.92, 183n.25, 183n.28, 185n.40, 186n.42, 191n.73
Böttger, P. C., 127n.12
Bousset, W., 131nn.57-58, 153-54n.1, 171n.149, 197n.17
Bouwman, Gijs, 91, 95-97, 176n.2, 181n.17, 186-87n.46, 188nn.54-55, 189nn.58-59, 192n.82, 194n.103
Braude, W. G. (G. Z.), 181n.17
Bremer, N., 177n.4, 178n.6
Bring, Ragnar, 61, 129n.40, 155n.18, 155-56n.19, 156nn.22-23, 157n.46, 166n.98, 185n.40
Broer, I., 124n.2 (Pref. '99), 183n.28, 184n.33, 188n.53, 188n.55, 195n.103
Brooke, G. J., 138n.148
Bruce, F. F., 160n.68, 181n.16, 185n.40, 192n.82, 195n.103
Bultmann, R., 6-8, 11, 17, 32, 126n.5, 130nn.50-53, 130n.55, 131nn.57-58, 131nn.62-63, 157n.47
Burchard, C., 143n.27, 144n.31, 144n.33, 145nn.37-38, 146nn.44-45, 148n.77, 148nn.80-81, 150n.90, 150n.92, 151n.95, 151n.100, 152n.106, 164n.82, 168n.121, 172n.154, 173n.165, 173n.167, 174n.170, 175n.191
Burton, E. de Witt, 156n.29, 156n.35, 161n.72, 171n.151, 197n.17, 201n.73, 204n.109, 204n.123

Callan, Terrance Dennis, 60, 62, 65, 154nn.3-4, 154n.9, 155n.17, 156n.29, 156n.32, 159n.52, 159n.63, 160nn.65-68, 161n.76, 162n.78, 163n.80, 164-65n.90, 165nn.92-93, 165n.96, 168n.123, 170nn.141-42, 171nn.147-48, 171nn.150-51, 175n.196
Callaway, M. C., 181n.16, 182n.21, 184n.32, 192n.82
Calvin, J., 196n.12
Collins, A. Y., 192n.79, 192-93n.86, 193nn.90-91
Constantin, Gottfried, 60
Corsani, B., 186n.46
Cosgrove, C. H., 131n.65, 140n.166, 151n.101
Cranfield, C. E. B., 127n.11, 130n.48, 135nn.112-13, 137n.136
Culmann, F. W., 155n.17

Dahl, Nils Alstrup, 60, 103, 196n.12, 197nn.18-22, 198n.30, 200n.53, 203nn.93-94
Dalman, G., 204n.112
Dalton, W. J., 174n.170
Davies, W. D., 162-63n.78, 197n.17, 201n.73, 202n.84
Déaut, R. Le, 184n.32
Dehn, G., 182n.21
Delitzsch, F., 148n.79
Delling, G., 158n.49, 185n.37
Deutsch, C., 192n.86, 193n.89, 193n.91, 194n.102
Dombrowski, B. W. W., 145n.38
Donaldson, T. L., 78, 142n.14, 143n.26, 174n.171, 187-88n.52, 198n.37
Dopp, J., 159nn.59-61, 161n.70
Dunn, J. D. G., 19, 23-24, 31, 32, 127n.9, 127n.11, 129n.29, 130n.48, 134n.99,

INDEX OF AUTHORS

138n.147, 140nn.1-2, 141n.3, 141n.5, 142n.12, 143nn.19-20, 145nn.38-40, 145n.42, 146n.44, 146n.48, 146n.51, 148n.74, 151n.100, 152n.109, 173n.167, 182n.21, 195n.6, 198nn.37-38, 200nn.56-57, 200n.59, 201n.73, 203n.97, 203n.101, 203n.104, 204n.107, 204n.114, 204n.120, 205n.125

Ebeling, G., 128n.17, 157n.47, 172n.157, 174n.178, 180n.16, 186n.46
Ego, B., 189-90n.61
Eisenman, R., 145n.39, 152n.2
Ellicott, C. J., 197n.17
Elon, M., 139n.156
Ensor, P. W., 149n.84
Esre, Shemone, 101
Estius, E., 196n.16
Ewald, G. H. A., 197n.17

Fiedler, P., 182n.20, 186n.46, 195n.103
Finkel, A., 139n.156
Fitzmyer, J. A., 125n.3 (Pref. '99), 152n.105
Flusser, D., 27-28, 145n.42, 146n.47, 147n.60, 147nn.64-65, 147nn.67-68, 150n.89, 150n.91, 151n.97, 152n.107
Frank, M., 155n.16
Frankemölle, H., 133n.87, 182n.20, 202n.77, 205n.126
Fricke, G. A., 155n.17
Fritsch, O., 154n.2, 154n.13, 155n.17, 156n.29, 165-66n.96, 174n.178
Füglister, R. L., 177n.4
Fuller, R., 127n.11

Gager, J. G., 186-87n.46, 194-95n.103, 197n.17, 201n.73
Gaston, L., 13, 127n.11, 130n.48, 131n.69, 134n.96, 135n.120, 137n.139
Geiges, F., 176n.3, 178nn.6-7, 179n.10
Giblin, Charles H., 71, 163n.80, 164n.90, 165nn.92-93, 166n.103, 168nn.122-23, 171n.149, 173n.167, 175n.196, 194n.101
Goldhorn, I. D., 155n.15
Goldin, J., 170n.136

Goodenough, E. R., 55
Gottstein, M. H., 139n.152
Gräer, E., 176n.2, 183n.28, 189n.59, 196n.12
Green, R., 178n.7
Greisenegger, W., 177n.4, 178n.6, 178n.8, 179nn.11-13
Grelot, P., 141n.2, 144-45n.37, 145n.43, 151n.99
Grotius, H., 196n.16
Gründler, J., 157n.46, 171n.149
Gundry, R. H., 127n.11, 193n.86
Gutbrod, W., 135n.115, 197n.21

Haacker, K., 177n.5, 185n.40, 190n.65
Hansen, G. W., 175n.196, 182n.21
Harnack, A. v., 180n.15
Hays, R. B., 182n.21
Heiligenthal, R., 127n.11, 128n.13, 132n.80, 133n.81, 133nn.84-87, 134n.101, 135n.111, 135n.113, 137n.145, 150n.87, 150n.90, 151n.102
Hengel, M., 133n.84, 138n.147, 139n.158, 139n.160
Hermelink, H., 128n.17
Hilgenfeld, A., 161n.72, 170n.137
Hirsch, E., 125n.3 (Ch. 1)
Hofius, O., 3, 126n.8, 127n.10, 128n.14, 175n.189, 189-90n.61
Hofmann, J. C. K. von, 197n.17, 203n.103, 166n.102, 169n.131
Hofstätter, H. H., 178n.7
Holsten, C., 160n.64, 174n.176, 196n.12
Holtz, T., 132nn.75-76, 133n.95
Horn, F. W., 193-94nn.93-95, 194n.100, 194n.102, 194n.97
Hübner, Hans, 63, 126n.5, 127n.11, 135n.111, 135n.117, 149n.82, 153n.8, 157nn.48-49, 159n.57, 163n.79, 167nn.109-10, 173n.165, 173n.167, 174n.176, 175n.194
Hüttenmeister, F., 203n.100

Jankowski, G., 176n.2, 185n.40, 191n.73
Jeremias, J., 192n.79
Jochum, H., 177n.5, 178nn.6-8, 180n.14
Joest, W., 129n.38

Index of Authors

Jowett, Benjamin, 61
Junghans, H., 128n.26, 129n.46

Kähler, M., 196n.12
Kampen, J., 146n.43, 148n.74
Kampling, R., 124n.2 (Pref. '08)
Kapera, Z. J., 138n.149
Kapstein, I. J., 181n.17
Karrer, M., 149n.87
Käsemann, E., 2, 12, 32, 126n.5, 135n.111, 135n.114, 137n.140
Kayser, C. L., 145n.37
Keel, O., 193n.90
Keil, K. A. G. (Keilius, C. A. T.), 155n.15, 155n.17, 165n.96, 166n.104
Keller, A., 171n.150
Kennedy, G. A., 185n.40
Kern, 161n.72, 171n.149
Kertelge, K., 126n.5
Kittel, G., 9
Klaiber, W., 196n.12
Klein, Günther, 63, 126n.5, 127n.11, 153n.8, 157-58n.49, 159n.51, 166n.99, 182n.20, 189n.57, 189n.59, 191n.69
Klijn, A. F. J., 190n.65
Klöpper, A., 153n.1, 161n.72, 164n.82, 165n.93
Koch, D.-A., 180-81n.16, 183n.21, 186n.46, 189n.57, 191n.67, 191n.71, 192n.82
Körkel-Hinkforth, R., 179n.8
Kraft, H., 132nn.72-73, 132n.75
Kraus, W., 108, 195-96n.9, 196n.12, 196n.15, 198n.32, 199n.46, 200n.61, 201n.67, 201nn.69-70, 202nn.77-78, 202n.88, 204nn.115-16, 204nn.118-19, 205nn.125-26, 205n.129, 205n.131, 205n.135
Kremers, H., 197n.17
Krummer-Schroth, I., 176n.3
Kubel, R., 154n.2
Kühl, E., 197n.17
Kuhli, H., 197n.17, 199n.51, 200nn.62-65, 201n.68, 201n.72, 202n.79
Kuhn, H.-W., 140n.2, 145n.43
Kuhn, K. G., 202n.79
Kunze, K., 176n.3, 178n.7, 179n.8

Ku, O., 196n.12

Lacan, M. F., 158n.49, 164n.90
Lagrange, M. J., 196n.12
Lambrecht, J., 6-7, 124n.1 (Pref. '99), 126n.9, 130nn.48-49, 142n.14, 143n.26, 152n.1, 174n.176, 186n.43, 188n.52, 198n.37
Lausberg, H., 164n.88, 167n.108
Lehninger, M., 173n.167
Levine, L. I., 152n.4, 153n.10
Lichtenberger, H., 139n.151, 139n.153, 141n.6, 142n.11, 189n.59
Lieberman, S., 170n.142, 171n.147
Liebers, R., 127-28n.12, 131n.68
Lietzmann, Hans, 65, 161n.71, 168n.117, 186n.46
Lightfoot, J. B., 157n.44, 166n.100, 183n.23, 196n.12
Lipsius, R. A., 196n.12
Lohmeyer, E., 3, 11, 13, 15, 27, 127nn.11-12, 128n.14, 128n.16, 131n.69, 132nn.75-76, 132n.78, 132nn.80-81, 133n.86, 133nn.89-92, 133n.94, 133-34n.96, 134n.99, 134n.102, 134n.104, 134n.106, 135n.119, 137n.136, 137nn.139-43, 149n.84, 150n.88, 151n.95, 193n.90
Lohse, E., 126n.6, 137-38n.146, 193nn.92-95, 201n.67
Longenecker, R. N., 162n.78, 163n.80, 169n.128, 170n.137, 171n.147, 172nn.154,157, 173n.167, 174n.177, 182n.21, 184n.32, 185n.41, 186n.41, 187n.47, 191n.73, 192n.82, 194-95n.103, 195-96n.9, 200n.55, 202n.91, 203n.94, 203n.103
Luck, U., 128n.19
Lücke, G. C. Friedrich, 60, 61, 62, 154n.5, 154n.12, 156nn.28-29, 156nn.31-35, 159n.53, 161n.68, 166n.102
Lührmann, D., 44, 47, 157n.47, 158n.49, 171n.148, 172n.155, 176n.2, 185n.37, 189n.59, 190n.65, 195n.5, 197n.17, 199n.45
Lull, D. J., 173n.167
Luther, Martin, 1-6, 8, 10, 11, 13-14, 17-18, 23, 60, 62, 125n.2 (Ch. 1), 125n.4 (Ch. 1), 128nn.17-28, 129nn.30-33, 129nn.40-46,

231

INDEX OF AUTHORS

130n.55, 136nn.125-28, 144n.36, 154nn.6-8, 156n.37, 180n.13, 180n.15, 188n.55, 196n.12
Luz, U., 176n.2, 182n.20, 183n.21, 188n.55, 189n.59, 191n.69, 196n.12
Lyonnet, S., 196n.12

Maa, H., 59
MacDonald, J., 171n.147
Mach, M., 158n.49, 162-63n.78, 163n.80, 175n.189
Maier, J., 145n.39, 146n.44, 146n.53, 148n.71
Maisch, I., 124n.2 (Pref. '08)
Malan, F. S., 181n.16, 182n.21, 185n.40
Mann, I., 129n.30, 154nn.6-7
Mann, J., 192n.82
Martínez, F. García, 145nn.38-39, 147n.58
Martyn, J. L., 180n.15, 184n.33, 185nn.40-41, 186-87n.46, 189n.59, 190n.65, 194n.103, 204n.121
Matera, F. J., 176nn.1-2, 182n.21, 183n.22, 185n.41, 186-87n.46, 190n.65, 195n.9, 196n.12, 199n.45
Mauser, Ulrich, 61, 156nn.20-22, 156n.24, 175n.196
McGrath, A. E., 125n.1, 125n.2 (Ch. 1), 129nn.38-39, 131n.59
McNamara, M., 184n.32
Meeks, W. A., 184n.32
Meiner, S., 150n.90
Melanchthon, P., 5-6, 129n.39
Menge, H., 137n.145
Merklein, H., 160n.66, 161n.72, 163n.79, 166n.97, 170n.136, 173n.166, 196n.12, 201n.67, 205nn.124-25, 205n.127, 205n.135
Metzger, B. M., 168-69n.124, 183-84n.29
Milik, J. T., 143n.18
Moo, D. J., 126nn.8-9, 127n.11, 128n.13, 129n.29, 129n.39, 134n.101, 134nn.105-6, 135nn.115-16, 138n.147
Moore, G. F., 131n.57
Morus, T., 197n.17
Müller, C., 126n.5, 196n.12
Münzel, G., 179n.8
Muner, Franz, 33, 64-68, 74, 76, 101-2, 104,

159n.54, 159-60n.63, 161n.69, 161n.72, 161n.75, 164n.82, 164n.89, 165n.90, 169n.128, 171n.154, 172n.157, 172n.160, 173n.165, 173n.167, 174n.178, 174n.187, 176n.2, 181n.19, 182n.21, 183n.22, 184n.32, 184n.35, 186-87n.46, 194n.103, 195nn.2-6, 196n.12, 197n.17
Mutius, H.-G. von, 153n.7, 172n.157

Naumann, T., 181n.16, 184n.32
Netzer, Ehud, 41, 58-59
Neusner, J., 152n.2
Newsom, C., 175n.188
Nicolai, Philipp, 192n.76
Nietzsche, Friedrich, 88, 181n.18
Noesselt (Noesseltus), I., 155n.17

Oepke, Albrecht, 61, 64, 73, 154n.14, 159nn.55-56, 159nn.62-63, 160n.64, 160n.66, 161n.69, 164n.82, 166n.100, 170n.134, 170n.139, 170n.142, 171nn.144-47, 174n.178, 176n.4, 177n.5, 178n.6, 179n.12, 182-83n.21, 196n.12, 199n.43, 199n.48, 199n.51
Ohly, F., 180n.15
Olyan, S. M., 161n.78, 163n.79, 175nn.188-89
Osten-Sacken, P. von der, 197n.17

Pannenberg, W., 125n.1
Pardee, D., 141n.8, 143n.18, 203n.98
Penna, R., 125n.3 (Pref. '99)
Perriman, A. C., 182n.21, 185n.40, 191n.69
Peters, A., 128n.24
Prigent, P., 152n.3, 152n.5, 153n.10

Qimron, E., 19, 138n.149, 139n.150, 139nn.152-53, 139nn.155-56, 139n.159, 140n.1, 141n.4, 141-42n.6-8, 142nn.9-12, 143n.18, 143n.24, 144n.32, 145n.38, 146nn.46-50, 147n.58, 147nn.60-62, 147nn.64-68, 148n.70, 151n.99, 203n.96
Quell, G., 171n.153

Radl, W., 172n.160, 183n.27, 184n.33

Index of Authors

Räisänen, H., 130n.54, 158n.49, 167n.109, 173n.165
Reeg, G., 203n.100
Reicke, B., 158n.49
Reithmayr, F., 161n.68, 165n.94
Rengstorf, K. H., 170-71n.142
Richardson, P., 103, 196n.12, 197n.17, 197nn.23-26, 198n.29, 200n.53, 201n.67, 202n.90, 203nn.103-5, 204n.107
Riesenfeld, H., 168n.121
Risch, E., 169n.128
Rissi, M., 193n.90
Ritschl, A., 158n.49, 160n.64, 161n.72
Rohde, Joachim, 64, 154n.7, 156n.35, 157n.44, 160n.66, 161n.69, 161n.72, 164n.82, 166n.100, 169n.128, 172n.161, 173n.167, 182n.21, 186n.46, 191n.73, 199n.46
Roloff, J., 102, 104, 196nn.10-12, 205n.124
Rosenmüller (Rosenmüllerus), I. G., 166n.96, 167n.113, 168n.121, 171n.149
Rückert, L. J., 196n.16
Ruether, R. R., 124n.1 (Pref. '99), 182n.20
Rusam, D., 158n.49, 187n.48

Sachs, H., 178-79n.8, 180n.14
Sack, K. H., 156n.31
Salvadori, L., 164n.89
Sanders, E. P., 7, 8, 11, 17, 33-34, 130n.48, 131nn.56-58, 131n.64, 152n.2
Sanders, J. T., 191n.73
Sänger, D., 159n.58, 161n.72, 170n.141, 171n.148, 188n.52, 200n.57, 200n.66
Schäfer, P., 175n.189, 197n.17
Scheel, O., 125n.2 (Ch. 1)
Schelkle, K. H., 197n.17
Schiffman, L. H., 139n.151, 145n.38, 147n.68, 151n.99, 177n.4
Schiller, G., 178nn.7-8, 179n.12, 180n.14
Schlatter, A., 130n.55, 140n.166, 197n.17
Schleiermacher, F. D. E., 159n.53
Schlier, Heinrich, 61, 64, 154n.2, 154nn.10-11, 157n.47, 158n.49, 159n.57, 161n.72, 162n.78, 163n.80, 165n.93, 173n.167, 174n.178, 183n.22, 183n.27, 184n.30, 184n.33, 185n.36, 188n.55, 194n.103, 195n.2, 196n.12, 197n.17
Schmid, C. F., 165n.96
Schmidt, H., 179n.8
Schmidt, M., 179n.8
Schmieder, H. E., 155n.17
Schnelle, U., 195n.103
Schoeps, H.-J., 163n.78, 181n.17
Schöttgen, C., 196n.16
Schrage, W., 112, 195n.5, 199n.51, 201nn.70-72, 205n.125
Schreckenberg, H., 177nn.4-5, 178-79nn.6-8, 179-80nn.11-13, 180nn.14-15, 181n.17, 183n.21, 187n.46, 190n.65
Schreiner, J., 192n.77
Schreiner, T. R., 127n.11, 128n.13, 129n.29, 130nn.48-49, 135n.109, 135n.120, 138n.147, 139n.161
Schrenk, G., 102-5, 108-9, 196-97nn.12-17, 197n.21, 198nn.28-31, 198nn.33-34, 199n.46, 199nn.49-53, 204n.111
Schulthess, J., 155n.17
Schürer, E., 35
Schweitzer, A., 131n.57, 158n.49
Schweizer, E., 158n.49
Schwier, H., 177n.5
Schwyzer, E., 168n.116
Seiferth, W., 177n.4, 179n.13
Sickenberger, J., 193n.90
Siebert, Wilhelm, 61-62, 154n.2, 155n.17, 156n.25, 156nn.26-27, 156n.29, 165n.96
Sieffert, Friedrich, 61-62, 156n.28, 154n.10, 154n.13, 155n.15, 156n.29, 156nn.37-39, 159n.55, 160n.64, 161n.69, 163n.79, 165n.94, 165n.96, 166n.98, 166-67nn.100-105, 168n.122, 169n.128, 172n.160, 173n.167, 174n.168, 174n.176, 196n.12, 199n.51, 204n.110
Siegert, F., 160n.65, 162-63n.78, 164n.83, 167n.107
Sloan, R. B., 130n.48
Söllner, P., 189n.57
Staerk, W., 204n.112
Stähli, H.-P., 36, 38-40, 152n.3, 152n.5, 153n.10

233

INDEX OF AUTHORS

Stählin, G., 191n.69
Stanley, C. D., 14, 136n.129, 136n.131
Stanton, G., 124n.3
Staudinger, F., 200n.56
Steck, Odil Hannes, 97, 191n.75, 192n.76, 192nn.78-81, 192n.84, 193n.90
Stegemann, E. W., 52, 135n.116, 138n.147, 189n.59, 191n.66, 201n.72
Stegemann, H., 141n.6, 141n.8, 145n.38, 146n.54, 147n.58, 162n.78
Stegemann, W., 127nn.11-12, 130n.48, 131n.55, 135n.120, 140n.166, 197n.17
Stegmann, A., 154n.1, 161n.76, 163n.80
Steinhauser, M. G., 184n.32
Stemberger, G., 58, 152nn.3-4
Stendahl, K., 128-29n.29
Steudel, F., 156n.31, 174n.168
Stolle, V., 76, 160n.65, 160n.67, 164n.90, 165n.92, 166n.97, 166n.99, 173n.163
Strack, H. L., 126n.9, 147n.59, 161-62n.78, 184n.32, 204n.111
Strecker, G., 150n.90, 151n.102
Stroumsa, G. G., 124n.2 (Pref. '99)
Strugnell, J., 19, 138nn.148-50, 139nn.152-53, 139nn.155-56, 139n.159, 140n.1, 141n.4, 141-42nn.6-8, 142nn.9-12, 143n.18, 143n.24, 144n.32, 145n.38, 146nn.46-50, 147n.58, 147nn.60-62, 147n.64, 147nn.66-68, 148n.70, 151n.99, 203n.96
Stuhlmacher, P., 126n.5, 185n.40, 189n.59
Stuhlmann, R., 201n.67
Suhl, Alfred, 89-90, 163n.79, 164n.80, 166n.97, 166n.103, 166n.105, 170n.136, 173n.165, 184n.30
Sussmann, Y., 142n.12, 143n.21, 144n.32

Thornton, C.-J., 142n.12
Tomson, P. J., 124n.1 (Pref. '08), 138n.147, 139n.158, 201n.67, 202n.73, 202n.79, 204n.117, 206n.137
Trummer, P., 127n.11
Tyson, J. B., 127n.11, 128n.14, 131n.69

Urbach, E. E., 175nn.188-89

Vanhoye, A., 154n.1, 164n.89
Vaux, R. de, 143n.18
Veijola, T., 152n.6
Vermes, G., 145n.38
Vielhauer, P., 158n.49

Wagner, G., 188n.55
Wallace, D. B., 158n.49, 159n.50, 165nn.92-93, 168n.123, 169n.128, 173n.165, 173n.167, 175n.196
Wallace, Edgar, 63
Wechsler, A., 124n.1 (Pref. '99)
Wehrhahn-Stauch, L., 178n.8
Weigand, G. H. F., 155n.17
Wei, B., 197n.17
Weiss, Ze'ev, 41, 58-59
Westerholm, S., 127n.9, 127n.11, 130n.48, 133n.81, 134n.104, 135n.108, 135n.112, 135n.120, 137n.143, 139n.161, 152nn.1-2, 157n.45, 158n.49, 175n.194
Wette, M. L. de, 196-97n.17
Wieseler, Karl, 60, 154n.7, 154n.9, 155n.15, 155n.17, 160n.68, 161n.69, 165n.94, 171nn.149-51
Wilckens, U., 7-8, 11, 17, 127n.11, 130n.48, 130-31n.55, 131n.62, 133n.88, 140n.166, 173n.167, 182n.20, 195n.103
Winer, G. B., 155n.17, 159n.53, 161n.72, 166n.102, 166n.104
Wise, M., 145n.39, 152n.2
Wolter, M., 145n.37, 148n.80
Wörner, E., 197n.17

Zahn, Theodor, 50, 105, 108, 132nn.75-76, 150n.87, 161n.72, 161n.76, 165n.93, 167-68n.116, 168n.117, 169n.128, 173n.165, 182n.21, 185n.40, 187n.50, 197n.17, 198n.34, 198n.40, 198n.43, 199nn.48-51, 200nn.55-56, 203n.103, 204n.111
Ziesler, J. A., 126n.5
Zimmer, K. F., 197n.17
Zöckler, O., 153n.1, 155n.15, 155n.17, 156n.27
Zwingli, U., 5

www.ingramcontent.com/pod-product-compliance
Lightning Source LLC
Chambersburg PA
CBHW030110010526
44116CB00005B/177